D0882882

# ARTICULATION LEARNING

by
## William M. Diedrich, Ph.D.

*Hearing and Speech Department,*
*School of Allied Health*
*College of Health Sciences and Hospital*
*University of Kansas Medical Center*

and
## Jeff Bangert

*Academic Computer Center*
*University of Kansas*

COLLEGE-HILL

College-Hill Press Houston, Texas 77035

Dedicated to

*Bet and Colette*

College-Hill Press
P.O. Box 35728
Houston, Texas 77035

*Library of congress Cataloging in Publication Data*
Diedrich, William M.
      Articulation Learning
      1. Articulation disorders in children. 2. Speech
therapy for children. I. Bangert, Jeff, 1938-
joint author. II Title.
RJ496.S7D53  618.92'85506  80-18405

ISBN 0-933014-59-7

# Contents

# Foreword

Articulation disorders have occupied the bulk of the time of speech-language clinicians throughout the study of communicative disorders. A number of important contributions have been made by researchers during these efforts. Winitz (1969) reviewed the first thirty years of articulation research applications. These developments may be characterized as having increasing specificity in testing and delineating articulation features and error patterns. The efforts also now extend to the analysis of phonology, a branch of linguistic science, so that we not only study sound formants but also the phonological rule features and the consistency of the child's deviant rule use.

Strategies for the remediation of articulation disorders also have been summarized (Sommers & Kane, 1974). However, the practice of articulation therapy has remained largely an art. The techniques used and the data recorded seem to be largely a matter of individual preference for clinicians. The broad guidelines for such activities are taught and generally followed. However, the basic refinements for a science of instruction have been slow to evolve.

Consequently, it is significant that Diedrich and Bangert have brought statistics and data processing into the realm of articulation therapy. And in so doing they have given speech-language clinicians a methodology to evaluate their own effectiveness, and they have provided administrators with a tool to monitor the progress of speech-handicapped children and the competency of public school speech clinicians.

Sixty-one speech clinicians working in different speech therapy settings in the Midwest furnished data on 1,108 elementary school children. These children were provided therapy for defective /r/ and /s/ phonemes over one school year. That data from the therapy given those children forms the basis for this project.

One major result of the work Diedrich and Bangert describe in this book was the development of a functional accountability procedure for school speech clinicians to use with large articulation therapy caseloads. Another unique contribution is a procedure to quantify clinician performance levels. This is a process that can be carried out by clinicians as they work with children.

The book further addresses practical clinical issues in articulation learning in matters that relate to number of sessions per week, lesson plans, generalization, and termination criteria. The procedures which generated four distinct articulation learning curves also can be applied to the progress of other children in other settings.

Diedrich and Bangert make a significant contribution to both the process of articulation therapy and the field of data analysis. Their book is testimony to years of hard work and to the common conviction of the authors that systematic data collection and descriptive data analysis could be merged to further our understanding of the articulation learning process.

Richard L. Schiefelbusch
*University of Kansas*

# Acknowledgments

Just as a good bird dog sniffs the wind, the investigator tests many different currents to determine the future direction of study. This project was influenced by many personal friends and some persons unknown to us. Their presence was sensed on many winds.

The project was supported primarily by the Office of Education, Special Projects Division, Washington, D.C. OEG-0-261293-3406 (031) and OEG-0-71-1689 (603) for six years (1969-75). Without that financial assistance and encouragement, this effort would never have been completed. Additional support came through the Kansas Center for Mental Retardation and Human Development (Grant HD-02528) and the University of Kansas.

Many experts were consulted on this project for a great many things. Perhaps most notable among them was Jack Irwin (now at Memphis State) who was the co-principal investigator during the first year of the project. Ogden Lindsley and his colleagues contributed the behavior chart and the notion of systematic data collection over time. Karl Koenig supplied the Port-A-Punch idea and format. Ralph Shelton and his colleagues originated the Sound Production Tasks and pioneered the evaluation of articulation learning. Heartfelt gratitude goes to Marge Denes, Mary Elbert, Joe Ann Levine, and Virginia Wright for their ideas, support, and discussions over several years. Appreciation also is due Gary Holdgrafer, Jane Reed, Linda Schmidt, Judy Spencer, Cathy Weinand, Kathy DeYoung, and Sharon Haack for their contributions.

A special thanks to Ross Copeland, Ed Zamarripa, and Louise Farrell from the Bureau of Child Research, University of Kansas, who provided administrative support for the project, and to Bob Hoyt and Bob Gardner for technical development of the 16mm film *Counting and Charting Target Phonemes from Conversation*, and the 2x2 slide and audio cassette program, and to Zilpha Bosone for the program booklet, *Charting Speech Behavior*.

The authors are indebted to Marilyn Barket who spent many hours cross-checking, polishing and coordinating the many aspects of manuscript and proof preparation.

We particularly want to acknowledge the enormous amount of help we received over the life of the project and the years of book writing from Paul J. Wolfe, Coordinator of Academic Computing at the University of Kansas and from all of the Academic Computer Center staff. All of the years of getting special output at 3 a.m. and special typing at 8 a.m. are appreciated.

Personnel from the University of Kansas Computation Center who worked many extra hours include Jim Frane, Judie Koontz, Bill Thornton, Ron Oliver, George Gunnels, Pete Klammer, Janet Erickson, Barbara Mulroy, and Merilyn Bowman. Dave Nordlund was responsible for the Tone Keyboard.

A special word of thanks to Jim Church for statistical advice and consultation.

We are especially grateful for the cooperation of administrators in the schools, supervisors of speech and hearing programs, the 61 speech clinicians, and the more than 1,700 children who participated in this study.

All the original clinician-child project numbers have been recoded to preserve the anonymity of those who provided the data for this study.

Publication of this book was made possible by generous contributions from the University of Kansas Academic Computer Center and the Bureau of Child Research. It was Paul J. Wolfe, director of the Academic Computer Center, and Richard L. Schiefelbusch, director of the Bureau of Child Research who gave the last boost of support that led to the publication of this work.

# Preface

It takes the natural sciences many years to describe and begin to control any aspect of our physical environment, yet progress in science is made continuously. A common sequence of events is: the isolation of a new or previously unnoticed phenomenon; the creation of a theory; design of new measurement tools to test the theory; and the application of the new tools to the phenomenon. The last step often produces both a validation of the theory and new unexplained phenomena, and the cycle begins again.

The behavioral and social sciences are still in their infancy. Our subject (humans and their behavior) seems infinitely more complex than the physical universe. This complexity creates difficulties in each step of the scientific cycle. There is disagreement about which are the most interesting phenomena to study. Theories flourish like weeds in a garden. The best tools we have for measuring behavior must strike a balance between reliability and relevance. It is often difficult and expensive, if not immoral, to apply the best tools to the appropriate phenomena. Thus, what often results from the application is increased confusion.

Still, we maintain the belief that the application of scientific method to human behavior is worthwhile, since the subject (humanity) is the most important one we know. We believe that our own area, speech pathology, needs better, more reliable, and more complex measurement tools to describe what happens in the therapy process. It is the purpose of this study to propose some ideas to advance us toward that goal.

At the start of the project we needed a method to acquire information about how speech clinicians perform articulation therapy. We were interested in the clinician's planning moves (cognitive lesson plan) as well as behavior and feelings of the clinician and the child during therapy. This was our first problem.

The next problem was data acquisition (methodology). How should we measure articulation? How should we obtain frequent speech responses from the child during the course of therapy in the school year? Given the large number of children to be studied, how could we make the articulation measurements available for data processing with minimal effort on the part of the child, clinician, and investigators? (First phase of the study.)

The next problem was how to learn about clinician-child interactions. Should we interview the clinician about what she[1] does right after it happens? Should we audio- or videotape the therapy sessions and then describe what occurs later? Should we place an observer in the room to take notes?

We wanted a system to describe the therapy process and provide data to be automatically decoded for processing. Could the clinician or child tell us what was happening, as it was happening? And if a procedure was found whereby the clinician-child could describe to us what was occurring during therapy, would this process interfere with therapy? Or worse, would the instrumentation hinder the child's learning? (Second phase of the study.)

---

1. Because the majority of the clinicians chosen for this study are women, we use the feminine reference throughout our report. This does not imply any disregard or disrespect for the male clinicians who also contributed to the study.

Plutchik (1968, p. 19) has summarized the basic process of naturalistic studies with which we had to contend in this project:

> Naturalistic studies, sometimes called field studies or clinical studies, are usually concerned with an accurate description of an individual's behavior as it is found to occur outside of the laboratory. They are concerned with relations between the individual and his environment as well as with relations between individuals. . . .
>
> In an effort to make more manageable the continuous flow of behavior, the observer selects categories of events to be observed. These categories are selected either on theoretical grounds, practical grounds. . . , or empirically by grouping observations that have something in common. . . . In addition, various sampling plans are used to condense the total flux into a workable portion.

The focus, then, of this investigation was to collect from public school speech clinicians systematic data about their therapy and to determine if certain principles of therapeutic intervention were manifested. As with most studies, we discovered some interesting results, we did not develop any panaceas, and we generated additional questions. Scientific progress is usually made in increments and not moonleaps. We believe this study makes an incremental contribution to the understanding of the clinical process in speech pathology. We trust our colleagues concur.

W.M.D.
J.B.

CHAPTER 1

# Introduction

This chapter introduces the statement of the problem and project questions. Goals and accomplishments of each project year are summarized for the reader. Chapter 2 (Methodology) details the essential procedures used to collect the data, select clinicians, and choose children during the course of the project. Chapters 3, 4, and 5 (Results) deal with the primary findings of the dependent and independent variables and their interactions. In Chapter 6 data unique to project Year 4 is discussed. Chapters 7 and 8 include subanalyses of certain segments not considered in the two major data reductions. Finally, Chapter 9 is a summary of the major conclusions of this investigation.

For definitions of special terms and symbols used in this project refer to Appendix G in this book.

## Statement of the Problem

Most textbooks discuss the management of clinical problems on the basis of the author's clinical experience. There is nothing wrong with "on the basis of my clinical experience" statements as long as the reader understands that other applications of those techniques or procedures must go through some metamorphosis. Furthermore, the fledgling clinician (or experienced one for that matter) who is looking for new clinical skills must also realize that the techniques of the clinic supervisor or professional colleague are subject to personal bias, prejudice, and blind spots. This study obtained empirical and objective descriptive data from many clinicians about articulation learning and the process of articulation therapy.

Other researchers have tackled the problem of making naturalistic observations of human behavior (Barker and Wright, 1955) in studying the ecological functions of children within a community, descriptions of the classroom (Flanders, 1965; Bellack, Kliebard, Hyman & Smith, 1966; Smith and Meux, 1970), and analyzing lesson plans (Herbert, 1967). To date, no major study has made field observations of speech therapy in the schools. Yet children with articulation problems are being helped in the schools. What are the conditions under which successful children learned? Is it possible to obtain good naturalistic data on these processes? Can information from large numbers of clinician-child interactions be sifted and unique therapy experiences gleaned from the analyses?

The elements of the therapy experience are the clinician, the child, and their interactions. Since each of these is variable, is it possible to establish some general principles of therapy? If data were collected on many clinicians, children, and therapy sessions, would enough substantive material emerge from the therapeutic crucible to predict clinician decision-making and therapy management?

The global strategy of the project described in this book was to identify effective teaching programs with children who achieved correct articulation performance in spontaneous speech. The clinician and child variables associated with the most effective learners were isolated. The project went through two phases:
1. The development of a system for assessing articulation progress from imitation and conversation during therapy. This was a basic demarcation from classical testing of articulation progress by evaluating the child at the beginning of

therapy and at the end of therapy from single word items sampled in the initial, medial, and final positions.
2. The second phase developed a methodology to describe the clinical events occurring between the clinician and the child during articulation therapy. (These two phases are discussed in Chapter 2.)

## Project Questions

The project addressed two major questions:
1. After establishing a method for tracking articulation learning for numerous children, would it be possible to isolate unique learning patterns?
2. Would it be possible to isolate factors important in articulation learning? There were four categories of variables:
a. Child characteristics (sound, previous therapy, IQ, etc.)
b. Clinician characteristics (age, years experience, rapport, etc.)
c. Therapy arrangements (number of sessions, number in group, etc.)
d. Therapy procedures (cognitive lesson plan, interactions, etc.)

## Goals and Accomplishments of Each Project Year

Each year some changes in methodology were made to sharpen the procedures used for studying the therapy process in articulation learning during the final data collection year (Year 4). The six years of the project are summarized below.

## Project Year 1

The basic task was to determine if systematic evaluation of the child's articulation learning could be done by field clinicians in the schools. Two probes, the Sound Production Task (SPT), an imitative speech task and counting target phonemes correct/wrong during three minutes of conversation (TALK), were taken on each child on a once-a-week or every-two-weeks schedule. The child's articulation learning was plotted on a chart. Data were collected in the field on IBM Port-A-Punch cards by the clinician, mailed to the project office and processed by a computer.

Clinician time spent on computing SPT/TALK, charting, and punching IBM Port-A-Punch cards was compared with another group of clinicians who used more conventional record-keeping procedures. No differences in total time were found. Reliability measures of clinician correct/wrong counts during conversation were satisfactory. The three-minute conversation provided a sufficient sample of /r/ and /s/ occurrences to reflect progress on the target phoneme. And finally, the speech sampled in three-minute TALK during therapy was representative of the child's speech when sampled (outside of therapy) by another non-clinician adult (Diedrich, 1971a). In the first year there were no restrictions on type of sound studied, but only the /r/ and /s/ were studied in the following three years. There were several reasons for studying only /r/ and /s/: 1) the high error incidence of both these sounds, 2) the high frequency of occurrence of /r/ and /s/ in conversation (8-10 times per minute), and 3) since we were interested in articulation learning, we needed two distinctly different phonemes.

## Project Year 2

During Year 1 we used the 30-item SPT for /r/. Since our interest was in the acquisition of /r/ and its many allophonic features, the SPT was enlarged to 60 items to sample a broader allophonic range of /r/. The new 60-item /r/ SPT was used in the next three project years. The 30-item /s/ SPT was not changed. The objective was to replicate the SPT/TALK probe and charting procedures on another group of clinicians and children—this time only with /r/ and /s/ defective children. Three project staff clinicians were charged with the task of developing a procedure to describe ongoing therapy interactions between the clinician and child.

The new group of clinicians was as reliable in correct/wrong counting from conversation as the first-year clinicians. They also confirmed the minimal time expended to record the data. Further evaluation of the TALK in other speaking environments confirmed that no differences were found in correct/wrong counts made from TALK samples obtained in therapy and those done elsewhere (child talking with the teacher in the classroom and with the parent at home). Furthermore, a major technical breakthrough was accomplished in Year 2 by discovering that the behavior events in therapy could be recorded by a touch-tone telephone keyboard, hereafter called the Tone Keyboard (TKB). The TKB eliminated the need to write all the interactions on paper. A system for describing the clinicians' lesson plan was also developed in Year 2.

## Project Year 3

Nine public school clinicians tested the TKB in group therapy. A procedure was detailed whereby they entered their cognitive lesson plan on the TKB before each session. At this stage of the project TKB decoding was not reliable, so a paper-pencil format was devised to enter the clinicians' cognitive lesson plan in Year 4. The therapy interaction behaviors of the clinician and child, as described by our coded system, could be entered during therapy by the clinician on the TKB. Audio tapes, recorded from the TKB were decoded later. The TKB was selected by the clinicians as a workable instrument to describe the therapy events with minimal interference in therapy procedures. There were shortcomings, but the TKB system was the most viable procedure.

## Project Year 4

Now we had a system for tracking children's articulation learning during the school year and a useable system for describing the clinician's lesson plan and the interactions with the child during therapy. By knowing which child achieved success we could go back and analyze the clinician's lesson plans and behavior during therapy to develop similar teaching behaviors across clinicians and children.

If principles of therapy management were to have across clinician-child viability, we would need to select clinicians and children from a larger geographic area. Therefore, since our first three years had been primarily with clinicians and children from the Kansas City area, we chose clinicians and children from three different locations: Minneapolis, Minnesota; Wichita, Kansas; and Jefferson County, Colorado (outside Denver).

To make our evaluation of the children more comprehensive, we gathered additional information on each child about auditory discrimination, language, and school achievement. In addition, we developed a procedure to evaluate the daily feelings of the clinician and child before and after each therapy session.

## Project Years 5 and 6

Realizing we had three years (Year 2, 3, 4) of data with the same measures of speech progress, 30-item /s/, 60-item /r/ SPT, and three-minute TALK for over 1200 /r/ and /s/ children, we decided to do two major analyses: 1) over three years of the project and 2) a detailed evaluation of the more comprehensive Year 4 data on 242 children. Some special aspects of the data were given additional analysis:

1. Analysis over the three years.
   a. The SPT/TALK was used as the source of the main dependent variables on all the children.
   b. Independent variables for all children included sound, sex, grade, previous therapy, sessions per week, number in group, project year, and geographical location of school.
   c. The following independent variables on the 61 clinicians were available: age, years experience, education, American Speech and Hearing certification, self-ratings about their clinical skills and ability to discriminate /r/ and /s/ phonemes, and an Educational Opinion Inventory (EOI) indicative of rapport.
2. Detailed evaluation of the comprehensive Year 4 data. Additional child characteristic variables included:
   a. Auditory discrimination, language ability, school achievement, and socio-economic status.
   b. Clinician cognitive lesson plan.
   c. Interactions of the clinician and child during therapy.
   d. Daily feelings of the clinician and child.

# CHAPTER 2

# Methodology

This chapter describes the development of a system for tracking articulation learning. Children's articulation performance was our basic dependent variable. Articulation was assessed in both imitation and conversation. The reasons for this choice are detailed. The classical independent variables (clinician and child characteristics) are then outlined. New independent variables for studying articulation learning are also included. These are labeled cognitive lesson plan, clinician-child interactions, and the affective record of clinician-child daily feelings.

The next section provides the reader with details about how the data were collected. The selection process for the clinicians and children is also examined.

Finally, the reader is introduced to the various reliability procedures used in this project. Determination of "reliability" was an intriguing, if not frustrating, experience.

For definitions of special terms and symbols used in this project refer to Appendix G in this book.

## Development of a System for Tracking Articulation Learning (Dependent Variables)

Our purpose was to develop a system for tracking children's articulation learning over time (the dependent variable). The focus was children with articulation problems. We wanted to observe how the clinician and child, working together, solve articulation problems. We were interested in the process of acquiring articulation skill. Thus we needed to create a means for accounting for articulation development through the school year.

First, a slight digression is in order. In recent years accountability has become a household word. Leaders in education search for better methods to evaluate the learning process. Business and industry have quality control procedures. Medicine uses 24-hour monitoring of vital signs in intensive care. All of these are forms of accountability. Many professionals in education and the behavioral sciences believe that accountability is an externally imposed concept. Sometimes it is. This book proposes to create yet another form of accountability.

Sometimes an administrator comes to a teacher with new forms to be filled out, and new measurements to be taken in order to provide what seems to be just more paper for the bureaucratic maw. The teacher may view this paperwork as completely external to the process of teaching. Much of our work is directed toward the numerical evaluation of articulation ability. If our ideas are received with approval, it is likely that some speech clinicians will be filling out more forms. Some speech clinicians may have negative attitudes toward this activity. What we propose as researchers is that evaluation is an essential part of all work. None of us can work in a social vacuum. All accountability procedures are intended to answer the question "What is the worth of what the worker is doing?" The basic answer to this question is a simple, personal assertion of value by the worker himself. In today's world this usually is not enough. We are concerned with thousands of clinicians and hundreds of thousands of children with speech problems. The "work" we are concerned with here is the improvement of the whole field of speech pathology. This work is performed by clinicians, administrators, college and university teachers and researchers. We ask the reader (whether administrator or clinician) to consider the energies and workloads of all these persons concerned with all of these children. With this perspective, we think that the basic answer to the accountability question can be improved by a systematic numerical scoring and by a few forms.

In particular, what we see as needed is a procedure that allows the speech clinician supervisor to assess the worth of his or her clinicians without relying entirely on personal impression. By looking closely at the performance of each child we have a starting point for evaluating the performance of the clinician. The child's performance is the issue in this section and in subsequent sections and chapters.

We first asked if it were possible to develop an on-line procedure to obtain a speech progress readout (called a probe). The procedure would be a basic demarcation from the classical single word, articulation testing of the child at the beginning and end of therapy. The tasks should be designed to be cheaply administered, in short periods of time, at frequent intervals, to large numbers of children. The probes should reliably reflect the child's total speech ability at any given time, and optimally reflect that speech in all speaking environments. These measures, if plotted, could provide a record of progress for clinician, child and parent. We also hoped to be able to make predictions about the likelihood of success for different children, clinicians and therapy procedures.

Systematic probing of the target phoneme by both imitation and conversation were developed in Project Years 1 and 2. One of the measures, the Sound Production Tasks (SPT) was comprised of sounds, words, and phrases spoken by the clinician and imitated by the child (Elbert, Shelton, and Arndt, 1967; Shelton, Elbert, and Arndt, 1967; and Wright, Shelton, and Arndt, 1969). There were 30 items for /s/ and 60 items for /r/ (See Appendix C and, for an analysis of SPT items, see Chapter 8). The second measure was a three-minute sample of spontaneous speech (TALK) between clinician and child. The clinician counts the target phoneme correct or wrong while the child is talking (Diedrich, 1971b, 1972b, and 1973b). Children who were in therapy once a week were probed once a month, twice a week children were probed every other week, and in block therapy (four times per week) probed once a week. In this manner the SPT and TALK probes were given during every fourth therapy session.

The probes spaced in this manner were sensitive enough to reveal the different learning patterns of the children on different therapy schedules. The SPT was to be given three times as baseline data before therapy was begun. By combining the correct and wrong counts from the imitative articulation task (SPT) and from conversation (TALK) a Unified Score was derived (Diedrich and Bangert, 1972). The Unified Score was the total number of target phonemes correct on TALK and SPT over the total number correct and wrong. Drash, Caldwell, and Leibowitz (1970) have discussed the reliability and sensitivity of using correct and wrong counts as a dependent variable in speech. Thus, the Unified Score can be computed at any time during the school year by giving the child SPT/TALK.

Examination of the imitative and spontaneous speech tasks used for this study yielded a positive correlation of .79 between the children's midyear SPT scores and TALK midyear scores. It would have been possible to analyze SPT and TALK separately, but there is the likelihood of obtaining similar results (also see

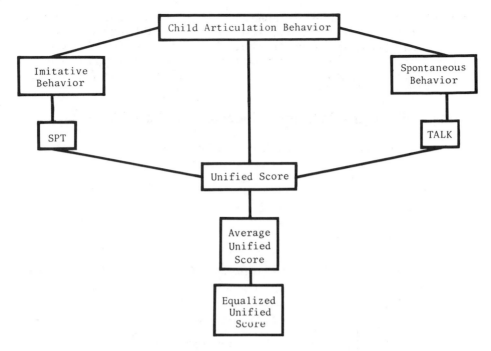

FIGURE 2.1 Structure of the dependent variable.

Chapter 7). Therefore, each pair of scores was combined in the Unified Score, resulting in an articulation score of both imitative and conversation skill for a given target phoneme (Figure 2.1).

Advantages of the Unified Score include combining two scores to give more information in one number. It is a more reliable indicator of the total speech behavior than a single number. Second, adopting the use of one number improves communication among speech pathologists. This concept is similar to that of IQ scores which combine verbal and performance skills. Third, the Unified Score provides comparability of results. Fourth, the Unified Score clarifies complex data analyses because it is easier to deal with one variable than with several. The fifth and last advantage is economy in time and money. It is very tedious and costly to work with both numbers on large amounts of data (even in the computer world).

The McDonald Screening Deep Test of Articulation (1968) was given to all project children at the beginning, middle, and end of the school year. It was not used as a dependent variable in the overall analysis strategy of the combined project years. There were several reasons for this decision. Analyses of data in Year 2 showed pre-test (September) McDonald Total Error scores correlated with midyear January scores (.79) and post-test (May) Total Errors (.65), but only –.22 with post-test TALK. Another difficulty is how to quantify the phoneme errors detected on any articulation test for an overall measure of severity. Are all phonemes equal in weight, and how do you weigh errors of omission or substitution? McDonald (1974) stated that his investigations of an overall articulation severity score (over several phonemes) had not been predictive of any future articulation learning on a given phoneme error. Another limitation was that we were interested in more continuous learning measures of a specific target phoneme. Also, since the McDonald Screening Test evaluates nine different sounds, it did not lend itself to systematic probe measures. We used the McDonald Deep Test (1964) for sampling /r/ and /s/ improvement, and used the Sound Production Tasks (SPT) to provide in-depth analyses of a given phoneme. (See Chapter 8 for analyses of the McDonald data.)

## Standard Measures (Independent Variables)

Informational questions were asked for all clinicians and children who participated in the project:

## Clinician Characteristics

a. Age
b. Sex
c. Education (BA or MA)
d. Years experience
e. American Speech and Hearing Certificate of Clinical Competence (Yes, No, Pending)
f. Self-concept on:
   1) discrimination of /r/ and /s/
   2) ability to teach /r/ and /s/
   3) ability to teach /r/ and /s/ in comparison with other clinicians.
   (Item f. was accomplished by having the clinicians rate their ability on a one-to-five scale from poor to excellent.)
g. Educational Opinion Inventory (Appendix A).
   We were interested in obtaining an evaluation of personality or attitude of the clinician. We did not want to use obvious psychological measures such as the Minnesota Multi-Phasic Inventory or California Personality Scale. In searching for a suitable instrument we found the Educational Opinion Inventory (EOI) by Krasno (1972) developed at the Stanford Center for Research and Development in Teaching.

> A scale was evolved from 300 EOI items with related EOI responses to the criterion variable of teacher-student support (R Scale). The purpose was to identify a set of items which would differentiate between prospective teachers who could establish immediate rapport with students as measured by the Pupil Inventory and prospective teachers who were not successful in establishing rapport. The validity of each EOI item for inclusion in the R Scale was thus defined as to the degree which it differentiated between two groups of potential teachers (p. 44).

The 62 items differentiating teachers with high and low rapport were administered to all our speech clinicians. If the Educational Opinion Inventory (EOI) indicated the speech clinician's ability to establish rapport, would it also show that speech clinicians who were successful in modifying /r/ and /s/ phoneme behavior had high rapport? Furthermore, since we were measuring the clinician's daily feelings, we would try and correlate the EOI rapport measure with daily feelings and see if it might be a predictive test. Since the EOI was not discovered until after Year 4 began, it was administered to all project clinicians from Years 2, 3, 4, in the early part of Year 4.

## Child Characteristics

a. Sex
b. Grade
c. /r/ or /s/ sound
d. Weeks of previous therapy on /r/ and /s/
e. Number of children in therapy group
f. School Record Information (Year 4 only)

School achievement tests in reading, spelling, arithmetic were pulled from the child's school records. In different schools different tests were used (even within the same city). However, we decided not to attempt to teach speech clinicians to give a standard school achievement test (for example, the Wide Range Achievement Test). We believed we could obtain a better in-depth index for a given academic area by using existing school tests, whether they were Stanford Achievement Test, Gates Reading Test, etc., than could be obtained by a survey instrument such as the Wide Range Achievement Test. Therefore, the reading percentiles from the school records actually reflect several different tests. The most recent score was used if more than one existed. It was interesting to note that despite the geographic differences, many of the schools used the Stanford Achievement Test in reading. School records were too incomplete to obtain information on spelling and arithmetic. In addition to the achievement tests, we requested information on intellectual tests, but found few children who had complete intellectual tests. That item was abandoned.

Additional questions were asked about the child's family and whether others in it had speech problems; whether the parents were deceased or divorced; whether they came from a minority group, and whether or not the child was from a low income group (less than $5,000 per year). This information was obtained from school personnel records, and from personal contact between the clinician and the family. Formal interviews were not held with the parents. Therefore, many of the responses were "don't know."

g. Auditory Discrimination (Goldman-Fristoe-Woodcock, subtest in noise, 1970). Duguay (1971) found this subtest sensitive in identifying discrimination problems in children with articulation disorders.

## Clinician-Child Interactions

### Cognitive Lesson Plan

Before a therapy session each clinician had some idea of what she planned to do. We simply put on paper, in a formal descriptive manner, her cognitive lesson plan for each of the children (when necessary the clinician could change her plan during therapy).

The ACTIVITY is the chronological order of the stimulus materials presented to the child during the therapy session. Table 2.1 summarizes the descriptions collected. The definitions of all activities and the instructions are in Appendix C.

### Behavior of the Clinician and Child During Therapy

The cognitive lesson plan provides a skeletal outline of what the clinician *intended* to do. The outline does not report what she actually *did*. A different procedure was used to obtain information about the specific behaviors the clini-

NAME OF THE ACTIVITY
      Free Conversation, Structured Speech, Reading, Drills (Standard, Game,
Rate, Transfer, Response Shaping), Discrimination, Self-Monitoring, Negative
Practice, Chart, Fun Time, Review and Give Assignments, Teacher or Parent
Conference, our test battery (articulation, language, voice), and probes
(Talk Task, Sound Production Task).

STIMULUS
      Auditory Model, Picture, Model and Picture, Graphic, Tape Recorder,
Other Equipment, Objects, Child Generated, Sentence Completion, and Chart

CONTENT
      Isolation, Syllable, Word, Phrase/sentence, Mixed

POSITION
      Initial, Medial, Final, Mixed, Blends

CONTINGENCY SCHEDULE
      Token Reinforcement and Token Cost

LENGTH OF TIME for each activity to the nearest minute.

DAILY FEELINGS
      Clinicians and child without knowledge of the other's choice, each
indicate before and after every session their mood at that time.


TABLE 2.1. CHILD ACTIVITY information obtained by each clinician on every child for all therapy
     sessions.


cian and child performed. There were no constraints placed on the clinician as to
type of therapy plan (materials, program steps, or equipment). The clinician was
asked to use a typical case management program in a group speech therapy
setting. A system gradually developed to describe the INTERACTIONS between
the speech clinician and the child. The specific second-to-second stimulus provided by the clinician, the response of any given child in the group, and the
consequation by the clinician are listed (Table 2.2). The clinician described the
therapy process as it actually occurred. We have developed two ways of obtaining
this information: 1) a paper/pencil procedure, 2) for Year 4 we used a Tone
Keyboard that allowed the clinician to make a running record of what she and the
child did as therapy occurred. The telephone touch-tones produced by the clinician were recorded and later decoded at the University of Kansas Academic
Computer Center (Appendix C).

CLINICIAN RESPONSES
    Again
    Wrong
    Approximation
    Correct
    Feedback to child about articulators
    Verbalization (all other talking was called verbalization)


CLINICIAN AUDITORY MODELS
    Isolation
    Syllable
    Words
    Phrase or sentences


SHAPING PROCEDURES


CRITICAL EVENT


CHILD RESPONSES
    Discrimination
    Wrong
    Approximation
    Correct
    Verbalization (all other talking was called verbalization)
    Keys 1-4 tell which child made the response

TABLE 2.2. On the 16-key Tone Keyboard the following information was recorded in real time to the nearest second by the clinician while therapy was in progress.


## Affective Record (Daily Feelings)

Finally, we wished to obtain some barometer of the clinician's feelings and the child's feelings on a day-to-day basis. The methodology had to be simple and require only a brief time to get a judgment of how the clinician and children were feeling before therapy and after therapy. No psychological test measures provided the kind of information we needed. Therefore, this procedure was followed: Before each therapy session the clinician answered the following questions: "How do you feel today about . . . child 1, child 2, child 3, yourself, therapy, conditions, and things generally?" There were three grades of feelings: good, soso, and lousy. The clinician checked her responses on the CHILD IDENTIFICATION, ACTIV-ITY, and FEELING sheet just before therapy and just after each therapy session. The children were presented with a magic slate on which had been drawn three faces; happy face, neutral face and sad face. They were told to circle the face that described how they felt at that moment. A piece of paper was used to cover the first response and the slate was placed under their chair. At the end of therapy the children were again asked to indicate how they felt and were told to circle one of the three faces. The clinician took the magic slate from each child and checked the appropriate box on the CHILD IDENTIFICATION, ACTIVITY and FEELING sheet for the before and after therapy feelings for each child in the group. These data were collected for each therapy session on all Year 4 clinicians and children throughout the school year (Appendix C).

## Data Collection Procedures

### Dependent Variables

In Years 2, 3, 4 the correct/wrong counts on the Sound Production Tasks (SPT) and three-minute TALK tasks were recorded on IBM Port-A-Punch cards and mailed each week to the project office. The McDonald Screening Deep Test of Articulation was completed at the beginning, middle, and end of the year. Responses were recorded on IBM Port-A-Punch cards and mailed to us.

The three-minute TALK tasks used for reliability checks and other analyses were tape recorded on all children at baseline and midyear and mailed to our office. All taped material was recorded at 3.75 ips and obtained in the clinician's therapy room on a Realistic Model 505, Sony TC-104A, or the clinician's own recorder.

### Independent Variables

In Years 2, 3, 4, paper/pencil data were collected on the clinicians' age, sex, education, years experience, ASHA certification, therapy skill self-concept, and rapport (EOI). These were mailed to us and keypunched at a later date for analysis. Child characteristic information on sex, grade, error sound, previous therapy, and number in therapy group was similarly collected.

In Year 4 additional child characteristic data were compiled on paper/pencil forms and later keypunched. This included school information, auditory discrimination (G-F-W), dental, and language battery (Appendix B).

### Cognitive Lesson Plan (Identification, Activity, and Feeling Sheet)

This was a paper/pencil format collected only in Year 4 and mailed weekly to our office to be keypunched. (see Appendix C)

### Tone Keyboard

Year 4 clinicians mailed (each week) audiotapes of touch-tone responses recorded at a speed of 1.875 ips on a Realistic Model 505 A taperecorder. The material was decoded at a speed of 7.5 ips (Appendix C).

## Selection of Clinicians

Two different strategies were used in the selection of clinicians for the project. In Years 2 and 3 all the clinicians came from the greater Kansas City Area (Missouri and Kansas). This eased the difficulties of project management and reduced the cost of training and the dissemination of materials. In Year 4, we decided to broaden the distribution of clinicians and children, so personnel were chosen from school districts in Wichita, Kansas, Minneapolis, Minnesota, and Jefferson County, Colorado (a Denver suburb). In our subsequent data analysis, a variable called GEOG identifies the geographical location of clinicians and children.

Prior to the beginning of project Year 2 speech clinicians in the greater Kansas City area were solicited by mail to determine their interest in the project. Out of the responses, twenty were chosen. An attempt was made to obtain a cross-section of school district size and socioeconomic status, although no formal check was made on these two criteria. The selection was made primarily on the basis of the project staff's familiarity with the area.

The result was 18 female and two male clinicians. Because of the small number of males, the sex of the clinician is not used in the statistical analyses. There were three black clinicians. Again, race was not used in the statistics.

Three part-time staff clinicians were added to the twenty in Year 2, making a total of 23 clinicians. Each staff clinician worked with a caseload of 20 children in the public schools. Their primary goal was to develop a methodology for describing therapy procedures as therapy was in progress. Note that a full set of data pertaining to all the clinicians is presented in Chapter 5, with an accompanying explanation of variables. The project Year 2 clinicians are numbered 1-23 in Appendix E Table E.21.

At the end of Year 2 we asked for volunteers to continue with the project. Out of the 20 nonstaff clinicians, seven volunteered to continue into Year 3. In Appendix E Table E.21, under variable YEAR, these are marked 23, indicating that they participated in both Years 2 and 3 of the project. Two clinicians (34 and 37) with whom we had maintained contact from Year 1 also volunteered to participate in the project.

To provide control, we arranged for nine new clinicians. They were to carry out regular clinical procedures with their caseloads, but were not taught to systematically count target phonemes like the project clinicians. The children's articulation progress was probed by our staff clinicians. These control clinicians were selected by the staff clinicians from among those available in the schools where the staff clinicians were working. The important criterion was the geographical accessibility of the children to the staff clinicians. These nine control clinicians are numbered 91-99. This produced a total of 18 clinicians whose children were to be studied in Year 3.

In Year 4, having chosen different geographical areas (Wichita, Denver area, and Minneapolis), the coordinators in each area were asked to choose clinicians who were willing to participate in the project. We asked the coordinators to choose clinicians with diverse educational backgrounds, a varied number of years of experience, and who used different therapy models and procedures. We did not intend to recruit clinicians from a population about whom we needed to make inferences. Thus, we also asked for participants in Year 4 who had, in the coordinator's estimation, provided successful therapy to children. This last characterization may cause the reader some trouble when we discuss the abilities of our clinicians relative to other clinicians. We can only hope that someone will soon do a similar experiment with a truly random sample of clinicians from an identified population.

The demographic breakdown of clinicians in Year 4 is similar to Year 3: 3 male, 24 female, all white. A range of socioeconomic school settings were included in the data, but that was not checked.

# Training of Clinicians

## Years 2 and 3

Prior to the school year, all clinicians received training in counting and charting target phonemes for conversation. The charting procedures are detailed elsewhere (Diedrich, 1971b; 1973b). The children were shown the results of the SPT/TALK probe and their progress on the chart. The clinicians practiced administering the McDonald Screening Deep Test of Articulation, Sound Production Tasks, and tape recording conversation for future reliability checks. They also learned how to use the IBM Port-A-Punch cards and were given instructions on mailing data to the project office.

In Year 3, the nine clinicians (seven from Year 2 and two from Year 1) in the Kansas City area collected data on the Tone Keyboard (TKB). The purpose was to refine the therapy data collection procedures in field conditions and to determine if the TKB methodology could be used on a larger scale in the last project (Year 4). The clinicians in Years 2 and 3 received a stipend for the year, plus per diem for participation in the several workshops (Table 2.3).

In Year 3 a group of nine new clinicians consented to have our staff clinicians administer SPT/TALK tasks to their caseload. This created a control group of clinicians and children who were not counting and charting. These nine clinicians received no training in any of the project procedures. This enabled us to have a group of children who were not receiving any regularly administered SPT/TALK tasks, i.e., were not having their progress systematically charted by the clinician every other week. These clinicians did not use the TKB during therapy.

## Year 4

For their participation in the project, clinicians in Year 4 had the opportunity (for a fee) to receive graduate credit through the University of Kansas Extension Division. They received a stipend and per diem payment to attend the several workshops. In addition, they could keep the different diagnostic tests used in the project during that year.

We conducted workshops in each of the three cities to instruct the clinicians in how to use the TKB (Appendix C). They received six to eight weeks practice in preparation for their participation during the next academic year. The clinicians during this period also practiced how to count target phonemes during conversation (our three-minute TALK task) with their children. No progress charting was done in this last year. The nine clinicians who piloted the TKB during project Year 3 became fairly comfortable with the TKB after six to ten hours of practice. The clinicians needed to use the TKB a minimum of twice a week to maintain their skills. In addition, the clinicians observed that it was not efficient to try to use the TKB for every therapy session in any given day. Four hours a week seemed to be a comfortable amount to handle. Consequently, we established the use of the TKB on a twice-a-week basis for four groups. That amounted to about four hours per week of therapy data being collected in that manner.

Data were collected on the IBM Port-A-Punch cards during the first three years of the project. In Year 4 this recording medium was not used because the clinicians had to master the operation of the TKB. We did not want to add another new "system" of data collection. It seemed wiser to obtain SPT/TALK data via conventional paper/pencil methods which were later keypunched.

| Year | Geography | Number of Clinicians and Children | | SPT/TALK Probes Done by | Variables[f] |
|---|---|---|---|---|---|
| | | Clinicians | Children | | |
| 1[a] | Kansas | 10 | 300 | clinician | |
| 2 | Greater Kansas City | 20 | 600 | clinician | |
| 2 | Staff clinicians | 3 | 61 | staff | |
| 2[b] | Greater Kansas City | 0 | 61 | staff | |
| 3[c] | Greater Kansas City | 9 | 176 | staff | |
| 3 | Greater Kansas City | 9[d] | 207[e] | clinician | TKB |
| 4 | Jefferson County | 7 | 65 | clinician | TKB |
| 4 | Minneapolis | 10 | 93 | clinician | TKB |
| 4 | Wichita | 10 | 84 | clinician | TKB |

a. Year 1 data not used because articulation sampling procedures were changed in subsequent years.

b. Parochial school children who received no speech therapy that year; staff clinician made monthly SPT/TALK probes. None of these or Year 1 children are included in the data analysis of 1108 children.

c. Nine control clinicians who provided therapy, but staff made monthly SPT/TALK probes.

d. Seven clinicians were from Year 2 and two clinicians from Year 1.

e. Twenty-eight children were the same children treated in Year 2.

f. The SPT/TALK probes were made by counting live child correct/wrong responses. The Tone Keyboard (TKB) was piloted in Year 3 and implemented in Year 4. See Chapter 8 for further discussion of counting/charting variables.

TABLE 2.3. Distribution of clinicians and children during the project.

Just prior to the beginning of the school year (August), a two-day workshop was scheduled in each of the three cities. During this time the following topics were presented and reviewed: Selection of project children, scheduling of tests, learning how to complete the Child ID, Activity and Feeling sheets, reviewing TKB procedures, and finally, all the tests were explained and practiced (for example, the Goldman-Fristoe-Woodcock Auditory Discrimination Test, the Token Test, etc.). In addition, specific administrative procedures were outlined for submitting testing materials, obtaining probes, and mailing TKB tapes, Child ID, Activity and Feeling sheets, and SPT/TALK sheets to the project office. Each clinician was given a five-inch, reel-to-reel tape recorder and instructed in its use. A workbook was prepared for each clinician detailing the steps, tests, and procedures. When school began we had 10 participating clinicians from Wichita, 10 from Minneapolis, and seven from Jefferson County (Denver) Colorado for a total of 27 clinicians.

The first of November another one-day workshop was held with the clinicians in each of the three cities to review their testing materials and schedules and to answer questions regarding the project operation. Reliability checks on their use of the TKB were also made at this time. A coordinator was chosen from the clinicians in each city so that questions could be channeled through this person and communicated to the project office for answers. Since many of the clinicians had similar questions, this was an efficient way to manage most problems. However, each clinician also had direct access to the project office via telephone or mail so specific queries could be answered promptly.

A third workshop was conducted with the clinicians during the latter part of January and mid-year checks and evaluations were reviewed. Additional questions and problems were covered at that time.

The last one-day workshop was held in the beginning of May to review the end-of-year tests and to provide the clinician with replacement forms and materials that had been expended during the year. The Educational Opinion Inventory was administered to all clinicians and they completed a questionnaire about their participation in the project.

## Selection of Children

The selection of children for this project is best seen as a hierarchical procedure with a large base population that is steadily refined down to the 1,108 children on which our analyses are based. Because this is a naturalistic study, the selection procedure is not random at every step, but we believe that ours is a realistic sample of United States children with articulation problems.

The basic selection procedure was established in Year 2. We began at a level of abstraction somewhat removed from our final sample. In Year 2 the original subjects were children in the greater Kansas City area (Missouri and Kansas) grade schools with articulation problems. Using the procedure described in the previous section, we chose clinicians to work in the project. The clinician-choice effectively makes a first selection from this basic population of children. We now may think of our pool of children as being the total caseload of the clinicians selected. Inasmuch as these are representative clinicians with representative caseloads, we propose that this reduced population is equivalent to the original.

Out of their total caseload, clinicians were instructed to select children with primary /r/ or /s/ errors for therapy. Children with other phoneme errors were acceptable as long as the /r/ or /s/ was the primary error and was one which, in the clinician's opinion, required therapy. The McDonald screening test was used on the children selected to see if large numbers of children had both /r/ and /s/ problems. It was found that only 11% of 584 children in Year 2 had errors on both the /r/ and /s/ sounds. By this we mean four or more errors on /r/ and four or more errors on /s/ (also, see McDonald Test data presented in Chapter 6). It was decided to allow the clinician to label these children with the primary phoneme error, /r/ or /s/. This is the target phoneme and is labeled SOUND.

Thus the group of children was reduced to those who were part of the selected clinician's caseloads with /r/ or /s/ problems. The clinicians scheduled their groups according to their normal practice. Each clinician mailed to the project office a list of their /r/ or /s/ children placed in therapy groups (/r/ or /s/ children were not placed together). The project office then selected groups for the project. It was first decided to select approximately 30 children from each clinician's list. These were to be roughly 15 /r/ and 15 /s/. The next problem was selection of grade.

We were aware of the criticism of the effects of speech therapy versus maturation. Earlier studies noted that articulation development was not complete until 6, 7, or 8 years of age. Therefore, we chose children who were in the third grade. We could not get all the subjects we needed (especially in project Years 1 and 2), so other grades were added. Grade order was 3, 4, 2, 5, 1, 6. Thus, all of the clinicians' third graders were selected. If the total of third graders was 30, the procedure stopped for that clinician. If not, fourth graders were selected. If the total of third and fourth graders reached 15 /r/ and 15 /s/, the procedure stopped, otherwise second graders were selected and so on.

Recent developmental studies in articulation by Prather, Hedrick, and Kern, (1974) and Arlt and Goodban (1976) give evidence that mastery of phonemes may start sooner and mature earlier. The two sounds (/r/ and /s/) with which we were primarily concerned were shown by Sander (1972) with the early Wellman and Templin data to have 90% completion by six years of age for /r/ and eight years of age for /s/. Arlt and Goodban observed 75% completion by four years for /r/ and five years for /s/ (90% completion was not provided). Prather et al. found by four years of age 91% completion for /s/, 100% for final /r/, but only 62% for initial /r/ (48 months was the oldest age group).

Poole's (1934) 100% completion data showed both /r/ and /s/ took until seven years six months. It appears that most children (75%) develop /r/ and /s/ by five years, but those who do not may be those speech clinicians teach in first, second, and third grades. Sander's (1972) point is well taken. Maturation of articulation skills takes place over a long period of time. There are still problems with predicting which children should get therapy and which will master their articulation skills without therapy by 6 to 8 years of age (see Chapter 7).

The final sample was selected from the above pool (Table 2.3). While measuring each child's learning curve (see Chapter 3) some children were dropped who did not have enough raw data or whose data had extreme variation. Lack of data was probably caused by moving or illness. This introduces a small bias. Wide variations in raw scores probably represent errors in the recording and data collection procedures and thus does not introduce much bias.

The procedure for Year 3 was the same as Year 2, except that each clinician had 20 children instead of 30. This was done because Year 3 clinicians were learning how to use the TKB.

In Year 4 we wanted to determine whether there were differences in teaching approaches with children who had a year or more of therapy compared with children who had no previous therapy on that phoneme. Therefore, we chose four sets of children, two /r/ and two /s/ groups, one /r/ group and one /s/ group had previous therapy, one /r/ group and one /s/ group had no previous therapy. It was noted in Year 3 that the use of the TKB was comfortable with two or three children in a group, but four children in a group overloaded the system. Therefore, each clinician had approximately 10 children for whom she collected data.

In the fourth year, the clinicians randomly chose their groups for the project. In order to increase the "randomness" of clinician selection of children, they were given the following instructions.

> Establish a therapy schedule for the year as usual, then look at the groups and see if they match any of the four above groups. Keep in mind that it's to your advantage to have them in as few schools as possible; scheduled twice-a-week, but not on Friday. (From our past experience children scheduled on Friday had too many days of missing therapy data because of holidays, teacher conferences, etc.) If your first attempt at scheduling does not provide the four groups, then rearrange the children as necessary to make the four groups. If you have more than the necessary number of groups, then assign an identification number to each group, place on a piece of paper, and choose them at random. For example, perhaps you have one Group 1 - no previous /s/ therapy; one Group 2 - previous /s/ therapy; one Group 3 - no previous /r/ therapy; and three Group 4's - previous /r/ therapy. Identify each of the three Group 4's on three pieces of paper. Blindly select from a box one piece of paper and this becomes your selection for Group 4.

Our preliminary data analysis showed little difference in articulation learning scores from therapy conducted once-a-week, twice-a-week, or block scheduling. Therefore, in Year 4, we selected children who were seen twice-a-week since this seemed to be the more common practice across the country (Bingham et al., 1961).[1] Each clinician's groups were composed of two to three children from grades one to six seen twice-a-week.

Additional requirements for selection of the children were the following:
1. *Hearing*: The child must not be labeled by the parent, teacher, clinician, nurse, or physician as having a hearing loss. No more than an average of 20 dB loss may be present in the better ear at 500-2000 Hz if audiograms were available.
2. *Special Education*: The child must not be in a special education class and not identified by a physician or school system personnel as a cerebral palsy, mentally retarded, emotionally disturbed, or hard-of-hearing child. A child classified as learning disability could be included if the child attended regular class (only a few were included in this classification).
3. *Combined Speech Problems*: In the opinion of the speech clinician, if articulation (/r/ or /s/) was the primary problem being treated, a child with voice, stuttering, or language problems was acceptable.
4. *Age*: As previously described, grade order selection was 3, 4, 2, 5, 1, 6.
5. *Organic*: Any child whose articulation problem appeared to be caused by a physical defect was not included, e.g., cleft palate or diagnosed central nervous system disease.

1. This practice may not be effective or justifiable for many children.

6. *Itinerants*: Children were not chosen from families who were subject to almost certain moves.
7. *Family Relationships*: No selection of twins. Only one sibling from the same family could participate in the project.

## Reliability Measures of Conversation

When any researcher draws conclusions, he or she wants the conclusions to be valid for situations outside the framework of the project, and for times after the end of the project. Our project involved the articulation learning of 1,108 children in numerous school settings, with 61 clinicians. We intend that the various conclusions drawn about the effect of /s/ and /r/ problems, and previous therapy, etc., will apply to more children, in different schools, for the foreseeable future of articulation therapy.

The primary tool for ensuring the validity outside our particular framework is statistical inference. We have a large sample of children, and we have been careful in our use of statistical techniques. A second tool is the estimation of the reliability of individual measurements. Following Cronbach et al. (1972), the most useful attitude is one of careful generalization. Given an articulation measurement on one particular child by one particular clinician, how much can we infer about that child's articulation, if measured sometime in the future, or in a different setting, or with different instruments, or by a different clinician? In each case, we want to generalize a single measurement, or set of measurements outside the immediate context.

Such generalization has classically fallen under the study of reliability. It is unfortunate that the methods of Cronbach et al. (1972) were not known to us when we conducted these reliability experiments. Ideally, a clinician could set up a reliability experiment for child articulation, specify the factors to be generalized, and then estimate the error of each individual measurement. This error could then qualify each mean difference, and thus, most of the conclusions. Instead, we will report standard reliability measures, and hope the reader will agree that (with a relatively large sample size) most of our conclusions are valid.

A summary of our findings are presented below. For more extensive information, the reader should refer to the data included in Appendix D.

## Other Studies

Other studies are difficult to compare with our work because they used typescripts, percent agreements, or the clinicians were not judged. For example, in Bankson (1970) and Bankson and Byrne (1972) typescripts of the first 40 words spoken in conversaion containing the target phoneme were prepared and then the judge listened to the tape-recorded conversation with the specific word and target phoneme underlined for them to judge. They had agreements ranging from 61-96%. In the Freilinger (1973) investigation, the word containing the target phoneme was on typescript and the judge listened to the words spoken from samples of conversation previously recorded and randomly dubbed on a master tape. He had 78.5% agreement over a total of 1,200 judgments. Shelton, Johnson, Arndt (1972) did not use typescripts and the mean percentage of agreement was 81% for the TALK tasks when heard from tapes. The Pearson intercorrelation for the judges was .96. They did not compare the clinician with the judges.

Stephens and Daniloff (1977) had six experienced judges listen to six defective /s/ and eight normal /s/ speakers. They heard speech samples both live and under maximum fidelity audio tape conditions. The judges knew the material (they were to slash out the /s/ target words if misarticulated). Under the live situation all judges agreed that the defective /s/ subjects were consistently in error; however, under the audio conditions these six listeners judged the defective /s/ speakers as being correct 24-75% of the time. They judged all normal subjects as correct live and 90-99% correct on audio judgments. The authors clearly stated ". . . that live listening conditions are absolutely critical for appropriate judgments of these /s/ misarticulations."

## Summary of Project Reliability Studies

a. Satisfactory reliability does not depend upon typescripts. Groups (four or more) of persons (clinician, non-clinician, etc.) can make reliable correct/wrong judgments (live or taped) of children's conversation (interreliability .70's to .90's, but only .54 for any individual). These are samples of speech from children unknown to the listener.
b. Clinician judgments of children they treat in therapy may be low (.30's to .70's) when compared to other observers (clinicians or non-clinicians). Frequency of total sounds heard in conversation are usually judged the same. After children have been in therapy (midyear or later), clinicians generally judge more correct and fewer wrong than the other observers.
c. Clinician's judgments are usually less reliable (stable) at baselines (September samples were .60 for /r/ and .30 for /s/) than at midyear (January samples were .76 for /r/ and .49 for /s/). This may be a demonstration of temporal effect and developing a self-internal standard.
d. Judgments made from tapes of /s/ are usually less stable (reliable) than /r/. Clinicians frequently counted /s/ for /z/ and poor audio tape fidelity are contributing factors.
e. Better reliability was obtained with the clinician in the live therapy situation than from tape observations.
f. Reliability of imitative Sound Production Tasks (SPT) was higher than for samples of conversation.
g. Once a correct/wrong standard is developed by a listener it remains relatively stable even after many hours of additional judgments carried out for short periods of time (25 hours in one week) or longer periods of time (66 hours over 11 weeks).
h. Reliability measures judged on children in therapy between clinicians and neutral observers may be low, but high reliability does not preclude experimenter bias (Kent et al., 1974).

The results reported above demonstrated that the /s/ sound was much more difficult to judge than the /r/. There are at least three major sources of error that contribute to poor reliability of /s/ judgments. One source is that frequently /z/ is counted for /s/ (e.g., trees). In a typescript analysis we found that the clinicians consistently counted more /s/ sounds than were available in the sample. Secondly, not all the trouble is in the ear of the listener. Costley and Broen (1976) have noted that

> . . . ambiguous productions tended to lie near the phoneme boundary for voice onset time . . . ambiguous productions tended to display unusual acoustic characteristics

. . . results suggest that it is not always valid to assume that the disagreement lies in the accuracy of the listener.

Voice onset time (VOT) then, may be a factor in /s-z/ confusions. Also it is difficult to make good audio tapes in the field to obtain adequate fidelty for /s/ reproduction. Our tape speed was 3.75 i.p.s. and adjoining classroom noise did not help improve the quality. Sharf (1968) demonstrated that groups of listeners obtained only 70% correct identification of /s/ from an Ampex tape recorder at 7.5 i.p.s. speed in a soundproof room. Neither our recording or listening conditions were that well controlled.

Finally, two other types of studies relate to the problem of making reliable perceptual judgments of repeated speech samples. Tekieli and Lass (1972) cited Warren (1961) as describing a "verbal transformation effect" from continued listening to auditory stimuli. They confirmed the transformation phenomenon and concluded ". . . that no single statement can be made concerning the consistency of subjects' reported verbal transformations as a function of either the meaningfulness or phonetic complexity of the repeating stimulus." On a similar topic of listener consistency to the same target phonemes Shelton, Johnson, and Arndt (1974) stated that

> Variability in judgment of articulation correctness by persons listening to repetitions of the same utterance does not appear to be universal. Nevertheless, shifts were made with sufficient frequency by several judges to support the opinion that research should be directed to observers' judgments of articulation adequacy under conditions where observers listen to repetitions of similar stimuli.

The transformation phenomenon may be yet another factor that influences listener reliability.

In their study of /s/ Stephens and Daniloff (1977) recommended that subjects repeat sentences varying in context at least three times in order to obtain a stable and adequate sample. They also suggested that judgments be made live and on a dichotomous acceptable/unacceptable scale. The three-minute TALK data judged live by the clinician in the field fulfills these requirements. The samples of conversation on the average will elicit 20-30 samples of the /r/ or /s/ in many contexts (see Chapter 7). Also, the clinician makes correct/wrong judgments live during therapy. The systematic SPT/TALK probes every two weeks across the school year provided considerable replication of the phenomenon being studied (target phonemes). Finally, our data reports on large numbers of children and clinicians. Any large individual variances have been washed out by statistical measures of central tendency. Also, the results seem to make sense and all this contributes to believeability of the data.

Therefore, we are willing to accept the fact that point for point agreement for any given child at any given time by any given group of clinicians or other listeners will be less than perfect for correct/wrong counts made during conversation. Clinical investigations should continue with the realization that the aseptic condition of the laboratory or statistical elegance of the agronomist's latticed field work will not usually obtain. Even with all the loopholes of clinical reliability, progress is being made and suggestions regarding articulation treatment should be given with the best evidence available.

A quote from Kenney (1975) seems appropriate here:

We would all prefer to have the testimony about an event from a sighted man over a blind man. But when we have only the blind man, we would not dismiss his testimony, especially if he were aware of his biases. . . .

The difference between the true experiment and the quasi-experiment is of the magnitude of the difference between sight and blindness. We must often grope in the darkness with quasi-experimental designs, but this blindness both forces us to compensate for biases and helps us develop a newfound sensitivity to the structure of the data. Finally, it makes us appreciate the clarity of true experimental inference.

## Tone Keyboard Reliability

### Reliability I

In order to determine that each project clinician had mastered the use of the Tone Keyboard (TKB) and the coding system (Appendix C) before they began therapy, a Criterion Tape was made. The Criterion Tape was a recorded 14-minute simulated therapy session. A "Clinician" and two "Artics" (adults) with an /r/ misarticulation participated in three therapy activities. These activities were planned so that most of the TKB coding system could be employed.

At the workshop in the fall (end of October) and prior to starting therapy, a project staff clinician visited each of the three participating cities and carried out the first TKB reliability measure. The tapes were collected and decoded and printouts were made.

A typescript was made of the 14-minute simulated Criterion Tape and each utterance was labeled according to the TKB coding system. This master guide of simulated keyboard entries was compared to each clinicians' keyboard entries. The comparison was made on a point-to-point correspondence. Any omission, addition, or substitution of touch tones was considered an error. From this comparison a percentage of agreement was obtained for each clinician. Anyone who had less than 75% agreement (arbitrary cutoff) was asked to redo the Criterion Tape.

The agreement scores from 26 clinician ranged from 99% to 67% (Appendix D, Table D.15). Only four of the clinicians scored below 75% and two of these clinicians had mechanical difficulties at the listening session. These people repeated the Criterion Test and all scored above the 75% criterion cutoff level on the second attempt. It is clear on the basis of these procedures that the project clinicians were able to reliably use the Tone Keyboard coding system.

### Reliability II

The second reliability measure was performed in December and January (depending on when our workshops could be scheduled) to determine how well the clinicians were utilizing the TKB system while they were actually performing their therapy sessions. Another project clinician in each city observed each clinician during one therapy session. She brought her own TKB, tape recorder, and tape so that two TKB recordings could be made simultaneously (one from the observing clinician and one from the actual clinician). These pairs of tapes were sent to the Computer Center for decoding and printing.

There were two classes of errors. Class I errors were indicated by the absence of a code on one printout which was present on the other. For example, when the observer does not agree due to attention (something happened) during therapy while she was looking at her TKB, Tone Keyboard failure, decode failure, etc. Class II errors (presence of a different code on both printouts) represent a clear cut difference in definition of category (Appendix D, Table D.15). The mean agreement for all clinicians was 73%. There was a total of 4,736 agreements, 1,820 Class I disagreements, and 14 Class II disagreements. Class I errors may be due to a mechanical problem, or to an "interpretation" of a category. For example, there were many times when one clinician would push the "vocalization" key and another clinician might push the "again" key (where the clinician says "try it again"). These two behaviors are very similar since they both represent a verbal utterance on the part of the clinician. The overall pattern of the TKB decoding is not affected with Class I errors (i.e., gross errors in category interpretation are not made). Class II errors are obvious conflicts in the use of a category, and if they had occurred with great frequency, would have provided a serious problem in reliability.

The calculation for percentage of agreement was as follows:

$$\text{Percent agreement} = \frac{\text{Agreements}}{\text{Agreements} + \text{Disagreements}}$$

## Reliability III

A third and final check was conducted in the latter part of March and beginning of April of the school year. In this procedure each project clinician made an audio tape of one therapy session with their project children and later in the day or week they listened to this audio tape and placed their responses on the TKB using another tape recorder. The computer TKB printouts were then compared to the audio recordings by the project staff. Since Johnson (1969) observed that 80% of the events in speech therapy were auditory and 20% visual it was believed that this reliability procedure of audio material would check most of the therapy interactions. The total number of therapy minutes was divided in thirds. Lingwall and Engmann (1971) had determined that therapy interaction in the middle third of a session was optimal for examining therapy process interaction events. For our reliability check an activity beginning closest to the middle third was chosen for analysis which amounted to approximately ten minutes of therapy.

The audio tape of therapy was played and the TKB printout was examined simultaneously for accuracy. All the possible codes were checked by a project staff person. The correspondence between the audio tape therapy events and the printout were noted. If a printed code agreed with the audio event it was checked as being PRESENT AND CORRECT. Each time a printed code was noted that did not agree with the audio event it was checked as being PRESENT BUT INCORRECT. If an audio therapy event was noted that had not been put on the TKB it was checked as MISSING. For the selected therapy session sample, the percentage of agreement was computed by dividing the number PRESENT CORRECT by the total number (PRESENT CORRECT, plus MISSING, plus INCORRECT). There was a mean agreement for all clinicians of 91% (range 52-100%) for audio tape of the therapy session with the clinician TKB printout (Table D.15). A total of 265 incorrect and/or missing TKB responses was found from a possible 3,415 responses. In other words, there was an error of approximately 8%.

A second check of reliability was possible by comparing the TKB touch tone audio tape with the computer TKB printout. This enabled a reliability check of the computer decoding system. All audio tones were counted and compared with the visual printout for the entire therapy session. The number of audio tones not printed was divided by the total number of audio tones. A mean agreement of 92% was observed for all clinicians (range 75-100%). There was a total of 999 missed printed codes from a total of 12,494 recorded audio tones which represents an error of 8.6% in the decoding system (Appendix D, Table D.15).

CHAPTER 3

# Results: Child Dependent Variables

We focus on one important question—How to measure articulation learning and use it as a subject of research? Starting from TALK and SPT, we build a series of derived variables. The final measures, the Equalized Unified scores or EU numbers, will be the dependent variables upon which we will focus in the next three chapters. Each of the four EU numbers is an estimate of the child's articulation ability at a particular point in the year. The four together show the level at which the child started the year and how the child learned.

Using the EU numbers we take one more step in deriving dependent variables. GAIN is defined as the difference between final and baseline score. It represents the child's total improvement during the year. Children do not solve their articulation problems at the same speed. Two may have the same initial and final score but have completely different learning experiences through the year. To discriminate differences between learning, we introduce GAMMA, a quantitative measure of speed of learning. It is derived from the EU numbers.

Each of these new variables will show us some particular aspect of the child's articulation learning. We summarize them statistically, giving means, standard deviations, and plots showing how they interact.

These variables allow us to get a clear view of various aspects of learning. To deal with learning as a whole, we create one more variable, called KLMO. This divides the children into five groups based on the shape of their learning curve. "K" children learn quickly. "L's" are successful in solving their articulation problems during the school year, but they do not learn as fast as "K's". "M's" are the ones who start the year with fairly good articulation and finish with good articulation. "O" children start with poor articulation and do not get much better. A fifth category, the "others," holds the children whose learning curve does not fit one of these patterns. KLMO will be used along with the other dependent variables in the following chapters. The reader who is comfortable with analysis of variance will pay most attention to the EU numbers, GAIN, and GAMMA in our results. The reader more familiar with chi-square and two-way tables will look at the statistical results from KLMO. It turns out that each of these variables has something to reveal about articulation learning.

For definitions of special terms and symbols used in this project refer to Appendix G in this book.

## Introduction

We have described the characteristics of the children and clinicians in this study. These are our measurement tools. In order to proceed, we must carefully choose those measurements or combinations of measurements that are our main interest. We must choose our dependent variables.

At first glance this seems simple. There should be one dependent variable—the child's articulation ability. All of us understand generally what is meant by articulation ability, but when we get down to specific measurements, it is not so simple.

The complications arise when we consider two questions:
1. What measure of articulation ability shall we use?
2. At what time shall we measure the child's ability?
The first question was covered in Chapter 2, Methodology. We have chosen to use SPT (imitative speech) and TALK (spontaneous speech) as the primary probe

measures. To balance their effects, we combine them in a Unified Score (US). Articulation ability for a given child, at a given time, is measured by this US. The US is not perfect. There are difficulties associated with the different sensitivities of SPT and TALK. There are those inherent sources of unreliability, but the US is the best single measure we have.

## The Child's Learning Curve

We presented two questions above. The choice of the US answers the first one. The second is at what time should we measure?

It would make the rest of this study much simpler if we could specify a particular day of the year, say May 15, as *the* day on which to measure the speaking ability of all our children. We might call this Good Speech Day. All children having a problem with their speech would come to school and be tested. This would be very much like an IQ test or National Merit Scholarship test. If this had happened during our project we could relate the effect of sound, grade, etc., to the US from that one day.

We know that this scheme will not work. Articulation is not like IQ. Articulation ability changes from week to week. Whatever one's opinion about IQ changes, articulation changes much more, for the problem child. And articulation ability is not a well-established criterion, unless the child is at 100%. To say that a child has a 110 IQ at a particular time in the sixth grade to some extent characterizes the child's mental ability. To say that a child has a US of 67% on a particular day does not really tell us much. The number 67 has much less significance than the number 110.

Articulation not only changes, but it may change radically from week to week. We will show examples of children who were speaking at a 20% ability in one week, and six weeks later were measured at 90%. There are also some apparent rapid changes that may result from unreliability. Sometimes a child shows an 87% ability, and a few weeks later, zero. Thus, our US *appears* to change wildly for some children.

Finally, any improved articulation ability is important, but we are also interested in the amount of change. To report a child's level on May 15 is interesting, but we also want to know where he was at the beginning of the year. We feel differently about two children, each scoring 93% correct on May 15, but one of whom started the year at 80%, and the other starting at 10%.

Most of the above arguments are simple. We list them so clinicians will see why they must measure a child's ability several times during the year. Two times is not enough. The analysis of the data will get fairly complicated because we have several measures for each child. What we have established is that a good measure of a child's articulation ability at a given time is the US. In order to best describe the child's articulation behavior, measurements should be taken throughout the school year, and the US calculated each time. The result is called the child's *learning curve*. This set of numbers is the first level of the dependent variable for our analysis.

An example of the data for one child and the associated learning curve are shown in Table 3.1 and Figure 3.1. We will use this example as we further refine the concept of the dependent variable. At this point we will look only at the calculations leading to the US. The data labeled 'AU Numbers' and 'EU Numbers' will be discussed later.

| SPT | C | 0 | 0 | 27 | 27 | 29 | 30 | 29 | 30 |
|---|---|---|---|---|---|---|---|---|---|
|  | W | 30 | 30 | 3 | 3 | 1 | 0 | 1 | 0 |
| TALK | C |  | 0 | 1 | 14 | 28 | 9 | 21 | 14 |
|  | W |  | 29 | 42 | 14 | 3 | 10 | 3 | 2 |
| US |  | 0 | 0 | 38 | 71 | 93 | 80 | 93 | 96 |
| Week |  | 6* | 6 | 11 | 16 | 20 | 28 | 32 | 37 |

Example of Unified Score calculation for week 11:

    SPT      27 correct     3 wrong

    TALK     1 correct    42 wrong

    Total phonemes = 1 + 42 + 27 + 3 = 73

    Total correct = 1 + 27 = 28

    Unified score = 28/73 x 100 = 38

| AU No. | 0 | 55 | 87 | 95 |
|---|---|---|---|---|
| AU Week | 6 | 14 | 24 | 36 |
| EU No. | 0 | 45 | 86 | 95 |
| EU Week | 6 | 12 | 24 | 36 |
| EU | EU1 | EU2 | EU3 | EU4 |

Example of AU number calculation:

    $AU2 = \frac{1}{2}(38 + 71) = 55$

    $AU\ Week = \frac{1}{2}(11 + 16) = 14$

Example of EU number calculation:

$$EU2 = \frac{12.56 - 6}{14 - 6} \quad x \quad (55 - 0) = 45$$

---

*All weeks were calculated from the first week of September. Clinicians generally had screening and therapy scheduling before starting their baseline testing of SPT and TALK for the project. Two SPT and one TALK were collected at baseline. In this example baseline testing began the middle of October.

TABLE 3.1. The derivation of unified scores (US), average unified scores (AU), and equalized unified scores (EU) for child #581, Year 2. SPT/TALK Correct (C) and Wrong (W) raw scores are included.

    The first line of Table 3.1 shows the child's SPT correct scores for eight successive probes. These measurements were made six weeks, 11 weeks, . . . , and 37 weeks after the beginning of the school year, as shown in the sixth line labeled 'Week.' We note that there is no regular interval between the child's probes. Between the fifth and sixth probe, there is an interval of eight weeks (28-20). Between the sixth and the seventh probe, there is an interval of four weeks (32-28). This varying interval between measurements is typical of naturalistic experiments done in the real clinical world.

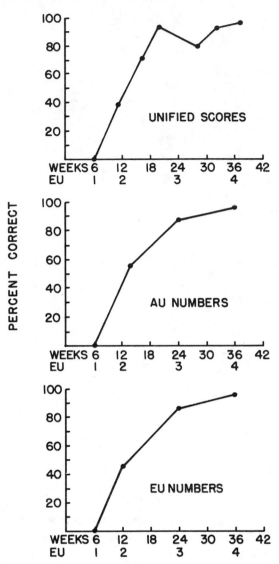

FIGURE 3.1. Example of learning curves for child 581 using Unified scores, AU numbers, and EU numbers.

The first line of Table 3.1, showing the child's SPT correct scores, indicates that the child had a severe articulation problem at the beginning of the school year. The first two measurements are both zero. The second line gives the SPT wrong. Note that there are 30 items on the SPT for /s/ so SPT C and SPT W will always add up to 30. The third measurement indicates that the child has made considerable progress by the eleventh week of school, the fifth week of therapy. At this point there are 27 corrects recorded and three wrongs. As measured by SPT, the child articulates the items in this imitative task quite well.

The third line of Table 3.1 gives the number of correct phonemes in three-minutes of spontaneous speech that we call TALK. Note that the clinician did not give a TALK test in the first baseline measurement. Sometimes there is only one of TALK or SPT, but this is to be expected in a realistic experiment. As we develop our dependent variables in some detail, it will turn out that one value of the dependent variable will be the average of several Unified Scores, and thus the average of several TALK and SPT scores. This averaging compensates for missing one test or the other.

If we look at the second baseline measure (the second column with Week = 6) we see that here there was a TALK given, and that it agreed with SPT. This child seems to have an articulation problem. However, at the third measurement, where SPT gives 27 correct and three wrong, TALK shows one correct and 42 wrong. The child performs the imitative task well, but does not articulate in spontaneous speech.

At this point all of our arguments for the US come into play. Our data are complicated enough by having to follow articulation on two dimensions, so we average TALK and SPT. This is shown below the TALK scores on the line labeled "US." The calculation of the US for week 11 is shown below US and Week. At this point in the school year the child has 73 total target phonemes recorded. Of these, 27 were correct out of SPT and one was correct from TALK, so the US was 38.

The other US's for this child are calculated in the same manner (Figure 3.1). This is what we call the child's "learning curve." The reader should look carefully at the figure to understand what is happening to the articulation level of this child. We have already seen that the child starts the school year with a severe problem. What the plot indicates is that the child makes steady, rapid progress, reaching a score of 93 in week 20. In the next probe, there is a little drift downward to 80, but the final two probes are at 93 and 96, so we would say that this child has almost solved his articulation problem by the end of the school year.

Returning to the main thread of the argument, what we are saying is that in this US sequence the child's learning curve forms the first version of our dependent variable. It is this sequence of numbers about which we want to make inferences using our statistical analyses.

The learning curve is the first version of our dependent variable, but not the last. The sequence of US's has several problems that must be solved to perform the statistical analyses. To solve these problems, we will use the learning curve to create new dependent variables, AU numbers, and finally EU numbers. The EU numbers will be our final dependent variables. These new variables will be the subject of the next two sections.

## Average Unified Scores—The AU Numbers

In the first section we asked two questions about the construction of the dependent variables. We have answered the first. The second asked what time shall we measure the child's articulation ability?

Given the conditions of the project, we did not have much flexibility about the times at which probes were done. Looking at Table 3.1, we see that probes were not equally spaced through the year. They were given to different children at different times. What is needed is to estimate each child's ability at the same times through the year. Knowing Mary's score in week 10, and Johnny's in week 12 does not help us very much when we want to compare Mary and Johnny.

We pursue this goal in two steps. First, we average the US's so that each child has the same *number* of data points. The result is the AU numbers. Second, we average further to estimate each child's ability at the same number of points, and *at the same time.* This final result is the EU numbers.

By looking at the number of US's each child had, and trying to arrange for our next scores to be averages of at least *two* US's, we decided that almost all children could have *four* average scores. This was the first logical step in the construction of the AU numbers.

The next choice was whether to average exactly two US's, or more than two. We chose the first because for many children the US were spread fairly far apart in time. Finally, it was decided to tie the averaging of the US's to the order of occurrence of the data, not the time of occurrence, and to average the times of occurrence along with the US's.

This process may be understood better from an example. Turn to Table 3.1. This child has eight US's. The AU numbers are constructed by averaging successive pairs. In the example, the second AU number is the average of the third and fourth US. Likewise, the second AU week is the average of the third and fourth weeks associated with the US's. Thus, we estimate this child's articulation ability as 55 at week 14. A glance at Figure 3.1 shows that this is not unreasonable.

The AU number lies on the line between the two US's—38 at week 11, and 71 at week 16. Since we know nothing about the articulation ability of this child other than what is contained in the US's, we use straightline interpolation to combine the data points. The reader should remember that the goal of all this is to produce *four* estimates of each child's articulation ability.

The full AU algorithm is as follows:
*Pairs* of US's are chosen as follows:
a.  The first two scores are averaged to produce AU1.
b.  The last two scores produce AU4.
c.  AU2 is averaged from two scores that are approximately a third of the way from the beginning of the child's participation in the study. Let the total number of scores for the child be N. Let I be the integer part of $N/3$. Then AU2 will be the average of scores numbered $I + 1$ and $I + 2$.
d.  Let J be the integer part of $(2N/3)$, then AU3 will be the average of scores numbered $J + 1$ and $J + 2$.
e.  If the child has five or less scores, he is dropped.
f.  If the child has six or seven scores, calculate AU1, AU2, and AU4 as above. AU3 is calculated by linear estimation (by hand) from a plot (graph) of the child's scores.

In all cases, where the two US's are averaged to create an AU number, the corresponding weeks are averaged to produce the *AU week.* What we are saying is that our best estimate of the child's articulation ability, if we had been able to take a measurement at the AU week, is the AU number. Again, the reader should look at Table 3.1 where there is a typical calculation of an AU number.

All of the AU numbers and raw scores were plotted by the computer and checked visually for reasonableness. About 100 children were rejected who had scores that were significantly different from their local averages. For instance, a sequence of scores 84, 93, 13, 97 was rejected.

The AU numbers have the following advantages:
1.  There are exactly four for each child. There are no "missing data."
2.  They seem to represent the real progress of most children, as indicated by the plots.
3.  Some variance which may be *error* or unreliability has been eliminated.

They also have a few problems:

1. The AU numbers are not similarly spaced for each child. AU2 for one child may be five weeks since the beginning of therapy, and eight weeks for another child.
2. Some children have been eliminated, and we are not able to check for possible bias in this process.
3. Some of the variance eliminated may be due to real variation in the child's ability.
4. To be more specific, if a child makes a rapid improvement, as shown by the US, the AU numbers will show an improvement, but it may not be as rapid as that shown by the US. This disadvantage is inherent in the process of obtaining averages of measurements in time.

## Equalized Unified Scores—The EU Numbers

The final step in our development of the dependent variable is to solve the first problem of the AU numbers. We want to estimate the child's articulation ability at each of four times throughout the school year, but these four times must be the same for each child, relative to the beginning of his therapy.

Our first task is to choose the time points. The solution is to average the AU weeks for all the children. The result is:

EU weeks—Relative to the Beginning
of School Year

| EU | 1 | 2 | 3 | 4 |
|------|------|-------|-------|-------|
| Week | 6.00 | 12.56 | 23.57 | 35.75 |

This means that the average AU2 was estimated about six weeks from the beginning of therapy.

We can now construct four estimates of articulation ability, called EU numbers, for Equalized Unified Score. These are calculated by linear interpolation from the AU numbers. This just means that we look at a plot of the AU numbers, draw lines between the scores, and say that our best guess for the child's scoring is those lines. Look again at Figure 3.1. EU1 is just AU1, the first AU number. In order to calculate EU2, we consider first the AU weeks. At week 6, we have estimated the child's articulation ability as 55. The EU week number we want to use is in the table above—12.56. Thus we want to use the AU numbers to estimate the child's ability just prior to week 14. This implies that the estimated score for week 12.56 will be a little less than 55. How much less? We use a proportion representing the amount of time elapsed from the beginning of therapy to the desired week number or $12.56 - 6 = 6.56$[1] divided by the amount of time elapsed from the beginning of therapy to the AU week or 14-6. The result is EU2 = 45, which is a little less than 55 as we had expected. This estimated ability of 45 at a week of 12.56 lies on the line drawn between the point representing AU1 and the point representing AU2 on Figure 3.1. Thus, this kind of calculation is called linear interpolation.

The precise rules for the EU numbers are:

EU1: = AU1

EU2: If the AU2 week came less than six weeks from the beginning of therapy,

---

1. The reader may wonder about the precision used in the calculation of EU numbers. Some intermediate calculations were rounded to two decimal places, like the average week 12.56. There is no logical explanation for this. We do not believe that it causes any problem with the estimation of each child's articulation ability.

then EU2 is the interpolated straight line average of AU1 and AU2. If the AU2 week came later than six weeks, then EU2 is the interpolated straight line average of AU2 and AU3.

EU3: Is similarly the straight line average of either AU2 and AU3 or AU3 and AU4.

EU4: If the AU4 week came less than 30 weeks from the beginning of therapy, then EU4 is the interpolated straight line average of AU3 and AU4. If AU4 comes later, then EU4 = AU4. We do this since most children do not make substantial progress immediately after the end of the year. In either case, EU4 is never allowed to exceed 100.

We have now created the EU numbers and they have certain advantages:
1. There are exactly four for each child.
2. They are similarly spaced in time. It is possible to compare EU2 for one child with EU2 for another child.
3. The EU numbers are weighted averages of possibly four raw Unified Scores, thus considerable error variance has been eliminated.

The EU numbers also have some problems:
1. As with the AU numbers, some children have been eliminated.
2. Some of the variance eliminated may be due to real child variation.
3. For a few children, we are estimating the child's ability at times when there are no nearby raw scores. Given the problems of data collection as discussed above, there was ultimately no way out of this problem.
4. To be more specific, if a child makes a rapid improvement, as shown by the US's, the EU numbers will show an improvement, but it may not be as rapid as that shown by the US's. This disadvantage is inherent in the process of obtaining averages of measurements in time.

The whole set of numbers, raw Unified Scores, AU numbers, and EU numbers were plotted (i.e., a graph was drawn) by the computer and checked visually. The major problem that occurred was that the EU numbers did not always replicate very rapid changes in the child's ability. Some children who improve very quickly at the beginning of the year are shown as improving a little less than was actually the case.

## Statistical Analysis of the EU Numbers

We have now created four variables: EU1, EU2, EU3, and EU4. We will use them to indicate each child's articulation level. They are an estimate of this ability at four times—at the beginning of therapy, about six weeks later, 18 weeks later, and at the end of the school year, 30 weeks later. We refer to these four as the "EU numbers" and as the child's learning curve.

We have discussed the construction of dependent variables. Certainly, in whatever clinical decisions are made in a school setting, it is useful to relate such a decision to the EU numbers, if they are known. One would like to say that a certain treatment procedure would raise the average EU2 of randomly selected children by 10 points, for instance. Or one would like to be certain that all children reached an EU4 of 100. Thus, the concept "dependent" is firmly attached to the EU numbers, but there is a distinction. EU1 is not really a dependent variable. It is an estimate of the child's baseline score, and thus is not a criterion. It is an indication of the material with which the clinician has to work at the start of the year. Thus, EU1 is an independent variable, and will be used to help predict the dependent variables in much of the subsequent analyses. However, for the sake of clarity, in this section, and sometimes elsewhere, we will deal with all four of the EU numbers together.

To begin, we consider the distribution of each. Figure E. 1a-d (Appendix E) shows the histograms of the four EU numbers. These give the basic statistical information about the EU numbers considered by themselves.

Look at the histogram for EU1, the baseline score. The first line of the plot indicates that 179 children started the year with a score of zero. The next line says that 191 children, 17.2% of our 1,108 children, had an EU1 score greater than zero, and less than or equal to five, while a total of 370 children, 33.4% had an EU1 of five or less. The other lines in the histogram can be interpreted similarly.

We are immediately struck by the fact that many children start out the year with a severe articulation problem. One-third have an EU1 of five or less. Half of the children have an EU1 of 15 or less. Thus, we are definitely working with children who need some kind of help. However, the child selection procedure described in Chapter 2 left us with a wide variation in the baseline articulation level since about one fourth (100.0 – 76.2 = 23.8%) of the children have an EU1 score above 40.

If we compare the histogram for EU2 with that of EU1, we see that considerable progress has been made in six weeks of therapy. Now only 14 children have a score of zero. Only 10.6% score five or less, and almost half of the sample (100.0 – 52.1 = 47.8%) is above 40.

This progress continues. The EU3 histogram is about the same shape as EU1, but reversed. Now most of the children are at the high end of the scale. Almost half (100.0 – 52.6 = 47.4%) are above 70. Finally, at the end of the year, we see about one-third (34.3%) of the children having an EU4 above 95.

As an overall conclusion, from looking at the distributions of EU numbers, we would say that the clinical system inputs many children with real problems, that some of the articulation problems are solved quickly, and that most of the children have their problems solved within one year.

The impressions given by the histograms are summarized by the univariate statistics shown in Table 3.2. We see immediately that the mean EU number

| Statistic | EU1 | EU2 | EU3 | EU4 |
|-----------|-----|-----|-----|-----|
| Mean | 26.7 | 44.9 | 64.9 | 76.5 |
| SD | 28.4 | 28.3 | 30.2 | 26.9 |
| Median | 15 | 43 | 73 | 87 |
| Minimum | 0 | 0 | 0 | 0 |
| Maximum | 100 | 100 | 100 | 100 |

TABLE 3.2. Summary statistics for EU numbers.

advances steadily through the year. This is shown graphically in Figure 3.2, which represents the average learning curve for our 1,108 children. Yet, because of the skewed distributions of EU1, EU3, and EU4, there is useful information in the median. Having dealt with the univariate statistics for the EU numbers, we now consider their joint distribution.

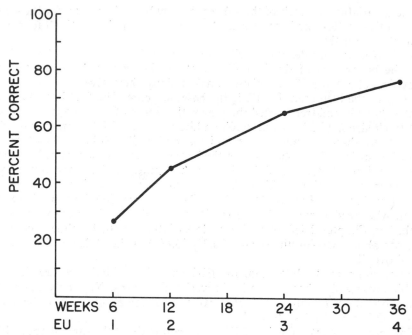

FIGURE 3.2. Plot of means of EU numbers which represent the average learning curve for 1108 children.

Table 3.3 gives the correlations between the EU numbers. We see that the EU numbers are, in general, correlated with each other. The smallest correlation, .37 is between EU1 and EU4, the largest, .89 between EU3 and EU4. The correlations closer to the diagonal seem to be larger. This is a general property of data measured in time: two measurements that are closer in time are often more correlated than two measurements that are farther away in time. We can say that if we know a child's score now, we can probably predict his score tomorrow. We have less ability to predict his score one week from now, and even less ability to predict six weeks from now. The EU1 and EU4 measurements are 30 weeks apart, and the $r^2$ for prediction is only .14.

The correlations get larger later in the year. The EU1—EU2 correlation, .72 is smaller than the EU3—EU4 correlation .89. This suggests that we are better able to predict the child's progress later in the therapy process, but this result is more simply explained by reference to the EU3 and EU4 histogram. In fact, many children score high on EU3, and it is easy to predict that they will get even closer to 100% at EU4.

The correlation, considered as a measure of the relationship between two variables, is most interpretable when the variables are both normally distributed, and their histograms look like bell-shaped curves. In our case, EU1, EU3, and EU4 do not appear to be normally distributed, Figure E. 1a-d, Appendix E, so we feel that a more detailed explanation of the joint relationship between the dependent variables is needed.

More detail is given in the scattergrams in Figure E. 2a-f, Appendix E. Here we have plotted the joint distributions of each pair of EU numbers. These scattergrams were done by computer, using the program BMDP6D (Dixon and Brown,

|      | EU1 | EU2 | EU3 | EU4 |
|------|-----|-----|-----|-----|
| EU1  | 100 | 72  | 47  | 37  |
| EU2  |     | 100 | 83  | 69  |
| EU3  |     |     | 100 | 89  |
|      |     |     |     | 100 |

TABLE 3.3. Correlations between EU numbers.

1977). Each point on the plot is either blank, showing that no child was there, or has a number or letter, giving the count of children. The number of children is indicated by "1" for one, "2" for two, . . . , "9" for nine, "A" for ten, "B" for eleven, . . . , and "Z" for 35. An "*" means 36 or more. At the bottom are the number of cases plotted and the correlation between the pair of variables. Below that are statistics for two regression lines, the first with the "X" or horizontal variable dependent, and the second with the "Y" or vertical variable dependent. In our case, the latter would be considered the most natural. Around the edge of the graph may be found two "X"s and two "Y"s. The regression lines for Y dependent passes through the two "Y"s, and similarly for the "X"s. For the reader who has less experience with scattergrams, we suggest looking first at the last plot (E. 3, Appendix E), where we have diagrammed the important areas.

Note that in each scattergram the horizontal axis is either EU1, EU2, or EU3. The vertical axis is EU2, EU3 or EU4, and the vertical variable is always *later* in time than the horizontal variable. Then we can characterize each important area as follows:

A. Children whose ability decreases from the earlier time to the later one.
B. Children who have a low score at the earlier time.
C. Children who make a moderate gain from one time to the later one.
D. Children who succeed, after not starting low.

Look now at area A in each of the scattergrams. There are very few children in this area. It is rare for a child's articulation ability to decrease from one time to the next. Most children make progress most of the time.

Look now at EU1 vs. EU2. Area B is somewhat filled in, whereas in EU2 vs. EU3 it is not. The children in B of EU1 vs. EU2 are those who start the therapy process with little articulation ability. They are the ones who need the most help. The fact that there are children in most of area B means that some make very rapid progress in just six weeks. This is a nice conclusion for the children who make the progress, but for us, as researchers, there is a problem: we may not be able to predict a child's EU2 score from his EU1 score if he starts low. This also contributes to the relatively low correlation between EU1 and EU2. In fact, if we look at area B in the EU1 vs. EU3 and EU1 vs. EU4 plots, we see that this area is very solidly filled in. This leads us to the unfortunate conclusion that we are unable to predict the EU3 score of children who start the year with low articulation ability. In EU1 vs. EU4, there are more children near the top of B than at the bottom, but the variation is still quite large. It will also be difficult to predict the final score.

The B area is less dense in each of the histograms that does not involve EU1. This means that after six weeks if the child still has a severe problem he is not likely to make *rapid* progress, although he may finish the year with no problem. Rapid progress can only come at the beginning of the year.

If you look at the EU2 vs. EU3 plot from some distance, it looks like a simple diagonal band. There are more children at the upper right corner of the band than at the lower left, but, as we move across the middle of the band from one point in the scattergram to another point there is about the same density of children. We conclude that from EU2 to EU3 children make from 0 to 40 points progress, but the amount of progress does not depend on where the child starts. This is another of our mixed results. It is good that the children make progress, but we may not be able to predict much about that progress without more information.

In EU3 vs. EU4, area C is *narrower* and less dense. We conclude that in the last 12 weeks of therapy much less progress is made. From the beginning to the end of the school year there is a decrease in the amount of progress a child is likely to make. This is another explanation for the observation that the correlations later in the year are larger than the earlier ones.

Finally, area D in EU1 vs. EU4 is very dense. Thus, many children succeed, irrespective of what their EU1 score is. This is good for the children, but their progress is unpredictable.

## Transformed EU Numbers

The rest of this book will discuss statistical analyses that have been performed on the EU numbers and the other dependent and independent variables. This will give the reader some feeling for each EU number as an estimate of the child's articulation ability measured at a particular time in the school year. Most readers will immediately see the differences between a child with an EU2 of 24 and a child with an EU2 of 89. The former will have some way to go and the latter child will have solved most of his or her articulation problems.

It is clear from looking at the histograms (Figure E. 1a-d, Appendix E) that the EU numbers, and in particular EU1 and EU4, are not well distributed. EU1 is skewed to the right and EU4 is skewed to the left. Thus, statistics calculated from these variables are open to question.

In order to make our statistical analyses a little more sensitive, we created transformed EU numbers, labeled EU1T, EU2T, EU3T, and EU4T. For each analysis reported in the text with EU numbers, a similar analysis is performed using the EUT variables. In most cases, the interpretation is the same. It is noted where there are different results using the transformed data.

The actual transformation process is complicated. There are four steps.

1. *Adjust zero and 100.* A child with an EU1T of zero is not able to make a correct phoneme in three minutes of conversation or on the items of the SPT. We do not, however, know if this same child might make a correct response in four minutes, if given a chance, or that he or she would not make a correct phoneme, even if given 10 minutes to try. It is possible that the SPT could have had more items in it and some children with zero could score higher if given more opportunities. For each test procedure, the score of zero does not tell us what the child's articulation ability really is. The same argument would hold for a child who scores 100. One child might have just solved his problem and managed, trying hard, to get a score of 100. Another child might have been articulating correctly for 19 weeks and have no difficulty with the test procedures. Again, the score of 100 does not tell us the precise nature of the child's articulation ability.

If a child scores zero on EU1, we do not know exactly what the articulation ability is, but we have one relevant piece of information—EU2. One child with an EU1 of zero and an EU2 of five probably had very poor articulation at baseline. Another child with an EU1 of zero and an EU2 of 70 probably had better articulation at baseline. Thus, it is reasonable to adjust the EU1 score of zero, based on the EU2 score. The actual transformation we see is:

If EU1 = 0, then EU1 (new) = .01 × EU2. Thus, the new EU1 score is just 1% of the EU2 score. The same transformation is performed on zeros in EU2, using EU3 and zeros in EU3, using EU4. Similarly, we transform the scores of 100: If EU4 = 100, then EU4 (new) = 99 + .01 × EU3. Again, the same transformation is applied to EU3 using EU2 and EU2 using EU1. Note that in each case, there is very little change to the raw numerical value of the variable.

2. *Folded Root Transformation.* Following McNeil (1977) and Tukey (1977), we note that the variables with which we are working are all derived from "counted fractions." It is recommended that they are transformed using the folded root transformation:

$$xnew = xold^p - (1 - xold)^p$$

Several powers were tried, attempting to achieve symmetry, and the value p = 0.14 as recommended by McNeil (1977) seemed to produce the best results.

The result of these two transformations is to make the distribution of each of the new EUT numbers very close to normal.

3. *Bring in Outliers.* Even after the first two transformations, there were a few observations that were off. Each of these was brought in to an arbitrary level. This operation was *ad hoc* and we depend on the large sample size to relieve any associated difficulties.

4. *Linear Transformation to Match EU.* The resulting variables had no necessary scaling. We then performed one simple linear transformation on all of them so the total mean and variance of the EU numbers matched the total mean and variance of the EU numbers. The results approximate the original data, except that now we have scores outside the original range.

Let us emphasize that the EUT numbers are used to check the results of the statistical analyses of EU numbers. Where there is a discrepancy, it is reported. The choice we make of not working with the EUT numbers throughout the text should make our readers comfortable with the interpretation of an EU1 of say 20, meaning low articulation ability. Discussion of EU1T with a value of −40 or EU4T with a value of 140 would be nonintuitive. In addition, where possible we relate the EU numbers and other dependent variables to be derived from them to practical clinical measurements. It would be more difficult to calculate the EUT numbers for use in clinical decisions.

The histograms of the EUT numbers are shown in Figure E. 4a-f, Appendix E. One is immediately struck by the apparent normality of distributions, especially when compared with the EU histograms. The progress of our 1,108 children is a movement of the bell-shaped curve steadily from left to right. Finally, the negative scores for EU1T and the scores larger than 100 were forced by the overall scaling of the EUT variables.

## Transformed GAIN and GAMMA

Transformed GAIN is the difference between transformed EU4 and EU1:

$$\text{GAIN} = \text{EU4T} - \text{EU1T}$$

For transformed GAMMA, we introduced a new complication. GAMMA is defined in a relatively simple fashion, using integer coefficients. If it is written as a linear combination of EU numbers it looks like:

$$\text{GAMMA} = (-1 \times \text{EU1}) + 1 \times \text{EU2} + 1 \times \text{EU3} + (-1 \times \text{EU4})$$

As we have seen above, the result is correlated with EU2. In performing the transformations, we decided to create a new GAMMA which would be:

    a. uncorrelated with EU2T
    b. uncorrelated with GAIN
    c. as close as possible to GAMMA, defined above.

This is a simple exercise in linear algebra, which results in:

$$\text{GAMMAT} = (0.84 \times \text{EU1T}) + 1.29 \times \text{EU2T} + 0.58 \times \text{EU3T} + (-1.13 \times \text{EU4T})$$

Thus GAMMAT, is conceptually similar to GAMMA, but is not related to GAIN and EU2. Unfortunately, it turns out that the statistical results are sensitive to the actual values of the coefficients, so we must qualify what we say about GAMMAT.

## GAIN, GAMMA, and LEVEL

In this section we will use the EU numbers to construct some new dependent variables. Out of the set of variables, including the EU numbers, four are dependent variables of primary interest. Later this number will be reduced to three. This is necessary because the EU numbers do not cover all the ideas associated with the learning curve when it is considered as a dependent variable. For instance, one is naturally interested in the child's gain in articulation from one time to another. All these new variables are defined in Table 3.4

We have chosen to use only linear combinations of the EU numbers because this is the simpler concept and because we do not believe that other methods of constructing dependent variables add to what is represented here. We now have

| Name | Definition | Meaning |
|---|---|---|
| GAIN | EU4 - EU1 | Articulation gain from the beginning to the end of the year. |
| GAMMA | (EU2 - EU1) - (EU4 - EU3) | A measure of the curvature of the learning curve. |
| LEVEL | ¼(EU1 + EU2 + EU3 + EU4) | The child's average articulation score throughout the year. |
| GAIN12 | EU2 - EU1 | Gain from baseline to six weeks. |
| GAIN23 | EU3 - EU2 | Gain from six weeks to 18 weeks. |
| GAIN34 | EU4 - EU3 | Gain from 18 weeks to 30 weeks. |
| GAIN13 | EU3 - EU1 | Gain from baseline to 18 weeks. |
| GAIN24 | EU4 - EU2 | Gain from six weeks to 30 weeks. |

TABLE 3.4. Definitions of new dependent variables.

four EU numbers and seven new variables, for a total of 11. There are only four dimensions of information here, so we know from the start that there must be redundant information in all these variables, considered together. However, this large set of variables can be used to examine different aspects of the information in the learning curves. Let us now provide the motivation for these new variables.

The focus of the dependent variables is on the child's learning curve. How can one measure a "good learning curve" or a "bad learning curve"? We are concerned with the child's articulation ability measured throughout the school year. We accept the idea that the EU numbers, which represent the child's learning curve, will be the basis for the dependent variables, but the EU numbers themselves are not quite what we want.

The new dependent variables are constructed to provide numerical measures. We will proceed by examples. We will look at the learning curves of several children and, in the process, motivate the construction of these new dependent variables.

In any study of change in which there is an optimum score, there is a fundamental dilemma: whether the best person is the one with the highest score at the end, or whether the best person is the one who gains the most. We are never sure whether to choose final score or gain score as our principal criterion. Consider our first example.

Example 1. Child No. 327. Year 2.

| EU1 | EU2 | EU3 | EU4 |
|-----|-----|-----|-----|
| 99 | 98 | 100 | 100 |

This child has the highest achievable final score. If final score is a criterion, then this is a good learning curve. However, we do not think that this is quite what we want since the child accomplished very little during the school year. We could ask why this child was in therapy at all.

This example shows that EU4 cannot be our most important dependent variable. Yet, we cannot neglect it entirely because bringing children to a high EU4 is what the therapy process is all about. A child with an EU4 of 50 cannot be said to have a "good learning curve."

Let us turn now to the child's overall gain. This is usually defined as the difference between the final score and the baseline score. In our notation this is EU4 – EU1. Here is a child with a good gain score.

Example 2. Child No. 220. Year 4.

| EU1 | EU2 | EU3 | EU4 |
|-----|-----|-----|-----|
| 0 | 29 | 82 | 100 |

This child has the best possible gain and the best possible final score. Over the school year he went from zero to 100. Yet, it is not possible to choose objectively whether child number 220 is better than child number 327. Number 220 made the most progress, but number 327 never really had a serious articulation problem, so number 220 has never articulated better than number 327. At any given moment during the school year (except at the end), if we got number 327 and number 220 together in the same room, we would say that number 327 had the better articulation. Under these circumstances, we cannot allow ourselves to say clearly that number 327 does not have a "good curve." This is the dilemma.

Another aspect of the problem appears when trying to decide how to reward clinicians. Their objective is to produce the best final score they can, but this means that they might want to work with children like number 327. We have already seen that children rarely decrease their score, and the clinician is going to be confident that number 327 will have a high final score by the sixth week or the 30th week. But, number 327 does not need our help. Rewarding clinicians on the basis of having more children like number 327 is silly.

On the other hand, if we tell clinicians that they will be rewarded on the basis of the progress that their children make, then clinicians will want to work with children like number 220. But number 220 starts at zero. Each clinician will want to get as many children as possible in her caseload who have a low baseline score so that they can make lots of progress. That discriminates against children who start at 50 but still need some help.

This situation makes it difficult to find a single, perfect dependent variable. We will have to work with several dependent variables, none of which can stand alone. Not only can we not choose objectively between final score and gain, but there is another problem illustrated by this example:

Example 3. Child No. 83. Year 2.

| EU1 | EU2 | EU3 | EU4 |
|-----|-----|-----|-----|
| 0   | 75  | 98  | 100 |

This child has the same final score and the same gain as number 220. But, any reasonable argument that number 220 has a "good curve" must lead to the conclusion that number 83 is better. This child learned faster than number 220. In the sixth week, number 83 had an articulation score of 75, where number 220 had only 29. If two children have the same initial and final score, then we would like to know which child can achieve a higher score sooner.

This case of two children with the same initial and final scores but different learning curves may be associated with the ideas of either "speed of learning" or with the curvature of the learning curve. Child number 83 learned faster than number 220. If we visualize their learning curves, that of number 83 curves upward and that of number 220 is less curved. We will thus use the terms "speed" and "curvature" interchangeably.

We have thus established that there are at least three general principles for choosing dependent variables: final score, gain and speed.

If we are looking at "good curves" and we consider speed and final score as criteria, then we note that what we have said means that a child who reaches 100 for EU4 may be good, but one who has an EU3 of 100 is even better, and the best child would be the one who reaches 100 at EU2.

This all leads us to think of the "final score" as not EU4 but maybe EU2. With EU2 as a dependent variable, we are certain to identify those children who may be dismissed from therapy quickly.

All of the above discussion has focused on the "good curve." If we turn our attention to the child with a "bad learning curve," the one with a greater articulation problem, then the choice of dependent variables changes.

Since children almost always improve from one time to another, the final score, EU4, is a sufficient criterion for the badness of a learning curve.

Example 4. Child No. 444. Year 2.

| EU1 | EU2 | EU3 | EU4 |
|-----|-----|-----|-----|
| 0   | 0   | 1   | 0   |

The fact that this child had an EU4 of zero would immediately lead us to believe that his prior EU numbers were probably not very high, and that he had never been able to articulate well. Thus, although we are inclined towards EU2 as a criterion for the good curves, EU4 seems to be the best choice for the bad curves.

We need to make an observation about EU4 which is partly statistics, and partly common sense. The histogram for EU4 shows that it is not normally distributed. It is skewed to the left. This makes us want to avoid it as a criterion variable. But, the data analyst may immediately suggest that we use our transformed EU4, which would improve the distributional properties. However, we have already seen that most children in this project are successful. Thus, *for most children, there is no real information in EU4*. No transformation changes the fact that many children have high EU4 scores and that differentiating among them is not very useful. For most children, EU4 provides some information, but it is specifically the few bad curves for which it is most useful. This leads us to a dilemma that must be resolved in a new way.

We want to know about children with "bad curves," so we consider just what we mean by "bad." Our intention is to qualify the articulation of the child *throughout the year*. In other words, the "bad curve" means the child, on the average, has poor articulation. We are thus led to the concept of the average articulation score of a child. Since a child's score cannot be negative, if his average score is low, we know that he must have low scores throughout the year. If his average articulation score is moderately low, we expect that he may have had some high score sometime, but we know that this will have happened most likely at the end of the year.

The use of the average score solves the problem of looking for a dependent variable to indicate children with bad curves. If the child's average score is low, then he must have a bad curve. But the average score is an average, a sum of other scores, and is likely to be fairly well distributed.

We now have four criteria for determining the dependent variable: final score (EU2), gain, speed, and average score.

Our original set of dependent variables seems to be the EU numbers, but here we must make the point that EU1 is not a dependent variable. It cannot be considered a criterion for treatment because it is the starting point for the therapy process. Later, we will use it to form our most important independent variable.

The first of our four conceptual dependent variables is final score. We have shown that EU4 or transformed EU4 are not desirable. We have chosen to neglect EU3 and concentrate on EU2 as our first primary dependent variable. From the above arguments, we know that a high EU2 is an indication of a good learning curve for those children who start low.

Our next concept is gain. There are many possible numbers that could be calculated from the data and called gain. We have chosen the simple gain over the whole year: EU4 – EU1. This is a simple difference between the baseline and end of year scores, ignoring the two scores between. In the text, it will be labeled GAIN. The units of GAIN are in percent correct. A typical score for a child would be 50. If this child started the project with an EU1 of 20 and his final EU4 score was 70, then GAIN = 70 – 20 = 50.

In our discussion above, we saw two children (number 220 and number 83) with high gain. Each of these made the maximum amount of progress throughout the year. But it must be remembered that a child with high GAIN must have started the year low. That means that GAIN is not just a simple measure of the child's progress, it also may indicate *where* he started.

In the scatter plots relating the EU numbers, we saw that most children do not decrease from one time to another. This implies that GAIN will be mostly positive. Child number 327 had a GAIN = 100 – 99 = 1. This child made no progress in the project, but we have already noted that this child may still be rated as successful. Child number 444 has a GAIN of zero and is unsuccessful. Thus, low GAIN may be associated with children who end up either good or bad.

One of our concerns is that the results should be applicable in clinical practice. Thus, we want to show how the clinician may measure the dependent variables in the school setting. To calculate GAIN, it is necessary to measure the child's average score (SPT + TALK) at the beginning of therapy and at the end of the school year. This latter measurement must be done whether the child has been dismissed from therapy or not. It will not give the same results if the clinician tries to get the GAIN measure with a final score before the end of the year.

GAMMA is a variable that is intended to deal with the speed of the child's learning curve. The easiest way to understand GAMMA is through examples.

| Child No. | Year | EU1 | EU2 | EU3 | EU4 | GAMMA |
|-----------|------|-----|-----|-----|-----|-------|
| 36 | 4 | 1 | 1 | 13 | 89 | –76 |
| 68 | 3 | 0 | 0 | 11 | 8 | 3 |
| 407 | 3 | 63 | 76 | 93 | 98 | 8 |
| 129 | 3 | 0 | 84 | 99 | 100 | 83 |
| 540 | 2 | 0 | 75 | 94 | 65 | 104 |

The examples above show five children arranged in order of increasing GAMMA. Child number 36 has a low articulation ability until near the end of the year. In terms of speed of learning, this is a slow learner. His GAMMA is very low. Child number 68 makes little progress throughout the school year. Child number 407 makes steady progress. On the other hand, Child number 129 is a fast learner. After six weeks of therapy, he has made it to the 84 percent correct level and could conceivably have been dismissed. This child has a very high GAMMA. The last example, Child number 540, warns us that there is an inherent problem in GAMMA. A high GAMMA results from the learning curve turning up very quickly, but GAMMA can go even higher, by having the curve turn down at the end. This is unfortunate, but we have already seen that most children do not decrease, so when we do the statistical analysis, this will not turn out to be a severe problem.

GAMMA was intended as a relatively simple measure of the curvature of the child's learning curve. The concept of gain is intended to measure how much a child improves. It is calculated as the difference between two scores. Curvature shows the change in the improvement, and is thus the difference of two gains. In our case, we chose the difference between the gain in the first period (EU2 – EU1) minus the gain in the last period (EU4 – EU3). Finally, the name GAMMA comes from the shape of the learning curve of the child with a high score, like Child

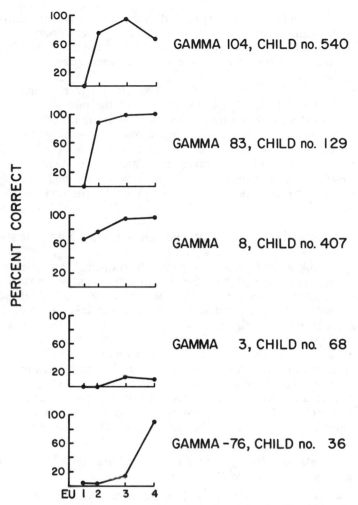

FIGURE 3.3. Illustration of different "speed of learning," GAMMA, for five children in the project.

number 129. This curve looks like a capital Greek letter gamma (Figure 3.3).

We found that to characterize the bad curve the best measure was the average score throughout the school year. We call this LEVEL. It is easily obtained. One simply probes that child's articulation for at least three points, including a baseline score and the end-of-year score, and averages the results. It is not necessary to have exactly four scores to average from, although there must be at least three.

We already have sufficient examples to show the possible spread of LEVEL.

| Child | 327 | 407 | 129 | 540 | 220 | 36 | 68 | 444 |
|-------|-----|-----|-----|-----|-----|----|----|-----|
| Year  | 2   | 3   | 3   | 2   | 4   | 4  | 3  | 2   |
| Level | 99  | 83  | 67  | 58  | 45  | 25 | 5  | 1   |

Since our scores are all in the range 0-100, we know that a low value of LEVEL shows a bad curve and a very high value indicates a child who had relatively good articulation throughout the year. On the other hand, an intermediate figure for LEVEL does not tell us much. A child with LEVEL between 20 and 70 may be a slow learner, may be a fast learner, or may have stayed at an intermediate level throughout the year.

The last block of variables (in Table 3.4) will not receive much attention. These variables (GAIN 12, 23, 34, 13, 24) are all the rest of the possible gain scores, besides GAIN for the entire school year. These are included for completeness. In the statistical analysis, we will bring in one of these only when it indicates a significant difference which cannot be dealt with in another way. We have decided that to include all these variables in all the statistical analysis would clutter the results unnecessarily. Summary statistics are provided for all dependent variables (Table 3.5) and the correlations among all the dependent variables (Table 3.6).

## Statistical Analyses of the Dependent Variables

When we look at our project as primarily statistical, our goal is to relate independent to dependent variables. For instance, we want to know whether the child's baseline score, an independent variable, influences EU2, a dependent variable. We have discussed the construction of our dependent variables. Before we discuss the independent variables and relate them to the dependent, we must consider the dependent variables as a group. As we discuss the effect of various factors on EU2 and GAIN, it will be useful to know how EU2 and GAIN are individually distributed, and how they relate to each other. Thus, in this section, we survey the dependent variables statistically.

We have created three nonexclusive sets of dependent variables: the EU numbers, except for EU1, the primary dependent variables EU2, GAIN, GAMMA, and LEVEL; and five other gain scores. Our focus in this and subsequent sections will be on the primary set.

*EU2*: This variable has already been discussed. Its distribution tends to be uniform, which will not be a problem.

*The distribution of GAIN scores*: In order to understand the distribution of GAIN, we need to look at the distribution of gain scores in general. The basic ideas here were discussed when we looked at the EU scattergrams, Figure 2a-f, Appendix E. The primary discovery was that a child's articulation score hardly ever decreases from one time to the next. This means that gain scores are rarely negative. However, if we look again at the scattergrams, we see that a few negative gains correspond to children in what we have called area "A" (Figure E. 3, Appendix E). In Table E. 1, Appendix E, we have counted these children.

The number of children with negative gain decreases with the length of the time interval. The smallest are GAIN, and GAIN24. The largest number corresponds to the shortest time interval, GAIN12. The longer the time interval, the less likely a decrease in articulation ability. Or, to put it more clearly, give the child enough time and his or her articulation will improve.

However, 3.1% of the children still show negative GAIN for the entire school year.

In the distribution of GAIN the mean and median are both 50. Thus, the average child makes a 50% articulation gain during the course of therapy in a

| | Variable | Mean | SD | Median | Minimum | Maximum |
|---|---|---|---|---|---|---|
| Primary | EU2 | 44.9 | 29.3 | 43 | 0 | 100 |
| | GAIN | 49.8 | 31.1 | 50 | -38 | 100 |
| | GAMMA | 6.6 | 28.4 | 2 | -76 | 104 |
| | LEVEL | 53.4 | 24.8 | 56 | 0 | 100 |
| Other gains | GAIN12 | 18.3 | 21.6 | 12 | -36 | 95 |
| | GAIN23 | 20.1 | 17.2 | 17 | -17 | 82 |
| | GAIN34 | 11.6 | 13.9 | 8 | -52 | 76 |
| | GAIN13 | 38.3 | 30.0 | 34 | -43 | 100 |
| | GAIN24 | 31.6 | 22.3 | 29 | -34 | 91 |
| Other EU | EU3 | 64.9 | 30.2 | 73 | 0 | 100 |
| | EU4 | 76.5 | 26.9 | 87 | 0 | 100 |

TABLE 3.5. Summary statistics for all dependent variables.

school year. From 0 to 100, the histogram (Figure E. 5a, Appendix E) is flat, but there are some large negative scores. One child is recorded as having lost 37 points during the year.

*GAIN and EU2*: The ideal mentioned above is almost reached by these two variables. Their correlation is −.06. Without considering the statistical significance, they are essentially unrelated. This can be visualized in the scattergram (Figure E. 6a, Appendix E). The children are uniformly scattered in the space of positive GAIN, with two exceptions: there are bites taken from the plot at the bottom and in the upper right corner.

| | EU2 | GAIN | GAMMA | LEVEL | GAIN 12 | 23 | 34 | 13 | 24 | EU 3 | 4 |
|---|---|---|---|---|---|---|---|---|---|---|---|
| EU2 | 100 | -06 | 55 | 94 | 41 | -24 | -47 | 16 | -48 | 83 | 69 |
| GAIN | | 100 | 39 | 06 | 70 | 68 | 29 | 90 | 71 | 34 | 53 |
| GAMMA | | | 100 | 41 | 88 | 13 | -66 | 71 | -31 | 61 | 34 |
| LEVEL | | | | 100 | 30 | 02 | -37 | 23 | -21 | 92 | 85 |
| GAIN12 | | | | | 100 | 17 | -23 | 82 | -01 | 50 | 45 |
| GAIN23 | | | | | | 100 | 00 | 70 | 78 | 34 | 38 |
| GAIN34 | | | | | | | 100 | -16 | 63 | -46 | 00 |
| GAIN13 | | | | | | | | 100 | 45 | 56 | 54 |
| GAIN24 | | | | | | | | | 100 | -02 | 30 |
| EU3 | | | | | | | | | | 100 | 89 |
| EU4 | | | | | | | | | | | 100 |

TABLE 3.6. Correlations between dependent variables.

The problem at the bottom is limited to the area with GAIN less than 25. Children with an EU2 below 20 make a small GAIN. The same is true for children with an EU2 above 70. But children with an EU2 between 20 and 70 have a tendency to make a GAIN above 25. Remember that the GAIN we consider is from the beginning of the year to the end. A child who has neither a high or low score at EU2 is likely to make overall progress, but there will still be a few whose abilities decrease through the year.

The area in the upper right portion of the scattergram represents children with a high EU2 and high GAIN. There are relatively few of these, and that is sensible, since high EU2 goes with high EU1 and thus low GAIN.

Another method of looking at this is to split the children into high and low EU2 groups. This means dividing the scattergram into left and right halves. In the left half are children with low EU2 (below 50). For them, EU2 seems to be positively related to GAIN. Higher EU2 (above 50), is associated with higher GAIN. In the right half of the plot, there is a negative relationship. High EU2 is associated with low GAIN. Since there is a certain amount of common sense in all of these interpretations, we accept them, but we note that GAIN and EU2 are not strictly independent normals. Nevertheless, we proceed as though they were unrelated.

*GAMMA*: Our measure of speed of learning is the difference between two gain scores, GAIN12 minus GAIN34. From our discussion of the distribution of gain scores, we know that there are a few negative gains. This causes GAMMA to have very long tails in both the positive and negative directions, as shown in the histogram (Figure E. 5b, Appendix E). This is a departure from the normal. Mean GAMMA is about 7, showing that the average learning curve has a curvature like that of either chld No. 407 or 68 in Figure 3.3. GAMMA is an approximation to the curvature of the learning curve, and thus is theoretically not sensitive to the overall curve or its slope.

*GAMMA vs. EU2*: Our idea of independent variables is not achieved in the case of GAMMA and EU2. Their scattergram (Figure E. 6b, Appendix E) shows that they are positively related, with a correlation of .55. But, when we consider that the scale values for the EU numbers are limited from 0 to 100, this begins to make sense. In fact, we know that many children start low but end up with high scores at EU2. These would have high EU2 and GAMMA, so there should be some children for which EU2 and GAMMA would naturally be associated. Because the scale is bounded, the mathematical possibility of children with high EU2 and low GAMMA does not occur, since these would have to start or end above 100. We are thus left with a measure of "final score" and a measure of speed of learning.

*GAMMA vs. GAIN*: The correlation here is moderate and positive at .39. The scattergram (Figure E. 6d, Appendix E) is roughly triangular, with few children in the lower corner of the triangle. These would be children with high GAIN and negative GAMMA, which would be like child No. 36 in Figure 3.3. This type of curve is rare, since the lower corner is not filled in. Thus, high GAIN is associated with high GAMMA, and the correlation is explained.

Above the upper edge of the triangle are a few outliers. These have very high GAMMA for moderate GAIN. This required the learning curve to turn down, like child No. 540 in the previously mentioned figure. Thus, the demarcation at the upper edge to this plot is another indication that children rarely have decreasing scores.

There are more outliers below the lower edge of the plot. These have moderate GAIN and very low GAMMA. These are children whose learning curve starts fairly high, then immediately decreases, then turns up, but overall shows low to moderate GAIN. The fact that there is a distinct lower edge to the triangle shows that these are unlikely. Again, we are shown that a decrease in articulation ability is not to be expected. Children in therapy get better.

*LEVEL*: Since LEVEL is an average of four variables, it is not surprising that it is distributed as shown in the histogram (Figure E. 5c, Appendix E). From the quality of the distribution, it would be an important variable, if it were not for the problem we face when we consider it with respect to EU2.

*LEVEL vs. EU2*: Our hope for four distinct dependent variables is not realized, since the correlation between EU2 and LEVEL is .94. This means that 88% of the variance of one is predictable from the other, and that a statistical analysis that is significant for one is likely to be significant for the other and to provide no new information. The scattergram (Figure E. 6c, Appendix E) shows that the range of values of LEVEL for a given value of EU2 is narrow, about 30 points. A child with an EU2 of 10 is likely to have a LEVEL of 25. A child with an EU2 of 90 is likely to have a LEVEL of 89 (these were both calculated from the regression equation). If we look at the scattergram more closely, it appears that the range of values of LEVEL for EU2 of 10 is larger than for EU2 of 90, and that the values of LEVEL are somewhat uniformly distributed with these ranges. A child with an EU2 of 10 may have a LEVEL in the range of 10 to 49.

We originally constructed LEVEL in order to deal with children who had bad learning curves. Now we see that EU2 is difficult to statistically distinguish from LEVEL. Thus we are inclined in the subsequent analyses to neglect LEVEL. The question of which factors may cause a child's learning curve to be bad will be dealt with partially by looking at EU2, and partially with a different kind of dependent variable, KLMO.

We conclude our discussion of LEVEL by quickly considering the two remaining scattergrams. GAIN vs. LEVEL (Figure E. 6e, Appendix E) should be compared with GAIN vs. EU2 (Figure E. 6a) but after it has been rotated around the diagonal. The major feature is the "bite" on the left of the GAIN vs. LEVEL plot, which corresponds to the bite discussed in the GAIN vs. EU2 plot. Children with intermediate values of LEVEL are unlikely to have zero GAIN. For instance, a child who starts the year at 50 and ends the year at 50 is rare. We can thus translate this bite into the "C" area of the EU1 vs. EU4 scattergram. Each picture shows that the child with an intermediate value of articulation ability is likely to be improving, while the child with a low articulation ability may remain a problem, and the child with high ability will remain high.

Finally, the GAMMA vs. LEVEL scattergram (Figure E. 6f, Appendix E) is compared with the EU2 vs. GAMMA plot, again rotated on the diagonal. As such there are no insights to be gained from the former.

*Statistics for Gain Scores*: We have said that not much time will be spent with the other gain scores. However, there are two points that can be made from the summary statistics and correlations. First, the mean gain scores are a measure of the average improvement over time. These have been divided by the average time interval, and multiplied by 10, to yield an expected value of improvement in articulation over 10 weeks (Table E. 2, Appendix E). Clearly, the highest rate of improvement comes in the first six weeks. After EU2, the rate of improvement is reduced, but this is not surprising, since so many children have reached a high level of articulation at EU2, and are not likely to improve much more.

The second point about gain scores is that some pairs of variables that are adjacent in time, like GAIN23 and GAIN34, have a very low correlation. This means that gain in the second period is unrelated to gain in the first period. Note carefully that this is not a statement about the EU numbers. If the child is high at EU3, he will be high at EU4. But the amount of change from EU2 to EU3 is not related to the amount of change from EU3 to EU4.

## Summary of Dependent Variables

This concludes our construction and statistical analysis of dependent variables. To summarize:

1. Articulation ability was measured by SPT and TALK probed throughout the year.
2. To simplify the analysis, SPT and TALK were combined into the Unified Score (US).
3. US's are averaged together to produce the Average Unified Scores, the AU numbers. These are not measured at the same times for each child.
4. Values are interpolated between the AU numbers to provide the Equalized Unified Scores, the EU numbers. These are considered subsequently to represent the child's learning curve. No further analysis will be done on TALK, SPT, or AU numbers in Chapters 3, 4, and 5.
5. Many children entered the project with low articulation ability. Most had achieved high ability by the end of the year. Almost all the time, most children improved their ability while in therapy.
6. The primary set of dependent variables are derived from the EU numbers:
   a. EU2—the child's average articulation ability after six weeks of therapy. This is considered as a final score, in place of EU4 or EU3 which are badly distributed.
   b. GAIN—the child's gain from the beginning to the end of the year.
   c. GAMMA—a measure of speed of learning.
   d. LEVEL—the average score over the whole year. It was originally created to deal with "bad learning curves," but was dropped from most of the subsequent analysis because it is correlated .94 with EU2.
7. EU2 and GAIN are not related. GAMMA is moderately correlated with both of the other variables.
8. Children with moderate articulation levels tend to improve during therapy. A few children with low articulation stay low. Children with high levels of articulation, of course, stay high.

## Factoring the Dependent Variables

A factor analysis (principle components using Kaiser's criterion for selection, followed by varimax rotation) was run on the total set of dependent variables. Although this set of variables is not suitable for factoring in the traditional sense, because the transformed variables were included, the analysis was still performed to see how the variables organized themselves.

The analysis produced three clear factors:

I. EU2—includes all EU numbers, but highest loadings are for EU2 and LEVEL.

II. GAIN—includes all GAIN scores except GAIN34. Highest loading is GAIN.

III. GAMMA—includes GAMMA raw and transformed and GAIN34.

The factor technique produces orthogonal factors. EU1 and EU1T are loaded on both factors I and II. GAIN24 and GAIN12 are loaded on factors II and III.

The analysis suggests that our choice of major dependent variables, EU2, GAIN, and GAMMA is at least consistent. Each of these is the primary variable on an orthogonal factor. The analysis cannot show that the choice of dependent variables is valid, since the selection of variables to be factored has some influence on the outcome of the analysis. We cannot show from this analysis that the three variables are useful, but it does appear that they are unrelated. It is reasonable to analyze them separately, because the factors they represent are orthogonal.

## Introduction to KLMO

We will now define a new dependent variable. A primary interest of the data analyst must be in the communication of results about the subjects of research. In our case, the most important goal is to discuss clearly what we have discovered about children and clinicians. In the process of doing data analysis it is desirable to use statistical techniques that are state-of-the-art and techniques from the most recent data analysis literature. Unfortunately, these state-of-the-art statistics may not be completely understood by our audience. Thus, the goal of being up-to-date in statistics and the goal of communicating clearly may be contradictory. Although in some cases there may be no way to resolve these conflicts, we would, when possible, prefer to work with two kinds of statistics: some that are state-of-the-art and some that are more easily communicated.

We have defined a full set of dependent variables representing several aspects of articulation ability and its changes. The source of all these variables is the EU numbers. The variables of primary interest are EU2, GAIN, and GAMMA. We propose now to create a new variable. The basis of this variable is the EU numbers, but we now focus on one particular concept: learning curve patterns. We will divide the children into groups based on the shape of their learning curves.

We will define four primary categories of learning curve and label them "K," "L," "M," and "O." The nominal variable that represents these categories will be called "KLMO." The name KLMO came about in an interesting manner. We did not know of terms in the common literature for learning curve patterns. A new term was needed and we noted that several scientific areas have created new terms from letters of the alphabet. We started with "A" and rejected it because it is used for grading in the schools. We then moved down the alphabet, rejecting letters until we got to "K." This, then, became the first label for our learning curve. Later we will note why there is no "N" in the patterns.

## KLMO Categories

In order to define the KLMO variable and its categories, we start with examples rather than an abstract definition. We will choose children from our study who are closest to the mean in each category on the EU numbers. The reader will be able to look at typical learning curves from children in each category. Following the examples we will give the precise definition of KLMO.

The histogram of EU1, Figure E. 1a, Appendix E, shows that many children start the year with low articulation ability. These are the children who could potentially make progress in therapy. They have an articulation problem that needs to be solved.

Among the children who start the year low, there are some who make rapid progress. They are fast learners. These are the children in the first category: "K." Children labeled "K" start the year with low EU1 baseline and have a high EU2. Our typical "K" child is shown in Figure 3.4. At the beginning of therapy, the child has a US of 8. In the next week, the US has risen to 19, and she is assigned an EU1 of 14. Then in nine weeks of therapy, the US has reached 74, and she gets an EU2 of 66. Thus, substantial progress has been made from EU1 to EU2. This progress continues until the end of the year. The EU4 of 98 indicates that the articulation problem was solved. The important thing here is the shape of the learning curve, which rises quickly at the beginning of therapy from a low baseline. This is what characterizes "K" children.

Of the children who start low, some do not make immediate progress, but do finally reach a high level of articulation. These children are labeled "L." Figure 3.5 shows a typical "L" child. Like the "K," the first US is very low at 7, with the baseline EU1 at 5. But this child, in the six weeks after therapy starts, has an EU2 score estimated at 21. The child is definitely making progress, but not fast enough to qualify for the "K" category. The last EU4 score of 87, means that the problem is being solved. This example is a real child, with real data. There is a slight turndown of the US at the end of the year, which is not reflected in the EU

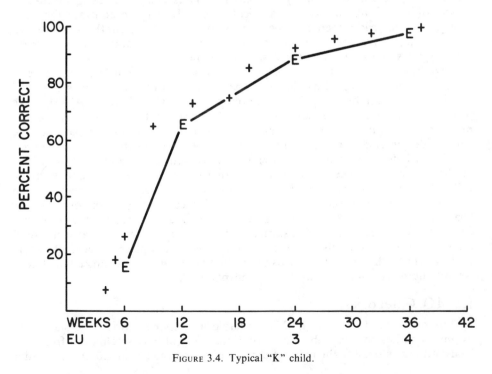

FIGURE 3.4. Typical "K" child.

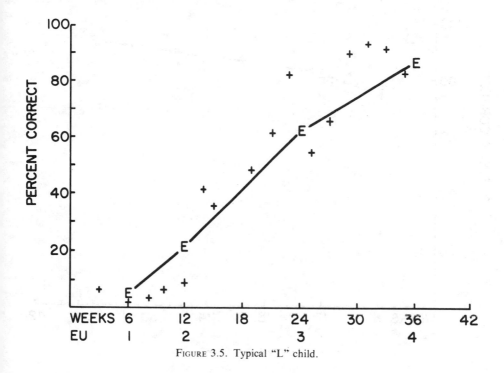

FIGURE 3.5. Typical "L" child.

numbers. This is a price we pay for having to make our numbers comparable across children.

Children in the "K" and "L" categories start the year with a low baseline score. The next category, "M," contains children who start the year high (Figure 3.6). Here the baseline score is 75, a level that suggests to some clinicians that the child might not need therapy. For the baseline level, the child progresses steadily upward to an EU4 of 97. Since, as we have seen (Figure E. 1a-d, Appendix E), almost no children have decreasing EU numbers, starting the year with a high baseline is sufficient to ensure that the child will reach a preset termination criterion.

It can be argued that some of the "M" children should not have been in therapy at all. We might have set up the child selection process to prevent the selections of "M's," but we know that this type of child does form part of the standard caseload of clinicians in the schools. It is better for our naturalistic study that this type is included.

The "M" children have a very flat learning curve, at a high articulation level. These children make relatively little progress. Our next category, "O," contains children who also have a flat learning curve, and make little progress, but at a low articulation level. Figure 3.7 shows the scores for a typical "O" who starts the year at a baseline of 6 and never gets above a level of 30. Looking at the learning curve, there is some indication of progress, but at the end of the year there is still a problem.

One may speculate about the causes for any particular child not overcoming an articulation problem. As we develop our statistical results, we will try to see what other variables may be related to the "O" learning. One may say that the "M"

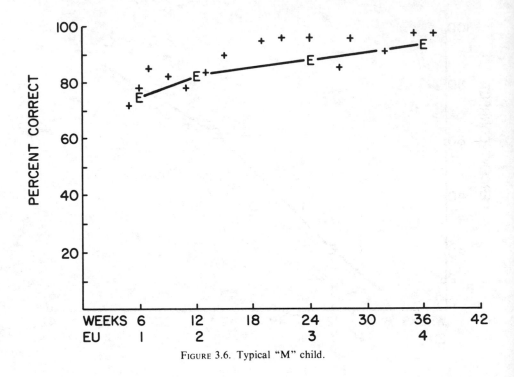

FIGURE 3.6. Typical "M" child.

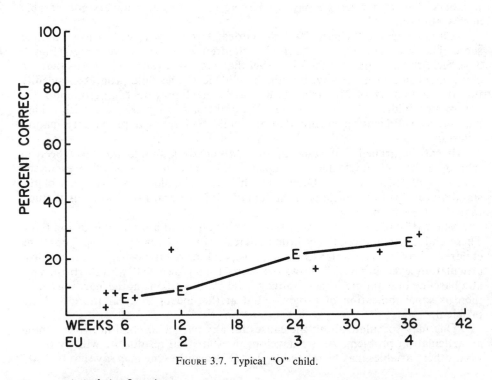

FIGURE 3.7. Typical "O" child.

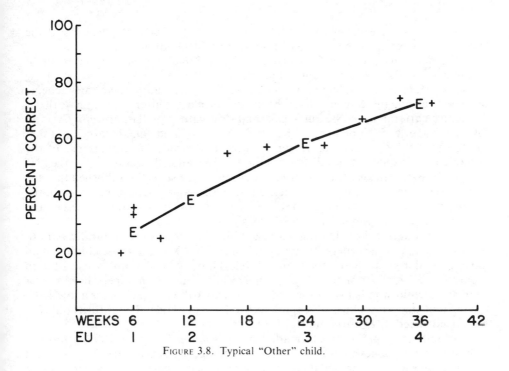

FIGURE 3.8. Typical "Other" child.

children do not need therapy in the first place. "O's" on the other hand are the ones who seem to need it the most.

We have constructed the variable KLMO and its associated categories in order to delineate the most distinctive child learning curves. Each child in each of the four categories goes through a learning process that should be identifiable by the practicing clinician. However, in order to make the categories distinctive, some learning curves must be left out. These are placed in a fifth category which we call "Other." Figure 3.8 shows a child near the mean of the children in the "Other" category. This child does not start low, nor end high. Some progress is made, but not a lot. Most clinicians would choose to continue the child in therapy next year, some would not. It seems most reasonable to view this as a "middle" child. We will be surprised in the subsequent statistical analysis if we are able to find variables that are strongly related to membership in the "Other" category. Yet, to make the analysis complete, we will not remove these children. In those instances where our statistical analysis is intended to explore the idea of prediction of KLMO, these "Other" children will be left in because we do not believe there is a crystal ball to tell us which children will be in the "Other" category prior to the beginning of therapy.

## KLMO—Definition

We have presented examples from the KLMO categories before precisely defining the variable because we feel that the reader's understanding of the learning curve patterns is more important than the mathematical definition.

The name of our variable is KLMO. It has five values: "K," "L," "M," "O," and "Other." Each child in our study receives only one value out of the five. Thus we end up with five groups: the "K's," the "L's," the "M's" the "O's," and the "Others." To repeat—one variable, five groups of children.

The definition of KLMO is given in Table 3.7 along with the number of children from the 1,108 in each category.

The reader may wonder about the lack of an "N" category. In an early scheme of classification, there would have been five primary patterns and an "other." These five patterns would be quick gain and slow gain, high flat, *medium flat*, and low flat. These were to be named "K," "L," "M," "N," and "O." It turned out that the fourth, "N," category was extremely rare, and would have made use of the variable in chi-square tables difficult because of small cell counts. Thus, the "N" category was eliminated, but the other categories were so well-established that the names were kept. The fact of "N" being rare is the same phenomenon seen in the scattergrams for EU2 vs. GAIN and LEVEL vs. GAIN. The area we called the "bite" in each case would have been "N's."

We are interested in children who start high and low, so we naturally want to use EU1 as one of the criteria to define KLMO. The "K's" are those children who have a rapid rise in their articulation level. Thus, we will want to use EU2 to separate the "K's" from the "L's." Finally, since the EU numbers hardly ever decrease, a child who is low at the end of the year will very likely have a low score throughout the year. Thus, we expect to use EU4 to define "O." It turns out that we do not need EU3 to define KLMO.

An important point must be made here. *The definition of KLMO is arbitrary.* The selection of values to delimit the KLMO categories is arbitrary. No statistical test was used, no external validity criterion was used. The categories were chosen to separate children with different learning curves, and to clarify the statistical results for readers who are more comfortable with discrete variables. Another set of researchers with the same data might choose different categories. We would not argue with them on a purely rational basis. Each of the categories could have been larger or smaller. Each category could have been modified to include curves with slightly different patterns.

Now let us review the details of the definition given in Table 3.7. Each column defines one category of KLMO. The actual number in that category is at the bottom of the column. The "K" category is defined as all those who have an EU1 below 32, and EU2 above 43, and an EU4 above 73. For this category, the first two criteria are the important ones. "K" children have to start low and reach a reasonably high level at EU2.

Note that there might be a "K" with an EU1 of 32, which is not very low. This same child may have an EU2 of 44, which is not much of a jump. The selection of values for our criteria was made to separate those children who might satisfy the "K" concept of fast improvement. Some of these will demonstrate faster learning than others.

The numerical values of the criteria were adjusted to get approximately the same number of children in each of the five categories. Several sets of criteria were tried. The one we used has 25% "Other," which is effectively unclassified, 18% "O's" and 19% of the 1,108 children in each of the other categories.

The difference between "K" and "L" is the EU2 criterion. "K's" must have an EU2 above 43, "L's" must be below. This means that there will be some "K" and some "L" who will have about the same learning curves. Most "K" children are successful and learn quickly. Most "L" children are successful but learn slower than the "K's."

|      | K    | L    | M    | 0    | Other |
|------|------|------|------|------|-------|
| EU1  | ≤32  | ≤32  | >53  | ≤32  |       |
| EU2  | >43  | ≤43  | >43  | ≤43  |       |
| EU4  | >73  | >73  | >73  | ≤54  |       |
| N    | 211  | 213  | 209  | 200  | 275   |
| %    | 19   | 19   | 19   | 18   | 25    |

TABLE 3.7. Criteria for definition of KLMO.

The criteria for "M" are the same as "K," except that "M's" must have an EU1 above 53. Because it is rare for our children to have decreasing EU numbers, this selects those who have a high score throughout the school year.

The criteria for "O" are the same as "L" except that EU4 must be below 54. Again, because EU rarely increases, this selects children who are low throughout the year.

## Relationship of KLMO to Other Dependent Variables

The variable KLMO is a dependent variable, constructed to bring some clarity to our analyses. We do not expect that this simple categorical variable will account for all of the variation in the EU numbers over all of the children, but it does have some explanatory power.

We would first like to see the average values of the EU numbers within each of our five KLMO categories. These means are shown in Table 3.8 and plotted in Figure 3.9. The pattern of these means confirms the ideas used to design the KLMO categories.

The average "K" child, true to his model as a fast success, starts at 12, and reaches a score of 64 in six weeks of therapy, a leap of 52 points. At EU3 he has reached 88, and by the end of the year, 94. This is a clear picture of a child who learns quickly and successfully solves his articulation problem.

Note that we have just described the average "K" child. There are children in the "K" category above this level, and children who are below. A few children on the border may have EU1 = 32, EU2 = 43, EU4 = 73. A child with scores like this would not be called a fast learner. However, there are very few children at the border of the category. More of them are near the mean. Thus, we can say that most of the children in the "K" category validate the ideas used to construct the category. In addition, there are many children who have an EU1 lower than the average and EU2 and EU4 higher than the average. They would certainly be called fast learners.

The average "L" child starts at about 8, near the "K" child, but by the sixth week his EU2 score is only 26, which is 38 points below the average "K." The average "L," a delayed success, moves steadily to an EU3 of 66 and finishes the year with an EU4 of 89. This child has solved his articulation problem, but he took longer than the "K" child. Looking at the plot, we see that the average "L" child makes a gain of about 2.7 points per week, every week. The reader should apply the same comments to the "L" child as were made about the "K" child, noting that

| Variable | K | L | M | O | Other | Total | $R^2$(x100) |
|---|---|---|---|---|---|---|---|
| EU1 | 12.2 | 7.5 | 75.3 | 6.8 | 30.2 | 26.7 | 78 |
| EU2 | 63.8 | 25.5 | 81.9 | 10.6 | 42.3 | 44.9 | 72 |
| EU3 | 88.1 | 65.8 | 91.4 | 18.7 | 59.9 | 64.9 | 69 |
| EU4 | 94.2 | 88.7 | 95.7 | 28.8 | 73.4 | 76.5 | 79 |
| | | | | | | | |
| GAIN | 82.0 | 81.1 | 20.3 | 22.0 | 43.3 | 49.8 | 72 |
| GAMMA | 45.4 | -5.0 | 2.3 | -6.4 | -1.4 | 6.6 | 45 |
| LEVEL | 64.7 | 47.0 | 86.2 | 16.3 | 51.6 | 53.4 | 79 |
| | | | | | | | |
| GAIN12 | 51.5 | 18.0 | 6.9 | 4.0 | 12.3 | 18.3 | 60 |
| GAIN23 | 24.4 | 40.3 | 9.5 | 8.2 | 17.7 | 20.0 | 44 |
| GAIN34 | 6.1 | 22.9 | 4.3 | 10.1 | 13.5 | 11.6 | 22 |
| GAIN13 | 75.9 | 58.2 | 16.2 | 12.0 | 29.8 | 38.3 | 64 |
| GAIN24 | 30.5 | 63.2 | 13.8 | 18.2 | 31.2 | 31.6 | 57 |
| | | | | | | | |
| N | 211 | 213 | 209 | 200 | 275 | 1108 | |

TABLE 3.8. Means of dependent variables for KLMO categories and percent of variance explained by KLMO.

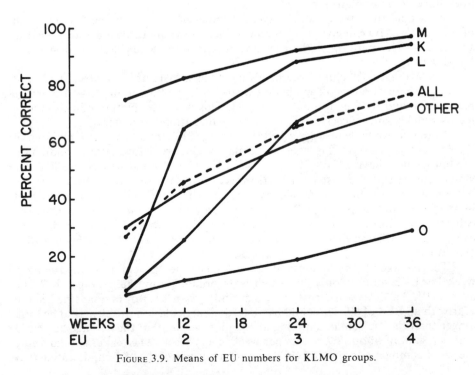

FIGURE 3.9. Means of EU numbers for KLMO groups.

we are talking about an average child, and that there will be some above the average and some below.

The typical "M" child starts at 75, then reaches 82 in six weeks. After EU3, his scores are at the same high level as the "K." Considering that some clinicians have recommended using 75% correct as a termination criterion, we see that the average "M" child might not even be considered for therapy. Certainly, those in the "M" category who are above the average curve, would not be thought of as learning much in the process of one year's therapy.

The average "O" child starts at about the same level as "K" or "L," but six weeks later has reached 11. By the end of the year, this child has managed to achieve only a 29% articulation ability. This is not a successful therapy experience. It must be assumed that the "O" child will be a candidate for more therapy in the next school year.

One quarter, 275, of our 1,108 children were not specifically categorized in KLMO. These are the children assigned to the "Other" group. It turns out that their scores through the year are very close to the average of all children in the study. They start the year at 30, and proceed steadily to an EU2 of 42, EU3 of 60 and end the year at EU4 of 73. There are many different kinds of learning curves within this "other" category. However, since the purpose of KLMO is to clarify the analyses, we will not discuss the patterns within "other" further.

In Table 3.8, we have also shown the means for GAIN and GAMMA. Children in the "K" and "L" categories have an average GAIN of about 81 points from the beginning to the end of the school year. Those in the other two categories have an average GAIN of 21. All the categories have an average GAMMA near zero, except "K." Given the mean and standard deviation of GAMMA in the whole population of 1,108 children, this means that some categories contain children with negative GAMMA. In fact many of these lie in the "L" category, because they are delayed but successful learners.

When we use KLMO as a dependent variable, although it is intended only for clarity, we would like some idea of how much of the variation in the dependent variables is accounted for by KLMO (Table 3.8). We can say that KLMO explains about 75% of the variation of all of the primary variables except GAMMA. The latter is not well explained by KLMO because of the problem with negative GAMMA's observed in the paragraph above. We claim "rough" estimates of the variance explained because most of these variables are not well distributed. "Rough" estimates of 75% are sufficient to meet our needs.

# CHAPTER 4

# Results: Child Independent Variables

In Chapter 3 we defined our basic measures of articulation learning, the dependent variables. In this chapter, we look at child independent variables. The question is—what is it about children that affects articulation learning? The variables are natural in the school setting. We are interested in baseline articulation, EU1; target phoneme, SOUND; grade in school, GRADE; and child's sex, KSEX; and whether the child has had previous therapy, PREVT. We look at these variables in some detail. It turns out that the combination of baseline and target phoneme called SNDEU1 will be the most important variable. SNDEU1 alone explains almost half of the variation in the child's articulation after six weeks of therapy. GRADE also turns out to be a useful variable. The sex of the child has no effect. All by itself, previous therapy status affects the dependent variables, particularly at the beginning of the year, but its effect is eliminated by knowing the child's baseline score. We show similar kinds of results when analyzing the learning curve variable KLMO.

For definitions of special terms and symbols used in this project refer to Appendix G in this book.

## Introduction

The independent variables in an experimental design are those under the control of the experimenter. For example, in working with school children one could choose a certain number of boys and a certain number of girls, thus controlling the independent variable, "sex." One could then choose to expose half of the sample to a certain teaching pattern, the other half to regular instruction. Thus "teaching method" would be another independent variable. In this experimental design, "sex" and "teaching method" would be independent variables under the control of the experimenter.

Our study is nonexperimental (naturalistic in the words of Plutchik, 1968, see Preface), but the idea of an independent variable remains the same. The independent variables are those the administrator, or the clinician *could control* in order to produce some desired effect in the dependent variables. For instance, a supervisor may decide to concentrate on just /s/ children, without therapy for /r/'s. This would have the probable effect of speeding up learning and producing quick success. It is possible that the /r/'s could be brought in later, after the /s/'s have been dropped. The independent variable in this example is the child's target phoneme and the dependent variable is GAMMA, our measure of speed of learning.

Our study is complicated because it is naturalistic instead of experimental. It is also complicated by having two units to observe: the child and the clinician. Thus, our independent variables will naturally fall into two groups, one that pertains directly to the children and one related to the clinician. The target phoneme noted above is a property of the child. But we can construct a related independent variable to be a property of the clinician. Consider all the children taught by a particular clinician in our study. Suppose this clinician had 20 children. Suppose that 15 of these had an /s/ problem. The $(15/20) \times 100 = 75\%$ of this clinician's children have /s/ as a target phoneme. This "75%" is a value of a variable that is a natural property of the clinician, which might be called "percent /s/." It is a clinician independent variable, but it is derived from a child independent variable. It is this kind of variable that sometimes complicates our study.

Note that there are several variables that are quite naturally clinician variables, including age, years of teaching experience, and ASHA certification. These should present no problems for the reader when they are properties of the clinician. However, we will also consider these same variables as properties of the children. We need to explain this.

One definition of a variable is "any property that divides the experimental units into groups." We have two experimental units—clinicians and children. Assume for the moment that the *child* is our basic experimental unit. It is clear then that EU1 is a variable since it divides our experimental units into groups—all the children with an EU1 of 0, all those with EU1 = 1, all those with EU1 = 2, etc. Someone else might use the temperature in Lawrence, Kansas as a variable, but we believe it has nothing to do with our children. A child's mother's age might have been a variable for our study, but we did not measure it.

In our study, the property of the clinician called DEGREE, the highest degree obtained, is a child variable because it divides the children into two groups. One group holds all the children taught by a clinician with a M.A. and the other holds all those whose clinician has a B.A. Since DEGREE divides the experimental units (children), into two groups, it is a *child variable*. It is also a clinician variable, because it divides the clinicians into two groups.

## The List of Independent Variables—Children

Table 4.1 is a list of the independent variables that pertain to children. Table 4.2 presents summary statistics for these variables. These statistics are discussed as we look at each variable in detail.

## Child Prior Variables

We now begin a detailed discussion of the variables in Table 4.1. In this section we describe the first block of variables. Statistics on these independent variables will be presented, then we will deal with statistical analyses of the effect of the independent variables on the dependent variables. The latter in some sense represents our first "final result," because it brings together the articulation learning patterns and some child-oriented independent variables. After we have dealt with this material, we will examine the effects of the clinician on the statistical analyses. We shall also look at the other blocks of child independent variables listed in Table 4.1.

The independent variables that apply to children fall naturally into three blocks—1) child prior conditions, 2) clinical decisions, and 3) experimental conditions. In this section we are concerned with the child prior conditions. We have labeled these EU1, CEU1, SOUND, SNDEU1, GRADE, PREVT, and KSEX.

The child prior conditions are properties inherent to the child before the beginning of therapy. These are not under the direct control of the clinician. They come with the caseload.

| Name | Values | Meaning |
|------|--------|---------|

Child Prior Conditions

| | | |
|------|--------|---------|
| EU1 | 1-100 | Baseline articulation score. |
| | | |
| CEU1 | | Categorized EU1. |
| | 1 | low, 0 - 6 percent correct |
| | 2 | medium, 7 - 33 percent correct |
| | 3 | high, 34 - 100 percent correct |
| | | |
| SOUND | | Target phoneme. |
| | 1 | /s/ |
| | 2 | /r/ |
| | | |
| SNDEU1 | | SOUND and CEU1 combined. |
| | 1 | /s/ low |
| | 2 | /s/ medium |
| | 3 | /s/ high |
| | 4 | /r/ low |
| | 5 | /r/ medium |
| | 6 | /r/ high |
| | | |
| GRADE | | The child's grade in the current year. |
| | 1 | first grade |
| | 2 | second |
| | 3 | third |
| | 4 | fourth, fifth, and sixth combined. |
| | | |
| PREVT | | Indicates whether the child has had therapy prior to the beginning of the project year. |
| | 1 | no previous therapy |
| | 2 | yes, some previous therapy |
| | | |
| KSEX | | Child sex. |
| | 1 | male |
| | 2 | female |

TABLE 4.1. Independent variables (children).

| Name | Values | Meaning |
|------|--------|---------|

**Clinician Decisions**

NGP — Number of children in this child's therapy group.

| | | |
|---|---|---|
| | 1 | individual therapy |
| | 2 | two children in therapy group |
| | 3 | three children in therapy group |
| | 4 | four children in therapy group |
| | 5 | five children in therapy group |

NOSESS — Number of sessions per week.

| | | |
|---|---|---|
| | 1 | once a week therapy |
| | 2 | twice a week therapy |
| | 3 | block therapy |

**Experimental Decisions**

YEAR — Year of project.

| | |
|---|---|
| | 2 |
| | 3 |
| | 4 |

GEOG — Geographical location of clinicians and children.

| | | |
|---|---|---|
| | 1 | Wichita |
| | 2 | Kansas City |
| | 3 | Denver |
| | 4 | Minneapolis |

**Clinician Prior Conditions**

DEGREE — Last academic degree.

| | | |
|---|---|---|
| | 1 | B.A. |
| | 2 | M.A. or M.S. |

ASHA — Clinical certification status in the American Speech and Hearing Association.

| | | |
|---|---|---|
| | 1 | Certified |
| | 2 | Pending |
| | 3 | Not certified |

TABLE 4.1. (continued).

| Name | Values | Meaning |
|------|--------|---------|
| AGE | 23-49 | Clinician age |
| CAGE | | Categorized AGE |
| | 1 | young, age < 28 |
| | 2 | middle, $28 \leq$ age < 40 |
| | 3 | old, $40 \leq$ age |
| YRSEXP | 0-18 | Years of clinical experience. |

Clinical Attitude

| | | |
|------|--------|---------|
| SELFR | 3-15 | Self concept concerning /r/ therapy. |
| SELFS | 3-15 | Self concept concerning /s/ therapy. |
| EOISUM | 93-137 | A paper/pencil attitude measure on clinician rapport. |
| CEOI | | Categorized EOI. |
| | 1 | low, EOISUM < 116 |
| | 2 | medium, $116 \leq$ EOISUM < 123 |
| | 3 | high, $123 \leq$ EOISUM |

TABLE 4.1. (continued).

EU1 is our measure of the child's articulation level at the beginning of therapy. It is the most important independent variable in terms of explaining variance in the dependent variables. Its derivation has been described as part of the dependent variables, but it is logically an independent variable.

From EU1 is derived Categorized EU1, or CEU1. This variable divides the children into three baseline groups of approximately equal frequency (Table 4.2). Since EU1 is the "pre" score in a study of change, it would have been possible for us to deal with it as a covariate, that is, as an independent variable whose effect is to be statistically removed from the dependent variables. However, there has been much criticism (Lord, 1969) of covariance analysis, so we have followed Winer's (1971) suggestion and created a categorized baseline score CEU1. It will be used as a factor in subsequent analyses.

The next child prior variable is SOUND, the child's target phoneme. This can be /s/ or /r/ under the conditions of this experiment. The variable called SNDEU1 or SOUND—CEU1 combines target phoneme and baseline categories. SNDEU1 divides the children into six categories. This variable was constructed to clarify the subsequent statistical analyses. When SOUND and CEU1 are used to explain the dependent variables, there is a large interaction effect. This is caused primarily by the special properties of children who have /r/ problems and start the year with a very low baseline score. Although we will see other interactions in our statistical analyses, this one is very strong and involves our two most important variables, so we choose to combine them from the start. It is this new variable, SNDEU1, that is the best single variable for explaining the articulation learning curves.

The next two variables in the child prior block are GRADE and PREVT. It is well known that older children have fewer articulation problems than younger ones. The frequency of problems for randomly selected children should decrease with age. As noted in Chapter 2, Methodology, we cannot discuss this hypothesis, because children were not selected randomly by age. However, we still are interested in age as an independent variable. The data available to us included both age and grade in school. These turned out to be highly correlated. To simplify the analysis, it was decided to drop age in favor of grade. In what follows, GRADE should be considered as a replacement for the age concept. GRADE itself is further simplified since there were few children in the high grades. Thus, the last GRADE category combines grades four, five and six.

PREVT indicates whether the child has had any *PREVious Therapy*. It is scored "1" for no and "2" if the child had some articulation therapy for that target phoneme (/r/ or /s/) prior to the beginning of the project year. In fact, what was recorded was number of weeks of prior therapy, but this number turned out to be very badly distributed. To make the data analysis more sensitive, weeks of therapy were reduced to the two values of PREVT. Less than 4% of the children had previous therapy on sounds other than /s/ or /r/.

The final child prior variable is KSEX, which records the child's (*Kid's*) sex. We have included this variable primarily because leaving it out would have caused many readers to question its absence. It has little effect on the dependent variables.

## Statistical Relationships Among the Child Prior Variables

We have listed the independent variables associated with the children as experimental units, and have defined the most important subset—the child prior variables. Before we relate the independent variables, we will look at the child prior variables, considering their joint statistical relationships. Since the project is a nonexperimental design, we will not make strong statements about significant effects among the independent variables. However, some of the results will help clarify our later analyses, and some may actually be statistically significant, if tested within a designed experiment, or in a whole population. Thus, we can learn from these analyses.

*EU1*: This is the child's baseline score, as recorded in the EU numbers. It was discussed and analyzed previously with the other EU numbers.

*CEU1*: The variable called CEU1 results from dividing the children into three approximately equal groups based on their baseline EU1 scores: Low, 0-6% correct; medium, 7-33%; and high, 34-100% correct. This categorization of EU1 eliminates the potential complications of using EU1 as a covariate. The counts and percentages for CEU1 are found in Table 3.12.

In most of the subsequent statistical analyses, we effectively use CEU1 instead of EU1. It is natural to ask, "What may be lost in the transition from EU1 to CEU1?" Table 4.3 shows the results of a one-way analysis of variance (ANOVA) relating the two variables. Most of the statistics contained in that table are found in standard ANOVA texts (e.g., Winer 1969). The use of R-square, the plot at the

| Name | Values | Meaning | N | % | Mean | Median | SD |
|------|--------|---------|---|---|------|--------|-----|
| EU1 | | | | | 27 | 15 | 28 |
| CEU1 | | | | | | | |
| | 1 | low | 398 | 36 | | | |
| | 2 | medium | 349 | 31 | | | |
| | 3 | high | 361 | 33 | | | |
| SOUND | | | | | | | |
| | 1 | /s/ | 539 | 49 | | | |
| | 2 | /r/ | 569 | 51 | | | |
| SNDEU1 | | | | | | | |
| | 1 | /s/ low | 210 | 19 | | | |
| | 2 | /s/ medium | 159 | 14 | | | |
| | 3 | /s/ high | 170 | 15 | | | |
| | 4 | /r/ low | 188 | 17 | | | |
| | 5 | /r/ medium | 190 | 17 | | | |
| | 6 | /r/ high | 191 | 17 | | | |
| GRADE | | | | | | | |
| | 1 | first | 304 | 27 | | | |
| | 2 | second | 365 | 33 | | | |
| | 3 | third | 248 | 22 | | | |
| | 4+ | 4,5,6 | 191 | 17 | | | |
| PREVT | | | | | | | |
| | 1 | no | 652 | 59 | | | |
| | 2 | yes | 456 | 41 | | | |
| KSEX | | | | | | | |
| | 1 | male | 667 | 60 | | | |
| | 2 | female | 441 | 40 | | | |
| NGP | | | | | | | |
| | 1 | | 9 | 1 | | | |
| | 2 | | 418 | 38 | | | |
| | 3 | | 458 | 41 | | | |
| | 4 | | 209 | 19 | | | |
| | 5 | | 14 | 1 | | | |

TABLE 4.2. Summary of all independent variables with the child as the experimental unit.

| Name | Values | Meaning | N | % | Mean | Median | SD |
|------|--------|---------|---|---|------|--------|----|
| NOSESS | | | | | | | |
| | 1 | once/week | 452 | 41 | | | |
| | 2 | twice/week | 556 | 50 | | | |
| | 3 | block | 100 | 9 | | | |
| YEAR | | | | | | | |
| | 2 | | 614 | 55 | | | |
| | 3 | | 300 | 27 | | | |
| | 4 | | 194 | 18 | | | |
| GEOG | | | | | | | |
| | 1 | Wichita | 76 | 7 | | | |
| | 2 | Kansas City | 914 | 82 | | | |
| | 3 | Denver | 43 | 4 | | | |
| | 4 | Minneapolis | 75 | 7 | | | |
| DEGREE | | | | | | | |
| | 1 | B.A. | 613 | 58 | | | |
| | 2 | M.A. | 436 | 42 | | | |
| ASHA | | | | | | | |
| | 1 | yes | 259 | 25 | | | |
| | 2 | pending | 111 | 11 | | | |
| | 3 | no | 679 | 65 | | | |
| AGE | | | | | 33 | 30 | 8 |
| CAGE | | | | | | | |
| | 1 | young | 342 | 33 | | | |
| | 2 | middle | 386 | 37 | | | |
| | 3 | older | 321 | 31 | | | |
| YRSEXP | | | | | 7 | 6 | 5 |
| SELFR | | | | | 12 | 12 | 2 |
| SELFS | | | | | 12 | 12 | 2 |
| EOISUM | | | | | 117 | 117 | 10 |
| CEOI | | | | | | | |
| | 1 | low | 327 | 34 | | | |
| | 2 | medium | 357 | 37 | | | |
| | 3 | high | 292 | 30 | | | |

TABLE 4.2. (continued).

Dependent Variable:  EU1
Independent Variable:  CEU1

$$R^2 = .82 \qquad N = 1108$$
$$LSD = 1.7 \qquad S = 2.2 \qquad ACS = 370$$

|       | SS     | DF   | MS     | F    | p     |
|-------|--------|------|--------|------|-------|
| CEU1  | 733023 | 2    | 366511 | 2516 | <.001 |
| Error | 160991 | 1105 | 146    |      |       |
| Total | 894014 | 1107 |        |      |       |

|       | Low  | Medium | High    |
|-------|------|--------|---------|
| CEU1  | 0-6  | 7-33   | 34-100  |
| Mean  | 1.7  | 18.2   | 62.4    |
| SD    | 2.0  | 8.2    | 19.4    |
| N     | 398  | 349    | 361     |

TABLE 4.3. Analysis of variance.

bottom, the least significant difference (LSD) statistic, Scheffe (S) and average cell size (ACS) are explained later. We may summarize the results by saying that CEU1 explains 82% of the variation of EU1, and that the means of the three groups are completely different.

*SOUND*: The next child prior independent variable is SOUND, which records the child's target phoneme, either /s/ or /r/. The various child selection procedures mentioned in Chapter 2 produced about the same number of /s/ (49%) as /r/ (51%).

*SOUND vs. CEU1*: When target phoneme is compared with categorized baseline, we find a chi-square of 4.4 with 2 df, which is not significant. Since the child selection procedures dealt with target phoneme and somewhat with baseline score, we can only say that our children show about the same level of baseline articulation ability whether they are /s/ or /r/. This may also be true of children in general.

*SNDEU1*: We now deal with a new independent variable whose creation is motivated by results contained in the next section. When we first began to run child prior variables against dependent variables, we found a very strong interaction between SOUND and CEU1. There is a considerable difference between /s/

and /r/ children who have a low baseline score. In order to deal with this inter-action, and simplify the data analysis, we decided to combine the two most important independent variables SOUND and CEU1.

Thus, we created SNDEU1, which has six categories, one for each combina-tion of target phoneme and baseline. The meaning of these categories is given in Table 4.1 and the counts in Table 4.2. The six categories have approximately equal "N," with /s/ low the largest, 19%, and /s/ medium the smallest with 14%.

It is this new variable SNDEU1 that we will use in most of the subsequent data analyses, instead of SOUND or CEU1. Clearly, this categorization loses little information.

*GRADE vs. SNDEU1*: Although neither GRADE nor SNDEU1 were randomly sampled, we need to know about any possible relationship between them for further analysis. We remind the reader that most of the subsequent analyses will be dealing with SNDEU1 instead of SOUND, EU1 or CEU1 separately.

GRADE and SNDEU1 are both discrete variables, so an appropriate analysis is a two-way table. This is given in Table E. 3, Appendix E. We have calculated chi-square and its associated probability, not as a test of the independence of the variables, but as an indication of their relationship.

If the reader is proceeding through the book, this will be the first complex two-way table. We suggest that the reader take some time to study it. Each cell of the table contains the number of children in the combined category of SNDEU1 and GRADE. For instance, in our study, out of 1,108 children, there were 49 who had an /s/ problem, started the year with a high baseline score, and were in the fourth, fifth or sixth grades. These 49 represent 4% of the total.

The large chi-square value indicates that GRADE and SNDEU1 are not unrelated. Chi-square is calculated by first assuming that there is no relationship between the variables and then estimating the number of children who should have been in each cell based on that assumption. This is called expected frequency and will not be printed in our tables. In the /s/ high, four+ cell, the expected frequency is 29. Since we have an observed frequency of 49, we would say that there are too many in this cell. Chi-square is the sum of the squared differences between the observed frequencies and the expected frequencies, divided by the expected frequencies.

Many people interpret two-way tables by just looking at the appropriate percentages. Following Habermen (1973) we always print the adjusted standard-ized deviation (ASD) in each cell. This number is related to the chi-square component, and can be interpreted as though normally distributed with mean zero and standard deviation one. In the cell we are looking at, its value is 4.3, which is very large (2.0 is significant at approximately the 5% level). By looking at the pattern of adjusted standardized deviations (ASD's) one can get an idea of what is going on in a two-way table. In our case we suspect that:
1. Children in the high grades tend to have a high baseline score.
2. The /s/ children in grade one tend to have low baseline.

These are not definite statistical conclusions, but simply a summary of what we have found. Since they correspond to common sense, they are not likely to be too far off the mark.

*PREVT—Previous Therapy Status*: At the beginning of the school year, we would expect the child's articulation level to be affected by his previous therapy. Thus, we expect the child's previous therapy status to be an important independent variable. It should affect EU1, the baseline score, and EU2, the sixth-week score, but it is not clear from the outset, whether PREVT will affect scores taken later in the year. Out of the 1,108 children, 652 (or 59%) had no previous therapy and 456 (or 41%) had previous therapy.

*PREVT vs. SNDEU1*: The problem here is to determine how previous therapy status affects baseline categories for /s/ and /r/. The statistical analysis is shown in Table E. 4, Appendix E. Looking first at the CEU1 categories for /s/ children, we see that 156 of those in the low category have not had previous therapy, while 42% who were in the high category have not had it. Looking at /r/, we see the same pattern, with slightly less strength. Thus, we can say that most children with low articulation ability probably have not had previous therapy. One notes that our conclusion certainly follows common sense, but there are two further thoughts that follow from it. First, this adds credence to the idea that therapy is successful. At the beginning of the year, children who have had therapy score higher than those who have not. Second, it opens a statistical question for our subsequent analysis: Which is the more important variable, baseline or previous therapy status? It is possible that both are not required to explain some of the variation of the dependent variables.

*PREVT vs. GRADE*: We now consider the previous therapy status of the children in each grade. The statistical results are given in Table E. 5, Appendix E. The youngest children, in grade one, are not likely to have had previous therapy. The opposite holds for older children in the high grades. In grade one, only 11% have had some therapy, while 70% of those in grades four, five, or six have some prior treatment. Statistically, this is a strong result, and we will not be surprised to find that either GRADE or PREVT is significant in explaining the dependent variables.

*KSEX*: This last child prior independent variable records the child's sex, of which we have 60% male and 40% female. It is possible that this particular sex ratio may be close to the one in the general population of grade school children who have /s/ or /r/ errors. For /s/ 64% are male, for /r/ 56% are male.

*KSEX vs. SNDEU1*: Table E. 6, Appendix E shows that sex is related to the target phoneme baseline categories. It appears that most SNDEU1 categories have about the same 60-40 split of male and female, except for /r/ low and medium, which have about half boys and half girls. We have no explanation for this phenomenon.

*KSEX vs. GRADE*: Table E. 7, Appendix E shows that grade and sex categories are completely unrelated.

*KSEX vs. PREVT*: Table E. 8, Appendix E shows a barely significant relationship with p = .05. There is a slight tendency for children with previous therapy to be male, and those with no previous therapy to be female.

## Summary of Results About Child Prior Variables

1. Our major variable is SNDEU1, which combines target phoneme and baseline categories.
2. Children in high grades have high baseline ability.
3. /s/ children in grade one have low baseline.
4. Low baseline children have not had previous therapy, while high baseline have.

5. Grade one tends to have no previous therapy, while high grades tend to have had some.
6. /r/ low and medium have a higher percentage of girls than the other categories.

## Relations Between Independent and Dependent Variables

The primary goal of the study is to discuss articulation learning. We have pursued that goal slowly and carefully. The conditions of the experiment have been described. The method of choosing children and clinicians was detailed in Chapter 2. Then we created the dependent variables from raw articulation scores. Next, we selected some important independent variables and related them to each other. We have now done all the preparation necessary to reach an important goal—the statistical analysis of the dependent variables as they are related to the independent variables.

Some questions now are: "Do /s/ children learn faster than /r/ children?" "What is the effect of previous therapy on the child's learning?" "Do the different grades learn differently?"

There is another question that is natural but must be dealt with more carefully. "What causes a child to learn faster?" The dangerous word in this question is "causes." It would be desirable if we could determine the basic, underlying factors that affect articulation learning. It would be very useful if we could delineate these "causes." Then we could tell clinicians what they could do to improve their teaching.

Unfortunately, we cannot identify causes in a naturalistic experiment. This is a very deep statistical concept and deserves some thought. We have observed what happened to children under certain conditions. We will see that some combination of conditions will be associated with more learning. But, this does not mean that if you change some factor to favor these conditions, you will necessarily get more learning. It is necessary to actually change those factors in a designed experiment before one can identify "causes." All we can do is identify factors associated with impaired or successful learning.

It is appropriate now to present the results of a sequence of analyses of variance (ANOVA). The focus is on the primary dependent variables EU2, GAIN, and GAMMA, bringing in other variables when they add to the analysis, and using the transformed variables when required to deal with the distributional problems of the primary variables. There will be several sets of ANOVA's using these dependent variables. In the first set, we will do one-way analyses with each of the child prior variables. At that point it will be clear that SNDEU1 is the most important child prior variable. Then we will run two-way analyses, using SNDEU1 and each of the other child prior variables. A typical question to be answered by one of these is—"What is the effect of GRADE, adjusted for SNDEU1?" Here we will discover that KSEX has very little effect on the dependent variables, and it will be subsequently neglected in the analyses. The final ANOVA will pit SNDEU1, GRADE, and PREVT against the dependent variables. This strategy is designed to give us the most information from a nonexperimental study. It does not seem appropriate to run just the large, three-way ANOVA, since the cells are very unbalanced and some cells have small counts. Thus, its validity in the context of a nonexperimental design is not clear. Furthermore, one wants to know what decisions to make if only limited information is available. What is the clinical supervisor to do if only baseline score, target phoneme and GRADE are known? The answer is not to be gained by looking at the large ANOVA, since it is unbalanced, and the effects are not independent.

Finally, we relate KLMO to the child prior variables. The reader with little background in statistics should find the discussion of counts and percentages more comfortable, although not all of the results from the ANOVA's will be duplicated in the KLMO analyses. Also, the concept of working with learning curves deserves attention by itself.

*ANOVA—EU2 vs. SNDEU1*: For the beneift of the reader with limited statistical experience, we will go into our first analysis of variance in some detail. The analysis has EU2, our sixth week score as the dependent variable and SNDEU1 as our independent variable. In the language of statistics, this is a one-way analysis of variance with six groups.

The most important part of any statistical analysis in the behavioral sciences is the subjects. In writing about statistics, we try to relate what we are doing to either the children or the clinicians.

Suppose we have some children with articulation problems and suppose that we know that their error phoneme is either /s/ or /r/. Also, we know their baseline articulation ability in three rough categories. Given this information, and no other, what do we expect to see six weeks after the beginning of therapy?

The answer to this question is contained in Table 4.4, which is discussed in some detail.

An ANOVA should tell us several things:
a. Does each independent variable (factor) have a significant effect on the dependent variable?
b. Are the significant effects strong enough to be important in prediction or making practical decisions?
c. How do the differences between individual group means relate to the overall significance?

The analysis of variance table, with sums of squares (SS), degrees of freedom (df), mean squares (MS), and F statistics, answers the first question. It is discussed in detail in several texts (e.g. Winer 1971). The only statistic that may not be familiar is "p," the probability or significance of "F." This is computed just to save looking it up in a table. Conventionally, a factor is considered significant when "p" is less than .05. In our study, we are inclined to see a particular factor as important when "p" is less than .001. We adopt this significance level because this is a naturalistic study, and because of the large "N."

When no factor in an ANOVA is significant, there is little more to be said. But, when a factor is significant, the second question becomes interesting. "Significance" merely means that an effect is not likely to have occurred by chance. We often want to know more because an effect may have practical significance or may be used for prediction. To answer these questions, we have printed the value of the multiple correlation R-square. This is the same R-square that is used in regression, the ratio of explained variance to total variance, corrected for the mean. It is not as common in ANOVA. In our case, we can say that SNDEU1 explains about half (48%) of the variation of EU2.

The third question above brings us into the area called multiple comparisons. We know from the F statistic that the means of the six SNDEU1 groups are

Dependent Variable: EU2

Independent Variable: SNDEU1

$R^2$ = .48    N = 1108

LSD = 4.3    S = 7.4    ACS = 183

|  | SS | DF | MS | F | p |
|---|---|---|---|---|---|
| SNDEU1 | 457617 | 5 | 91523 | 204 | <.001 |
| Error | 493654 | 1102 | 448 |  |  |
| Total | 951270 | 1107 |  |  |  |

Table of Means - EU2

| SOUND |  | /s/ |  |  | /r/ |  |
|---|---|---|---|---|---|---|
| CEU1 | Low | Medium | High | Low | Medium | High |
| Mean | 34.7 | 45.6 | 73.5 | 15.1 | 35.2 | 69.1 |
| SD | 26.0 | 23.2 | 18.5 | 18.3 | 19.2 | 20.1 |
| N | 210 | 159 | 170 | 188 | 190 | 191 |

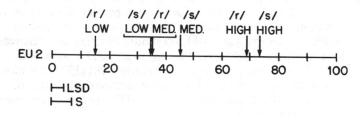

TABLE 4.4. Analysis of variance.

different. Now we want to answer questions such as, "Are the /r/ highs different from the /s/ highs?" In a designed experiment the best strategy is to plan just what mean comparisons are to be made before the data are gathered. Our experiment is not designed, and there are no planned comparisons, so we are exploring. We have one further difficulty in that we have a large number of ANOVAS to look at and no computer program to do the comparisons automatically.

Thus, we have adapted a strategy which differs from the standard literature. In each ANOVA, we plot the means, either on a simple scale for a one-way ANOVA, or in an interaction plot for a multi-way ANOVA. For our current example, this scale is found at the bottom of the table. This plot gives the reader a quick view of the relative position of the group means. It shows which means are relatively close to each other. What it does not show is whether the means differ significantly.

What is missing in this plot is a unit of distance. We have provided this in the two small scales at the bottom of the plot, and, in the process, provided an approach to the multiple comparisons problem.

The first scale is marked LSD and has a value of 4.3 in our example. This is the size of Fisher's Least Significant Difference (Ott, 1977) at the 5% level. The

*Results: Child Independent Variables*     71

other scale shows the value of Scheffe's S for a comparison of two average means at the 5% level.

The primary purpose of each of these two values—LSD and S, is to provide a sense of scale to the plot of means. These give the reader an intuitive view of how far apart the means are.

Fisher's LSD is a statistic used to compare two means. If the numerical difference between two means is less than LSD, then it is reasonable to say that they are not significantly different. In our example, the difference between /s/ low and /r/ medium is 35.2 – 34.7 = 0.5. This is much less than the LSD value of 4.3, so we say that the /s/ lows and the /r/ mediums have about the same mean. The /s/ highs and the /r/ highs differ by 4.4, so they are far apart. For the rest of this section and the next few sections, we will use LSD to establish a level, such that if two means differ by less than LSD, we will consider them to be essentially the same.

There is, however, a technical problem connected with sample size. In our naturalistic design, we expect that the cell sizes will not be balanced. For instance, there are 170 /s/ highs and 190 /r/ highs. If we were doing a designed experiment, we would try to make these numbers the same, and the analysis would be much easier. In particular, there would be a single value of LSD for comparing any pair of means. In our case, there are supposed to be different values of LSD for each pair of means. We have decided not to try to calculate all these LSD's, so we have provided a single one for each analysis, using the harmonic mean of the N's as the standard cell size. This is printed as average cell size (ACS) in the table. This means that the quoted LSD is accurate for any comparison between means whose cell sizes are average for the analysis. If, however, one of the cell sizes is much smaller than average, then the value of LSD should be expected to increase, and if both means have cell sizes much larger than average, LSD should be thought of as smaller than calculated here. The reader may consult Ott (1977) for more details, and may calculate the correct LSD for a given comparison using the ANOVA table. Remember that the whole purpose of LSD is to make the means comparison easier and clearer.

Fisher's LSD is a good choice for a liberal test of the difference between two means. We have also printed and plotted Sheffe's S as a conservative test. If two means are farther apart than S, then there is good reason to believe that they are different. In our example, /s/ medium and /r/ medium differ by 45.6 – 35.2 = 10.4, which is larger than the S value of 7.4. Theoretically, the technique used for Sheffe's S can be used to compare any combination of means. But we have used again the harmonic mean and adjusted the calculation to the comparison between a pair of means. The biggest problem with S is that it is designed to take into account all possible comparisons, and it grows with the number of cells. Thus, in the larger designs, it gets very large. This may also be considered as an effect of the degrees of freedom lost when estimating a large number of parameters.

One particular point of confusion sometimes arises when considering the practical importance of statistical results. One may ask, "Just how important can a difference of 7.4 points be?" One may visualize two children, and think of one having an ability measured by 10 on our scale, and the other by 18 on our scale. They are different, since they differ by more than 7.4 points. But, says the observer, who cares? A six or seven point difference on our scale is not likely to be detectable by the ear.

The confusion comes from the difference between what is claimed for an individual and what is claimed for a group. What this ANOVA says is that a group of about 200 children differs from another group of 200, if their means differ by 7.4 points. Very few of us can perceive the speaking ability of a group of children. One may think the speech handicapped children in one district are a little better than in another district, but this judgment is influenced by specific individuals. It is not a reliable assessment of the mean. This is an area where statistics help assess the abilities of a large number of subjects, with little influence from specific individuals. The clinician is probably correct in saying that a seven point difference between two children is not important. But what is discussed here is a seven-point difference between two groups of 200, and that is quite a different matter.

In summary, we plot the means and provide two scales to judge whether pairs of means are significantly different. If the difference between two means is less than LSD, then they should be thought of as close. If the difference is larger than S, then they are far apart. One must watch for cell sizes that are much smaller than average. This does not quite correspond to standard statistical practice, but it offers some clarity. The interested reader may perform more precise calculations using a standard reference like Ott (1977) and a hand calculator.

To summarize what we know so far about EU2 vs. SNDEU1: The children in the high baseline group, who start at 62 (Table 4.3) make about a 10 point improvement in six weeks, and there is little /s/ – /r/ difference. Those in the medium group, starting at 18, make about 22 points improvement, and the /s/ are 10 points higher than the /r/. Finally, /s/ and /r/ lows, both starting at about two, make completely different progress in six weeks. The /r/ low gets to only 15, which is 13 points improvement. And /s/ low gets to 35, for 33 points improvement. At this juncture, we cannot choose either group as the norm, so we cannot say that /r/ is lagging behind, with the implication they were supposed to be higher, or that /s/ is running ahead with the implication that they might have been lower. The groups are simply different.

*ANOVA – EU2 vs. SOUND and CEU1*: There are three reasons for looking at an analysis of EU2 against SOUND and CEU1. First, it is at this point that we can motivate the construction of SNDEU1, which was referred to earlier in the

Dependent Variable:  EU2

Independent Variables:  SOUND, CEU1

$R^2$ = .27    N = 1108

LSD = 5.1     S = 8.7     ACS = 183

|  | SS | df | MS | F | p |
|---|---|---|---|---|---|
| SOUND | 82512 | 1 | 82512 | 130.7 | <.001 |
| CEU1 | 203900 | 2 | 101950 | 161.5 | <.001 |
| SOUND X CEU1 | 32383 | 3 | 16191 | 25.6 | <.001 |
| Error | 695603 | 1102 | 631 | | |
| Total | 951270 | 1107 | | | |

TABLE 4.5. Analysis of variance.

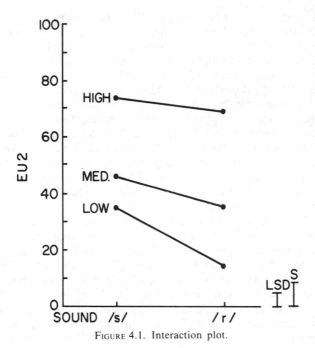

FIGURE 4.1. Interaction plot.

chapter. Second, this analysis gives us another view of the previous one. And, third, we can introduce a useful graphic device—the interaction plot.

Table 4.5 shows the results of the ANOVA. The means for this table are the same ones presented in Table 4.4. Clearly, both SOUND and CEU1 are highly significant. However, note that there is a very significant interaction between the two independent variables. It is this interaction that is of most importance to us here.

In an analysis of variance with more than one factor or independent variable, combinations of the factors may have an effect on the dependent variable over and above the effect of the individual factors. These combinations of factors are labeled "interactions." A simple graphic device called an "interaction plot" can help one see just what the significance of an interaction means. Figure 4.1 is the interaction plot for the analysis of EU2 with respect to SOUND and CEU1 (LSD = least significant difference; S = Scheffe; ACS = average cell size). What is plotted on the vertical axis is the group means. To construct an interaction plot for two factors having a significant interaction, one first chooses the factor with the *least significant* main effect. In our case, this is SOUND, with an F of 130.7. This effect is used as the horizontal axis for the plot. One then plots the group means and connects with lines those means that belong to the same category of the *other factor*. Thus, the upper left point in the plot represents the mean 73.5 for the /s/ high children (see Table 4.4 for the values). The upper right point represents the mean 69.1 of the /r/ highs. The line below that one represents the "mediums." And the bottom line is for the "lows."

In an interaction plot, a significant interaction is associated with the visual sense of the lines being *not parallel*. Here the line for the highs is almost flat, while

| SNDEU1 | EU1 | EU2 | EU3 | EU4 |
|---|---|---|---|---|
| /s/ low | 1.5 | 34.7 | 65.9 | 79.5 |
| /r/ low | 2.0 | 15.1 | 35.1 | 52.0 |
| /s/ medium | 17.6 | 45.6 | 70.6 | 81.4 |
| /r/ medium | 18.7 | 35.2 | 54.1 | 68.8 |
| /s/ high | 65.2 | 73.5 | 85.5 | 91.0 |
| /r/ high | 59.9 | 69.1 | 80.8 | 87.7 |

TABLE 4.6. Mean EU numbers for each SNDEU1 category.

the line for lows drops off at a steep angle. Thus the high line is not parallel to the low line. This is associated with the significant SOUND CEU1 interaction. A note of caution: it is not usually possible to judge the significance of an interaction directly from an interaction plot. One must have the ANOVA table. In the process of analyzing data some parallel lines are associated with significant interaction. On the other hand, some lines that seem not to be parallel are associated with nonsignificant interaction.

One can also visualize the main effects in an interaction plot. Note that an /s/ mean is always higher than the corresponding /r/, which illustrates the SOUND main effect. Also, the highs are higher than the mediums which are higher than the lows, showing the CEU1 main effect.

The particular means plotted here are the same as those plotted at the bottom of Table 4.4, thus showing that there is more than one way to look at data.

Finally, let us reiterate that there is a significant interaction, the lines are not parallel, and that this seems to be associated with the /r/ lows making much less progress in six weeks than the /s/ lows.

*SNDEU1 Means:* Although EU2, GAIN, and GAMMA are our primary dependent variables, we can add to our understanding at this point by looking at the means of all the EU numbers for each of the SNDEU1 categories. These are shown in Table 4.6 and plotted in Figure 4.2. We will refer to this plot as we proceed in the analysis. It is here that we can see clearly the difference between /s/ and /r/ learning. Those who start the year with a high baseline score show very little phoneme differentiation. For those who start low or medium, the /s/ pattern is completely different from /r/. In looking at the curves, one might be able to say that all children, *except /s/ low and medium*, make steady progress during the year. Highs gain about 25 or 30 points during the year, and others gain about 50. In contrast /s/ medium and low gain 25 or 30 points in the first six weeks of therapy, and reach a score of about 80, irrespective of where they started. Thus, most of these children, and by generalization, most /s/ children, should not need more than one year to reach a reasonable criterion.

*ANOVA – GAIN vs. SNDEU1:* In the last subsection, we looked at the relationship of baseline-target-phoneme to the six weeks score. Now we want to see the effect of the same categories on GAIN by systematically working with each of the three primary variables in turn.

The summary analysis of variance table, Table 4.7 indicates about the same thing as the table for EU2. SNDEU1 is closely related to GAIN, because the F is

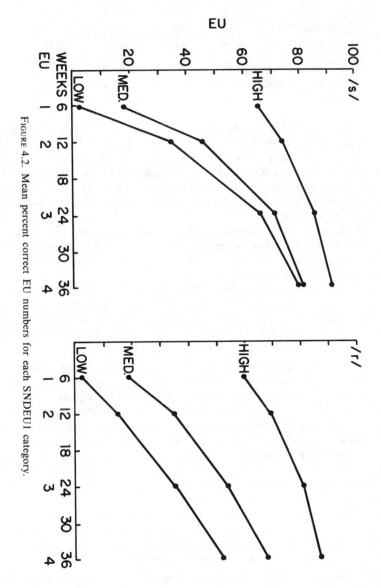

FIGURE 4.2. Mean percent correct EU numbers for each SNDEU1 category.

Dependent Variable:  GAIN
Independent Variable:  SNDEU1

$R^2$ = .36     N = 1108

LSD = 5.1     S = 8.6     ACS = 183

|        | SS      | df   | MS    | F     | p     |
|--------|---------|------|-------|-------|-------|
| SNDEU1 | 388266  | 5    | 77653 | 125.6 | <.001 |
| Error  | 681190  | 1102 | 618   |       |       |
| Total  | 1069456 | 1107 |       |       |       |

Table of Means - GAIN

| SNDEU1 |      | /s/    |       |      | /r/    |      |
|--------|------|--------|-------|------|--------|------|
|        | Low  | Medium | High  | Low  | Medium | High |
| Mean   | 78.0 | 63.7   | 25.8  | 50.0 | 50.1   | 27.8 |
| SD     | 24.8 | 22.0   | 19.2  | 32.3 | 26.3   | 21.5 |
| N      | 210  | 159    | 170   | 188  | 190    | 191  |

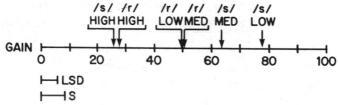

TABLE 4.7. Analysis of variance.

highly significant and the R-square is .36. More than a third of the variance of GAIN can be accounted for by SNDEU1.

The pattern of means here is quite different from the pattern in EU2. For one thing, the means are generally reversed in order. The /s/ highs have a lower mean than the /s/ lows. This is backward from EU2, but it makes sense. The data are saying that the /s/ highs make less progress over the whole year than the /s/ lows. We would naturally expect this, because the scale we use is limited and the highs start higher than the lows. If a child starts the year at 80, with a fairly good articulation ability, then the most he can get is a 20-point gain. If a child starts at 20, then he could make an 80-point gain in the whole year. Since most children make some progress, we are not surprised that those who start higher make less gain. Note that if we had used a scale with no maximum score, or a scale in which most children did not reach the maximum, this might not have been true.

The pattern of means for GAIN is not only reversed from that of EU2, but the structure is also somewhat different. One should look at /s/ high, medium, and

Dependent Variable:  GAMMA

Independent Variable:  SNDEU1

$R^2$ = .09    N = 1108

LSD = 5.5    S = 9.4    ACS = 183

|  | SS | df | MS | F | p |
|---|---|---|---|---|---|
| SNDEU1 | 84551 | 5 | 16910 | 23.1 | < .001 |
| Error | 805570 | 1102 | 731 |  |  |
| Total | 890121 | 1107 |  |  |  |

Table of Means - GAMMA

| SNDEU1 | /s/ | | | /r/ | | |
|---|---|---|---|---|---|---|
|  | Low | Medium | High | Low | Medium | High |
| Mean | 19.6 | 17.2 | 2.7 | -3.8 | 1.7 | 2.2 |
| SD | 36.5 | 32.2 | 19.3 | 25.9 | 24.3 | 18.3 |
| N | 210 | 159 | 170 | 188 | 190 | 191 |

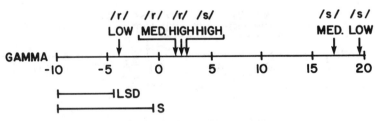

TABLE 4.8. Analysis of variance.

then low, and then /r/ high, medium, and then low. The /s/'s follow the expected pattern, going from left to right, but the /r/ lows are in the wrong place. In fact, they have the same mean as the /r/ mediums. It appears that they should have had a much higher GAIN than they do. We consider this to be the major result from this particular analysis. Children with an /r/ problem and low baseline do not make as much gain in articulation over a whole year when compared to the other subgroups.

*ANOVA – GAMMA vs. SNDEU1*: The ANOVA table for the third primary dependent variable is shown in Table 4.8. The major conclusion here is the low predictability of GAMMA as shown by the R-square value of 9%. This unpredictability is also associated with the wider intervals for LSD and S.

The pattern of means is quite different from the two previous patterns. Here, most of the groups have mean around zero, except for /s/ medium and /s/ low, which have an average GAMMA around 18. Since GAMMA is a measure of curvature, this pattern of means can be associated with the learning curves in Figure 4.2. As we noted previously, most of the groups show about the same straight line learning curve, except for the /s/ mediums and lows, which are curved upwards. It seems reasonable to repeat the generalization that these two groups seem to learn quickly.

One notes that the /r/ lows have the lowest mean GAMMA, but that their mean does not seem to be significantly different from the others.

## Summary of One-Way ANOVA's for Child Prior Variables

We have looked at SNDEU1 vs. each of the primary dependent variables. It would not be possible to go through the same one-way ANOVA for each child prior variable and each primary dependent variable. A typical question that might be answered here is whether GRADE had any effect on EU2. However, the effect of SNDEU1 is so strong that it is more important to look at the effect of GRADE, adjusted for SNDEU1, rather than the effect of GRADE alone. The same holds for the other child prior variables. We do not feel that the one-way ANOVA's are as important as the two-way ANOVA's with SNDEU1.

Thus, we only summarize the one-way ANOVA's in Table E. 9, Appendix E rather than giving the details. In looking at the latter table, one is immediately struck by the strength of SNDEU1 in predicting EU2 and GAIN. SNDEU1 is also the best predictor of GAMMA, although the R-square is only 9%. We also note that the child's sex has little influence on the dependent variables.

Table E. 10, Appendix E summarizes the one-way ANOVA's for the other dependent variables. Again we are struck by the importance of SNDEU1 in predicting dependent variables. GRADE is strongly related to all the variables, with the least effect on EU4. The effect of PREVT changes with time. It has the most effect at the beginning of the year, and no effect at all on EU4, which is quite sensible. However, we note that it is related to all of the gain scores. Although the means are not presented here, in all cases children with no previous therapy have higher gain scores. There is little effect on EU1. This will be discussed later when we see that there is also an unexpected interaction.

For our final look at the one-way ANOVA's, we state without details or summaries that all of the previous analyses have been run on the transformed EU numbers. These analyses did not suggest any changes in the conclusions. Table E. 11, Appendix E shows the mean EUT numbers for each SNDEU1 category. These means are plotted in Figure E.7, Appendix E. Comparing this with the EU means plotted in Figure E.6, Appendix E, we see that the learning curves are quite similar.

## Two-Way Analysis of Variance

*EU2 vs. SNDEU1 and GRADE:* We have now looked at the effect of the baseline-target phoneme variable on the dependent variables. The children who have an /r/ problem and start the year with little articulation ability seem to make relatively little progress, and are slow learners. Those who start the year with high ability remain high during the rest of the year, whether they are /r/ or /s/. They also do not seem to gain or to be fast learners. Children with an /s/ problem who start the year with baseline below 34 make rapid progress.

These are the results we derived by looking at each of the dependent variables in a one-way ANOVA with SNDEU1. Since this is a naturalistic study, we have looked only at the effects that were considered significant. Each of the characterizations of the children are reasonable, but incomplete. In each of these analyses, there are variables that have been ignored.

Now we will report a series of two-way analyses of variance, using each of the child prior variables in turn as one factor and SNDEU1 as the other. In this way we will review the effect of GRADE, PREVT, and KSEX, while adjusting for the effect of SNDEU1. The typical question we want to answer is—"What is the effect of grade on articulation learning?" However, when we look at grade, we want to take into account the possible effect that target phoneme and baseline may have in modifying the effect of grade. Thus, SNDEU1 will always be part of each of these analyses.

The statistics upon which these analyses are based are shown in Tables E.12 and E.13, Appendix E. The former displays the ANOVA tables, and the latter the means and standard deviations for the GRADE analyses. GRADE has a highly significant effect on EU2 and GAMMA, and is somewhat less significant for GAIN. The probability levels in Table E.12 should be compared with those in Table E.9. In the latter, we are looking at one-way ANOVA's for GRADE, ignoring other variables. In the former, we consider GRADE adjusted for SNDEU1. One result of adjusting for SNDEU1, is that the GRADE effect on GAIN is reduced in importance. The opposite is true of GAMMA, where the GRADE effect becomes more important when the effect of SNDEU1 is removed. In all cases, note that GRADE is never as strong in its effect as SNDEU1.

The EU2 means for GRADE and SNDEU1 categories are plotted in Figure E.8, Appendix E (LSD = least significant difference; S = Scheffe; ACS = average cell size). Our first problem is to interpret the main effect for GRADE. The /s/ medium curve shows what one would expect by common sense. Each grade has a higher mean EU2 than the previous one and the mean difference between grade four and grade one is significant, at least using LSD as a criterion. If we look at /s/ highs and /r/ highs, we see the same pattern, with less difference between grades one and four. Unfortunately, the same is not true of the other three curves. The /r/ lows show very little effect on grade. As we proceed, we will see that in general, the /r/ lows will be little affected by most variables. The /s/ lows show the pattern of increasing means for higher grades for one, two, and four+, but there is also a disconcerting "third grade bulge." The /s/ low third graders have a much higher EU2 than they should have. This same effect shows up in /r/ medium, which otherwise looks like /r/ low, in that the EU2 means for grade one, two and four+ differ by very little. We have no good explanation for the third grade bulge and are reluctant to investigate it further because the GRADE sampling was far from random. Thus, we prefer to see the effect of GRADE as simple: 1) grades one and two tend to have a lower mean than grades three and four, and 2) this effect is much stronger for /s/ medium and low, and 3) /r/ lows show little effect of GRADE.

*GAIN vs. SNDEU1, GRADE*: The interaction plot for GAIN is Figure E.9. The probability of the effect of GRADE on GAIN is .04. Throughout the book we mostly discuss effects that are significant at the .001 level, so we will not spend much time with this. There are a few things to say about this plot. Remember that we expect the effect of GAIN to be opposite that of EU2. Thus, the order of the low, medium, and high curves is opposite that of the EU2 plot. However, note that the "third grade bulge" is in the same direction as EU2 for /s/ low, /r/ low, and

/r/ medium. For each of these, the third graders have a slightly higher mean than seems reasonable. Note also a greater drift downward for /r/ than /s/, which is opposite to what happened for EU2, where the /s/'s drifted upward more than /r/. The EU2 picture would lead us to believe that there should be a general effect of GRADE on /s/ and that it should be lower for higher grades. However, as noted above, the significance of GRADE is not strong, so we are not inclined to state any of these as strong conclusions.

*GAMMA vs. SNDEU1, GRADE*: The effect of GRADE on GAMMA is highly significant, and the plot, in Figure E.10 shows some very interesting patterns when compared with the same plot for EU2 in Figure E.8, Appendix E. Remember that EU2 and GAMMA are somewhat correlated, so we expect to see similar patterns in the two dependent variables.

If we look first at /s/ and ignore for the moment the /s/ low fourth graders, we see a nice pattern of upward drift of mean GAMMA with GRADE. The older children learn faster. This is what we saw for the same children looking at EU2. However, let us remember the effect of baseline categories we saw previously when looking at GAMMA and SNDEU1. The order of curves is reversed from top to bottom. The /s/ low and medium have a lower EU2 than /s/ high, but learn faster.

Consider now /r/ first and second graders. They all have mean GAMMA near zero, using LSD as a criterion, the lows are different from the highs, but in the opposite direction from the /s/'s. These low children learn a little bit slower than high in the same phoneme, grade categories.

Clearly, there is a "third grade bulge" for /s/ low and /r/ medium as there was for EU2. We still have no explanation for this.

Let us compare the EU2 conclusions with those for GAMMA. 1) grades one and two definitely have a lower mean GAMMA, 2) this effect seems to be strong for all /s/ and for the /r/ medium children, and 3) all /r/'s show relatively less effect of GRADE than /s/.

*Primary Dependent Variables vs. SNDEU1, PREVT*: The next child prior variable is PREVT which represents the child's previous therapy status. The ANOVA tables are shown in Table E.14 and the means in Table E.15, Appendix E. Clearly, PREVT is not highly significant for any of these dependent variables, when adjusted for SNDEU1. At this point in our discussion, we suggest that the child's previous therapy status is of little help in predicting learning, given that the baseline category is known. Effectively, all of the variation which might be due to PREVT, is accounted for by SNDEU1.

Although it is only significant at the .011 level, we will take a quick look at the effect of PREVT on GAIN, in Figure E.11. We see that all /s/ and the /r/ medium groups show a consistently higher GAIN for no previous therapy. This makes sense, because no previous therapy children start the year with lower articulation ability. As in the previous analyses, there is no effect for /r/ lows.

*Selected Dependent Variables vs. SNDEU1, KSEX*: The analysis for the final child prior variable is summarized in Table E.11. If we look at just the main KSEX effect, we see that it is not significant. The child's sex does not seem to affect his articulation learning on the average. However, there is a significant interaction for EU2 and GAMMA. What does this mean? The means for the categories are listed in Table E.17 and plotted in Figure E.12 and E.13, Appendix E. An interaction is usually significant when some of the categories do not fit the pattern of the others.

Dependent

| Independent | EU2 | | GAIN | | GAMMA | |
|---|---|---|---|---|---|---|
| | p(F) | $R^2$ | p(F) | $R^2$ | p(F) | $R^2$ |
| SNDEU1 | < .001 | | < .001 | | < .001 | |
| GRADE | < .001 | | .039 | | .001 | |
| S X G | .626 | | .534 | | .796 | |
| All Factors | | .50 | | .38 | | .12 |
| SNDEU1 | < .001 | | < .001 | | < .001 | |
| PREVT | .566 | | .011 | | .392 | |
| S X P | .246 | | .141 | | .039 | |
| All Factors | | .48 | | .37 | | .10 |
| SNDEU1 | < .001 | | < .001 | | < .001 | |
| KSEX | .708 | | .456 | | .409 | |
| S X K | .001 | | .345 | | .002 | |
| All Factors | | .49 | | .37 | | .11 |

TABLE 4.9. Summary of ANOVA, p(F) and $R^2$ for SNDEU1 with each child prior variable from a two-way ANOVA, N = 1108.

Independent

| Dependent | GRADE | Interaction | PREVT | Interaction | KSEX | Interaction |
|---|---|---|---|---|---|---|
| EU1 | < .001 | .023 | .067 | .359 | .908 | .007 |
| EU3 | .012 | .860 | .230 | .032 | .156 | .032 |
| EU4 | .031 | .917 | .080 | .116 | .397 | .271 |
| GAIN12 | < .001 | .335 | .085 | .284 | .723 | .001 |
| GAIN23 | .022 | .457 | .253 | .049 | .083 | .220 |
| GAIN34 | .022 | .880 | .407 | .014 | .239 | .160 |
| GAIN13 | .185 | .631 | .041 | .037 | .170 | .090 |
| GAIN24 | < .001 | .852 | .145 | .080 | .545 | .069 |

TABLE 4.10. p(F) for two-way ANOVA. Independent variables are SNDEU1 with each child prior variable. N = 1108. Interactions are with SNDEU1. All SNDEU1 p's are < .001.

In the interaction plot, this is shown by some lines not being parallel to the others. The effect of KSEX is a good example of this. In Figure E.13 we see that the /s/ medium children are quite different from the others. In the rest of the SNDEU1 categories boys and girls have about the same EU2 score. But, the /s/ medium boys have a mean EU2 of 41, while the girls have a mean of 55. This difference causes the significant interaction. It appears that boys and girls are not significantly different and that the /s/ mediums are an unexplained anomaly.

Remember that EU2 and GAMMA are correlated, it is not unexpected to see that for GAMMA, the /s/ mediums show the same sex difference as in EU2. In addition, there is a small difference in /r/ lows. Again, we feel that the safest conclusion is to deny any sex difference, and to leave the /s/ medium effect for further experimentation.

## Summary of Two-Way ANOVA's for Child Prior Variables

Table 4.9 summarizes the effects of the child prior variables on the primary dependent variables. Clearly, SNDEU1 is always the most important variable. Next comes GRADE, which has a strong effect on EU2 and GAMMA. Previous therapy status seems not to be needed, given baseline, and the child's sex is only involved through an unexplained effect of /s/ medium girls.

The effect of child prior on other dependent variables is summarized in Table 4.10. Note that each of the entries in the table is an F probability for a two-way ANOVA with SNDEU1. The effect of SNDEU1 is always significant at less than the .001 level.

The effect of GRADE seems to decrease with time. At baseline it is quite strong, and there is an interaction. This is caused by the differing pattern of GRADE means in the CEU1 categories. All the "low" means are no more than one point apart. But, the "high" means differ by 10 points from grade one to grade four. GRADE has a strong effect on GAIN12 and GAIN24, both of which are connected to EU2.

PREVT and KSEX show few significant effects, and these are all caused by previously discussed patterns.

Dependent Variable

| Independent | EU1 | EU2 | EU3 | EU4 | GAIN | GAMMA |
|---|---|---|---|---|---|---|
| S | <.001 | <.001 | <.001 | <.001 | <.001 | <.001 |
| G | <.001 | <.001 | .005 | .006 | .056 | .006 |
| P | .425 | .006 | .019 | .037 | .110 | .030 |
| SG | .003 | .241 | .547 | .835 | .472 | .266 |
| SP | .657 | .169 | .068 | .125 | .083 | .003 |
| GP | .008 | .563 | .392 | .031 | .007 | .901 |
| SGP | .118 | .057 | .152 | .033 | .269 | .470 |

TABLE 4.11. Summary of ANOVA. p(F) for selected dependent variables in 3-way ANOVA, N = 1108. Independent variables: SNDEU1 (S), GRADE (G), PREVT (P).

We have run all of the ANOVA's using the transformed variables, and found no modifications to make in the major conclusions.

## Three-Way Analysis of Variance

*SNDEU1, GRADE, PREVT:* Our last ANOVA in this section is a three-way involving all of the child prior dependent variables except KSEX. The latter was left out because its main effects were completely nonsignificant in the previous analyses.

With a designed experiment, this analysis would be the major result of this chapter. In our case, the cell sizes vary so widely, from 3 to 77, that we are not able to make strong claims about the significant factors and interactions. We end up using this particular ANOVA just to make a tentative point about PREVT. From the previous material, the simple two-way ANOVA using SNDEU1, and GRADE is the most important.

Space does not allow us to present all analyses for all dependent variables, or even all of the primary variables. Thus, we present the ANOVA summaries first, and then select EU2 for further discussion.

Table 4.11 shows the F probabilities for ANOVA's using all of the EU numbers and GAIN and GAMMA. Looking at just SNDEU1 and GRADE, we see much the same significances we have seen previously, so they need not be discussed here. However, now there is a significant effect for PREVT under EU2. Since some cell sizes are so small, we have also included Table E.18, Appendix E, which is the same summary for the transformed variables. Let us remember that the transformations chosen made all of the EUT variables look normally distributed, and stabilized their variance. Thus, we are not surprised to find the SG interaction in Table 4.11 with a value of .003, and the same interaction in Table E.18 with a value of .162. This is one of the reasons for transforms; to make spurious interactions go away. Thus, noting that in the transformed dependent variable table there are no two-way significant interactions, we are left with the PREVT main effect and the three-way interaction to discuss.

We choose to look at EU2. In fact, we have plotted EU2 and EU3, both raw and transformed. Each plot suggests similar conclusions.

Table E.19 shows the ANOVA table for EU2. The means are printed in Table E.20, Appendix E. The point that we want to make is that there are many grades in which children with no previous therapy have a higher mean EU2 than children *with* previous therapy. Of the sets of first graders, all except /r/ low show this pattern. Since, in fact, there are very few first graders with previous therapy (33 out of 304), it is strange that almost all of them would have a low mean EU2. But, many young children may have therapy prior to our project year because of the severity of their problem. The mean of EU1 for the /s/ low children broken down by GRADE and PREVT varies from 1.3 to 2.6. At baseline we hypothesize that this can be considered as one homogeneous group, which is the effect of controlling for CEU1. Yet, at EU2 we have the mean no-previous-therapy first graders at 32, and the previous-therapy first graders at 19. Thus the seven children in the latter group must have had a very severe or long-term problem. The previous therapy given to them prior to the beginning brought their group average up to one, but after six weeks they lagged behind the no-previous-therapy children by 13 points. This is an interesting hypothesis that deserves further study, but our effective cell sizes are so small that we cannot pursue the idea further.

Finally, we must note our inability to clarify the significant three-way interactions for EU2T, EU3T, and EU4T. The plots of these variables have many similar characteristics to the plot of EU2, so we can only note that not all the patterns in each subplot are parallel.

## Summary of Results

Conclusions from this section are in one list. Following this, we use KLMO to explore most of the items.

1. SNDEU1 has the most influence of any child prior variable on each of the dependent variables.
2. Several positive characteristics apply to children who have an /s/ problem and a baseline score of less than 34, "/s/ medium and low." They have a high mean GAMMA (18), so they can be said to learn faster than the others. Their mean GAIN of 70 is high and they gain 31 points on the average in the first six weeks of therapy (GAIN12). At the end of the school year, these children have mostly solved their articulation problem. Their mean EU4 is 80.
3. Other children, the /s/ highs and the /r/'s, make steady progress during the year. The mean GAMMA of these other groups is near zero.
4. Low baseline children with an /r/ problem do not make as much GAIN as the others. The mean is 50. This is much lower than mean GAIN for /s/ low, 78. It is the same as the mean GAIN for /r/ medium, 50, whereas, /r/ low would be expected to be much higher. Among these same /r/ low children, other groups defined by child prior variables show relatively little mean difference on any of the dependent variables.
5. Grade one and two children have a mean EU2 of 40, which is much lower than the mean EU2 of children in the higher grades, 53.
6. Grade one and two have lower average GAMMA than higher grades. This same conclusion is particularly true for /s/ and /r/ mediums.
7. Among all the /r/'s there is less overall GRADE effect than among the /s/'s.
8. In the /s/ low and /r/ medium groups, the third graders have a relatively high EU2 and GAMMA compared to the other grades. This we call the "third grade bulge."
9. Most of the variation due to previous therapy status can be better explained by using baseline categories. PREVT has relatively little significance when the effect of SNDEU1 is eliminated.
10. Among all the /s/ children, and in the /r/ medium group, there seems to be a little more GAIN if the child has no previous therapy than if he has therapy.
11. The child's sex has no direct effect, but /s/ medium girls have a relatively high EU2 and GAMMA.
12. In many of the GRADE-SNDEU1 categories, particularly grade one, there is higher EU2 associated with no previous therapy. This may reflect an association between previous therapy and a more severe problem.

## KLMO Versus Independent Variables

We have now finished exploring the effect of child prior variables on articulation learning variables, using standard statistical tools of analysis of variance. The conclusions in this section summarize some of our results, using our categorical dependent variable KLMO. In the sense that KLMO defines categories of learning

Dependent Variable:  KLMO
Independent Variable:  SNDEU1
Cells are count over row percent

| SNDEU1 | K | L | M | O | Other | Total |
|---|---|---|---|---|---|---|
| /s/ Low | 74 | 78 | 0 | 31 | 27 | 210 |
| | 35 | 37 | 0 | 15 | 13 | 100 |
| /s/ Medium | 80 | 37 | 0 | 16 | 26 | 159 |
| | 50 | 23 | 0 | 10 | 16 | 100 |
| /s/ High | 0 | 0 | 108 | 0 | 62 | 170 |
| | 0 | 0 | 64 | 0 | 36 | 100 |
| /r/ Low | 12 | 50 | 0 | 100 | 26 | 188 |
| | 6 | 27 | 0 | 53 | 14 | 100 |
| /r/ Medium | 45 | 48 | 0 | 53 | 44 | 190 |
| | 24 | 25 | 0 | 28 | 23 | 100 |
| /r/ High | 0 | 0 | 101 | 0 | 90 | 191 |
| | 0 | 0 | 53 | 0 | 47 | 100 |
| Total | 211 | 213 | 209 | 200 | 275 | 1108 |
| | 19 | 19 | 19 | 18 | 25 | 100 |

Lambda =  .27

TABLE 4.12. Two-way table.

curve patterns, we answer the question of how the independent variables affect a child's learning curves. We expect that the reader with less statistical experience will find some of the summarized results easier to comprehend.

*KLMO vs. SNDEU1:* Our most important independent variable SNDEU1 divides the children into six categories according to their target phoneme and their baseline score. Using the five categories of KLMO (including "other") we will thus have 6 × 5 = 30 possible categories in which to place children when we relate KLMO to SNDEU1. The number in each of these categories is shown in Table 4.12. Thus we know that 74 children have an /s/ problem, started the year with an articulation score of six or less (CEU1 low), and had an overall learning curve categorized as "K," which means they were fast learners. Likewise, of the /s/ low children, 78 were categorized as having an "L" learning curve, meaning that they learned to solve their articulation problem but more slowly than the "K's."

Also included in this table are the KLMO percentages. The 74 /s/ low "K's" represent 35% of the total of 210 /s/ low's. The 78 /s/ low "L's" are 37% of the /s/ lows. It is reasonable to say that among the /s/ lows there are about the same number of "K's" and "L's."

Our interpretation of this table is based primarily on these KLMO percentages. At the bottom of the table, the four primary KLMO categories have about the same percentage of children. Thus, in a breakdown of the children by a child prior variable, we expect that each of the KLMO sub-categories to have about the same percentage of children if the child prior variable was *not* related to KLMO.

Thus, if SNDEU1 was *not* related to KLMO, we would expect the same number of "K's" as "O's" among the /s/ lows. The fact that there are more than twice as many "K's" as "O's" leads us to believe that there is a relationship between SNDEU1 and KLMO.

The method of construction of KLMO requires that children in the high baseline category cannot be "K," "L," or "O." Low and medium children cannot be "M." Thus, our interpretation of the percentages is modified. We do not expect about 19% in each category as we would in the usual two-way table, but an equal percentage in the remaining categories. Thus, the /r/ mediums show no preference for KLMO. Given that an /r/ medium cannot be an "M," the remaining three "K," "L," "O" primary categories are roughly equally distributed. (Note that there would be a few more "others" if there were strict independence, since there are more "others" than "K," "L," or "O.")

As a summary statistic for each of the tables in this section, we calculate lambda, a measure of prediction of improvement, rather than chi-square. The latter tests for strict independence and none of the tables in this section show anything close in independence. Each of the chi-squares is quite large. Lambda measures the improvement in prediction of KLMO which we get by knowing the categories of the other variable, SNDEU1 in this case. When we predict KLMO, we use the largest category in the appropriate row. If we do not know SNDEU1 we must use the "other" category because it is the largest. Then we would make an error 75% of the time. If we know SNDEU1, and if for instance a child was in the /s/ medium category, then we would predict that this child would be a "K," the largest KLMO category in the /s/ medium row. In this row, we would be expected to make an error only 50% of the time. Over the whole table we would expect to improve our prediction by 27% if we know SNDEU1, over not knowing it.

The alert reader will have already noted that the definitions of our two variables are (SNDEU1 and KLMO) related; even so, the interpretation of lambda is acceptable. First, it is a good descriptive measure. Second, it says that if we know the target phoneme and baseline categories at the beginning of the year, and if we make reasonable predictions, then we will expect an improvement over not knowing those categories. This latter statement is quite valid, even if the definitions of SNDEU1 and KLMO are related.

Finally, in these preliminary remarks about interpretation of KLMO tables, let us remember that the primary purpose of KLMO is clarity. We expect that some readers are not totally comfortable with the previous ANOVA's. We hope that a simple statement like; *there are relatively few "O's" among the /s/ lows—* will be much easier to deal with than the previous analyses.

Now let us deal specifically with the relation of KLMO to SNDEU1. The

TABLE 4.13. Three-way table.

Dependent Variable: KLMO
Independent Variables: SNDEU1, GRADE

| SNDEU1 | GRADE | K Count | % | L Count | % | M Count | % | O Count | % | Other Count | % | Total Count | % |
|---|---|---|---|---|---|---|---|---|---|---|---|---|---|
| /s/ | | | | | | | | | | | | | |
| Low | 1 | 22 | 26 | 34 | 40 | 0 | 0 | 13 | 15 | 15 | 18 | 84 | 100 |
| | 2 | 25 | 36 | 28 | 40 | 0 | 0 | 11 | 16 | 6 | 8 | 70 | 100 |
| | 3 | 19 | 54 | 10 | 28 | 0 | 0 | 4 | 11 | 2 | 6 | 35 | 100 |
| | 4+ | 8 | 38 | 6 | 28 | 0 | 0 | 3 | 14 | 4 | 19 | 21 | 100 |
| Medium | 1 | 15 | 38 | 15 | 38 | 0 | 0 | 4 | 10 | 6 | 15 | 40 | 100 |
| | 2 | 26 | 47 | 9 | 16 | 0 | 0 | 7 | 13 | 13 | 24 | 55 | 100 |
| | 3 | 24 | 58 | 9 | 22 | 0 | 0 | 4 | 10 | 4 | 10 | 41 | 100 |
| | 4+ | 15 | 65 | 4 | 17 | 0 | 0 | 1 | 4 | 3 | 13 | 23 | 100 |
| High | 1 | 0 | 0 | 0 | 0 | 13 | 54 | 0 | 0 | 11 | 46 | 24 | 100 |
| | 2 | 0 | 0 | 0 | 0 | 39 | 68 | 0 | 0 | 18 | 32 | 57 | 100 |
| | 3 | 0 | 0 | 0 | 0 | 29 | 72 | 0 | 0 | 11 | 28 | 40 | 100 |
| | 4+ | 0 | 0 | 0 | 0 | 27 | 55 | 0 | 0 | 22 | 45 | 49 | 100 |

Dependent Variable: KLMO
Independent Variables: SNDEU1, GRADE

| SNDEU1 | GRADE | K Count | % | L Count | % | M Count | % | O Count | % | Other Count | % | Total Count | % |
|---|---|---|---|---|---|---|---|---|---|---|---|---|---|
| /r/ | | | | | | | | | | | | | |
| Low | 1 | 4 | 6 | 17 | 26 | 0 | 0 | 37 | 57 | 7 | 11 | 65 | 100 |
|  | 2 | 3 | 4 | 18 | 27 | 0 | 0 | 35 | 53 | 10 | 15 | 66 | 100 |
|  | 3 | 4 | 9 | 14 | 31 | 0 | 0 | 20 | 44 | 7 | 16 | 45 | 100 |
|  | 4+ | 1 | 8 | 1 | 8 | 0 | 0 | 8 | 67 | 2 | 17 | 12 | 100 |
| Medium | 1 | 6 | 13 | 19 | 41 | 0 | 0 | 10 | 22 | 11 | 24 | 46 | 100 |
|  | 2 | 11 | 20 | 11 | 20 | 0 | 0 | 19 | 34 | 14 | 25 | 55 | 100 |
|  | 3 | 19 | 40 | 10 | 21 | 0 | 0 | 9 | 19 | 9 | 19 | 47 | 100 |
|  | 4+ | 9 | 21 | 8 | 19 | 0 | 0 | 15 | 36 | 10 | 24 | 42 | 100 |
| High | 1 | 0 | 0 | 0 | 0 | 20 | 44 | 0 | 0 | 25 | 56 | 45 | 100 |
|  | 2 | 0 | 0 | 0 | 0 | 31 | 50 | 0 | 0 | 31 | 50 | 62 | 100 |
|  | 3 | 0 | 0 | 0 | 0 | 23 | 58 | 0 | 0 | 17 | 42 | 40 | 100 |
|  | 4+ | 0 | 0 | 0 | 0 | 27 | 61 | 0 | 0 | 17 | 39 | 44 | 100 |
| Total | | 211 | 19 | 213 | 19 | 209 | 19 | 200 | 18 | 275 | 25 | 1108 | 100 |

most important comparison is between /s/ and /r/ within baseline categories. In this comparison, /s/ seems to come out consistently better than /r/. The /s/ lows are about three-fourths "K" and "L," while the /r/ lows are only one-third "K" and "L." The /r/ lows have half "O's," the /s/ lows are 15%. The /s/ mediums have half "K's" and 75% "K" and "L," while the /r/'s are one-fourth "K" and only 50% "L." Even the /s/ highs have a few more "M's," though we do not see this as important. Thus, /s/ learns consistently faster than /r/, and contains many less nonsuccessful "O's." Note that there are at least two ways in which a group of children can be said to be better than another. There may be more "K" and "L," or there may be less "O's." Both of these are true of the comparison between /s/ low and /r/ low. Further, there is another, more subtle way that one group can be better than another, and that is to have a higher proportion of "K's." This is true of the comparison between /s/ medium and /s/ low.

Now we use KLMO to survey the results from the previous ANOVA's. The strength of SNDEU1 is shown by the fact that one cannot achieve a high lambda without it. The high GAMMA for /s/ medium and /s/ low associates with the relatively high percent "K" for these categories in Table 4.12. This same high "K" percent can be related to the other items in conclusion number two. The result about other children having mean GAMMA near zero cannot be seen as clearly in the two-way table as in the interaction plot, because GAMMA for the other children is a result of a combination of factors. The problems of the /r/ lows in conclusion number four (p. 85) is shown clearly by the very low percent "K" and the high percent "O." /r/ lows do seem to have special problems.

*KLMO vs. SNDEU1 and GRADE*: We use essentially the same strategy in dealing with KLMO as with the ANOVA's. SNDEU1 is established as an important variable, and we thus use it in all the subsequent tables to adjust for the effect of the other child prior variables.

GRADE and SNDEU1 are shown in Table 4.13. This is essentially a three-way table, involving KLMO, SNDEU1, and GRADE. But, we have already dealt with SNDEU1, so we will use this primarily to interpret the effect of GRADE. To do this, we look at each vertical block of four GRADE percents. If these are about the same, we would say that this particular SNDEU1 category shows no GRADE effect, if they are different, then there is a GRADE effect. For instance, the "O" percents for /s/ low are 15, 16, 11, and 14. These are similar enough that we would not say that /s/ lows differ on GRADE. In contrast, the "K" percents for /s/ low are 26, 36, 54, and 38. Third grade /s/ lows are more than half "K's," which probably contributes to the "third grade bulge" in Figure E.8, Appendix E. It is this kind of interpretation we pursue throughout the table.

The purpose of looking at KLMO is statistical clarity. We think that for some readers this will be valid, but the analysis of the SNDEU1, GRADE is complicated. Consider conclusion number five (p. 85) which says that low grades have lower EU2 than high grades. This is primarily derived by looking at Figure E.8, Appendix E. The same thing can be seen in Table 4.13, but it is more difficult. Compare the /s/ lows in the figure with the GRADE percentages in the table. The "third grade bulge" is seen as the high percent "K" previously mentioned. But the drift upward of the other grades is a result of both "K" and "L." Note that the "K" percents for grades one, two, and four drift upward. For "L" they generally go down. When considering EU2, this makes sense, because a higher percent "K" is likely to make a group's mean EU2 go up, but a higher percent "L" is likely to make it go *down*. Thus, the curve in the figure is consistent with the percentages.

This analysis applies clearly to the /s/ mediums, in which the "K" percent goes strictly up with GRADE, and the "L" percent tends to decrease.

For the highs, the roles of "K" and "L" are taken by "M" and "other" respectively. In the /s/ high group, "M" percents drift up, with GRADE and the "other" percents drift down. This is consistent with the high curve. The fourth grade highs are more difficult to interpret. The /r/ high group shows the same pattern, here extended to the fourth grade.

The /r/ medium curve has a "third grade bulge," but is otherwise flat. This seems to be the result of a high "K" percent, combined with a low percent "O" and "other." The lack of effect for grades one, two and four is complicated. "K" drifts upward with grade, "L" drifts down, but "O" drifts up. The combination seems to result in the flat curve.

In the first three grades, the /r/ low grade percents are about the same for all five KLMO categories. This is consistent with the flatness for the /r/ low grade curve. But, fourth grade /r/ lows are two-thirds "O's." Since the "L" percent is small for this category, one would say that these children are "O" instead of "L." And, since "O" curves and "L" curves can be right next to each other, it is not strange that the EU2 means for grades three and four can be close. Note however, in Figure E.9 that the /r/ low curve dips at grade four. This is probably the result of the high percent "O's."

We have used the two-way table to "read" the interaction plot, and vice versa, for EU2. In the process we have thrown some light on conclusions number five and number eight (p. 85). We invite the reader to use this same two-way table to "read" the interaction plots for GAIN and GAMMA.

*KLMO vs. SNDEU1, PREVT:* Our conclusion number eight about the effect of previous therapy status was essentially negative. We claim that one does not need to use PREVT if CEU1 is available. This is generally born out in Table 4.14. In general, the percentages in the "no" and "yes" categories for each group are about the same. One can compare this table with Figure E.11, but we will not go into this further.

*KLMO vs. SNDEU1, KSEX:* In conclusion number 11, we said that sex has little effect, but that there was a problem with /s/ medium classification for girls. In Table 4.15 one can see both of these conclusions. In general, there is little difference between the male and female percents in each group, but the /s/ medium girls are almost three-quarters "K." Although this adds a little information to the sex anomaly, it does not aid in finding an explanation.

*KLMO vs. All Child Prior:* We come now to the last analysis in a very long section. In analyzing a set of data with a relatively large number of variables, it is desirable to combine the variables in a single analysis. Thus, one should be able to get at all potential interactions. When dealing with the ANOVA's we noted that the cell sizes were so small in even the three-way analysis that we were reluctant to draw strong conclusions. We decided not to try to analyze any higher way designs.

In the last parts of this section, we have been using the categorical variable KLMO primarily to add clarity to the discussion. However, recent developments in statistical methodology offer us the opportunity to use KLMO for a large analysis. We use a log-linear model to analyze the six-way table of counts combining KLMO with all of the child prior variables. In particular, we use the program BMDP3F, developed by Morton Brown at the UCLA Health Sciences Computing Facility (Dixon & Brown, 1977). Using Brown's program, the calcula-

TABLE 4.14. Three-way table.

Dependent Variable: KLMO

Independent Variables: SNDEU1, PREVT

| SNDEU1 | PREVT | K Count | % | L Count | % | M Count | % | O Count | % | Other Count | % | Total Count | % |
|---|---|---|---|---|---|---|---|---|---|---|---|---|---|
| /s/ | | | | | | | | | | | | | |
| Low | No | 59 | 38 | 57 | 36 | 0 | 0 | 20 | 13 | 20 | 13 | 156 | 100 |
| | Yes | 15 | 28 | 21 | 39 | 0 | 0 | 11 | 20 | 7 | 13 | 54 | 100 |
| Medium | No | 53 | 54 | 22 | 22 | 0 | 0 | 7 | 7 | 16 | 16 | 98 | 100 |
| | Yes | 27 | 44 | 15 | 24 | 0 | 0 | 9 | 15 | 10 | 16 | 61 | 100 |
| High | No | 0 | 0 | 0 | 0 | 43 | 60 | 0 | 0 | 28 | 39 | 71 | 100 |
| | Yes | 0 | 0 | 0 | 0 | 65 | 66 | 0 | 0 | 34 | 34 | 99 | 100 |
| /r/ | | | | | | | | | | | | | |
| Low | No | 11 | 8 | 33 | 25 | 0 | 0 | 75 | 56 | 15 | 11 | 134 | 100 |
| | Yes | 1 | 2 | 17 | 31 | 0 | 0 | 25 | 46 | 11 | 20 | 54 | 100 |
| Medium | No | 24 | 23 | 33 | 31 | 0 | 0 | 23 | 22 | 25 | 24 | 105 | 100 |
| | Yes | 21 | 25 | 15 | 18 | 0 | 0 | 30 | 35 | 19 | 22 | 85 | 100 |
| High | No | 0 | 0 | 0 | 0 | 45 | 51 | 0 | 0 | 43 | 49 | 88 | 100 |
| | Yes | 0 | 0 | 0 | 0 | 56 | 54 | 0 | 0 | 47 | 46 | 103 | 100 |
| Total | | 211 | 19 | 213 | 19 | 209 | 19 | 200 | 18 | 275 | 25 | 1108 | 100 |

Dependent Variable: KLMO

Independent Variables: SNDEU1, KSEX

| SNDEU1 | PREVT | K Count | % | L Count | % | M Count | % | O Count | % | Other Count | % | Total Count | % |
|---|---|---|---|---|---|---|---|---|---|---|---|---|---|
| /s/ | | | | | | | | | | | | | |
| Low | Male | 48 | 37 | 41 | 32 | 0 | 0 | 19 | 15 | 22 | 17 | 130 | 100 |
| | Female | 26 | 32 | 37 | 46 | 0 | 0 | 12 | 15 | 5 | 6 | 80 | 100 |
| Medium | Male | 42 | 40 | 31 | 29 | 0 | 0 | 14 | 13 | 19 | 18 | 106 | 100 |
| | Female | 38 | 72 | 6 | 11 | 0 | 0 | 2 | 4 | 7 | 13 | 53 | 100 |
| High | Male | 0 | 0 | 0 | 0 | 64 | 58 | 0 | 0 | 46 | 42 | 110 | 100 |
| | Female | 0 | 0 | 0 | 0 | 44 | 73 | 0 | 0 | 16 | 27 | 60 | 100 |
| /r/ | | | | | | | | | | | | | |
| Low | Male | 6 | 6 | 25 | 25 | 0 | 0 | 50 | 50 | 18 | 18 | 99 | 100 |
| | Female | 6 | 7 | 25 | 28 | 0 | 0 | 50 | 56 | 8 | 9 | 89 | 100 |
| Medium | Male | 24 | 25 | 25 | 26 | 0 | 0 | 24 | 25 | 24 | 25 | 97 | 100 |
| | Female | 21 | 22 | 23 | 25 | 0 | 0 | 29 | 31 | 20 | 22 | 93 | 100 |
| High | Male | 0 | 0 | 0 | 0 | 73 | 58 | 0 | 0 | 52 | 42 | 125 | 100 |
| | Female | 0 | 0 | 0 | 0 | 28 | 42 | 0 | 0 | 38 | 58 | 66 | 100 |
| Total | | 211 | 19 | 213 | 19 | 209 | 19 | 200 | 18 | 275 | 25 | 1108 | 100 |

Lambda=.32

tions for such a complex design are simple, but the interpretation of results is still difficult. The major reference for this analysis is Bishop, Feinberg, and Holland (1975).

We first collapse GRADE into two categories, 1, 2, and 3 through 6. This is in accord with conclusion number five above, but it does not allow us to get more insight into the "third grade bulge." Next, we notice in Table 4.12, that children in the high baseline category can only be "M" and "other," and that the medium and low categories contain no "M's." Thus, we break our analysis into two tables, one for the highs and one for the medium and low.

The results of fitting log-linear models to these two tables are summarized in Table 4.16. Each of the two models fits the data well, and no terms can be added or deleted. We offer some interpretation of what is happening here, but it must be considered tentative.

Our primary focus is KLMO. We are really not much interested in the interactions between the independent variables. With this focus, we conclude that the child's sex and previous therapy status are not needed to explain KLMO for low and medium baseline children. One derives this conclusion from the fact that there are no terms connecting KLMO directly with KSEX or PREVT in the model. Any effect of KSEX comes through SOUND (the XS term in the model). The effect of PREVT comes through GRADE (GP in the model), and CEU1 (PE in the model).

Therefore, we can collapse over KSEX and PREVT, producing Table 4.17. This is the last word about children with baseline below 34. In particular, the row percents are a reasonable estimate of the probabilities for KLMO for these children. For example, a child with an /r/ problem, low baseline, in grade one or two has a .55 probability of being an "O." The conclusions to be drawn from this table are similar to those from the SNDEU1, GRADE table, and will not be repeated.

Symbols

| KLMO | KSEX | GRADE | PREVT | SOUND | CEU1 |
|------|------|-------|-------|-------|------|
| K | X | G | P | S | E |

GRADE collapsed into Two Categories 1-2, 3-6

Model 1.   CEU1 = Low and Medium; KLMO = K, L, O, and Other        N = 747
                  KG, KS, KE, XS, GP, PE, SE
                  chi square = 115.4        p = .249        df = 106


Model 2.   CEU1 = High, KLMO = M and Other                          N = 361
                  KXS, GP
                  chi square = 20.3        p = .501        df = 21

TABLE 4.16. Models for KLMO versus child prior variables.

Dependent Variable: KLMO

Independent Variables: SOUND, CEU1, GRADE

| | | | Counts | | | | |
|---|---|---|---|---|---|---|---|
| SOUND | CEU1 | GRADE | K | L | 0 | Other | Total |
| /s/ | Low | 1-2 | 47 | 62 | 24 | 21 | 154 |
| | | 3-6 | 27 | 16 | 7 | 6 | 56 |
| | Medium | 1-2 | 41 | 24 | 11 | 19 | 95 |
| | | 3-6 | 39 | 13 | 5 | 7 | 64 |
| /r/ | Low | 1-2 | 7 | 35 | 72 | 17 | 131 |
| | | 3-6 | 5 | 15 | 28 | 9 | 57 |
| | Medium | 1-2 | 17 | 30 | 29 | 25 | 101 |
| | | 3-6 | 28 | 18 | 24 | 19 | 89 |
| | Total | | 211 | 213 | 200 | 123 | 747 |

| | | | Row percents | | | | |
|---|---|---|---|---|---|---|---|
| /s/ | Low | 1-2 | 31 | 40 | 16 | 14 | 100 |
| | | 3-6 | 48 | 29 | 13 | 11 | 100 |
| | Medium | 1-2 | 43 | 25 | 12 | 20 | 100 |
| | | 3-6 | 61 | 20 | 8 | 11 | 100 |
| /r/ | Low | 1-2 | 5 | 27 | 55 | 13 | 100 |
| | | 3-6 | 9 | 26 | 49 | 16 | 100 |
| | Medium | 1-2 | 17 | 30 | 29 | 25 | 100 |
| | | 3-6 | 31 | 20 | 27 | 21 | 100 |
| | Total | | 28 | 29 | 27 | 16 | 100 |

TABLE 4.17. Four-way table. M removed from KLMO, high removed from CEU1, GRADE collapsed into two categories. N = 747.

Finally, the high baseline children need only SOUND and KSEX (The KXS term) to explain KLMO. We can collapse over GRADE and PREVT, producing Table 4.18, which is merely an extraction from Table 4.15. As with Table 4.17, one may interpret the row percentages as probabilities. One anomaly is noted: /s/ high girls are almost three-fourths "M." One wonders if some extra care is directed toward girls, to have them thoroughly extinguish small articulation problems, where it may be recognized that /s/ problems are more easily solved than /r/, thus accounting for the SOUND effect. It is also possible that some mechanism like this may explain the /s/ medium girl anomaly.

Dependent Variable: KLMO
Independent Variables: SOUND, KSEX
Cells are count over row percent

| SOUND | KSEX | M | OTHER | TOTAL |
|-------|------|-----|-------|-------|
| /s/ | Male | 64 | 46 | 110 |
| | | 58 | 42 | 100 |
| | Female | 44 | 16 | 60 |
| | | 73 | 27 | 100 |
| /r/ | Male | 73 | 52 | 125 |
| | | 58 | 42 | 100 |
| | Female | 28 | 38 | 66 |
| | | 42 | 58 | 100 |
| | Total | 209 | 152 | 361 |
| | | 58 | 42 | 100 |

TABLE 4.18. Three-way table. Sample restricted to CEU1 = High, KLMO = M and Other. N = 361.

CHAPTER 5

# Results: Clinician Variables

The last chapter looked at the characteristics of children. Now we consider—are there measurable characteristics of clinicians that affect a child's articulation learning? We proceed with the statistical analysis of clinician characteristics. We also take one more step, one which we think is very important to the field. We construct measures of clinician peformance. These are called Clinician Performance Levels, CPL. There are two of them, CPL2 for performance after the child has had six weeks of therapy, and CPL4, after the whole year.

We begin by looking at various clinician characteristics like age, degree, etc. These turn out not to be as significant as one would like in affecting our results.

Then we turn to a more interesting question—what is the real meaning of a clinician dependent variable? The child's goal is perfect articulation. A child dependent variable like EU2 measures how close the child is to that goal at a particular time. The units are essentially percent correct. The goal of the clinician is to bring all of her children to perfect articulation. One's first idea of a clinician dependent variable might be average articulation level of the group of children in therapy. However, the clinician whose children all started with a low baseline would show low performance. The same clinician with high baseline children would show high performance. We take the logical step and remove the effect of the child's expected performance from the clinician performance measure. The result is CPL.

We provide simple tables for the calculation of the relative child performance, KPL. Given a group of children in therapy after six weeks or after the whole year of therapy, it is a simple task with a hand calculator to calculate the clinician performance.

We suggest that our overall strategy for deriving KPL and CPL may be used in other learning situations to derive measures of teacher performance. One only needs a numerical measure of child ability and a sample of children from which the most important independent variables are known.

Finally we do something which is not statistically kosher. We analyze our data pretending that we knew the CPL scores of the clinicians at the beginning of the project. Based on this analysis, we believe that the really important variables in determining articulation learning are baseline articulation, target phoneme (combined as SNDEU1), and the clinician.

The chapter concludes with statistical analyses of variables which are important to the clinician—number of therapy sessions per week and number of children in the therapy group. These were not set up to be statistically analyzed in the original project design. The best we can do is hope for a new project in which a large sample of clinicians have their CPL measured and are then carefully assigned to groups of children using different therapy plans.

For definitions of special terms and symbols used in this project refer to Appendix G in this book.

## Introduction

We have so far been dealing primarily with variables for which the primary observational unit is the child. The reader may now want to turn back to the beginning of Chapter 4, under the section *Independent Variables*. That section concerns the nature of variables and observational units.

Our discussion now turns to those variables for which the primary observational unit is the clinician and variables we can create by taking means or by calculating percentages of child variables. A typical variable of the first type is clinician age, which clearly has nothing directly to do with the child. An example of the second type of variable is the average baseline score EU1. If we take all of a clinician's children and calculate their mean EU1, we have a variable that differs over the set of clinicians and indicates the level at which each clinician's children entered the study. The group of children attached to a clinician will not be expected to do as well if their mean EU1 is not high. If it turns out that they have a relatively high EU2, the clinician probably does a good job in therapy.

The next three sections contain all of the statistical results that pertain to the clinician. All of the clinician variables are presented, but the focus is on independent variables. Next, we introduce a new idea that we consider to be a major result of this work—measures of performance for child and clinician. Finally, these measures of performance are used as dependent variables to further qualify the effect of the child prior variables, and deal with the other independent variables. Thus the sequence in the next three sections is, 1) clinician independent variables, 2) clinician dependent variables used to construct performance measures, and 3) statistical analyses using these performance measures.

Returning now to the main thread of this section, there are 61 clinicians in our study upon which we can define about 43 variables. This allows us to present in Table E.21, Appendix E the full set of clinician data. Following this, in Table 5.1, is a list of all these variables, giving name, range, and the meaning of the variable, along with the meaning of each value for discrete variables. This table corresponds to Table 4.1 which gives the same information about the child variables.

We will spend less time with the statistical analyses of the clinician variables than with the child variables. There are two reasons for this, the smaller number of clinicians (61) and the lack of a sampling scheme for clinicians.

Many studies in the educational and behavioral sciences report results from samples of teachers much smaller than ours. Thus, some readers may see our sample of 61 clinicians as "large." Our position is that one must have a larger designed sample in order to make inferences about several variables.

Our most important results are the techniques for estimating clinician performance. It is unfortunate, but for the best estimate, we needed a controlled sampling of clinicians from some well-defined population. Ideally, we should have a sample of clinicians chosen to randomize their teaching ability. But this would be circular, because prior to our work we did not know of measures of clinical ability or performance.

Thus, we suggest that the reader accept our sample of clinicians as representative, and imagine what we have displayed are techniques for measuring performance. Those techniques are close to ideal, but they should be applied in a new experiment where the clinicians are chosen by a sampling scheme. The measures may not be too far off, but they can be improved.

## Independent Variables

This section surveys the clinician independent variables found in Table E.21. The dependent variables are dealt with in the next section.

Table 5.2 gives univariate summary statistics for all the clinician variables. This forms the basis for our survey. We have presented the same statistics that were calculated for the child variables in Table 4.2. For each discrete variable, the counts and percentages for each value are given. Note, however, that there are

| Name | Values | Meaning |
|------|--------|---------|
| Prior Conditions | | |
| CLIN | 1-99 | Identifies each clinician in the project |
| DEGREE | | Last academic degree |
| | 1 | B.A. |
| | 2 | M.A. or M.S. |
| ASHA | | Clinical certification status in the American Speech and Hearing Association. |
| | 1 | Certified |
| | 2 | Pending |
| | 3 | Not certified |
| AGE | 23-49 | Clinician age |
| CAGE | | Categorized age |
| | 1 | $AGE < 28$ |
| | 2 | $28 \leqslant AGE < 40$ |
| | 3 | $40 \leqslant AGE$ |
| YRSEXP | 0-18 | Years of clinical experience |
| SELFR | 3-15 | Self concept concerning /r/ therapy |
| SELFS | 3-15 | Self concept concerning /s/ therapy |
| EOISUM | 93-137 | A paper/pencil attitude measure of clinician rapport |
| CEOI | | Categorized EOISUM |
| | 1 | $EOISUM \quad 116$ |
| | 2 | $116 \leqslant EOISUM < 123$ |
| | 3 | $123 \leqslant EOISUM$ |
| Clinical Environment | | |
| YEAR | | The project year involving this clinician. |
| | 2 | Year 2 |
| | 3 | Year 3 |
| | 4 | Year 4 |
| | 23 | Both means years 2 and 3. |

TABLE 5.1. Clinician variables.

| Name | Values | Meaning |
|------|--------|---------|
| NOSESS | | Average number of sessions per week |
| | 2 | once a week therapy |
| | 3 | twice a week |
| | 4 | block therapy |
| NOKIDS | 4-51 | Number of children from this clinicians caseload who were involved with our project. |
| CASELOAD | 20-125 | Total clinical caseload while clinician was involved with involved with our project. |
| MEAN NGP | | Average number of children in a therapy group for this clinician. |
| | 1 | individual therapy |
| | 2 | two children in the therapy group |
| | 3 | three children |
| | 4 | four children |
| | 5 | five children |
| GEOG | | Code for the geographical location of this clinican. |
| | 1 | Wichita, Kansas |
| | 2 | Kansas City, Kansas |
| | 3 | Jefferson County, Colorado (A Denver suburb) |
| | 4 | Minneapolis, Minnesota |

Averages of Child Independent Variables

| | | |
|---|---|---|
| % S LOW | 0-57 | Percent of this clinicians children, who were involved in the project and had /s/ problems, and had a low baseline score. The next five variables are defined similarly. |
| % S MED | 0-57 | |
| % S HIGH | 0-33 | |
| % R LOW | 0-58 | |
| % R MED | 0-50 | |
| % R HIGH | 0-75 | |

TABLE 5.1. (continued).

| MEAN GRADE | 13-34 | Average child grade. |
| % PREVT | 0-95 | Percent of project children who had previous therapy. |
| % MALE | 14-94 | Percent of project children who were male |

Averages of Child Dependent Variables

| MEAN EU1 | 6-78 | Average EU1 score for all project children belonging to this clinician. The next five variables are defined similarly. |
| MEAN EU2 | 22-85 | |
| MEAN EU3 | 34-94 | |
| MEAN EU4 | 46-97 | |
| MEAN GAIN | 18-78 | |
| MEAN GAMMA | (-30)-59 | |
| % K | 0-86 | Percent of project children who fell in the "K" category on the KLMO variable. |
| % L | 0-44 | |
| % M | 0-100 | |
| % O | 0-59 | |
| % Other | 0-67 | |

Clinician Performance Measures

| CPL2 | 21-53 | Clinician performance measure based on EU2. |
| CPL2 RANK | 1-61 | Rank of each clinician based on CPL2. |
| QCPL2 | | Categorized CPL2. |
| | 1 | not good |
| | 2 | OK |
| | 3 | good |
| CPL4 | 17-42 | Clinician performance measure based on EU4. |
| CPL4 RANK | 1-61 | Bank of each clinician based on CPL4. |
| QCPL4 | | Categorized CPL4. |
| | 1 | bad |
| | 2 | OK |
| | 3 | not bad |
| NO. B | 2-25 | Number of project children from this clinician who were classified as "B". |

TABLE 5.1. (continued).

missing data. In Table E.21, for example, the entry is blank for clinician 91, under DEGR. This means that we do not know this clinician's terminal degree. There are four clinicians, 91, 93, 97, and 98 in Year 3, who did not return the questionnaire which was sent to them, and thus these prior variables are missing. In addition, CASELOAD was obtained two years after the end of the project by telephoning the clinicians, and there are four missing values for clinicians who could not be reached, or who did not remember their caseload. Thus, in Table 5.2, DEGREE adds up to only 57, indicating that four clinicians are missing in this variable. The percentages however are calculated for all the non-missing clinicians, so they will add to 100, except for rounding error.

For each of the continuous, or nondiscrete variables we show the mean, median, standard deviation, minimum, and maximum. These should give a rough picture of the distribution of values for these variables.

The first block of variables, labeled "Clinician Prior" holds all those that pertain to some clinician quality that is known, or fixed, prior to the beginning of a project year. These correspond to the "child prior" variables. Thus, the clinician's terminal degree is certainly a property of the clinician, and is known prior to the beginning of the project year. We have more BA's than MA's.

The variable labeled ASHA indicates membership in the American Speech-Language-Hearing Association. It may represent a different level of clinical competence than the degree. At the beginning of the respective project years, 17 of the clinicians were clinically certified, six had requested certification but not yet received it (pending), and 34 (60%) were not certified (or members). Curlee (1975) reported on a survey conducted in 1973 (which corresponds to Year 4 of our project) which estimated that 56% of the total speech and hearing work force (28,250) were members of ASHA. Approximately 65% of the clinicians who work in the public schools were non-ASHA members. Therefore, our sample contained approximately 5% more ASHA clinicians than the national average.

Our clinicians ranged in age from 23 to 49, with a median of 30. Curlee (1975) noted a median age of 29.3 years for nonmembers and 33.2 years for ASHA members. The clinical experience, which was expected to be correlated with their age, ranges from zero to 18 years, with a mean of 6.3 years. The variable AGE was categorized into three groups for statistical analyses, just like EU1 (see Child Prior Variables—Statistics). This new variable is called CAGE, for Categorized AGE.

The clinicians were asked to rate themselves on their self-concept on: 1) discrimination of /r/ and /s/, 2) ability to teach /r/ and /s/, and 3) ability to teach /r/ and /s/ in comparison with other clinicians. Each question was scored on a one to five scale. These three scores were added to produce the variables SELFR, which measures the self-concept for /r/, and SELFS, the self-concept for /s/. Each of these has a mean near 12, which represents the middle of the scale.

EOISUM is a measure of rapport. It was also categorized into three groups to create the new variable called CEOI. Note that a high score on both EOISUM, and CEOI represents high rapport.

The next block of variables is labeled "Clinical Environment." These do not pertain directly to the clinician, but to the situation in which she is found. Two of these variables YEAR and GEOG are really part of the project setup. YEAR is the value of the project year in which each clinician worked. As explained in Chapter 1, the first year of the project was used to try out data analysis and testing procedures. The 1,108 children come from project Years 2, 3, and 4. As noted in Chapter 2 there were seven clinicians who were in Year 2, and who continued into

| Name | Values | Meaning | N | % | Mean | Median | SD | Min | Max |
|------|--------|---------|---|---|------|--------|----|----|-----|
| **Prior Conditions** | | | | | | | | | |
| DEGREE | 1 | BA | 33 | 58 | | | | | |
| | 2 | MA | 24 | 42 | | | | | |
| ASHA | 1 | Cert. | 17 | 30 | | | | | |
| | 2 | Pend. | 6 | 10 | | | | | |
| | 3 | Not. Cert. | 34 | 60 | | | | | |
| AGE | | | | | 32.0 | 30 | 7.7 | 23 | 49 |
| CAGE | 1 | 28 | 22 | 39 | | | | | |
| | 2 | 28-39 | 21 | 37 | | | | | |
| | 3 | 40 | 14 | 25 | | | | | |
| YRSEXP | | | | | 6.3 | 6 | 4.4 | 0 | 18 |
| SELFR | | | | | 11.7 | 12 | 2.0 | 8 | 15 |
| SELFS | | | | | 12.2 | 12 | 1.8 | 5 | 15 |
| EOISUM | | | | | 119.3 | 120 | 9.3 | 93 | 137 |
| CEOI | 1 | 116 | 16 | 29 | | | | | |
| | 2 | 116-122 | 17 | 31 | | | | | |
| | 3 | 123 | 22 | 40 | | | | | |
| **Clinical Environment** | | | | | | | | | |
| YEAR | 2 | | 16 | 26 | | | | | |
| | 3 | | 11 | 18 | | | | | |
| | 4 | | 27 | 44 | | | | | |
| | 23 | | 7 | 12 | | | | | |
| NOSESS | 2 | Once/wk | 15 | 25 | | | | | |
| | 3 | Twice/wk | 42 | 68 | | | | | |
| | 4 | Block | 4 | 7 | | | | | |

TABLE 5.2. Statistical summary of all clinician variables.

| Name | Values | Meaning | N | % | Mean | Median | SD | Min | Max |
|------|--------|---------|---|---|------|--------|-----|-----|-----|
| NO. KIDS | | | | | 18.2 | 16 | 13.2 | 4 | 51 |
| CASELOAD | | | | | 75.5 | 78 | 29.9 | 20 | 147 |
| MEAN NGP | | | | | 2.65 | 2.6 | 0.61 | 2.0 | 4.2 |
| GEOG | 1 | Wichita | 10 | 16 | | | | | |
| | 2 | G KS City | 34 | 56 | | | | | |
| | 3 | Jeff. Cty. | 7 | 12 | | | | | |
| | 4 | Minn | 10 | 16 | | | | | |

Averages of Child Independent Variables

| Name | Mean | Median | SD | Min | Max |
|------|------|--------|-----|-----|-----|
| % S LOW | 18.4 | 17 | 13.9 | 0 | 57 |
| % S MED | 13.7 | 13 | 12.6 | 0 | 57 |
| % S HI | 15.2 | 14 | 10.4 | 0 | 38 |
| % R LOW | 15.5 | 14 | 14.7 | 0 | 58 |
| % R MED | 17.7 | 14 | 12.3 | 0 | 50 |
| % R HI | 19.5 | 16 | 15.9 | 0 | 75 |
| MEAN GRADE | 2.36 | 2.3 | 0.44 | 1.3 | 3.4 |
| % PREVT | 44.0 | 44 | 21.4 | 0 | 95 |
| % MALE | 59.5 | 59 | 17.2 | 14 | 94 |

Averages of Child Dependent Variables

| Name | Mean | Median | SD | Min | Max |
|------|------|--------|-----|-----|-----|
| MEAN EU1 | 28.8 | 28 | 13.0 | 6 | 78 |
| MEAN EU2 | 48.4 | 47 | 14.9 | 22 | 85 |
| MEAN EU3 | 69.1 | 69 | 15.0 | 34 | 94 |
| MEAN EU4 | 80.0 | 82 | 13.0 | 46 | 98 |
| MEAN GAIN | 51.1 | 50 | 15.6 | 18 | 87 |
| MEAN GAMMA | 9.0 | 6 | 15.8 | -30 | 59 |
| %K | 20.4 | 15 | 20.0 | 0 | 86 |
| %L | 19.6 | 17 | 14.6 | 0 | 83 |
| %M | 22.5 | 17 | 18.6 | 0 | 100 |
| %O | 15.2 | 14 | 15.4 | 0 | 59 |
| % OTHER | 22.4 | 22 | 15.4 | 0 | 67 |

TABLE 5.2. (continued).

Year 3. These are labeled 23. They had 26 children who were carried from Year 2 to Year 3. They were counted as different in the 1,108. Most clinicians come from Year 4.

Before Year 4, we attempted to detect geographic differences among groups of clinicians and children in different parts of the country. Thus, we created the

| Name | Values | Meaning | N | % | Mean | Median | SD | Min | Max |
|------|--------|---------|---|---|------|--------|-----|-----|-----|
| Clinician Performance Measures | | | | | | | | | |
| CPL2 | | | | | 30.8 | 30 | 5.9 | 21 | 53 |
| CPL2 RANK | | | | | 31.0 | 31 | 17.8 | 1 | 61 |
| QCPL2 | 1 | Not Good | 20 | 33 | | | | | |
| | 2 | OK | 21 | 34 | | | | | |
| | 3 | Good | 20 | 33 | | | | | |
| CPL4 | | | | | 30.5 | 31 | 5.5 | 17 | 42 |
| CPL4 RANK | | | | | 31.0 | 31 | 17.8 | 1 | 61 |
| QCPL4 | 1 | Bad | 20 | 33 | | | | | |
| | 2 | OK | 21 | 34 | | | | | |
| | 3 | Not Bad | 20 | 33 | | | | | |
| NO. B | | | | | 9.1 | 8 | 6.7 | 2 | 25 |

TABLE 5.2. (continued).

variable GEOG to record where the clinician worked. Unfortunately, the geographic effect was swamped by the clinician effect, so we do not know whether there are geographic differences.

The variable CASELOAD is the value of each clinician's total caseload in the project years. For the seven clinicians who were in both Years 2 and 3, it is the sum of their two years' caseloads. This is the total sample from which the project children were drawn. The average caseload was 75.5 which compares favorably with the Curlee (1975) guideline of 70 children per clinician.

The number of project children for each clinician is the value of NOKIDS. We suggest turning back to Table E.21, Appendix E to see how this varies. Clinicians who had children in just Year 2 had about 25 on the average in the project. Those in both Years 2 and 3 had about 50. Those in Year 3 had about 17, and the Year 4 clinicians had about seven, because of the Tone Keyboard. Thus, the number of children available to assess each clinician's performance varies considerably. This is a weakness in the design.

The final two variables in this block NOSESS and MEAN NGP represent clinical decisions. NOSESS gives the value of the number of sessions per week of therapy by each clinician. A value of 2 represents one session per week, 3 means two sessions, and 4 means block therapy (four sessions per week). It is unfortunate that only four clinicians used block therapy. Such a small number precludes any strong statistical statement about the effect of this therapy pattern. NGP represents the number of children who were in the group receiving therapy.

The next block of clinician independent variables is the average of the child prior independent variables. We have already discussed the idea of averages of child variables. The first six variables here are the percentages of SNDEU1, one variable for each value. Turn again to Table E.21. Under % S LOW, clinician 1 had an entry of 14. This means that 14% of this clinician's children were /s/ lows. Similarly, 21% of these 43 children were /s/ medium. The meaning of each of the other four variables is similar. Except for rounding error, the sum of these six will be 100.

The statistics of the % SNDEU1 variables show little variation. They each have a mean between 13-20. Four have a maximum between 50 and 60. The variable % S HI has a more limited range, from 0-38. The % R HI would have about the same range as the others, except for two clinicians, 50 and 52. Clinician 50 has three of her four children in the /r/ high category, and clinician 52 has two-thirds of her six children in that category. In the case of 50, all of her children were in the high baseline category.

The next variable in this block is MEAN GRADE, which is just the average value of the variable GRADE for each clinician's project children. This is almost the average grade, but not quite, since grades 4, 5, and 6 are scored in our data as 4. This variable has a mean of 2.36. It ranges from a value of 1.3 for clinician 50 to 3.4 for 56.

The next two variables are percentages. The percent of project children who had previous therapy is indicated by % of PREVT. This has a wide range, from zero to 95. The percent of project children who were male is given by % MALE, which ranges from 14 to 94.

We could discuss MEAN EU1 in this section, since it is logically an independent variable, but we prefer to deal with this variable with the other average EU numbers in the following section.

## Relationships Among the Clinician Independent Variables

After reviewing each clinician independent variable, the next logical step is to deal with their interrelationships. But since, as noted above, this is not a random sample of clinicians, the analysis of relationships between clinician variables is interesting but not to be associated with strong statistical statements.

Another problem associated with the clinician variables is that they are not strongly related to each other, except for certain pairs that are by their nature related. Table 5.3 summarizes the relationships between the clinician prior variables, using simple two-way tables for the analysis. Each of the entries is a significance level for chi-square. For the purposes of this analysis, SELFR, SELFS, and YRSEXP were each divided into three approximately equal frequency groups.

SELFS and SELFR are strongly related in the expected fashion. Clinicians who have a positive self-concept for /r/ tend to have a positive self-concept for /s/ and vice versa. Likewise categorized age (CAGE) is related to YRSEXP. Older clinicians have more experience than younger. DEGREE is related to ASHA. Some 79% of MA clinicians are in the categories *certified* or *pending*, while only 12% of the BA clinicians are in the same category. ASHA is related to YRSEXP. Certified clinicians have more experience. These are statistics that would be expected to be significant, and offer no surprises.

In this summary table, what is not there is as interesting as what is there. ASHA and CAGE are only significant at .023. Older clinicians tend to be certified. Curlee (1975) found ASHA members to be older than nonmembers. What is not there is a significant relation between DEGREE and CAGE or YRSEXP.

YRSEXP relates to SELFR. Clinicians with less than four years experience tend to have a lower self-concept for /r/. This would make sense, except that there are no other significant relationships with self-concept.

The greatest shortcoming in this table lies in the statistics for CEOI. Clinician rapport does not relate to anything else. This could be positive. Clinicians of all shapes, sizes, and personalities may be found who have good rapport. On the

|        | DEGREE | ASHA  | CAGE  | YRSEXP | SELFR | SELFS |
|--------|--------|-------|-------|--------|-------|-------|
| ASHA   | <.001  |       |       |        |       |       |
| CAGE   | .323   | .023  |       |        |       |       |
| YRSEXP | .139   | <.001 | <.001 |        |       |       |
| SELFR  | .532   | .235  | .270  | .018   |       |       |
| SELFS  | .582   | .980  | .897  | .143   | <.001 |       |
| CEOI   | .144   | .218  | .212  | .878   | .756  | .413  |

TABLE 5.3. Summary of the interrelations between clinician prior variables. Chi-square probabilities for two-way tables. YRSEXP, SELFR, and SELFS are divided into three categories.

other hand, we are not able to add deeper meaning to this concept, thus we are not able to guide clinicians in the improvement of their level of rapport.

The clinician prior block includes many discrete variables. They were analyzed using two-way tables and chi-square. The next block of variables, the averages of the child independent variables, are all continuous, so correlations relate them. These are shown in Table E.22, Appendix E.

The correlations of the last three variables, MEAN GRADE, % PREVT, and % MALE, with the other variables and with themselves all lack significance at the .01 level. Although they seem to be unrelated, let us remember from the earlier analysis that there were some strong relationships between the corresponding child variables. Thus, for example, if we consider GRADE and PREVT, we know that a child in grade one is not likely to have had previous therapy. When we look at a clinician's caseload, on the average, we do not expect less previous therapy to be associated with a lower average grade, since the correlation between MEAN GRADE and % PREVT is .10, which is not significant. This is true only of average caseloads, chosen in some manner similar to the way our project children were chosen (which put some emphasis on the third grade). In contrast, if a clinician had a caseload of only first graders, we would expect most of them to be without previous therapy. Our data indicate that our groups of project children were never structured to include only first graders.

The SNDEU1 variables have some high correlations and some low. For instance, in our sample of groups of children, there was a strong negative relationship between % R LOW and % R HI. In fact, all of the pairs of variables are negatively related except % S LOW with % R LOW, % S MED with % R MED and % S HI with % R HI. The last three pairs are positively correlated, but are not significant. This means that if you look at all of the project groups, those with more /s/ lows may or may not have /r/ lows, but they will have less of every other SNDEU1 category on the average. It is not clear what this means. It may be an artifact of our child selection procedure.

Our final task in this section is to relate the two blocks of variables, clinician prior, and child averages. The correlations are presented in Table E.23. Most are not significant. As in the previous table of correlations, there are no significant correlations for the three variables MEAN GRADE, % PREVT, and % MALE. There are some significant correlations associated with DEGREE, ASHA, YRSEXP, SELF, and EOISUM. Because of the complexity of the child selection mechanism, these are not simple to interpret. For instance, the correlations with DEGREE could be interpreted as meaning that clinicians with an MA may be assigned the more difficult children, the /r/ lows and mediums, and that these clinicians are not given the easy ones, the highs. But the positive correlation of ASHA with % S HIGH, and the negative correlation of YRSEXP with % R MED, make such an interpretation very tenuous.

# Measures of Clinician Performance

## Clinician Dependent Variables

This section begins a block of sections that lead to one goal: the establishment of clinician performance measures. We will discuss the clinician dependent variables, then we will explain how one goes about using data like ours to measure performance. Next, we will construct the measures, and evaluate our clinicians on them. Finally, we use the performance ratings to further analyze the children, getting more insight into the factors affecting the learning process.

Using this section as an introduction to the next three sections requires only one piece of logic: clinician performance must have something to do with child performance. However we are going to rate the clinicians, the rating scheme must have something to do with the child dependent variables. Or, to be more specific, the average EU2 of a clinician's children should be one of the factors in our performance measure. This average EU2 is called MEAN EU2 in Table E.21, Appendix E and it is one of the clinician dependent variables. Thus, this section surveys the clinician dependent variables.

The reason for EU2 being called a child "dependent" variable should be clear from our previous discussion. Calling MEAN EU2 a *clinician* dependent variable may not be as clear, so let us start by discussing this idea.

For the child, EU2 is obviously a dependent or criterion variable, because it is a score we want to increase for each child. Any reasonable method that will improve a child's EU2 score would be useful.

For the clinician, MEAN EU2 is the average of all the EU2 scores of all of the children. For instance, clinician number 3, saw 28 children whom we are analyzing, and the average of all the EU2's for those children is 54. This clinician's MEAN EU2 is 6 points above the mean of all the clinicians.

We call MEAN EU2 a clinician *dependent* variable because it is possible to use it as a criterion for selecting clinicians. If we have some applicants for a position, and if we know all of their MEAN EU2 scores, and if we believe that they have all been treating the same kind of children with the same baseline level of articulation problem, then we should hire the clinician with the highest MEAN EU2. Our selection would be based on the common sense notion of average child ability after six weeks of therapy (EU2). Thus MEAN EU2 is a dependent or criterion variable for choosing clinicians. In the next section we will go much more deeply into the criteria for choosing clinicians. For the moment, we note that all other MEAN EU scores in Table E.21, Appendix E would also be suitable as potential clinician selection criteria (except, of course, MEAN EU1).

The block of five variables starting with % K may also be considered as clinician dependent variables, but here the concept is a little more complicated. The variable % K is just the value of the percentage of project children who were "K's" for that clinician. Clinician 1, for instance has a % K of 23. This means that out of this clinician's 43 project children (look under NOKIDS), 23%, or 10 of these children were in the "K" category of the variable KLMO. This clinician had 10 children who started low and made a rapid gain in their articulation ability.

Similarly, % L is the percent of the clinician's project children who were in the "L" category. Likewise for % M, % O, and % OTHER.

If we look only at % K for the moment, we can begin to see why this might be a clinician dependent variable like MEAN EU2. If we had a choice of hiring clinician 8 or 9, say, and if the only thing we knew was that 8 had 43% "K" children and 9 had 10% "K" children, we would prefer clinician 8. Her children seem to learn faster. However, the old problem of KLMO, that the definition of the categories uses EU1, applies here. A clinician who has lots of "K" children must have low MEAN EU1. Requiring that a clinician's children start with low ability is not relevant to clinician skill.

Note also that if we neglect the problem of the involvement of EU1 in KLMO, the variable % O would also be a potential clinician dependent variable. In this case, we want to choose a clinician who has a *low* % O, over another clinician with high % O. It is difficult to decide just what to do with the other variables in this block. The % L, if high, means that the clinician's children learned slowly, *but they did learn.* The % M, if high, means that the children did not make much progress, but they ended the year at a very high level. The % OTHER would not have much use as a dependent variable.

With the above discussion of the concept of *dependent* as it applies to the clinician variables, we can look at the summary statistics in Table 5.2. At this point we will include MEAN EU1. Subsequently, it will be used as an independent variable.

The mean EU numbers follow the expected progression, 29, 48, 69, and 80. These numbers define a learning curve that is the average of the average of the project groups. These numbers are, of course, quite close to the EU means given in Table 3.2.

One of the statistical problems with the EU numbers was their poor distributions, EU1 is skewed to the right, and EU4 to the left. One of the standard results in statistics, called the "central limit theorem," says that means of means are likely to be normally distributed, and this is true for the variables we are considering. The mean EU numbers and MEAN GAIN and GAMMA have much better distributions than the corresponding variables from which they are averaged. There are only a few problems. Clinician 50 has a MEAN EU1 of 50, which is a definite outlier. In fact, this same clinician has the maximum score on MEAN EU1, EU2, and EU3, but the values of the maximums do not represent outliers for the other two variables. MEAN EU4 has a few clinicians below 50, which skews the distribution a little to the left. On MEAN GAMMA, clinician 23 is a little far to the right, but not enough to cause real trouble. Because of the low level of distributional problems, we will not need to deal with the averages of the transformed variables over the clinicians.

In contrast to the mean child dependent variables, the KLMO percentages are quite poorly distributed. The % K is skewed to the right by four clinicians with more than 60% "K." The % L has one outlier, clinician 55 at 83%. Likewise, % M has an outlier, clinician 50, as expected from our previous discussion. The % O is definitely skewed; 19 clinicians have no "O's." The others range from 4% to 59%. The % OTHER is skewed to the right by four clinicians above 50%. However, with all these problems, we choose to leave the % KLMO variables alone. This will simplify the analysis. The reader should consider again that we have only 61 clinicians and that statistics on these five variables should be interpreted carefully.

The interrelationships among these clinician dependent variables is shown in

Table E.24. Most of these correlations are significant at the .05 level. For most of these variables, there is some other variable with a strong relationship. The correlations between each of the MEAN EU numbers can be compared with the child data in Table 3.3. The two matrices have the same pattern, but in the clinician matrix, the high correlations are higher, and the low correlations are lower. Thus, the interpretation of the EU numbers as a series of measures which indicates a temporal relationship is carried over here. For any two MEAN EU numbers, if the pair is close together in time, the correlation is low. Also, toward the end of the school year the correlations get larger.

Two of the variables, % M and % OTHER, are not strongly related to the others. They each have significant correlations with the MEAN EU numbers, but none over .42 in magnitude. These two are unrelated to the other variables.

The other KLMO variables show expected relations with the EU numbers. The % K is highly correlated with GAMMA. Both of these are sensitive to the shape of the learning curve, and both emphasize the "K" curve used to name GAMMA.

The % M is highly correlated with MEAN EU1. Whether a clinician has a large proportion of "M's" in her group of children is largely a matter of her children's average baseline. Note that this result suggests that % M should not be strongly associated with the idea of a dependent variable, since MEAN EU1 has the quality of an independent variable. One is not as interested in predicting or controlling % M as % K or % O.

Finally, % O is correlated with the last two EU numbers, MEAN EU3 and EU4. This certainly fits with the design of the "O" category. It is primarily a measure of the final score and the proportion of children who were low in articulation ability at the end of the year. As a dependent variable, one's effort would be directed to reducing % O.

## Clinician Performance—What is a Good Clinician?

There are several theoretical arguments for constructing clinician performance measures to rate our clinicians. These same measures are suitable for rating the performance of other clinicians. This section contains those arguments. In the following two sections, these arguments are applied to our data. Then the performance measures are used to further analyze the children.

Because rating clinicians is such an important issue, this section proceeds slowly and carefully. Some arguments are strong and some are weak. Examples to illustrate the points made are drawn from our data, and thus, results from the calculations in the subsequent sections will be assumed. But, since we use the statistical results as examples, we do not think that the reader will need to turn back and forth from this section to the next two.

Our argument starts with a statement that is a warning. We will be using *our data* to construct our performance measures. The reader may be weary of reading about problems with our data, primarily the lack of a sampling plan, the naturalistic design, and the small sample of clinicians, but it is at this point that these problems assume crucial importance.

We see child selection and the lack of a careful sampling plan as the least of the problems. Another caution is the reliability of the SPT/TALK scores and clinician bias (Chapter 2). But we do have 1,108 children and we are inclined to rely on the large sample size to mitigate the biases. This will not help us if we are involved in breaking the units into very small cell sizes.

The fact that this was a naturalistic and not a designed experiment may be a plus. We can argue that these children were selected and given therapy in conditions that were realistic school therapy conditions. Such choices as therapy mode and group size were done according to the clinician's judgment, and thus our data comes from a realistic source.

However, since there are interactions between child characteristics and therapy modes, this is not really a valid argument. It is possible, for instance, that more /r/ lows may have been assigned to once a week therapy than to twice a week. It is possible that this causes some difficulty for /r/ low learning. Thus, it is possible that the poor showing of these children is the result of clinician decisions and their scores should have been higher. But, we will use these scores to calculate our performance measures. Again, we do not think this is a serious problem with our data, but it clearly would have been better to randomize the decision variables in our experiment.

The third problem, the small number of clinicians, is much more difficult to explain away. We indicated earlier that there were about 5% more MA clinicians in our study than reported nationally in the public school work force. Also, persons who volunteer their services for projects of this kind may not represent the average clinician. It is possible that all of the clinicians are much better than average, or much worse. It is possible that /r/ lows were preferentially assigned to bad clinicians, and their scores really do not reflect their ability. These are potential difficulties that we cannot explain away by sample size, because it is only 61 and not randomly chosen.

In fact we have no way to make this problem disappear. We can only offer two comments. First, the reader may want to go through our clinician data and decide whether it fits her experience. The % KLMO variables may be useful. Our average clinician had 20% of her children rated as "K." This represents children who started the year at about 12% correct and reached 64% correct on their target phonemes in six weeks. Is this reasonable? If this fits the reader's clinical experience, then it gives some confidence in our data and the performance measures derived from it. The second comment is that we feel we have accomplished something by presenting arguments and a theoretical structure for measuring performance. We will thus show how another experiment can be performed, using our techniques and solving our data problems. This next experiment can then be considered as the one that establishes the better set of parameters for calculating performance. This is a valid comment insofar as there is a real possibility of performing the proposed experiment.

We end these warnings with the hope that the reader will discount the problems with child selection and agree either that our clinicians comprise a reasonable sample or that our arguments are useful.

The next step is to deal with the basic ideas of performance measurement. Clinician ratings are calculated from the data we have, but the question is how? What do we mean when we say that a clinician has done a good job with a child in therapy? Or, more generally, what do we mean when we speak of a "good clinician?"

Clinician performance will be measured by child performance. When we speak of a good clinician, we mean that this clinician's children did well in therapy. This is a strong place in our argument leading to performance measurements. We expect that the reader will find it obvious, but as we have said, we are trying to be as careful as possible.

Since the measures of child performance are the dependent variables, the EU numbers, GAIN, GAMMA, KLMO, and the others, we expect that our clinician performance calculations will involve these variables. We should be able to rate the clinicians using the dependent variables, but the question is "how?" To answer this question we will discuss a series of possible methods, showing how each does not do quite what we want it to, except for the last one.

Start with a simple idea. Suppose there was a miraculous clinician, call her C1, who always got her children to 100% in six weeks of therapy. Suppose that C1 worked with many children, with a range of baseline articulation levels. All of them reached 100% correct articulation in six weeks. If there were such a person, C1 would be the perfect clinician. We could then measure other clinician's performance by seeing how they compared to C1. Our natural measure of performance would be:

## Performance Measure 1:
### MEAN EU2

Look at the clinician data in Table E.21. If MEAN EU2 is to be our performance measure, then our best clinician is 50, with a rating of 85. As we saw in the last section, this is an outlier, far ahead of the other clinicians.

Will the reader accept 50 as our best clinician? We hope not. Look at MEAN EU1. This clinician's children started the year at 78, the highest average baseline score. They were all "M's." They may have done well after six weeks of therapy, but *we expected them to do well*. We would have been surprised if they had not done well. We do not normally give a gold star for doing what is expected. We would be happier with a clinician who did better than expected.

The quality of clinician performance relates to children doing better than expected. We want the clinician to solve articulation problems, but we do not want to give a high rating for doing what comes naturally. Our analysis of the data shows that high baseline children are likely to have a high EU2. We cannot label a clinician "good" for starting with high baseline and ending up with high EU2. Thus, MEAN EU2 is not satisfactory as our measure of clinician performance. Clinician 50 is not the best.

What is needed is a deeper understanding of the term "expected." We are concerned with the child's level of articulation. This will naturally be measured by the EU numbers. In common speech, when we talk of "expectation," we are placing ourselves at a particular point in time and looking to the future. We have some knowledge of the child's situation at this particular point and we expect a different situation to develop.

Our expectation of the child's articulation level involves predicting a particular EU number from information known before the EU number is to be measured. For instance, at the beginning of therapy, when we know the baseline score, we might predict what the EU2 score would be six weeks in the future. Or, we could predict EU4 from the other EU numbers. We only need to specify the point we want to predict and the point we are predicting from. This is what we mean by the expectation of the child's articulation level.

What do we mean by "better than expected?" The answer to this question forms a numerical basis for our prediction measure. Suppose we have predicted that a child will have an EU2 of 80, using the baseline score EU1 (how we made the prediction will be explained shortly). We now put the child in therapy, and six

| Clinician | Child | Predicted | Observed | Residual |
|-----------|-------|-----------|----------|----------|
| 1 | 1 | 60 | 75 | 15 |
|  | 2 | 80 | 72 | -8 |
|  | 3 | 90 | 92 | 2 |
|  | 4 | 75 | 96 | 21 |
|  | 5 | 93 | 82 | -11 |
|  | Average | 79.6 | 83.4 | 3.8 |
| 2 | 1 | 71 | 65 | - 6 |
|  | 2 | 90 | 87 | - 3 |
|  | 3 | 86 | 92 | 6 |
|  | 4 | 63 | 62 | - 1 |
|  | 5 | 89 | 86 | - 3 |
|  | Average | 79.8 | 78.4 | - 1.4 |

TABLE 5.4. Demonstration of residuals and Performance Measure 2 using hypothetical data.

weeks later, measure the child's articulation level. Thus, we get an observed EU2, say 95. We predicted that EU2 would be 80, and observed 95. It is common sense to say that the child did better than expected, but at this point we have a numerical measure of "better than expected," which is that the child is precisely 95 – 80 = 15 points better than expected. The process we just went through is called calculating a residual:

$$\text{Residual} = \text{Observed} - \text{Predicted}$$

If the child had only made an EU2 of 75, then the residual would have been 75 – 80 = –5. Negative residuals mean that the child did worse than expected. This also means that the observed score was less than the predicted score.

Clinician performance can be measured by the average of residuals over all of the clinician's children. If we think of each child as having a predicted and observed score, we can calculate a residual for each of the clinician's children, and then average them. This leads us to a second performance measure.

## Performance Measure 2:

### Average (Observed EU2 minus Predicted EU2)

Technically, this is MEAN EU2 minus average predicted EU2, and is an adjustment of the first performance measure.

Since residuals are important for our performance measures, we offer in Table 5.4 some hypothetical data for illustration. Here are two clinicians each with five children. For each child we show predicted and observed EU2. The residual is calculated using the formula above. For the clinicians we have the averages for each of the columns. The main point is that clinician 1's children did better than expected, and clinician 2's did worse. If we were to use performance measure 2, then clinician 1 would get a higher score than clinician 2. All of our subsequent performance measures, including the last one, will use this concept of residual, so all of the measures will give a higher score to clinician 1 than to clinician 2.

The obvious problem with performance measure 2 is that it does not say how to predict EU2. We will deal with this in detail below, but first we need to discuss an implication of the use of residual.

The formula for residuals can be rearranged to

$$\text{Observed} = \text{Predicted} + \text{Residual}$$

Thus, the observed score is in two components. The predicted part of the score is related to child properties like baseline, sound, etc. The residual is related to clinician performance. It would be better if we could break the observed score down further.

Observed score equals:

> controlled child property effect +
> uncontrolled child property effect +
> controllable clinician effect +
> clinician individual effect +
> other controllable effects +
> pure random error

The *controlled child property effect* is what we have been calling "predicted." It is typically the value of EU2 predicted from EU1. We will deal with this in detail below. It offers no difficult problems.

The *uncontrolled child property effect* is a problem. This is an effect due to child variables we did not measure or control. For instance, a child's sensitivity to peer pressure might affect articulation learning. This is something we did not measure or control. Ideally, children are assigned at random to clinicians, so this effect is *averaged out* when computing performance measure 2. Or, one might give some test to the children to assess their sensitivity to peer pressure, then adjust for this test score. Neither was done, and thus our performance measure is potentially biased. There is nothing to be done about this problem in our data, so this represents a specific weak point in our argument.

By *controllable clinician effect* we mean an effect due to some property of the clinician that might be used to adjust a performance measure. For instance, suppose we had a raw performance measure and discovered that clinicians with more experience had higher scores. It does not seem reasonable to score a clinician down for lack of experience, something that she cannot change, so we might adjust for this effect. This encourages potentially good clinicians. Unfortunately, one would need a large sample of clinicians to detect this kind of effect, and we do not have that large sample. This is a problem, but not a difficult one.

The *clinician individual effect* is the most important of the clinician effects. This is the part of the child's learning that is due to the clinician as an individual and not as a member of a group, for instance, the group of experienced clinicians. We will see later that this effect is very strong. It is the effect for which the clinician performance measure was designed. In the ideal situation, only this and the controlled child property effect would really be involved with articulation learning. The others would be controlled for or would be randomized.

*Other controllable effects* might include clinical environment, teaching method,, etc. In other experiments, each of these might be studied to determine their influence on articulation learning and on clinician performance. We will consider teaching method later (Chapter 6), but will not relate this topic directly to produce an adjustment for clinician performance.

This simple formulation of residuals lumps together the uncontrolled child property effect, the controllable clinician effect and the other controllable effects with the clinician individual effect and calls them the clinician effect. With our relatively large sample, it is possible that the child effects are averaged out, unless there was a strong bias in child selection for particular clinicians. Other controllable effects are not so strong. Thus, if the reader accepts these assumptions, the use of residuals to rate clinicians is reasonable. If not, we hope that we have provided enough discussion to help the reader delineate the various effects in other ways.

We can return now to our proposed performance measure 2. The problem is that we have not been specific about how to predict EU2. This is easy to solve. Our earlier analysis has shown how the child prior variables affect EU2. In many of these analyses, the R-square was fairly high, so some level of prediction is possible. This makes it reasonable to define:

## Child Performance Measure 1:

EU2 observed minus EU2 predicted from child prior variables.

We are applying our ideas about residuals and their interpretation as performance measures directly to the child data. For instance, if the child has a low baseline and is an /r/, then we will predict a low EU2. If the observed EU2 comes out higher than expected, we say that the child learned better than expected. The residual will be positive. If we now interpret the observed EU2 in Table 5.4 as predicted from child prior variables, each of the residuals can be interpreted as Child Performance Measure 1.

We are designing the performance measures to be used in the schools. They are not purely theoretical. Thus, we are concerned about the ease of interpretation of our measurement scales. Many persons find working with negative numbers difficult. Thus, the numbers produced by Child Performance Measure 1 may not be easy for school clinicians. Thus, we will transform this scale, using a simple linear transformation which does not change any of the scale's statistical properties. We can now take advantage of our large sample size and use the sample estimated residual variation (mean square for error) to adjust the residuals to mean 10, standard deviation 3. These will be recorded as integers.

## Child Performance Measure 2:

Performance measure 1 adjusted to mean 10, standard deviation 3, and rounded to the nearest integer.

The result of this adjustment will be numbers in the range of 0 to 20. A 10 child is average with respect to our children, 13 is good, 16 is very good, 7 shows poor performance and the 4 child did much worse. This scale is easy for clinicians to use. Later, by choosing only a few child prior variables for our prediction of EU2, we will present a table for the calculation of this number, so that no arithmetic is involved.

A note of caution: The child performance measure must *not* be used to grade the child. The child's task is to solve an articulation problem. The important score is the EU number. The R-square which results from our prediction of EU2 is not very high, and thus there is much unexplained individual variation in children. The goal of therapy is a high EU2 and EU4, not a high performance measure. For instance, if an /s/ high child reaches 75 at EU2, that is what may be expected. One might at that point terminate the child. The therapy would be rated as successful, but the child's performance is only average. Remember that EU2 measures one thing, articulation level, and our performance measure measures something else. It measures child articulation learning, compared to other children in the study.

Before we specify our final child performance measure, we have to solve a conceptually difficult problem. In this whole section, we are dealing with two different goals.
1. To devleop the formulas for clinician performance measures.
2. To use these measures to score our clinicians and make further statistical analysis.

The problem is that we should avoid trying to accomplish these two goals *using the same data*. Imagine using a very small sample, say two clinicians with five children each. If we use the same data to calculate the prediction equations for child performance and clinician performance, then we turn around and use these equations to score the clinicians, we shall see very exaggerated effects.

What we would like to have is two sets of children, and two sets of clinicians. With the first set of children, we would establish the prediction equations. With the second set, we would use those equations to rate clinicians and to measure the effects of those performance ratings on child learning. We do not have this two-set situation in our experiment, but we can simulate it.

We randomly divide our children into two samples, matched on baseline EU1, and target phoneme, SOUND. These two samples, called "A" and "B" will simulate separate experiments.

A sample—to calculate the prediction equation for child performance.

B sample—to rate the clinicians and for statistical analysis.

We can now define our final child performance measure, which will be called KPL for Kid Performance Level:

## Child Performance Measure 3, KPL2:

EU2 observed minus EU2 predicted, adjusted for mean 10, standard deviation 3; where EU2 predicted is calculated from sample A.

The "2" in KPL2 means that it was calculated using EU2. After some argument, we will create one more KPL score.

We can now return to a consideration of clinician performance measures. Using KPL2, we can improve the precision of the last definition.

## Performance Measure 3, MEAN KPL2:

KPL2 averaged over all of the children taught by one clinician.

Starting from this definition, there are only two corrections to make before we reach a final clinician performance measure.

The range of variation of Performance Measure Three is affected by the number of children used to calculate it. To understand this, take two extremes. First, a clinician with only one child. Then MEAN KPL2 has the same distribution as KPL2 (they are the same number). The standard deviation of MEAN KPL2 for this clinician will be three, since that is how we adjusted KPL2. At the other extreme, imagine clinician number two with 100 children. The standard deviation of this person's MEAN KPL2 will now be three divided by the square root of 100, which is $3/10 = .3$. If clinician one were to be evaluated repeatedly over the years, always using one child, then most of the time her scores would lie in an interval 12 points wide (using normal theory, $2 \times 1.96 \times$ standard deviation). Clinician number two's scores would lie in an interval 1.2 points wide. This does not seem to be right.

MEAN KPL2 will be corrected by multiplying by the square root of the number of children in the caseload.

## Performance Measure 4:

### MEAN KPL2 × square root of N.

This can be interpreted as either a simple correction as above, or as a t-test. It turns out that the t to test the hypothesis that MEAN KPL2 is zero, using standard normal assumptions is strictly proportional to our Performance Measure 4.

Finally, we will adjust the scale of Performance Measure 4. Again, we see the possibility that our performance measure will be used in the schools. KPL2 was adjusted to have mean 10 and standard deviation three. Clinicians who use this measure may get to recognize an "8 child" or a "15 child," just as many people react to, say, a 120 IQ. We believe that it would not be good practice to place the children and clinicians on the same scale, so we have decided to adjust the clinician performance measure to have mean 30, and standard deviation three. This is the final step.

## Performance Measure 5, CPL2:

### ([MEAN KPL2 – 10] × square root of N + 30)

CPL2 stands for Clinician Performance Level, using EU2. As with the children, we expect possible recognition of a "30 clinician," which is average, a "36 clinician" which is very good, or a "24 clinician" which is not very good.

CPL2 is a final choice as a performance measure. Let us summarize what led to it. We start by deciding to use our own data, even though it has problems. In particular, the performance of the child is used to rate the clinician. Thus, MEAN EU2 is a candidate for a performance measure, since our perfect clinician has 100 EU2. But, the raw EU number does not take into account the expectation of child performance, so we adjust it by using the residual, which is the difference between observed and predicted (expected). Our performance measures will all be adjusted residuals. The use of residuals may average out uncontrolled effects, but there may also be bias. A child performance measure KPL2 is defined as the residual from EU2, predicted with child prior variables and calculated on one half of a random split of our children. KPL2 is adjusted to mean 10, standard deviation three. Then the clinician performance measure CPL2 is KPL2 averaged over the clinician's children, adjusted for number of children, and adjusted to mean 30 standard deviation three. We propose this as a measure of clinician performance which should rate our perfect clinician very high, since it uses only EU2 among the EU numbers.

The details of the calculation of CPL2 and KPL2 follow. We conclude this section by looking at one final problem. CPL2, which is associated with EU2, is only sensitive to six weeks of therapy. If CPL2 is high, we have a good clinician, but what if CPL2 is low? What if the clinician's average child learns less than expected after six weeks? Is there not still the possibility that the children may reach a high level of articulation later in the school year? Or, the other possibility remains that the children will do worse than one would expect at EU4.

When CPL2 is high, we definitely have a good performance, but when CPL2 is low, it is still possible for subsequent learning to be higher or lower than expected. A consistent rating of CPL2 is associated with a good clinician, but CPL2 low does not specify that the clinician does badly. CPL2 low means merely "not good."

Thus, we offer a second measure of clinician performance.

## *Performance Measure 6, CPL4:*

This is the same as CPL2, using EU4 instead of EU2.

There is also an associated child performance measure KPL4.

We offer CPL4 for completeness. It should, in theory, allow a better assessment of potential and actual performance. Unfortunately, the two measures turn out to be highly correlated, just as EU2 and EU4 are highly correlated. Adjustment of CPL4 for CPL2 was considered, but this would not preserve the ease of calculation we required. We leave it in our analysis because we think that it may have practical, human importance as a "second chance" for clinician rating. If, with a particular caseload, a clinician has a low CPL2, then there is still the possibility of improving on CPL4. The only real purpose of any kind of rating system is to improve performance. Any rating system that reveals problems without indicating possible solutions is pointless.

One final caution. If our system is used, and if it is effective, as we expect that it will be, then the statistics obtained will be different from ours. For instance, the mean EU2 in schools where our rating system is used may be much higher than our mean EU2. All other statistics will be different. The statistical norm upon which our rating system is based will be destroyed by the use of the system. This is as it should be. We do not want children to have a mean EU2 of 45 like ours. We want clinicians to rate themselves, improve their therapy procedures, and end up with mean EU2 of 60 or higher. Thus, there is no point in preserving the statistical structure of our sample.

## The Prediction of EU Numbers

In the previous section we laid out the arguments leading to the child and clinician performance measures, KPL and CPL. We now present the details of the regressions used to create KPL2 and KPL4.

There are several steps in the process, the first of which is the establishment of the sample upon which we predict the EU numbers. In the last section, we explained that we did not want to use the same children to predict the EU numbers and to score the clinicians. Thus, our total sample of 1,108 is split into two approximately equal parts that we call "A" and "B." The "A" sample is the one we will use to predict EU numbers.

The AB split is to be done randomly, but we want two samples that are fairly well matched on the important variables, target phoneme and baseline. Thus, the split was performed as follows. Each group of children belonging to each project clinician was dealt with separately. Within each group of children, the /s/ and /r/ were also dealt with separately. Within each target phoneme group, we ranked the children according to their baseline EU1 score. Then, in the first pair of the EU1 ranking, one child was randomly assigned to the A group and one to B. Likewise, in the second pair, one went to A and one to B. This continued until either we ran out of children in this group or had one left. In the latter case, it was randomly assigned to A or B.

The result is an A group and a B group for each clinician matched on target phoneme and baseline. Combining the children into two groups, we ended up with 553 A's and 555 B's. All of the other child prior variables were compared across the two groups and were found to be nonsignificant.

In fact, we have such a relatively large sample, that it is possible to argue against the AB split procedure on the grounds that the two samples are too closely matched. One really does not see different results in the two groups. However, we continued to use the two groups for the reasons given in the last section.

Having the basic A sample on which we want to do our prediction, we next consider the choice of variables. Our first task is to predict EU2, using information known prior to the six weeks' therapy mark. Thus, we have available to us, EU1, SOUND, GRADE, PREVT, and KSEX.

As noted in the previous section, one criterion for the prediction process is that we can end up with a tabular presentation of the results, so that school clinicians can determine KPL without calculation. We wanted our tables to be small. These restrictions led to the selection and modification of the variables.

First, EU1, and SOUND must obviously be part of the set of predictors. To reduce arithmetic, we decided to divide EU1 into six equal frequency groups. At this point, use of CEU1, with its three groups would have resulted in the loss of too much information. More categories would have produced tables that were too large. At the same time it was decided to divide EU2 and EU4 into six groups for similar reasons.

There is one more variable, grade, in the prediction. KSEX clearly added little information so it was not used. Our earlier results indicate that the effect of PREVT is mostly contained in the baseline effect, so it was not used.

To the variables EU1, SOUND and GRADE, we also add interactions. We use the term interaction here in the sense it is used in analysis of variance. The interaction between two discrete variables is a set of variables formed by the products of the indicator variables. Thus, we add to the list of potential independent variables in our regression the products of EU1, SOUND, and GRADE. The reader will remember that one of our first results showed that the interaction between EU1 and SOUND was highly significant, largely because of the /r/ lows. Using the product of EU1 and SOUND in the KPL regressions allows the resulting prediction to be sensitive to effects like this.

Finally, the three way product was not included in the final regression because it has no significant effect on the dependent variable. There is also a minor complication in the coding of EU1, EU2, and EU4. As noted above, each of these was divided into six categories. These categories were assigned values which were approximate percentile values as shown in Table 5.5. Thus, for example, a child with a zero EU1 was given a score of .08 for the regression. A child with an EU4 of 90 was assigned a score of .58 for EU4 in the regression. Clearly, the values of the percentiles are approximately equally distributed, so that integer values, 1, 2, 3,

| EU1 | | EU2 | | EU4 | | |
|---|---|---|---|---|---|---|
| Category Limits | N | Category Limits | N | Category Limits | N | Coded Values |
| 0 | 84 | 0-11 | 100 | 0-46 | 91 | .08 |
| 1-5 | 100 | 12-26 | 83 | 47-73 | 90 | .25 |
| 6-15 | 85 | 27-43 | 93 | 74-87 | 93 | .42 |
| 16-32 | 94 | 44-60 | 91 | 88-96 | 107 | .58 |
| 33-60 | 97 | 61-79 | 95 | 97-99 | 84 | .75 |
| 61-100 | 93 | 80-100 | 91 | 100 | 88 | .92 |

TABLE 5.5. Coding of EU1, EU2, and EU4 for KPL regressions. N = 553 ("A" Sample).

etc., could have been used, but this complication is irrelevant in practice, since all calculations use the tables in the next section.

The results of the KPL regressions are shown in Table 5.6. For each of the two dependent variables EU2 and EU4, we give the regression coefficients, the simple correlation, and the significance level of the regression coefficient. Thus, the first column under each dependent variable is the coefficients we use to predict EU2 and EU4, and thus to calculate KPL2 and KPL4.

The interpretation of these coefficients is not easy. As noted in Mosteller and Tukey (1977) the value of a regression coefficient depends on all the variables used to form the equation, not just the variable to which the coefficient is attached. Thus, the coefficient of $-.438$ for EU1 in predicting EU4 does not mean that EU1 has a negative relationship with EU4. The correlation of .33 shows that the relation is, in fact, positive. What the negative coefficient means is that EU1 has a negative relation with EU4, when the effect of all the rest of the independent variables has been eliminated. Likewise, one would not say that EU1 had no effect on EU2 based on the nonsignificant regression coefficient. Instead, it appears that the inclusion of the other variables, and particularly the EU1 SOUND interaction makes EU1 an unimportant variable in the prediction.

The interpretation is clearer when we look at SOUND. It is an important variable, and its relationship with EU2 and EU4 is negative. Thus, since SOUND is coded "1" for /s/ and "2" for /r/, we can say that the /r/'s show a lower expected EU2 and EU4 than /s/'s even with the other variables eliminated.

GRADE adds a little to the EU2 prediction and has some effect on the EU4 prediction through its interactions. The interactions themselves are not easy to interpret. Clearly, EU1 × SOUND is an important variable in the prediction equation. This is probably connected with the SOUND × EU1 interaction discussed under child prior independent variables.

## Child and Clinician Performance—KPL and CPL

How to measure the performance of a clinician in /s/ or /r/ articulation therapy? That is the question to be finally answered in this section. In Chapter 5 our goal has been the creation of a method for measuring a performance.

The KPL regressions discussed in the previous section are not suitable for clinical use. Too much calculation is required, even with a hand calculator. Thus, we set up the categorized EU numbers, and made our selection of independent variables so that KPL can be looked up in a table (Table 5.7).

| Independent Variable | EU2 (6 levels) | | | EU4 (6 levels) | | |
|---|---|---|---|---|---|---|
| | Regression Coefficient | Correlation with Dependent | p(F) for Coefficient | Regression Coefficient | Correlation with Dependent | p(F) for Coefficient |
| EU1 (6 levels) | 0.155 | .68 | .177 | -0.438 | .33 | .003 |
| SOUND (/s/ and /r/) | -0.223 | -.18 | <.001 | -0.256 | -.24 | <.001 |
| GRADE (1,2,3,4+) | 0.067 | .24 | .028 | 0.026 | .06 | .507 |
| EU1 X SOUND | 0.330 | .50 | <.001 | 0.411 | .20 | <.001 |
| EU1 X GRADE | 0.014 | .59 | .624 | 0.077 | .28 | .038 |
| SOUND X GRADE | -0.031 | .06 | .065 | -0.042 | -.10 | .046 |
| Constant | 0.439 | | | 0.782 | | |
| $R^2$ | 0.54 | | | 0.23 | | |
| Standard Error Est. | .197 | | | .249 | | |

TABLE 5.6. Regression to create a model for child performance, using EU2 and EU4 dependent, and selected child prior variables as independent. "A" sample (N = 553).

To use the table to calculate KPL numbers, one first notes that it is divided into two large sections, one for KPL2, and one for KPL4. The first half (KPL2) estimates child performance after six weeks of therapy, using EU2 as the dependent variable in the regression, the second half of the table estimates KPL4, the child's performance at the end of the school year, using EU4.

After working with a child during the first six weeks of the school year, one can use the KPL2 table. The baseline EU1 score is needed at the beginning of therapy. The calculation of EU1 is discussed at the beginning of Chapter 3. The major point is that at least one three-minute TALK, preferably two, and at least one SPT, better two, need to be scored, preferably within a one-week period. All of the TALK and SPT scores are then averaged together to produce EU1.

One also needs to know the child's target phoneme, /s/ or /r/, and grade in school. Remember that grades 4, 5, and 6 are combined in our calculations. After six weeks of therapy, another measure of articulation level (EU2), is obtained, using the same techniques as EU1.

With these four pieces of information: EU1, SOUND, GRADE, and EU2, one can look up KPL2 in the table. You will note that there are eight sections in the table marked KPL2, one for each combination of SOUND and GRADE. One of these eight is selected for the particular child. Then use EU1 to select a row, and EU2 for a column. The entry in that cell that is common to the row and column is the KPL2 for that child.

As an example, suppose a child has the target phoneme /r/, grade one, and an EU1 of 3. Thus, we look at the section of the table labeled KPL2 R-CHILDREN, GRADE 1. The second row of the table corresponds to an EU1 of between 1 and 5. If this child has an EU2 of 80, then we look in the last column, which corresponds to EU2 scores between 80 and 100. Thus, the KPL2 for this child is 21, which represents a high level of achievement, relative to our sample, since mean KPL2 is 10 and standard deviation is 3.

### KPL2 — S - CHILDREN, GRADE 1

| EU1\EU2 | 0–11 | 12–26 | 27–43 | 44–60 | 61–79 | 80–100 |
|---|---|---|---|---|---|---|
| 0– 0 | 7 | 9 | 12 | 14 | 17 | 20 |
| 1– 5 | 5 | 8 | 11 | 13 | 16 | 18 |
| 6– 15 | 4 | 7 | 9 | 12 | 14 | 17 |
| 16– 32 | 3 | 6 | 8 | 11 | 13 | 16 |
| 33– 60 | 2 | 4 | 7 | 9 | 12 | 14 |
| 61–100 | 0 | 3 | 6 | 8 | 11 | 13 |

### KPL2 — R - CHILDREN, GRADE 1

| EU1\EU2 | 0–11 | 12–26 | 27–43 | 44–60 | 61–79 | 80–100 |
|---|---|---|---|---|---|---|
| 0– 0 | 10 | 13 | 15 | 18 | 20 | 23 |
| 1– 5 | 8 | 11 | 13 | 16 | 18 | 21 |
| 6– 15 | 6 | 9 | 11 | 14 | 16 | 19 |
| 16– 32 | 4 | 7 | 9 | 12 | 14 | 17 |
| 33– 60 | 2 | 4 | 7 | 9 | 12 | 15 |
| 61–100 | 0 | 2 | 5 | 7 | 10 | 12 |

### KPL2 — S - CHILDREN, GRADE 2

| EU1\EU2 | 0–11 | 12–26 | 27–43 | 44–60 | 61–79 | 80–100 |
|---|---|---|---|---|---|---|
| 0– 0 | 6 | 9 | 11 | 14 | 16 | 19 |
| 1– 5 | 5 | 7 | 10 | 12 | 15 | 18 |
| 6– 15 | 4 | 6 | 9 | 11 | 14 | 16 |
| 16– 32 | 2 | 5 | 7 | 10 | 13 | 15 |
| 33– 60 | 1 | 4 | 6 | 9 | 11 | 14 |
| 61–100 | 0 | 2 | 5 | 7 | 10 | 12 |

### KPL2 — R - CHILDREN, GRADE 2

| EU1\EU2 | 0–11 | 12–26 | 27–43 | 44–60 | 61–79 | 80–100 |
|---|---|---|---|---|---|---|
| 0– 0 | 10 | 13 | 15 | 18 | 20 | 23 |
| 1– 5 | 8 | 11 | 13 | 16 | 18 | 21 |
| 6– 15 | 6 | 8 | 11 | 13 | 16 | 19 |
| 16– 32 | 4 | 6 | 9 | 11 | 14 | 17 |
| 33– 60 | 2 | 4 | 7 | 9 | 12 | 14 |
| 61–100 | 0 | 2 | 5 | 7 | 10 | 12 |

### KPL2 — S - CHILDREN, GRADE 3

| EU1\EU2 | 0–11 | 12–26 | 27–43 | 44–60 | 61–79 | 80–100 |
|---|---|---|---|---|---|---|
| 0– 0 | 6 | 8 | 11 | 13 | 16 | 18 |
| 1– 5 | 4 | 7 | 9 | 12 | 14 | 17 |
| 6– 15 | 3 | 5 | 8 | 11 | 13 | 16 |
| 16– 32 | 2 | 4 | 7 | 9 | 12 | 14 |
| 33– 60 | 0 | 3 | 5 | 8 | 10 | 13 |
| 61–100 | 0 | 1 | 4 | 7 | 9 | 12 |

### KPL2 — R - CHILDREN, GRADE 3

| EU1\EU2 | 0–11 | 12–26 | 27–43 | 44–60 | 61–79 | 80–100 |
|---|---|---|---|---|---|---|
| 0– 0 | 10 | 13 | 15 | 18 | 20 | 23 |
| 1– 5 | 8 | 10 | 13 | 15 | 18 | 21 |
| 6– 15 | 6 | 8 | 11 | 13 | 16 | 18 |
| 16– 32 | 4 | 6 | 9 | 11 | 14 | 16 |
| 33– 60 | 1 | 4 | 6 | 9 | 12 | 14 |
| 61–100 | 0 | 2 | 4 | 7 | 9 | 12 |

### KPL2 — S - CHILDREN, GRADE 4+

| EU1\EU2 | 0–11 | 12–26 | 27–43 | 44–60 | 61–79 | 80–100 |
|---|---|---|---|---|---|---|
| 0– 0 | 5 | 8 | 10 | 13 | 15 | 18 |
| 1– 5 | 4 | 6 | 9 | 11 | 14 | 16 |
| 6– 15 | 2 | 5 | 7 | 10 | 12 | 15 |
| 16– 32 | 1 | 4 | 6 | 9 | 11 | 14 |
| 33– 60 | 0 | 2 | 5 | 7 | 10 | 12 |
| 61–100 | -1 | 1 | 3 | 6 | 8 | 11 |

### KPL2 — R - CHILDREN, GRADE 4+

| EU1\EU2 | 0–11 | 12–26 | 27–43 | 44–60 | 61–79 | 80–100 |
|---|---|---|---|---|---|---|
| 0– 0 | 10 | 13 | 15 | 18 | 20 | 23 |
| 1– 5 | 8 | 10 | 13 | 15 | 18 | 21 |
| 6– 15 | 5 | 8 | 11 | 13 | 16 | 18 |
| 16– 32 | 3 | 6 | 9 | 11 | 14 | 16 |
| 33– 60 | 1 | 4 | 6 | 9 | 11 | 14 |
| 61–100 | 0 | 1 | 4 | 6 | 9 | 12 |

TABLE 5.7. Two forms of child performance level—KPL2 and KPL4—for categories of baseline, target phoneme, and grade.

Let us look at another example. Consider a child with an /s/ problem in grade 3. EU1 is 0 and EU2 is 59. This child is found in the third section of the KPL2 table, first row, fourth column. KPL2 is 13. The performance here was better than average.

These examples show how the table is used. The reader should now be able to apply them in practice. Our next subject is interpretation. To gain some insight into what the table means, we need to see how it is constructed.

One can state quickly how the numbers in the table are calculated. They are the values of Child Performance Measure 3, given in the previous sections. We doubt that this rapid characterization is sufficient. Let us go into more detail. Table 5.8 shows the complete calculation of a child's KPL2 using the regressions. We will go through this in detail, but the reader should remember that this is for explanation only. It will not be necessary to do this calculation in practice.

## KPL4    S - CHILDREN, GRADE 1

| EU1\EU4 | 0-46 | 47-73 | 74-87 | 88-96 | 97-99 | 100-100 |
|---|---|---|---|---|---|---|
| 0- 0 | 5 | 7 | 9 | 11 | 13 | 15 |
| 1- 5 | 5 | 7 | 9 | 11 | 13 | 15 |
| 6- 15 | 5 | 7 | 9 | 11 | 13 | 15 |
| 16- 32 | 4 | 7 | 9 | 10 | 13 | 15 |
| 33- 60 | 4 | 6 | 8 | 10 | 12 | 14 |
| 61-100 | 4 | 6 | 8 | 10 | 12 | 14 |

## KPL4    R - CHILDREN, GRADE 1

| EU1\EU4 | 0-46 | 47-73 | 74-87 | 88-96 | 97-99 | 100-100 |
|---|---|---|---|---|---|---|
| 0- 0 | 8 | 10 | 12 | 14 | 16 | 18 |
| 1- 5 | 7 | 9 | 11 | 13 | 15 | 17 |
| 6- 15 | 6 | 8 | 10 | 12 | 14 | 16 |
| 16- 32 | 5 | 7 | 9 | 11 | 13 | 15 |
| 33- 60 | 4 | 6 | 8 | 10 | 12 | 14 |
| 61-100 | 3 | 5 | 7 | 9 | 11 | 13 |

## KPL4    S - CHILDREN, GRADE 2

| EU1\EU4 | 0-46 | 47-73 | 74-87 | 88-96 | 97-99 | 100-100 |
|---|---|---|---|---|---|---|
| 0- 0 | 5 | 7 | 9 | 11 | 13 | 15 |
| 1- 5 | 5 | 7 | 9 | 11 | 13 | 15 |
| 6- 15 | 4 | 6 | 8 | 10 | 12 | 14 |
| 16- 32 | 4 | 6 | 8 | 10 | 12 | 14 |
| 33- 60 | 4 | 6 | 8 | 10 | 12 | 14 |
| 61-100 | 4 | 6 | 8 | 10 | 12 | 14 |

## KPL4    R - CHILDREN, GRADE 2

| EU1\EU4 | 0-46 | 47-73 | 74-87 | 88-96 | 97-99 | 100-100 |
|---|---|---|---|---|---|---|
| 0- 0 | 9 | 11 | 13 | 15 | 17 | 19 |
| 1- 5 | 7 | 10 | 12 | 14 | 16 | 18 |
| 6- 15 | 6 | 8 | 10 | 12 | 14 | 17 |
| 16- 32 | 5 | 7 | 9 | 11 | 13 | 15 |
| 33- 60 | 4 | 6 | 8 | 10 | 12 | 14 |
| 61-100 | 3 | 5 | 7 | 9 | 11 | 13 |

## KPL4    S - CHILDREN, GRADE 3

| EU1\EU4 | 0-46 | 47-73 | 74-87 | 88-96 | 97-99 | 100-100 |
|---|---|---|---|---|---|---|
| 0- 0 | 5 | 7 | 9 | 11 | 13 | 15 |
| 1- 5 | 5 | 7 | 9 | 11 | 13 | 15 |
| 6- 15 | 4 | 6 | 8 | 10 | 12 | 14 |
| 16- 32 | 4 | 6 | 8 | 10 | 12 | 14 |
| 33- 60 | 3 | 5 | 7 | 9 | 11 | 13 |
| 61-100 | 3 | 5 | 7 | 9 | 11 | 13 |

## KPL4    R - CHILDREN, GRADE 3

| EU1\EU4 | 0-46 | 47-73 | 74-87 | 88-96 | 97-99 | 100-100 |
|---|---|---|---|---|---|---|
| 0- 0 | 9 | 11 | 13 | 15 | 17 | 19 |
| 1- 5 | 8 | 10 | 12 | 14 | 16 | 18 |
| 6- 15 | 7 | 9 | 11 | 13 | 15 | 17 |
| 16- 32 | 6 | 8 | 10 | 12 | 14 | 16 |
| 33- 60 | 4 | 6 | 8 | 10 | 12 | 14 |
| 61-100 | 3 | 5 | 7 | 9 | 11 | 13 |

## KPL4    S - CHILDREN, GRADE 4+

| EU1\EU4 | 0-46 | 47-73 | 74-87 | 88-96 | 97-99 | 100-100 |
|---|---|---|---|---|---|---|
| 0- 0 | 5 | 7 | 9 | 11 | 13 | 15 |
| 1- 5 | 5 | 7 | 9 | 11 | 13 | 15 |
| 6- 15 | 4 | 6 | 8 | 10 | 12 | 14 |
| 16- 32 | 3 | 5 | 8 | 9 | 12 | 14 |
| 33- 60 | 3 | 5 | 7 | 9 | 11 | 13 |
| 61-100 | 2 | 4 | 6 | 8 | 10 | 12 |

## KPL4    R - CHILDREN, GRADE 4+

| EU1\EU4 | 0-46 | 47-73 | 74-87 | 88-96 | 97-99 | 100-100 |
|---|---|---|---|---|---|---|
| 0- 0 | 10 | 12 | 14 | 16 | 18 | 20 |
| 1- 5 | 8 | 10 | 13 | 14 | 17 | 19 |
| 6- 15 | 7 | 9 | 11 | 13 | 15 | 17 |
| 16- 32 | 6 | 8 | 10 | 12 | 14 | 16 |
| 33- 60 | 4 | 6 | 8 | 10 | 12 | 14 |
| 61-100 | 3 | 5 | 7 | 9 | 11 | 13 |

TABLE 5.7. (continued).

This child's baseline is 91, which is very high. Our ability to construct a table for KPL2 comes from the fact that we categorized EU1 and the other two relevant EU numbers, instead of using them raw. Six categories were chosen. The category limits are found in Table 5.5. Thus, EU1 is first converted to one of six values, in our case to 0.92. We shall suppose that this is a child in grade 4, so SOUND is coded as 1, and GRADE is coded as 4.

The coded values of EU1, SOUND, and GRADE are multiplied to get the interactions. For instance, the EU1 by GRADE interaction has a value of 3.68, 0.92 times 4. Thus, we have six values for the independent variables. These are multiplied by the regression coefficients from Table 5.6, and the products are added with the constant to produce an estimate of the converted value of EU2. The value of the estimate in our case is 0.859 (Table 5.8). The observed EU2 for this child was 76. We note in passing that this child does not fit the usual pattern of

Regression:

| Independent Variable | Raw Score | Converted Score | Regression Coefficient | Product |
|---|---|---|---|---|
| EU1 | 91 | .92 | .155 | .143 |
| SOUND | 1 | 1 | -.223 | -.223 |
| GRADE | 4 | 4 | .067 | .268 |
| EU1 X SOUND | | .92 | .330 | .304 |
| EU1 X GRADE | | 3.68 | .014 | .052 |
| SOUND X GRADE | | 4 | -.031 | -.124 |
| Constant | | | .439 | .439 |
| | | | Sum | .859 |

Residual:

| Observed EU2 | Converted EU2 | Predicted EU2 | Residual (Difference) |
|---|---|---|---|
| 76 | .75 | .86 | -.11 |

Converted to Mean 10, SD 3:

$$\frac{\text{Residual}}{\text{Standard Error Estimate}} \times 3 + 10 = \frac{-0.11}{.197} \times 3 + 10 = 8.32$$

Rounded to Nearest Integer:

KPL2 = 8

TABLE 5.8. Example of KPL2 calculation for child No. 1, Year 4.

increasing EU numbers. The observed EU2 is converted (using Table 5.5) to 0.75. We can now calculate our residual, –0.11. This child had less than average articulation after six weeks of therapy, given the target phoneme, baseline, and grade.

We have shown that this residual is the basic performance measure that we want, but that it is not expressed in convenient terms. Thus, it is transformed, so that the set of performance measures from our A sample will have mean 10 and standard deviation 3. The formula for transformation uses the fact that the standard deviation of the residual is the regression standard error of estimate. The result of this transformation, rounded, is 8, the child's KPL2, which can be checked in our table.

The point is that the entries in the table are calculated using precisely the methods in the above example. EU1, EU2, and EU4 are converted to six categories, the regression estimate of EU2 or EU4 is calculated, the residual is obtained, and finally, the KPL2 or KPL4 is the transformed residual.

Now that we understand the use and construction of the KPL table, let us discuss the meaning of the individual entries, and the overall entry patterns. It is important to remember here that the average child performance level for the "A" children is 10. Most (about 95%) of the entries will be between 4 and 16. Four is 2 SD's below the mean and 16 is 2 SD's above.

The point is that the KPL table can be used to interpret the regressions and vice versa. Consider the variation in either KPL2 or KPL4 associated with the three basic independent variables EU1, SOUND, and GRADE. Clearly, change in EU1 causes the most change in KPL, if all the other variables are held constant. For instance, /s/ children in grade 1, may have a KPL2 of from 0 to 7, depending on their EU1. But, for EU1 held constant at 0, in grade 1, /s/ has a KPL2 of 7, and /r/ has a KPL2 of 10, a change of only 3 points. Similarly, for /r/ children, with EU1 still held at 0, KPL2 ranges from 5 to 7 with grade.

At this point, we expect the reader to wonder about the range of values of KPL. We have said that most of the scores should be between 4 and 16, yet the table has entires from –1 to 23. Consider the –1 entry in the table for /s/ children in grade 4. To get this score, a child must start the year at 61 or higher and end the year at 11 or lower. This is clearly extremely unlikely. Our previous analyses suggest that this is a practical impossibility. Thus, we have entries that are mathematically possible, but unlikely in practice. We also see that we must be careful in interpreting the entries in table 5.7. We can say, however, that an entry outside the range 4 to 16 represents a score that children are not likely to get.

The regression interpretation of the table should now be easier. Look at the regression results in Table 5.6. For EU2 (KPL2), EU1 is the most important variable, but it enters into the equation through its interaction with SOUND. Thus, we see in table 5.7 that EU1 causes the most variation, but that the pattern for /s/ children and /r/ children is slightly different.

The /r/ children can achieve higher KPL2 scores for low EU1 than /s/ children. The entries in Table 5.7 in the upper right corner, are higher for /r/ than /s/. The fact that the entries are in the table does not mean that they are likely to be achieved. In fact, this difference in the /s/ – /r/ pattern simply means that it is more difficult for the /r/ child to get a high EU2 with low baseline than it is for the /s/ child—a result that we have seen many times previously. The /s/ child in grade 4, starting at 0 and reaching 80 at EU2, gets a KPL2 of 18, 2.67 standard deviations above the mean. This is not likely, but it is possible. The /r/ child starting at 0, who obtains 80 at EU2, is supposed to get a 23 KPL2, but this is 4.33 standard deviations above the mean, which we would rate as almost impossible. If we look along each row of each table, and assume that most children will end up in the range 4 to 16, then the difference between /s/ and /r/ is apparent. In grade 1, an /s/ with a baseline of 0 may reach 60, an /r/ only about 43.

What is the effect of grade? According to the KPL table, not much. The entries in the small tables, compared across grades, change at most by two points. This is consistent with the regressions, where we saw that GRADE has a significance of only .028 in the EU2 equation. The reader may be wondering why the children one sees in different grades have different articulation levels. Why does grade not have more effect? The answer is that the effect of grade was never as large as that of EU1 or SOUND, and these two factors, particularly EU1, take care of most of the GRADE effect. What one sees in clinical practice is different children with different baseline levels. We have already shown that the higher grades have higher baseline on the average.

Up to this point, we have been primarily concerned with KPL2. When we look through the KPL4 part of Table 5.7 most of what was said about KPL2 is still applicable. The biggest difference is in the effect of the EU1 SOUND interaction. Note that the four parts of the KPL4 table which refer to /r/ children look much like the KPL2 part of the table. In contrast, the /s/ part of the KPL4 table shows very little effect of EU1. The KPL4 score for /r/ children is determined almost completely by EU4.

We have been discussing the interpretation of the KPL table. Now we will deal with some apparent problems. The table was designed to simplify the calculation of KPL for the clinician, but in choosing the methods of simplification, some information has been lost.

In order to make the table easy to use, we chose a small number of categories, six, for the EU numbers. The disadvantage of this small number is that there are some gross changes. Child number 244 in Year 2, SOUND /s/, GRADE 2, has an EU1 of 81, and an EU2 of 89. The child does not make much progress, yet the KPL2 score is 12, which is above the mean. Should not this child get a lower KPL score? In fact, if we look at the appropriate entry in the table, we see that, if a child has a baseline above 60, and an EU2 above 79, the KPL2 is 12. It is possible for a child to have an EU1 of 100, and an EU2 of 80, and still get that KPL2 of 12. Thus, we see that a child may make no gain, or may decrease in measured ability, and still get a good KPL score.

There are several reasons for this. First, the individual categories for the EU scales are wide. We are looking at one row, where the range of EU1 children for that row may be from 61 to 100, 39 points. Thus, the formula we use for regression is only loosely covered by this wide range. However, the reader must realize by now that we are talking about children with a *baseline* score of 61 to 100. Only 16% of our children had such a score. For example, only 17 children fit in the row which has the /s/ phoneme, grade 2, and EU1 above 60. Thus, this particular problem does not occur frequently.

The second cause of the problem is that the regression formula does not fit all children. For each of KPL2 and KPL4, only seven parameters were fit, six regression coefficients, and the constant. The models explain about half of the variation of EU2 and about a quarter of EU4. Thus, any particular child may not fit the model and may get a KPL that does not seem to be appropriate. All we can really claim is that when we look at a large number of children the errors will average out. The reader must realize that KPL is computed primarily as a tool to get CPL. We may miss the assignment of a KPL score to one child, but when CPL is calculated for a clinician with an ordinary caseload, then the KPL problems average out. *Do not depend on KPL to assign performance levels to children.*

Once reminded that only seven parameters were used to get KPL, the reader may ask why not use more. Ultimately, the answer lies in the choice of regression variables, which was discussed above. The final choice was a matter of judgment and convenience. But, we do not believe that more parameters would have improved the situation.

A third problem is that the KPL numbers are not simply measures of either articulation level or of gain. Thus, child 244 did not make much gain in six weeks, but, in fact is receiving a good KPL2 for having an EU2 of 89. This is not a bad state of affairs.

The final subject of this section is the clinician performance level (CPL). The ideas leading up to it and the essential formula were discussed under Clinician Dependent Variables. In that section, we chose performance measures 5 and 6 as our final methods. These are presented in Table 5.9, which is to be used by the clinician or the administrator to calculate the two CPL numbers. We have not constructed a table for the calculation of CPL, since it seems to be so simple. As of

1. Given the clinician's /s/ and /r/ caseload, containing N children.
2. Calculate KPL2 and KPL4 for each child.
3. Average KPL2 over all children, /s/ and /r/, to get MEAN KPL2
   and the KPL4's to get MEAN KPL4.

$$\text{MEAN KPL2} = (\ \Sigma\ \text{KPL2})/N$$
$$\text{MEAN KPL4} = (\ \Sigma\ \text{KPL4})/N$$

4. $\text{CPL2} = (\text{MEAN KPL2} - 10) \times \sqrt{N} + 30.$

   $\text{CPL4} = (\text{MEAN KPL4} - 10) \times \sqrt{N} + 30.$

   Round both to the nearest integer.

TABLE 5.9. Method of calculation of clinician performance levels CPL2 and CPL4.

this writing, a hand calculator which has a square root key can be purchased for less than $10, and this is all that is needed.

Table 5.10 shows the CPL numbers calculated for one clinician. Most of the work will come from calculating the two mean KPL's. The results can be checked in our table of clinician data, Table E.21, Appendix E. Again, we remind the reader that CPL has been adjusted to have mean 30 and standard deviation three. Since the mean minus two standard deviations is 24 and plus two standard deviations is 36, we expect most CPL scores to lie in the interval from 24 to 36. We would tend to rate a clinician with a score of 33 and above as good, and a clinician who scores below 27 as not good. We suggest the reader look over all of the CPL scores listed in the Table E.21. It is helpful to get an overview of the distribution of

| Child Number | 1 | 5 | 7 | 8 | 10 |
|---|---|---|---|---|---|
| Phoneme | /s/ | /r/ | /r/ | /s/ | /s/ |
| SOUND | 1 | 2 | 2 | 1 | 1 |
| GRADE | 4 | 1 | 2 | 3 | 3 |
| EU1 | 91 | 3 | 91 | 0 | 0 |
| EU1 Converted | .92 | .25 | .92 | .08 | .08 |
| EU1 X SOUND | .92 | .50 | 1.84 | .08 | .08 |
| EU1 X GRADE | 3.68 | .25 | 1.84 | .24 | .24 |
| SOUND X GRADE | 4 | 2 | 4 | 3 | 3 |
| EU2 | 76 | 80 | 96 | 67 | 59 |
| EU2 Converted | .75 | .92 | .92 | .75 | .58 |
| EU4 | 99 | 99 | 99 | 99 | 99 |
| EU4 Converted | .75 | .75 | .75 | .75 | .75 |
| KPL2 | 8 | 21 | 12 | 16 | 13 |
| KPL4 | 10 | 15 | 11 | 13 | 13 |

N = 5       MEAN KPL2 = 14.0       MEAN KPL4 = 12.4

CPL2 = 39       CPL4 = 35

TABLE 5.10. Example of KPL and CPL calculations, clinician No. 39, Year 4.

these scores now. They will be discussed in more detail in the next section, when we talk about the statistical analysis of the CPL variables.

One more question may be asked—how can you combine /s/ and /r/ to make one performance measure? We have shown that /s/ and /r/ children learn differently. But, the major difference we found is in the area of SOUND EU1 interaction. This is precisely what is taken care of in the regression equation. Thus, it is possible to combine children with the two target phonemes, since their special learning patterns are compensated for in the regression.

Four other variables are associated with the CPL numbers and listed in Table E.21. These are RANK CPL2, RANK CPL4, QCPL2 and QCPL4. The first two are obtained by ranking the clinicians on the corresponding CPL number. The ranks are arranged with 1 designating the lowest score and 61 the highest. Thus, for example, we see that clinician 23 has the best score on CPL2, with rank 61. This same clinician scores next to the top on CPL4 with a rank of 60.

The two variables QCPL2 and QCPL4 each divide the clinicians into three groups based on the corresponding CPL numbers. These will be used in the next section for statistical analysis. The construction and justification for these two is similar to other grouped variables like categorized EU1 (CEU1) and categorized EO1 (CEO1). There is a difference in that the QCPL codes were constructed by dividing the clinicians into three equal groups (except for the one clinician beyond 60). Thus, there are clinicians in adjacent categories who happen to have the same CPL numbers. For example, clinicians 13 and 41 both have CPL2 scores of 29, but one is arbitrarily assigned to the first QCPL2 group and the other to the second. Since we will be using the QCPL numbers purely for our own analysis, and not recommending their use beyond this study, we feel that this construction is justified.

In the last part of Table 5.2 we have listed the names assigned to the QCPL categories. These reflect the thinking discussed at the end of the section on Clinician Dependent Variables. There we justified the construction of CPL4 as a possible help to the clinician. If CPL2 is low, it is still possible for the clinician to put in extra effort and bring up the KPL4 and CPL4 scores. We have labeled the lowest category of QCPL2 as "not good," intending to indicate that a low CPL2 does not mean poor performance, merely performance that is not good. Likewise, the highest category of QCPL4 is labeled "not bad," meaning performance that may be very good. What the latter means is that the clinician's children had high KPL4 on the average. We want this to be rated good, but it would have been even better to have a high average KPL2, and thus a high CPL2.

The reader who has looked through the CPL scores in Table E.21 will see that CPL2 and CPL4 are correlated. We will explore this in more detail in the next section, but we admit that our clinicians rated high on CPL2 tend to be rated high on CPL4, and thus the conceptual difference between the two measures does not show up in the data. Still, we feel that the idea of the clinician being able to work to get a high CPL4 after a low CPL2 is useful. As we have said before, we do not expect that other clinical data will average out like ours. Our data should be used only as a standard against which to gauge improvement in therapy methods.

## Statistical Analysis of the Effect of the Clinician

We have constructed a technique to assess the performance of clinicians. This involves the measurement of two variables—CPL2 and CPL4 for each clinician.

Although the reader may still have misgivings about the meaning and applicability of these two variables, we proceed in this chapter to deal with their statistical relationship to the rest of our variables.

We will first relate them to the other clinician variables, trying to determine whether it is possible to predict clinician performance. (You are not to be left in suspense here, the answer is no.) Then we use the categorized variables QCPL2 and QCPL4 to divide the clinicians into three groups with differing performances. Using these groups, we can begin to assess the effect of the clinician on the child variables. Here we look at such questions as whether or not the relationship between EU2 and SNDEU1 holds after adjusting for the clinician effect. Finally, we are able to deal with clinical and experimental variables, using the categorized CPL numbers. These variables, NOSESS, NGP, YEAR, and GEOG, have been left to this point, since they each seem to be related to the clinician. This will conclude our basic exposition of the statistical results of the study.

## Statistical Summary of CPL

We start by looking at basic statistics concerning CPL2 and CPL4, and the associated categorical variables, QCPL2 and QCPL4. For means, standard deviations, and counts, the reader is referred to the last part of Table 5.2, Clinician Performance Measures.

The means for CPL2 and CPL4 are 30.8 and 30.5 respectively. These approximate the values to which we adjusted the means by the algorithm we used. They are as expected.

To deal with the standard deviations, we must introduce a new topic, one that is important in this section. The reader will remember that we constructed the CPL numbers so they would each have mean 30, and standard deviation three. It seems that the measured standard deviations are 5.9 and 5.5 for CPL2 and CPL4. This is a considerable discrepancy. Values that are near six are supposed to be near three.

This discrepancy between the measured and theoretical standard deviations is caused by one simple observation—*the clinician is a major source of variation in articulation learning.* For example, we will see in the next section that QCPL2 explains 14% of the variation of EU2 on the B sample. We will also see that there is no difference between the EU1 means across the QCPL2 categories. Thus, it is differences between clinical groups, and, we infer, between clinicians, that determine a large part of the variation in learning patterns.

Our theory (that the standard deviations for the CPL numbers should be three) required that the clinical groups, that is, the caseloads, be random samples from our population of children. It also required that they be treated similarly. Based on the EU1 means, we can deal with the caseloads as though they were random samples although they were treated differently. The clinician seems to make the difference. The result is a large standard deviation in the CPL variables.

Note that the largest CPL2 score (53), is 7.7 theoretical standard deviations away from the mean. However, the large observed standard deviation for the CPL numbers is definitely not the result of outliers. The standard deviation remains high when outliers are removed.

The statistics for the RANK variables are entirely a result of construction. Likewise for the QCPL numbers. Each depends only on the relative order of clinicians, and not on the value of the actual CPL score. These will be used later, since both the RANK and QCPL variables have some apparent "noise" removed, relative to the CPL numbers.

Having considered the univariate statistics for the CPL numbers, the clinician performance variables, we now turn to the relations between these and the other clinician variables. The reader will remember that the sample size here is at most 61 (the number of clinicians), and our conclusions cannot be very strong.

Table 5.11 gives the correlations of the CPL numbers with the clinician prior variables. We have already introduced the theme of the strong effect of the clinician on the child dependent variables, shown by the large CPL standard deviations. Here we discuss another theme—the relative lack of effect of other clinician variables. Our creation of the clinician performance measures was partly motivated by the usefulness of the idea itself, and partly by discovering that other clinician variables are weak in effect. In the table, only two correlations are significant, at no more than the .05 level. And, noting that CPL2 and CPL4 are themselves highly correlated, we do not see these two correlations as representing different

|  | CPL2 | CPL4 |
|---|---|---|
| CPL4 | .77** | 1.00 |
| DEGREE | -.02 | .05 |
| ASHA | -.10 | -.15 |
| AGE | .14 | .14 |
| CAGE | .06 | .06 |
| YRSEXP | .03 | .05 |
| SELF R | .20 | .20 |
| SELF S | .17 | .17 |
| EOI SUM | .19 | .23 |
| CEOI | .29* | .30* |

*significant at .05
**significant at .01 level

TABLE 5.11. Correlations between CPL numbers and selected clinician variables. N = 54 clinicians.

effects. What we can conclude is that these clinician variables are not related to clinician performance, but that there may be a weak effect from the EOI measure (rapport), at least when it is categorized.

We can also look at the possible relationship of the CPL numbers with the clinician independent variables by calculating chi-squares on two-way tables of QCPL variables versus DEGREE, ASHA, CAGE, and CEOI. These will not be shown, since the results can be stated simply—there are no significant effects at even the .20 level. We also tried categorizing the three variables YEARS, EXPERIENCE, SELF R, AND SELF S. This again produced no significant effects.

The unfortunate conclusion is that, with the sample size we have, and our selection of variables, it is not possible to find a good predictor of clinician performance. The only barely significant relationship is between CEOI and the CPL variables, and this clearly could not be used for prediction.

Given no single clinician prior variable that is strongly related to the CPL numbers, is it possible that all the clinician prior variables taken together will be able to predict some of the CPL variance? The answer is, again, no. We ran two multiple regressions, one for each CPL variable. The independent variables were the clinician prior variables. The overall regression was not even significant, so we will not report the details. We are forced to the conclusion that, among the clinician variables that we measured, there is no single one, and no combination, that will allow us to predict clinician performance. If nothing else, this suggests to us that it will be very important in any future study of articulation learning to have some prior measure of clinician performance ability. As we shall see, the clinician effect is strong, and we cannot see how to carry out a valid experiment in this area without taking account of it.

We would like now to survey the joint relationship of the CPL variables with all of the other clinician dependent variables. The latter set includes all the MEAN variables in Table E.21, Appendix E and all the variables giving the percent breakdown for the KLMO categories. Table 5.12 shows the correlation matrix for these variables. In order to provide some organization for this table, we ran a simple factor analysis (principal components followed by varimax). Note that we use this statistical technique only for descriptive purposes, not to test any statistical hypotheses. Table E.25, Appendix E shows the results of this factor analysis.

It seems easier to deal with the factors in reverse order. Consider the correlations. They tend to be high in value. These variables tend to be jointly correlated. The exceptions are % L and % OTHER. If you look at all the correlations for these two variables versus the others, you will see that the values tend to be low. These two variables are unrelated to the others. It is a common phenomenon in

| | MEAN EU4 | MEAN EU3 | MEAN EU2 | CPL4 | % M | CPL2 | % K | MEAN GAMMA | MEAN GAIN | % L | % OTHER |
|---|---|---|---|---|---|---|---|---|---|---|---|
| % O | -92 | -85 | -70 | -58 | -30 | -54 | -46 | -45 | -51 | -11 | 07 |
| MEAN EU4 | | 94 | 77 | 74 | 38 | 67 | 53 | 57 | 60 | 12 | -35 |
| MEAN EU3 | | | 84 | 71 | 38 | 72 | 57 | 72 | 54 | 00 | -35 |
| MEAN EU2 | | | | 52 | 58 | 69 | 52 | 64 | 16 | -40 | -30 |
| CPL4 | | | | | 12 | 77 | 50 | 61 | 68 | 18 | -40 |
| % M | | | | | | 15 | -21 | -11 | -40 | -28 | -37 |
| CPL2 | | | | | | | 66 | 82 | 58 | -12 | -38 |
| % K | | | | | | | | 82 | 67 | -24 | -35 |
| MEAN GAMMA | | | | | | | | | 66 | -16 | -32 |
| MEAN GAIN | | | | | | | | | | 43 | -28 |
| % L | | | | | | | | | | | -19 |

N = 61, 25 - sig. at .05; 33 - sig. at .01 level

TABLE 5.12. Correlations between clinician dependent variables. The variables are rearranged to emphasize relationships.

factor analysis for such unrelated variables to come out on the last factor. The last factor is just % OTHER and the third factor is just % L.

The third factor also has a .57 loading MEAN GAIN, but the correlation between MEAN GAIN and % L is only .43. We would not conclude that there is a strong relationship between these two variables, or between MEAN GAIN and the third factor.

Factors one and two cover the rest of the variables, but there is some overlap between the two. In the language of factor analysis, we do not seem to have "simple structure." Since the second factor has its highest loadings on % K, MEAN GAMMA, and MEAN GAIN, and CPL2, we tend to see it as measuring some variation of speed of learning. The first factor is loaded on % O, MEAN EU4, MEAN EU3, and MEAN EU2. These together make us think of a kind of final score. This is the same idea discussed when we introduced the primary dependent variables in Chapter 3.

Since our focus in this section is on the CPL numbers, we conclude by suggesting that CPL4 seems to contain both the concepts of final score and speed of learning. CPL2 on the other hand, though it is correlated with CPL4, relates mostly to the idea of speed of learning.

## Child Prior and Dependent Variables
## Adjusting for the Clinician

The important use of the CPL variables is to assess the quality of clinician performance in practice. In a sense, as we write this, we wait for you, our readers, to apply these ideas in your own clinical practice. We naturally see the potential improvements in articulation learning as justification for the difficulties we have gone through in creating these variables.

There is another use of CPL that we can apply directly to our data. We want to assess the effect of the clinician on the child dependent variables. The question is, "How does the performance of the clinician affect the child's learning?" This is the question pursued in this section. It is, however, a question that we know from the outset cannot be clearly answered by our experiment.

The problems were discussed when we argued for the construction of the CPL numbers. Ideally, we would have had the values of the CPL numbers *before* the beginning of our experiment, and we would have randomly assigned children and treatment conditions to a random selection of clinicians. None of this holds, so the reader must take the remainder of this section with a grain of salt. We do believe that it will be useful to pursue our question using our own data, as long as the reader realizes that all of the statistical results in this section are biased because the formulas for the CPL variables were created under the same conditions as were the dependent variables. We have tried to alleviate this problem with our random split of the data into the A and B samples. The CPL formulas and scores used the A sample. In this section we will use the B sample to do the statistics.

What we will do is look at the effect of the clinician alone, and then at some of the child prior variables adjusting for the clinician. The latter are the primary results. Would the conclusions still hold if clinician performance were used as an additional independent variable? We will show that the clinician is an important variable, but that the statistical results do not change.

Within this section, the most interesting variables are the two categorized clinician performance variables: QCPL2 and QCPL4. These divide the clinicians into three equal sized groups. For QCPL2, the high group are those who have the best performance, and the low group contains those clinicians whose performance after six weeks of therapy is lowest. QCPL4 is arranged similarly after 30 weeks of treatment (an entire school year). These two are our primary independent variables.

Let us remember our earlier discussion in which we noted that a clinician variable can naturally be considered a child variable. In this section, the clinicians are divided into three groups by each of the QCPL variables, but the children are also divided into groups. For instance, the high QCPL group holds those children who were taught by a clinician who showed high performance. Thus, we use the QCPL variables as independent variables for the children. In the experiment we would like to perform, the QCPL values would be known at the beginning, just as the child prior variables are known.

In that ideal experiment, our first question would be, "What is the effect of the clinician on the children's learning?" For our data, Table E.26, Appendix E suggests an answer. In the first entry in the first column, we see that there was no difference between the means of the three QCPL2 groups at baseline. This is exactly as we would want it, but, of course, using real data, one must insert a caution. The CPL scores were constructed using a regression that eliminated the baseline effect. Certainly, CPL was created on the A sample and we are now working with the B sample, but we must still refrain from claiming strong statistical justification for our results.

While there is no difference at baseline, at EU2, the difference is strong enough to explain 14% of the variance. For each of the dependent variables we have listed, either QCPL number explains from 8 to 20% of the variance. The groups of clinicians may be used to predict some of the variation in articulation learning. This major result was anticipated in the last section where we saw that the standard deviation of CPL2 and CPL4 is twice as high as it should be if the children were randomly assigned to clinicians after their therapy.

The QCPL variables divide the children into three groups. What would happen if we divided the children into 61 groups, one for each clinician? The results of this analysis are shown in the last column of Table E.26. Here the independent variable is CLINO, the clinician identification number. Now we can explain from 25 to 35 percent of each dependent variable. We intend the latter to show the strength of the clinician effect. It is not quite the analysis that should be performed, since, in our ideal experiment, the clinicians would be considered a random effect. We do not think such analysis is necessary to convince the reader that there is great variation between clinicians and that this variation strongly affects articulation learning. In any future experiment, or in any plan to improve articulation therapy, the effect of the clinician must be taken into consideration.

The next question is, "Given that the clinician has a strong effect, does that change any of our conclusions about the effect of child variables?" To answer this question we reran the analyses (described under Primary Results for Child Prior Independent Variables), adding QCPL variables to the independent variables. Since we would have to do this on the B sample, and because many of the analyses already have small cell sizes, this is not always possible. We have, however, run some of these and have found that the conclusions do not change.

We conclude this section with a few examples. Table E.28, Appendix E summarizes the means and standard deviations for SNDEU1 and QCPL2. Table E.27 shows the results of two-way ANOVA's using SNDEU1 with CPL4. These can be compared to the series of ANOVA's using just SNDEU1, starting with Table 4.4. Our summary, Table E.27, can be compared to the first row of Table E.9.

An immediate conclusion from Table E.27 is that QCPL2 and QCPL4 seem to have approximately the same effect. To save space, we discuss only QCPL2.

The next conclusion is likely to be that QCPL adds quite a bit to the explained variance. For EU2 we have now gone from 48% to 60% by adding QCPL2. There is a similar improvement for GAIN and GAMMA. Again, we see how important the clinician variables can be.

Finally, we note the absence of an interaction for EU2 and its presence for GAIN and GAMMA. Figures E.14 and 15, Appendix E should help us understand this. The EU2 plot shows that for each SNDEU1 category there is better EU2 associated with the better clinician performance. However, when we look at GAIN we see that there is no apparent effect of clinician category on the high baseline groups. The better clinician does not get more gain from the children who start the year with a high baseline. Second, the clinician performance category definitely affects /r/ low and medium children. The /r/ lows have a 50-point GAIN difference, depending on whether they are taught by good or not-so-good clinicians. We get this same kind of result for GAMMA.

Once again we remind the reader that our conclusions in this section are tentative because QCPL2 was constructed using the same measures that we are now using as dependent. But, we suggest that /r/ children with a baseline score below 33%, should be assigned to better clinicians. And that clinicians with less expected performance could be given the children with high baseline scores. Of course, this implies that the clinician's past performance has been measured, something we are clearly recommending.

## Clinical Decision Variables—NOSESS and NGP

It is possible that the reader is tired of statistical analyses that are overly qualified, and especially tired of analyses that offer some glimpse of an interesting and useful result through a fog. We ask you to bear with us, for we have two more important variables to discuss. As usual, there will be heavy qualifications to our results. But these particular variables are of direct practical importance to the therapy process.

NOSESS records the number of therapy sessions employed per week: once a week, twice a week, or block. NGP records the number of children in the small therapy groups, from one to five. In this section we would like to answer the question, "How should one best arrange for therapy with different children?"

Now comes the qualifications. We have with NOSESS a different kind of problem, one we have not dealt with before. The problem with this variable is that clinicians are nested within it. With one exception, clinicians taught children using only one pattern of sessions per week. The data under the NOSESS column in Table E.21, Appendix E records the exact therapy pattern for each clinician. We are also reminded that in Year 4 only twice-a-week therapy was used.

In our ideal experiment one would not confound clinician skill with NOSESS. One would ideally assign clinicians randomly to therapy patterns or have each clinician teach children at each of the patterns. Clearly this is not what happened in our case. We have no way of knowing whether, for instance, all of our

Independent Variables: QCPL2, NOSESS

Cells are count over row percent over asd

N = 555 (B Sample)

|  | NOSESS | | | |
|--------|------|-------|-------|-------|
| QCPL2 | Once | Twice | Block | Total |
| Not good | 151 | 78 | 14 | 243 |
|  | 62 | 32 | 6 | 100 |
|  | 9.0 | -7.6 | -2.2 | |
| OK | 39 | 94 | 12 | 145 |
|  | 27 | 65 | 8 | 100 |
|  | -4.0 | 4.0 | -0.3 | |
| Good | 37 | 107 | 23 | 167 |
|  | 22 | 64 | 14 | 100 |
|  | -5.9 | 4.3 | 2.7 | |
| Total | 227 | 279 | 49 | 555 |
|  | 41 | 50 | 9 | 100 |

chi-square = 83.8,    df = 4    p < .001

TABLE 5.13. Joint distribution of QCPL2 and NOSESS.

"good" clinicians chose block therapy because they might be more effective that way or whether they chose once a week because that is easier.

We will use as the clinician independent variable QCPL2. We have already found that results using QCPL4 duplicate those with QCPL2. Given that clinicians are nested within the NOSESS, our first question is to see how NOSESS is related to the QCPL categories. Since we are ultimately interested in the children, not the clinicians, we count up the children as they are categorized by QCPL2 and NOSESS. The results are in Table 5.13. Clearly, the two variables are highly related. The reason for this is also clear. Those clinicians rated in the lowest performance category are mostly doing therapy once a week. Note also that there are relatively few clinicians and children having block therapy, a fact inherent in the design of the experiment, and one that causes difficulty.

Returning to the main result, the observation that our high performance clinicians used twice a week therapy has no clear conclusions. As we noted above, it is possible that twice a week therapy improves clinician performance. It is also possible that good clinicians tend to choose to work with children twice a week. It is not clear that if a good clinician were to be assigned to see children once a week she would not still do well. These important matters must be left for another experiment.

We turn now to the main question—"How does NOSESS affect articulation learning?" If we perform a one-way ANOVA (not shown) we find significant differences between the means of the NOSESS categories on all the primary dependent variables. But, this does not turn out to be the last word. Table E.29 shows the results of two-way ANOVA's with NOSESS, adjusting for QCPL2. The

| | | EU2 | | GAIN | | GAMMA | | |
|---|---|---|---|---|---|---|---|---|
| QCPL2 | NOSESS | Mean | SD | Mean | SD | Mean | SD | N |
| Not Good | Once | 32.1 | 26.9 | 37.0 | 28.6 | -3.8 | 21.1 | 151 |
| | Twice | 35.8 | 27.4 | 46.6 | 29.0 | -3.2 | 27.1 | 78 |
| | Block | 44.6 | 32.1 | 36.3 | 36.9 | 1.2 | 21.8 | 14 |
| OK | Once | 48.0 | 26.2 | 50.4 | 28.5 | 12.8 | 26.1 | 39 |
| | Twice | 47.3 | 27.4 | 51.6 | 31.5 | 5.8 | 23.9 | 94 |
| | Block | 39.2 | 23.4 | 66.5 | 28.9 | -0.8 | 38.8 | 12 |
| Good | Once | 49.0 | 28.6 | 63.6 | 30.7 | 10.3 | 26.6 | 37 |
| | Twice | 61.6 | 25.9 | 61.8 | 31.0 | 25.4 | 28.0 | 107 |
| | Block | 70.0 | 28.3 | 63.3 | 28.6 | 42.1 | 38.8 | 23 |
| Total | | 45.1 | | 50.0 | 30.7 | 7.7 | | 555 |

TABLE 5.14. Means and standard deviations of primary dependent variables for each combination of QCPL2 and NOSESS. N = 555 (B Sample).

means and standard deviations are in Table 5.14. If we adjust for clinician performance, there is no main effect for NOSESS. In general, this means that one should know the performance level of the clinicians, and if one does, then number of sessions per week does not affect learning. One wonders about the significant interaction for GAMMA. This is plotted in Figure E.16. We must remind ourselves again of the relatively small sample size of both clinicians and children under block therapy. In the figure, there are only 23 children in block therapy who were taught by a high performance clinician, but they did remarkably well. This suggests that it would be very useful to do a study using block therapy, knowing the clinician performance levels.

We would like to have investigated the effect of NOSESS with other variables, particularly SNDEU1, but our sample size was not large enough for that. We are left with the conclusion that the best thing to do is another experiment to study the effect of NOSESS, but barring that, it appears to have been mostly eliminated by the clinician effect.

Number of children in the therapy group, NGP, turns out to be analyzed quite similarly to NOSESS. The major difference is that effects are not strong. There are two differences. Each clinician tends to have several sizes of groups, so we do not have the nesting problem. The second difference is that effects that were strong for NOSESS tend to be weaker for NGP.

Table 5.15 shows how children are distributed with respect to QCPL2 and NGP. The largest effect we see is that good clinicians tend to work with children in groups of four. The next strongest effect is that clinicians rated *not good* tend to use groups of three. The better clinicians tend to work with two in a group. As usual, we cannot infer cause here. We do not know if these conclusions are the result of the inherent performance levels of the clinicians, or whether this was one of the factors that caused clinicians to be rated high or low in our data. In any case, what final conclusions might be drawn about NGP is not clear.

Note one small discrepancy between the analyses. There were some children with NGP recorded as 5, and as 1 (individual therapy). In Table 5.15, these are not counted, thus reducing the sample size to 543. In subsequent analyses, five in a group was added to four, and individual therapy children were added to two per group. The numbers are too small to affect the results.

Table E.30, Appendix E summarizes the two-way ANOVA of NGP adjusting for QCPL2. The means and standard deviations are in Table E.31. As with NOSESS, a one-way ANOVA (not shown) would show significant differences between NGP categories. But, when adjusting for clinician performance, there is no significant NGP effect for EU2 and GAIN.

GAMMA, on the other hand has a mildly significant NGP effect and interaction. The means are plotted in Figure E.17. The figure is not easy to interpret. For children in groups of two, the clinicians line up as they might be expected from high to medium to low performance. But in groups of three, high performance clinicians seem to be associated with much faster learning. The same is true of groups of size four. A tentative conclusion would be that it would not hurt to assign good clinicians to large therapy groups where they would be more effective. Combining this with the NOSESS results, we would suggest that good clinicians work with children in block therapy and in large groups. But, our strongest suggestion is for someone to perform an experiment to test this.

Independent Variables:  QCPL2, NGP

Cells are count over row percent over asd

N = 555 (B Sample)

|  |  | NGP |  |  |
| --- | --- | --- | --- | --- |
| QCPL2 | Two | Three | Four | Total |
| Not good | 82 | 123 | 34 | 239 |
|  | 34 | 51 | 14 | 100 |
|  | -1.8 | 3.5 | -2.2 |  |
| OK | 68 | 60 | 17 | 145 |
|  | 47 | 41 | 12 | 100 |
|  | 2.4 | -0.5 | -2.4 |  |
| GOOD | 59 | 51 | 49 | 159 |
|  | 37 | 32 | 31 | 100 |
|  | -0.4 | -3.3 | 4.8 |  |
| TOTAL | 209 | 234 | 100 | 543* |
|  | 38 | 43 | 18 | 100 |

chi-square = 31.4,   df = 4,    p < .001

*12 observations not counted which had NGP of 1 or 5.

TABLE 5.15. Joint distribution of QCPL2 and NGP.

# Experimental Condition Variables—YEAR and GEOG

The last two variables in this section are YEAR and GEOG. These are labeled "experimental conditions" for want of a better term. Clinicians are nested within each of them, so it is reasonable to use our QCPL numbers to adjust them. Our look at them will be cursory, since it will turn out that they do not, of themselves, affect articulation learning.

The variable YEAR records the project year in which each of our clinicians worked and in which the children had therapy. For children, the values of YEAR are 2, 3, and 4. There were twenty-eight children who were continued from Year 2 to 3, but we chose to deal with these as though they were distinct children. Seven clinicians worked in both Year 2 and 3 of the project. These are recorded in Table E.21, Appendix E.

One hypothesis we might explore in analyzing YEAR would be that we have three replications of the experiment. This would imply that all of the child prior and clinician prior variables would show no differences across the project years. We analyzed two-way tables for YEAR against SNDEU1, GRADE, PREVT, and KSEX. There were no significant differences except for PREVT. In Year 4, a few more children had previous therapy than expected. Thus, we would say that the children tend to be similar across the project years.

What is different is the clinicians. When we ran YEAR against the clinician categorical variables, CAGE, CEOI, and DEGREE showed significant differences. These can be summarized as; Year 4—younger, with more rapport; Year 3—More MA's; and Year 2—more BA's.

Table E.32 shows the results of comparing YEAR with QCPL2, using the children as observational units. Again we have differences between the years. Year 4 tends to have children taught by "OK" clinicians, and "not good" clinicians. Year 3 is high on "not good." Year 2 has a few more "good's" than would be expected.

The question we are most interested in is, "Was the articulation learning different across the project years?" The answer is yes, but it is mostly caused by the clinician differences. We are seeing a pattern similar to NOSESS and NGP. When we run a simple one-way analysis of the dependent variables across the project years, we get significant effects. But, when we run the two-way ANOVA, adjusting for QCPL2, there are no significant effects for YEAR or the interaction for the primary dependent variables, EU2, GAIN, and GAMMA. The only significant effect is the YEAR main effect for EU3 and EU4. These two disappear when we run a three-way analysis, including SNDEU1. Thus, we conclude that differences across years are mostly caused by clinician differences.

Without going into detail, we can say that the same pattern of effects is true for geographical differences. Because of the sample size problem, what was analyzed was the two-level variable that recorded whether the child or clinician was in the Kansas City area or not. Again, there were clinician but not child differences. There were differences between the areas when clinician performance was ignored, and these differences were no longer significant after adjusting for clinician. Once again: the most important variable in articulation learning after the child prior variables (sound and baseline score) is the individual clinician and her level of performance.

# CHAPTER 6

# Data Unique to Project Year 4

An enormous amount of data collected over one school year from 27 clinicians and 194 children regarding their daily feelings (mood) is condensed in this chapter. Many data analysis procedures were used to summarize this information.

Additional child characteristic information, not collected in Years 1, 2, 3, was obtained for Year 4 to complete our analysis. These data added another dimension in our search for child characteristics to explain the clear-cut differences obtained in /r/ and /s/ articulation learning discussed in Chapter 4. The reader may be surprised at our results.

This chapter attempts to find relationships between the clinician's lesson plan and the distinctive articulation learning curves reported in Chapter 3. It also reports the lesson plan results of clinicians classified according to their high or low performance scores (CPL) described in Chapter 5.

Finally, data collected on the Tone Keyboard (TKB) by the clinician is presented. This information includes clinician stimuli, children's responses, and clinician reinforcement. Our results are contrasted with those reported in the literature.

For definitions of special terms and symbols used in this project refer to Appendix G in this book.

Year 4 of the project was to be the last year in which data were to be taken. Our focus was on clinician lesson plans and clinician-child interactions through the use of the Tone Keyboard to record what was happening in articulation therapy. But, because this was to be our last year, we also asked ourselves if there were other variables we might measure that might affect articulation learning.

Since there was nothing else about the clinician that we could measure conveniently, we naturally turned to thinking of child properties. We constructed a list of child property variables that could be measured without too much difficulty. These are listed in Table 6.1.

The question also arose whether it was possible that some aspect of mood might be affecting therapy. And, of course, whether that could be measured. Thus, we created the measure of Clinician and Child Daily Feelings, described in Chapter 2. In this section, we will deal first with the Daily Feelings, and then turn our attention to the child properties.

## Daily Feelings

It is unfortunate, but nothing seems to have come of our statistical analyses using the Daily Feelings variables. After trying several possibilities, we ended up using six variables recorded over the 194, Year 4 children. Each one of these measured the value of either the average mood or the change in mood over the whole school year. Each referred to either the clinician's attitude toward the child, the child's mood, or the clinician's attitude toward herself. The regression of these against the three primary dependent variables (EU2, GAIN, GAMMA) was not significant.

We do not conclude that mood does not affect learning. More powerful data analysis techniques may still find something useful in the Daily Feeling variables.

| Variable | Description* and range of scores |
|---|---|
| GFWP | Goldman-Fristoe-Woodcock Test of Auditory Discrimination (subtest in noise), Percentile (0-98) |
| PPVTIQ | Peabody Picture Vocabulary Test IQ (68-168) |
| TOKEN | Token Test (part V), total score (0-21) |
| DETROIT | Auditory Attention Span for Related Syllables (12-93) |
| READ | Reading Test, percentile score (1-99) |
| SIBLINGS | Number of siblings (0-9) |
| DIVORCE | Are the parents divorced? |
| MINORITY | Is the child from a minority group? |
| POOR | Is this child from a low income family, (i.e., less than $5,000/year)? |
| DDKK | Diadochokinetic rate ("da" in 15 seconds) (19-84) |
| BITE | 1 = yes, open bite; 2 = no, open bite |
| TOTT | Total Tongue Thrust Score (higher score represents more problems) (11 items) |
| TOTD | Total Dental Score (higher score represents more problems) (six items) |

*For more detail see Appendix

TABLE 6.1. Child property variables from Year 4 data.

The data are longitudinal, but irregularly spaced, so some form of smoothing (followed by the application of newly developed time-series techniques) may produce useful results.

## Child Characteristics

Let us return now to the child property variables. What we will report is a relatively simple analysis directed toward the question, "Will the child property variables help in predicting articulation learning?" We note from the outset that the answer is "yes."

When we survey statistics on the family variables, SIBLINGS, DIVORCE, MINORITY, and POOR, it turned out that they tended to be poorly distributed, and so were not included in the analysis. We feel that a larger sample, or an experiment specifically designed to deal with these variables would be useful.

Table 6.2 shows the results of regressions using the remaining child property variables as predictors for the dependent variables. Note that we have not attempted to introduce clinician or child prior variables for adjustment, since this would greatly complicate the analysis.

Each of the three dependent variables has a significant relationship with the set of independent variables. The least significant is GAIN, for which the significant predictors are PPVTIQ and TOTT. Both EU2 and GAMMA have a much

Dependent Variables

| Independent Variables | Mean | SD | EU2 | | | GAIN | | | GAMMA | | |
|---|---|---|---|---|---|---|---|---|---|---|---|
| | | | r | β | p(β) | r | β | p(β) | r | β | p(β) |
| GFWP | 26.5 | 22.8 | .00 | -.06 | .464 | .13 | .04 | .602 | .12 | .00 | .972 |
| PPVTIQ | 102.9 | 14.4 | .00 | -.04 | .594 | .21 | .19 | .028 | .16 | .08 | .322 |
| TOKEN | 15.7 | 3.0 | .21 | .22 | .008 | .04 | -.05 | .531 | .28 | .22 | .008 |
| DETROIT | 48.3 | 16.0 | .11 | -.02 | .802 | .08 | -.01 | .924 | .19 | -.02 | .850 |
| READ | 51.6 | 30.1 | .10 | .08 | .304 | .16 | .08 | .346 | .21 | .12 | .137 |
| DDKK | 45.3 | 12.5 | .15 | .10 | .170 | .07 | .07 | .352 | .21 | .15 | .046 |
| TOTT | 2.9 | 2.0 | .00 | .06 | .445 | .15 | .19 | .016 | .08 | .15 | .048 |
| TOTD | 1.0 | 1.0 | -.19 | -.21 | .006 | .06 | -.01 | .923 | -.12 | -.18 | .020 |
| $R^2$ | | | .11 | | .007 | .09 | | .037 | .16 | | <.001 |

TABLE 6.2. Regression of primary dependent variables on Year 4 child variables (N = 186) with means, standard deviations, correlations (r), standardized regression coefficients (β), and significance levels of regression coefficients.

stronger relationship with the child property variables. Remember that EU2 and GAMMA tend to be correlated. Note also the contributions of TOKEN and TOTD on EU2 and TOKEN, DDKK, TOTT, and TOTD on GAMMA. We conclude that child properties appear to be useful for predicting articulation learning, and suggest that adjusting for SNDEU1 (six categories of baseline score) and clinician performance level (CPL) might eliminate these effects.

| Variables | /s/ Mean | SD | /r/ Mean | SD | t | p |
|---|---|---|---|---|---|---|
| Dependent Variables | | | | | | |
| EU1 (baseline) | 27.9 | 33.4 | 35.1 | 29.7 | 1.59 | NS |
| EU2 (6 weeks) | 54.6 | 26.9 | 50.1 | 29.8 | 1.10 | NS |
| EU3 (18 weeks) % correct | 81.1 | 20.9 | 70.9 | 27.8 | 2.87 | < .01 |
| EU4 (30 weeks) | 90.2 | 15.6 | 82.7 | 23.1 | 2.63 | < .01 |
| Gain | 62.2 | 32.6 | 47.5 | 28.3 | 3.37 | < .01 |
| | | | | | | |
| Therapy Arrangements | | | | | | |
| Grade (1-4) | 2.5 | 1.0 | 2.2 | 1.0 | .93 | NS |
| No. sessions/week | Forced equal--all children had therapy twice/week | | | | | |
| No. in group (2 or 3) | 2.3 | 0.5 | 2.2 | 0.4 | 1.16 | NS |
| | | | | | | |
| Clinician Characteristics* | | | | | | |
| Age (23-49) | 30.4 | 6.8 | 31.1 | 7.3 | 0.66 | NS |
| Years experience (0-12) | 5.2 | 3.3 | 5.1 | 3.4 | 0.15 | NS |
| EOI (rapport) (97-138) | 120.8 | 7.2 | 122.2 | 7.7 | 1.29 | NS |
| | | | | | | |
| Child Characteristics | | | | | | |
| PPVT IQ (68-168) | 102.6 | 15.4 | 102.4 | 13.8 | 0.08 | NS |
| GFW (percentile) (0-98) | 26.5 | 24.0 | 25.5 | 21.4 | 0.30 | NS |
| DETROIT (12-93) | 49.5 | 15.9 | 47.1 | 16.1 | 1.02 | NS |
| TOKEN (total score) (0-21) | 15.8 | 3.1 | 15.5 | 2.8 | 0.68 | NS |
| READING (percentiles: 1-99) | 53.5 | 29.2 | 49.2 | 30.4 | 1.02 | NS |
| DDKK (/da/ in 15") (19-84) | 44.9 | 14.0 | 44.6 | 12.6 | 0.14 | NS |
| TOTD (6 items) | 1.1 | 1.0 | 0.9 | 0.9 | 1.43 | NS |
| TOTT (11 items) | 4.2 | 2.1 | 1.9 | 1.6 | 8.79 | <.001 |
| BITE** | 1.8 | 0.4 | 2.0 | 0.2 | 3.78 | <.001 |

*Range in parenthesis.

**Means are calculated on 1 = yes, open bite; 2 = no open bite.

NS indicates significant evidence was not obtained.

TABLE 6.3. Means, standard deviation, and significance levels for 92 /s/ and 101 /r/ children in Year 4 on several dependent and independent variables.

Another way to look at the child prior variables is to ask, "Are these variables responsible for the learning differences noted between /s/ and /r/ children?" Table 6.3 illustrates the comparisons. We note in passing that both /s/ and /r/ groups started baseline at the same level. Grade level or therapy sessions per week were not factors that determined the differences in /s/ and /r/ learning in Year 4. In another analysis we noted that previous therapy also was not different between the two groups. Also, less than four percent of the children in Year 4 had previous therapy on sounds other than /s/ or /r/. There are no differences between the two groups on therapy arrangements, clinician characteristics, or most of the child characteristics. It is interesting to note that /s/ children demonstrated more indices of tongue thrust (TOTT) and had more Open Bite (space between upper and lower incisors) than the /r/ children. However, we are unable to account for the /s-r/ learning differential on the basis of these results. We believe that there should be some variables that account for articulation learning differences. Therefore, since those we looked at have not been completely successful, future investigators should look at additional variables.

The daily lesson plan is a recording device used in project Year 4 to detail the clinician's cognitive plan. The lesson plan is discussed in this chapter, as is the therapy interaction as tracked by the Tone Keyboard (TKB). We also consider the possibility that, if learning patterns emerge in target phoneme acquisition, then it would be appropriate to make an analysis of the clinicians' lesson plan or therapy interaction.

## Clinician Daily Lesson Plan and Articulation Learning

### All Data from Year 4

As described in Chapter 2 (Methodology), 27 clinicians completed a form (Appendix C) that specified their cognitive lesson plan for each child for every therapy session during the year. Data were mailed each week to our project office to be keypunched. Descriptions of lesson plans were gathered on 212 children for over 19,000 activities for that year. The absolute and relative frequency of each category is indicated in Table 6.4.

The activity name with the highest occurrence is number 12—Standard Drill (20.2%), followed by number 1—Free Conversation (13.4%). The next most frequent were the standard probes used to measure our dependent variable over the school year, number 26—TT (10.2%) and number 27—SPT (11.7%). This was followed by number 13—Game Drill (7.9%), number 10—Chart Time (5.0%), and number 2—Structured Speech (4.7%).

It can be seen from this tabulation that number 17—Discrimination and number 18—Self-Monitoring made up only 3.2% of the activities. Because Van Riper's book (1978) has been a basic text since 1939, it was surprising to find that his cardinal step in ear training was not often utilized. Or, if listening skills are important, these clinicians believed that discrimination training can be accomplished in a very few trials.

Another observation is that these public school clinicians did not spend much time with parents or teachers, either in training or conference. The notions of Transfer Drill, Rate Drill, Negative Practice, and Response Shaping were seldom used. Fun Time—a period when clinicians engaged in a game activity that was not speech structured—was also rare.

| Name | | Absolute Frequency | Relative Frequency (Percent) |
|---|---|---|---|
| 0. | Missing Cards | 54 | 0.3 |
| 1. FC | Free Conversation | 2553 | 13.4 |
| 2. SS | Structured Speech | 902 | 4.7 |
| 3. Rdg | Reading | 864 | 4.5 |
| 4. RA | Review Assignment | 449 | 2.4 |
| 5. GA | Give Assignment | 858 | 4.5 |
| 6. PP | Parent Participation | 7 | 0.0 |
| 7. TP | Teacher Participation | 0 | 0.0 |
| 8. PC | Parent Conference | 27 | 0.1 |
| 9. TC | Teacher Conference | 5 | 0.0 |
| 10. ChT | Chart Time | 954 | 5.0 |
| 11. FT | Fun Time | 176 | 0.9 |
| 12. SD | Standard Drill | 3856 | 20.2 |
| 13. GD | Game Drill | 1498 | 7.9 |
| 14. RD | Rate Drill | 168 | 0.9 |
| 15. TD | Transfer Drill | 130 | 0.7 |
| 16. TTh | Tongue Thrust Drill | 183 | 1.0 |
| 17. Dis | Discrimination | 531 | 2.8 |
| 18. SM | Self Monitoring | 70 | 0.4 |

| Name | | Absolute Frequency | Relative Frequency (Percent) |
|---|---|---|---|
| 19. NG | Negative Practice | 51 | 0.3 |
| 20. Sh | Resp. Shaping | 223 | 1.2 |
| 21. ShD | Directions | 22 | 0.1 |
| 22. ShA | Auditory | 6 | 0.0 |
| 23. ShV | Visual | 6 | 0.0 |
| 24. ShK | Tactual | 1 | 0.0 |
| 25. MD | McDonald Articulation Test | 328 | 1.7 |
| 26. TT | Talk Task | 1946 | 10.2 |
| 27. SPT | Sound Production Test | 2237 | 11.7 |
| 28. TThD | Tongue Thrust Dental | 258 | 1.4 |
| 29. VS | Voice/Speech | 152 | 0.8 |
| 30. LB | Language Battery | 405 | 2.1 |
| 31. GFW | Auditory Discrimination* | 93 | 0.5 |
| 32. | Combination SM-SS | 5 | 0.0 |
| 33. | Combination SD-SM | 4 | 0.0 |
| 34. | Combination GA-SD | 2 | 0.0 |
| 35. | Combination TT-SPT | 27 | 0.1 |
| 36. | Combination SS-GD | 2 | 0.0 |
| | TOTAL | 19053 | 100.00 |

*Clinicians did not always indicate on their lesson plan (Activity Cards) "tests" administered once or twice during the school year; consequently, items like #31 (GFW) show fewer cards (93) than total children tested (212).

TABLE 6.4: The absolute frequency and relative frequency (percent) of activity NAME categories for all clinicians, /r/ and /s/ children, and for all therapy sessions during the year.

| | Name | Absolute Frequency | Relative Frequency (Percent) |
|---|---|---|---|
| 1. M | Model (auditory) | 2316 | 21.0 |
| 2. P | Picture | 2633 | 23.9 |
| 3. MP | Model Picture | 281 | 2.6 |
| 4. T | Tape Recorder | 46 | .4 |
| 5. E | Other Equipment | 38 | .3 |
| 6. O | Objects | 12 | .1 |
| 7. G | Graphic | 2339 | 21.2 |
| 8. CG | Child Generated | 2823 | 25.6 |
| 9. SC | Sentence Completion | 49 | .4 |
| 10. Ch | Chart | 234 | 2.1 |
| 11. GM | Graphic/Model | 138 | 1.3 |
| 12. PG | Picture/Graphic | 120 | 1.1 |
| | Total | 11,029 | 100.0 |

TABLE 6.5. The absolute frequency and relative frequency (percent) of all activity STIMULUS categories for all clinicians, /r/ and /s/ children, and for all therapy sessions during the year.

The STIMULUS categories used by the clinicians are detailed in Table 6.5. The most frequent item was Child Generated (25.6%). This means that the clinician did not provide a specific stimulus (e.g., pictures) and the child was expected to "make-up" the words or sentences. Use of Pictures (23.87%) was the next most frequent stimulus followed by Graphic (21.21%) and then Auditory Model (20.99%). A surprising stimulus was Model and Picture which occurred only 2.55% of the time. Auditory-Picture occurred more than Pictures alone, but clinicians apparently permit children to self-initiate speech more often than they expect imitative (echoic) behavior. This is probably a good clinical procedure.

The CONTENT categories are listed in Table 6.6. The Phrase/Sentence (53.96%) occurred the most, which was surprising. This indicated that clinicians

| | Name | Absolute Frequency | Relative Frequency (Percent) |
|---|---|---|---|
| 1. I | Isolation | 527 | 4.9 |
| 2. S | Syllable | 673 | 6.2 |
| 3. W | Word | 3623 | 33.5 |
| 4. Ph | Phrase/Sentence | 5845 | 54.0 |
| 5. SW | Syllable-Word | 11 | .1 |
| 6. X | Mixed | 48 | .4 |
| 7. SI | Syllable-Isolation | 36 | .3 |
| 8. WP | Word-Phrase | 69 | .6 |
| | Total | 10,832 | 100.0 |

TABLE 6.6. The absolute frequency and relative frequency (percent) of activity CONTENT categories for all clinicians, /r/ and /s/ children, and for all therapy sessions during the year.

| | Name | Absolute Frequency | Relative Frequency (Percent) |
|---|---|---|---|
| 1. I | Initial | 1892 | 18.0 |
| 2. M | Medial | 341 | 3.2 |
| 3. F | Final | 689 | 6.6 |
| 4. X | Mixed | 7343 | 69.7 |
| 5. Bl | Blends | 268 | 2.5 |
| | Total | 10,533 | 100.0 |

TABLE 6.7. The absolute frequency and relative frequency (percent) of activity POSITION categories for all clinicians, /r/ and /s/ children, and for all therapy sessions during the year.

do provide practice with more than just words. Phrase-sentence drill is useful in establishing carryover of the target phoneme into more complex linguistic contexts. Words were second most frequent at 33.45%. Isolation (4.87%) and Syllable (6.21%) make up the remaining content categories.

The POSITION categories are in Table 6.7. The Mixed position (i.e., the target phoneme is in the Initial, Medial, Final, or Blend Position) was by far the most common at 69.71%. Initial Position (17.96%) was second, the Final (6.55%) and Medial (3.24%) were next. These data suggested that clinicians typically start training the /s/ and /r/ phoneme in the Initial position and then switch to the Mixed position. The Medial and Final positions were not frequently used as discrete programming steps. This point will be discussed later in more detail.

One question we asked at this point was "Do clinicians use the same activities for training the /s/ and /r/?" We selected six clinicians at random and compared the ACTIVITY NAME category for analysis. Table 6.8 illustrates the analysis. Numbers in the left column refer to the actual number of times a Name Category appeared. The corresponding frequency is in the right column. The symbols indicate whether the Name Category is greater (>) or less than (<). The chi-square indicates whether the differences were significant or not.

It can be seen that two clinicians (C and D) did not use any different activity categories for their /s/ and /r/ therapy. The other four clinicians did use significantly different activity structures. For all clinicians, Standard Drill (SD) was used more frequently with /r/ therapy than with /s/. Free Conversation (FC) and Structured Speech (SS) were more common with /s/ training than with /r/. Reading was used equally. It was surprising to find that tongue thrust (TTh) therapy was used with /r/ children by clinicians A and B. Two explanations were possible: 1) some /r/ children also had /s/ errors and the clinician was working on both, or 2) an /r/ child could also have had tongue thrust (without /s/ errors) and the clinician was working to eliminate the "habit."

## Analysis of Lesson Plan According to Child Learning Curve

In the previous section we analyzed lesson plans from the entire Year 4. The next step was to determine if differences in cognitive lesson plans would emerge when summarized for the different KLMO learning curves. We also had the problem of summarizing the data. How can you describe the progression of lesson plans across time? We attempted to solve this by summarizing the data according to EU1-2 (first six weeks), EU2-3 (next 12 weeks), and EU3-4 (last 12 weeks).

| Name | A (.01) /s/ /r/ | B (.05) /s/ /r/ | C (non-significant) /s/ /r/ | D (non-significant) /s/ /r/ | E (.001) /s/ /r/ | F (.05) /s/ /r/ |
|---|---|---|---|---|---|---|
| FS | 74 > 57 | 22 = 22 | 22 > 17 | 71 > 47 | | |
| SS | 38 > 20 | 9 < 35 | | 12 > 8 | | |
| Rdg | 33 > 15 | 7 < 21 | | | 68 > 35 | 15 < 36 |
| Cht | 63 > 42 | 38 < 93 | | | 18 > 7   8 < 13 | |
| SD | 88 <121 | 52 < 86 | | 24 < 33 | 88 <209 | 108 <155 |
| GD | | | 17 > 13 | 45 > 28 | | |
| T̄ Th | 10 > 7 | 8 < 10 | | | | |
| Other | 7 > 2 | 8 = 8 | | | 67 >38 | 34 > 24 |

TABLE 6.8. The distribution of selected activity NAME categories for all therapy sessions for /r/ therapy and /s/ therapy for six selected clinicians. The chi-square values represent significant differences in the frequency of occurrence of lesson plan activities between /r/ and /s/ therapy for each clinician. Activity categories which had low level occurrence are dropped from the program and appear as blanks.

Extracting the data from the voluminous computer printout had to be done by hand and we were limited in time and money. We used KLMO categories to select children with distinctive learning curves. We chose as many clinicians from the three different geographic areas as possible. We also wanted to use clinicians who had more than one type of learning curve. Once those decisions had been made, then selection of children from a given caseload was done randomly. When data analysis time was exhausted we had 17 different clinicians represented as can be observed in Table E.33, Appendix E. Several clinicians (number 39, number 42, number 62) had "K" /s/ and "L" /r/ curves. Two clinicians (number 46, number 48) had "L" /s/ and "O" /r/, and one clinician (number 48) had "L" /s/, "L" /r/ and "O" /r/. Eight "K" /s/, eight "L" /s/, nine "L" /r/, and seven "O" /r/ children were selected. No "M" children were chosen because their baseline scores were higher than KLO. It was believed that study of the KLO patterns would provide us with the most information at this time about possible differences in teaching procedures.

## Comparison of "K" /s/ versus "L" /s/

In order for the reader to compare the eight "K" /s/ and eight "L" /s/ children, their personal characteristics are summarized in Table E.34, Appendix E. There were no significant differences between the two groups on baseline scores (EU1), Peabody IQ, reading percentile, Detroit Memory for Syllables, geography, and number in therapy group. The "K" /s/ group was significantly better on the Token Test ($< .01$) and they had older ($< .05$) children. The "L" /s/ group had a few more children with previous therapy. Figure 6.1 illustrates the K-L curves for the 16 /s/ children and L-O curves for the 16 /r/ children.

The summary of the two groups on ACTIVITY NAME, STIMULUS, CONTENT and POSITION for the three periods during the school year are presented in Table E.35, Appendix E. The numbers represent the frequency of occurrence of all categories for every child during the specified time period. These values were summed horizontally for the total within each cell. Percentage values were then computed. They total 100% in each case except for the CONSEQUATION cell. For this, a percentage was determined by tallying all occurrences of reinforcement (or token cost) and dividing by the number of activities counted for that time period.

What are the main differences between the "K" and the "L" learner? It appears from these descriptive data that the clinicians utilized similar teaching strategies (lesson plan), but by definition the "L" children took longer to learn the response. In other words, the response capability of the child seemed to determine the progression of stimuli that could be presented through the school year. There does not appear to be a qualitative difference in the teaching arrangements (ACTIVITY NAME, STIMULUS, CONTENT, POSITION), but rather, one of a temporal difference. That is, when the child was able to produce one level of response the clinician then moved to the next level of stimuli presentation in some systematic progression. That is most clearly seen through the year by increased spontaneous speech (FC, SS, RDG) and decreased drill activity (SD, GD) under ACTIVITY NAME. There were fewer auditory and more picture, plus child generated STIMULI. Under CONTENT there was a progressive use of Isolation, Syllable, Word, Phrase/Sentence and a predominant shift from the Initial to Mixed with little use of the Medial or Final Position.

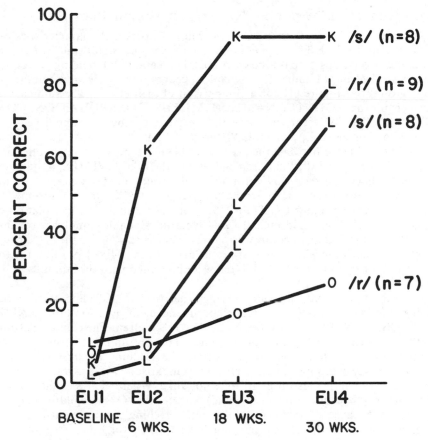

FIGURE 6.1. Illustrates average KLMO curves for selected /s/ and /r/ children whose lesson plans were analyzed for the year. Percent correct for Unified Score (SPT/TALK) and weeks of therapy are indicated.

There is one interesting difference between the K-L /s/ groups. "K" makes 56% GAIN during the first six weeks of therapy. In checking lesson plans the "L" children can make the sound in isolation by the end of six weeks. Why do they not like the "K" group, make a similar 56% GAIN during the next 12 weeks which is twice as long as the "K" children's first six week period? Instead, the "L" group makes only a 31% GAIN.

By inspecting the lesson plan data (and the Tone Keyboard data described later) it is evident that two things occurred: 1) During the EU2-3 period, the "L" children received more auditory stimuli than the "K" group during the first six weeks, and 2) the "L" learners had more practice at the Initial Position of words and less practice with words in the Mixed position. Clinicians tend to provide too many auditory models when they should permit children to self-generate more responses via picture or graphic (written) materials. The other point, which will be discussed later in more detail, is that there is greater learning when the target phoneme is embedded in the Mixed Position in words and phrases.

## Comparison of "L" /r/ and "O" /r/ on Lesson Plan Data

The nine "L" /r/ and seven "O" /r/ children's personal characteristics are summarized in Table E.36, Appendix E. There were no significant differences between the two groups on baseline scores (EU1), Peabody IQ, reading percentile, Token Test, Detroit Memory for Syllables, geography, grade and number in therapy group. See Figure 6.1 for a comparison of their curves. The summary of the two groups on ACTIVITY NAME, STIMULUS, CONSEQUATION, CONTENT, and POSITION for the three time periods during the school year are presented in Appendix E, Tables E.40 through E.50.

The big difference between the /r/ "L" and "O" learners was seen in the first six weeks of therapy. The "L" children had 54% of their ACTIVITIES in Standard or Game Drill compared to 39% for the "O" group. Fifty-six percent of the stimulus was auditory (M + MP) for the "L," but only 48% for the "O" group. The "L" children received under CONTENT 57% of their stimulation in Isolation or Syllable, but the "O" /r/ children had a 26% Isolation-Syllable stimulus. Note that for the "L" group, Initial Position was 64% compared to 47% for the "O" group. Also observe that only 22% of the stimulus came in the Mixed position for the "L," but 47% of the time the "O" children were presented with the stimulus in the Mixed Position.

These descriptive data provide evidence that the /r/ "O" children were not receiving the same qualitative teaching arrangement (ACTIVITY NAME, STIMULUS, CONTENT, POSITION) as the "L" children. The causal question: Was this the reason for their not learning? The presumptive answer is yes. Contrary to the /s/ K-L comparison, where the teaching arrangements were similar for the two groups, in the /r/ L-O comparison, the program teaching arrangements (cognitive lesson plan) were not alike. Where "L" /s/ children may not have learned because of intrinsic (child) reasons, the "O" /r/ children may not have learned because of intrinsic or different teaching arrangements. And of course, children in both groups may not have learned for other reasons.

## Comparison of "L" /s/ and "L" /r/ on Lesson Plans

We have discussed /s/ K-L and /r/ L-O learning curves. Now let us look at the same learning curve (L) with two different phonemes, /s/ and /r/ (Tables E.35 and E.37, Appendix E).

There is considerable qualitative similarity between the /s/ and /r/ "L" pattern of percent for the activity name, stimulus, content, and position. The difference appears to be that /s/ children had more auditory stimulation (especially in the first 18 weeks of therapy). The /r/ children got more stimulus presentation in the word/phrase categories. They also received more practice in the medial, final and blend positions. However, both the /r/ and /s/ "L" curves had far more initial and mixed stimuli than medial or final, indicating that once the target phoneme was produced in the initial position, clinicians generally emphasized embedding the phoneme in the mixed position in words and phrases.

## Summary of Time, Sessions, and Activities for KLO Learning Curves

Each clinician noted on the lesson plan the time to the nearest minute spent in therapy. Total time does not include the probe tasks (SPT took three to five minutes and TALK was three minutes) which came every two weeks. A summary of these data for the four groups of learners for the school year is in Table E.38, Appendix E. It is clear that the "K" /s/ learners had the least amount of therapy time (6–9 hours) followed by "L" /s/-/r/ (9-10 hours), and "O" /r/ had the most time with 12 hours. The most striking observation is that all children were scheduled for twice a week therapy, 20-30 minutes in length. With this schedule they should have received in 30 weeks (most schools have a 36 week year) anywhere from 20-30 hours of therapy. Our records show that in the /s/ "K" groups all eight children were in therapy less than 30 weeks (range 12-29, $\overline{X}$ = 22), six of the eight /s/ "L" were less than 30 weeks, three of the nine /r/ "L" were less than 30 weeks, and all seven /r/ "O" children were in therapy for 30 weeks. All children started therapy after October 1, 1972, and none went beyond May 30, 1973 (approximately 31 weeks, minus the week for Christmas, equals 30). Screening and scheduling were done in September. Looking more closely, we see that the "K" /s/ group had an average of 24 sessions and a mean of 22 therapy weeks for the year. For the "O" /r/ group, all children were seen for the entire year (30 weeks) with an average of 40 sessions which amounts to 1.3 sessions per week. This means that there was no real difference in the amount of therapy impact received by the fast or slow learners, both were actually seen in therapy slightly more than once a week. Dublinske and Bruntzel (1974) reported in a work study of 143 clinicians in the state of Kansas, that two-thirds of their time was spent in remediation (therapy) which did not include diagnostic evaluations, consultations, or screening. The difference in real time spent in therapy reported by our clinicians is quite different from the expected projected time. It indicates that holidays, school events, sickness, transfer from class to speech office, and "getting ready" for therapy all subtract from real therapy time.

The average session length was 17-18 minutes for all children and an ACTIVITY averaged seven to eight minutes. Clinicians utilized an average of two to three activities for each therapy session. No real differences were apparent across the groups.

From another point of view, speech therapy time with the "K" and "L" children was surprisingly brief. The hours reported were for group therapy and therefore reflected the total time the child was in therapy. Some individual therapy programs boast correction in three to six hours. These "K" /s/ children did almost as well in group therapy. We continued to be impressed with the observation that public school therapy was relatively efficient in getting many children to criterion (high percent correct in conversation), but clinicians fail to dismiss the children from therapy after reaching criterion (see discussion under Termination Criteria, Chapter 7).

In a survey of 15 school clinicians which asked them to estimate the average length of time in hours it takes to teach a child to be 85-90% correct in ten minutes of conversation, the following average times were obtained (the range is in parenthesis):

| | | |
|---|---|---|
| Frontal Lisp | 38 hours | (8-195) |
| Lateral Lisp | 55 hours | (7-200) |
| Consonant /r/ | 38 hours | (5-130) |
| Vowel /r/ | 53 hours | (5-210) |

The clinicians of course qualified their estimates by such statements as "it all depends upon the child," etc. Nevertheless, their estimates suggested that the average /s/ or /r/ child takes at least a full year of therapy. These clinicians also reflected the prevalent notion that frontal lisp is easier to correct than lateral lisp and consonantal /r/ easier than vowel /r/ (see Chapter 8 for additional data on this point).

## Analysis of Lesson Plan Data According to Clinician Performance

By comparing lesson plan data with the child's learning curve we hoped to do a *post hoc* analysis of the clinician's lesson plans to isolate differences in therapy approaches. Although some trends were observed and discussed, another analysis seemed appropriate. In Chapter 5 we reported on the great differences in clinician performance level (CPL) found in our study. We were curious about what would be discerned in lesson plan programming if we divided the 27 clinicians in Year 4 into high and low CPL groups. We had lesson plan data only on clinicians from Year 4. We chose for comparison seven clinicians who had the highest and seven who had the lowest CPL scores in that year. These two groups of clinicians had significantly ($< .001$) different scores at both CPL2 (6 weeks) and CPL4 (30 weeks). Table E.39, Appendix E illustrates the distribution of the /s/ and /r/ children and dependent variables for the two groups of clinicians. There were no significant differences between the baseline (EU1) scores of the children in the two groups. There were significant differences between high and low performance clinicians on EU2 (six weeks after therapy began), GAIN for the school year (after 30 weeks), and speed of learning GAMMA. Would this comparison reveal any differences in the cognitive planning done by the clinicians over the school year?

A similar analysis of the clinician lesson plans (as reported above) was made. These data were analyzed by ACTIVITY NAME, STIMULUS, CONTENT, and POSITION for EU1-2 (first six weeks of therapy), EU2-3 (next 12 weeks), EU3-4 (last 12 weeks). One additional breakdown was included. It divided the children's baseline scores into low (0-6%, Table E.40, Appendix E), medium (7-33%, Table E.41, Appendix E), high (34-100%, Table E.42, Appendix E), and finally, in order to increase the size "N," grouping low and medium (Table E.43, Appendix E) baseline children together.

## Analysis of High/Low CPL with /r/ Children

Because there were only four baseline /r/ children for the low CPL group (Table E.40) comparisons may not be valid. It is instructive to note that during the first six weeks of therapy, the low CPL group planned much more training of the target phoneme /r/ in isolation drill (33% to 11%) and high CPL planned less use of the phoneme in the Initial Position (38% to 59%) and much more in the Final Position (19% to 5%).

Looking at Table E.41, Appendix E there were eight medium baseline children in each group. Under ACTIVITY NAME, the high CPL group planned more standard drill (SD) in the first six weeks than the low CPL group (44% to 28%). The high CPL group planned under STIMULUS more (M) modeling (50% to 37%), and less (G) graphics (10% to 34%) than the low CPL group. Under CONTENT high CPL anticipated practicing less time on the sound in (I) isolation (6% to 11%) than the low CPL group. Finally, during the first six weeks, the high CPL group under POSITION planned much less use of the target phoneme in the (I) Initial (26% to 41%) and more use in the (F) Final (15% to 4%) compared to the low CPL group. The consonant /r/ was defined as initial CV (run) and blends (truck), with the allophones stressed vocalic / ɝ / (girl) and unstressed post vocalic / ɚ / (board) in the Medial Position, and unstressed / ɚ / (mother) generally in the Final Position. Words such as "carrot," depending upon pronunciation, may have both unstressed / ɚ / and consonant /r/. The point is that words that contain so-called medial and final /r/ sounds are richer in a variety of the /r/ allophones than just use of the initial /r/. Whether the more frequent use of "Medial" and "Final" POSITION in the high CPL during the first six weeks is important or not is unknown. Also, note that both high and low CPL used the same high percentage of words in all (mixed) positions (53% and 54%). In the next twelve weeks of therapy (EU2-3), the high CPL group surpassed the low group (65% to 57%) in mixed position, which may be reflected by the increased use of phrases under content (46% to 38%). The more frequent planned use of isolation drill and the Initial Position by the low CPL groups appeared in the high baseline group during the first six-week period (Table E.42, Appendix E). And when the data were collapsed for both low and medium baseline children for the entire year (Table E.43, Appendix E), the two most apparent differences were the lesser planned use of Initial Position (16% to 32%) and greater use of the Mixed Position (64% to 54%) by the high CPL group.

Summary observations of clinicians who had high performance levels versus low performance levels for /r/ children (Tables E.40 through E.44, Appendix E) include the following.

*Activity Name*: Free conversation (FC), structured speech (SS), and reading (Rdg) activities have different use between the two groups. High CPL planned less FC and much more SS and Rdg in therapy. They also used fewer game drill (GD). The rest of the scheduled activities were very similar for the two groups.

*Stimulus*: High CPL used more picture (P) and fewer auditory models (M) than low CPL.

*Content*: During the first six weeks of therapy, high CPL planned less Isolation (I) and more word (W) Content for the /r/ low baseline group; and less Isolation and more Phrases (Ph) for the high baseline group compared to low CPL.

High CPL used more phrase/sentences than low CPL throughout the year (first six weeks, next 12 weeks, and last 12 weeks of therapy).

*Position*: High CPL used fewer Initial (I) and more Final (F), blends (Bl), and Mixed (M) Position than low CPL. The latter clinicians appeared to dwell on the Initial Position whether early in therapy (first six weeks) or with high, medium, or low baseline children. The use of "final" (usually unstressed / ɚ /) and "medial" (stressed / ɝ / and unstressed / ɚ /) increases the practice of those vowel allophones of /r/. The Initial and Blend Position contain the consonant /r/. High CPL used more blends.

*Consequation*: No particular pattern could be discerned.

## Analysis of High/Low CPL with /s/ Children

Table E.45, Appendix E summarizes /s/ low children. Few disparities between the two groups were noted for ACTIVITY NAME and STIMULUS. The most obvious and interesting differences between high and low performance clinicians were in the first six weeks where the planned use of isolation under CON-

TENT occurs twice as often for low CPL than high CPL (25% to 12%). High CPL anticipated using less Initial and more Mixed Position than low CPL. Eye-balling subsequent time periods (EU2-3 and EU3-4), one may observe the systematic percentage increase in isolation, syllable, word, and phrases under CONTENT and, at first, the high use of Initial Position, but predominant use of Mixed Position high CPL group. The low CPL group seems to start that way but in the next two time periods (EU2-3 and EU3-4) they use more Initial Position (Tables E.45 and E.46, Appendix E). We presume that is because the children were not acquiring the /s/ phoneme as quickly as those children in the high CPL group.

Table E.47, Appendix E was not very informative because only three high /s/ children existed in each group. By combining the /s/ low and medium children, Table E.48, Appendix E illustrates more clearly that during the first six weeks, the high CPL planned less Initial and more Mixed Position activities than the low CPL. Since the children with high CPL made their greatest improvement in the first six weeks of therapy it was surprising to see so little difference in the clinician's lesson plans during this period. Analysis of the data over the entire year for low and medium children (Table E.49, Appendix E) and all the children (low, medium, and high) also were not very revealing (Table E.50, Appendix E).

Summary statements from clinicians who had high performance levels versus clinicians with low performance levels for /s/ children are presented in Tables E.45 through E.50, Appendix E.

*Activity Name*: Not much difference to be seen between high and low CPL.

*Stimulus*: High CPL used fewer auditory models, more pictures, and more reading.

*Content*: During the first six weeks of therapy, high CPL used fewer isolations and more syllable drill. They also used more phrases than words compared to the low CPL. When working with the low baseline children (0-6%), the low CPL used isolation drill twice as often as high CPL during the first six weeks of therapy.

*Position*: High CPL used fewer Initial and more Mixed Position than low CPL at early-mid-late therapy time as well as with high, medium, and low baseline children. Both high and low CPL used Medial and Final Position less than 7% of the time as separate drill categories.

## Conclusion

The differences observed in the cognitive lesson plans between the high and low performing clinicians were not dramatic. They were in fact disappointing, since we hoped to demonstrate more clear-cut differences in the lesson plan data to account for the significant differences in the children's performance (EU2 scores, GAIN, and GAMMA, Table E.39, Appendix E). Elbert and McReynolds (1975) demonstrated no particular pattern of generalization after training on four /r/ allophones. Their study would tend to diminish the effect of position or context in /r/ learning. Our less-than-obvious results reported above would lead one to speculate that reasons other than content and position (or any other lesson plan variable) may be more important in determining why some clinicians and children do better than others. This was true for both the /r/ and /s/. As with many analyses in this study, we continue to fail to uncover unitary variables that can explain gross differences in articulation learning in /r/ and /s/ children.

Multiple factors—in their aggregate—appear to have specified effects (Chapter 4 and 5).

## Summary Discussion of Lesson Plan Materials

The high use of the mixed position category observed with "L" /r/ and /s/ was also found in the "K" /s/ group. Since both "K" and "L" children were successful, this observation should be carefully considered by clinicians in their programming. Once the sound is successfully produced in the initial position, then to achieve the best (speed and stability) generalization, the clinician should arrange target phoneme practice materials in a variety of (mixed) positions at the word and phrase/sentence level.

The literature is supportive, but not entirely clear (or conclusive) on this point. McLean (1970) found that institutionalized retarded subjects did not generalize the trained phoneme to a word position different from that in which it was trained. One study (Powell and McReynolds, 1969) evaluated the generalization of initial, medial, and final position training with /s/ and another (Elbert and McReynolds, 1975) evaluated the training of four /r/ allophones. Both studies concluded that normal elementary school children will begin to emit the sound in positions other than the trained position.

Aronin (1971) found across-position generalization for /s/ but not for /l/ after imitation training with five normal children, age 4 years-5 months to 5 years-9 months. An increase in the number of same position generalizations occurred after the children completed spontaneous training. He concluded that across-position generalization is less predictable than same position generalization.

In the study by Elbert and McReynolds (1978) across-position generalization was obtained for five subjects with /θ/ for /s/. The effect of context in training was less than expected and they suggested that the development of stimulability (ability to imitate), practice, and individual error patterns may influence generalization.

Raymore and McLean (1972) trained four institutionalized subjects in the initial, final, and medial, positions and in a randomized presentation of all three positions. The level of responding was higher and more stabilized with the randomized treatment. Finally, McLean and Raymore (1972) observed that training to 100% criterion at the word level in nine normal elementary school children did not necessarily result in generalization of correct responses to sentences and conversation. Training in words, sentences, and conversation appeared to be necessary for some children. Across-position generalization and generalization to untrained words occurred for some subjects. Also, when a five week vacation was instituted, regardless of the program phrase, subjects made gains in correct phoneme production.

McReynolds (1972) found no generalization after isolated /s/ training, but the children did learn from initial and final syllable drill. Gains from medial syllable /asa/ practice were difficult to interpret because "it may not have functioned as a new articulatory response to be learned." She concluded that generalization was more apt to occur when the correct sound was trained in the context of other phonemes and by changing the position of the phoneme.

Ruscello (1975) trained six elementary school subjects who were not initially stimulable on /s/ in isolation. He began training in isolation, then in words using the McLean (1970) stimulus-shift paradigm. Some children did generalize to formerly misarticulated words after training in isolation alone. He also found that children who had training in initial, final, and medial positions had more words correct on test probes than those trained only in the initial position.

McLean's stimulus-shift program used with normals (McLean and Raymore, 1972) takes the child who is stimulable on the target sound and begins training at the word level (imitation of the clinician with the sound in the initial position). This procedure is different from Gerber (1973) who recommends that the target phoneme be practiced in nonsense syllables and nonsense words until skill is obtained before moving to real words. Winitz (1975) recommends training the target sound in nonce (nonce words, then nonce words in conversational speech, transfer nonce words to English words, then phrases, sentences, and conversational speech).

In contrast to isolation or nonsense syllable drill, the paired-stimuli technique described by Irwin and Griffith (1973, p. 175) trains the target phoneme by the use of key words.

> A key word is defined as one in which the subject produces the target phoneme in a socially acceptable manner; it must have the target phoneme in it only once, in either the initial or the final position.

Key words are paired with words that contain phoneme errors. The effectiveness of generalization from paired-stimuli training was tested by the McDonald Screening Deep Test (1968). Significant improvement was noted for only the target phoneme trained in both initial and final position, not for other phonemes that were in error. In essence then, two-word combinations containing the target phoneme when uttered spontaneously on the Screening Deep Test were significantly improved between pre- and post-paired stimuli intervention periods.

The above studies indicate considerable variability of performance in generalization. Whether the variability is due to individual differences in children, clinicians or designs of the studies is impossible to say at this time. Further work is needed but the studies suggest the following:
1. Some children generalize from isolation drill to words. Others need to practice nonce syllables and then words.
2. Some children generalize from word drill to conversation. Others need practice in phrases and sentences before conversational drill.
3. It is more likely that a child will have greater generalization to words that contain the target phoneme in sentences and conversation, if he has previous training in different positions (I, M, F) or allophones.

The only way to determine how well the child is performing at different levels is to systematically probe his productions under a series of specified conditions (McReynolds, 1972; Costello, 1977; Elbert and McReynolds, 1975 and 1978). The early work of Wright, Shelton, and Arndt (1969) empirically demonstrated that specific probe measures during speech therapy provided information about the transfer of the target phoneme in imitation (SPT), reading, and spontaneous speech. The SPT and TALK probes used in this study provided the clinician with bi-weekly feedback about the progress of each child throughout the school year. The SPT evaluated imitative skill at the isolation, syllable, word, and phrase level and helped the clinician determine how well the child was performing in spontaneous conversation. As one develops skills in listening to conversation, different allophones or contexts can be distinguished in connected speech. The clinician can then tailor the stimulus presentations to the individual needs of the child.

The K-L curves represent children who were successful in acquiring their target sound in conversation. From studying their lesson plans these clinicians planned to utilize isolation, syllable, word, phrase/sentence, and conversation in their therapy. Most training begins at the isolation level, then goes to the initial syllable or word position, then the mixed positions (I, M, F), and finally phrase/sentence drill. Little use seemed to be made of the medial and final positions as specific practice steps. The high occurrence of the mixed positions and the considerable practice in connected (FC, SS, Rdg) speech suggest that these procedures were used for carryover (transfer generalization[1]) of the target sound into conversation. We stress "suggest" because we do not know exactly what each child received in therapy. The lesson plan, as noted earlier, represented the clinicians' intentions, but does not necessarily describe the therapy interactions. In spite of this admonition, most children who are successful in carryover still need production practice of the target phoneme in the mixed position in conversation. As we have indicated in Chapter 7, once the child can produce the sound correctly at better than 75% in conversation for two consecutive probes one week apart, he can be dismissed from therapy with better than an 80% chance of not having a remission.

Sommers and Kane (1974) summarized thoroughly the major (and minor) articulation therapy models and procedures used in this country over the past 50 years. They reported varying degrees of emphasis on carryover training at the conversation level by the different authors. It is difficult to evaluate therapy procedures by different authors or carried out in practice by clinicians, but during the past 5-10 years, there has been an increase in the practiced use of conversation in therapy. Gerber (1977) reviewed nine articulation programs that have emerged in the past 10 years. Six of them utilized conversation as a test probe. This is quite different from the more traditional pre-post testing done on a standard articulation test (the Templin-Darley or McDonald for example). The lesson plan data reported here confirm the notion that clinicians specified free conversation (13% of the therapy activities) second only to standard drills (20%) as a category of therapy. Many workers in the vineyard (as Van Riper likes to say) are providing practice of the target phoneme where the terminal objective should be—in conversation.

What has caused this shift in therapy emphasis (if indeed there is one)? Three forces have been active in the past 15 years. First, psycholinguistics has made an impact on our field with attention placed on the study of the phoneme in context, morphology, and syntax. Notions of coarticulation and distinctive features are now common. Evaluation of the phoneme in complex linguistic units made the study of connected speech in conversation a natural step. Second, operant psychology has emphasized programming, baseline measures, and systematic probes during treatment to evaluate effects. This has focused our thinking on the ultimate result of speech therapy which is, of course, correction of the target phoneme at the conversational level, not just on a single word articulation test. Third, account-

---

1. Griffiths and Craighead (1972) reserved the term *carry-over* for the measure of generalization that occurs from training in therapy to spontaneous speech. Mowrer (1971) defined carry-over "as used by clinicians generally refers to the transfer of correct articulation in speaking situations outside the clinical setting."

| K | | | L | | | M | | |
|---|---|---|---|---|---|---|---|---|
| Clinician | Child | Sd | Clinician | Child | Sd | Clinician | Child | Sd |
| 39 | 5 | /r/ | 39 | 3 | /r/ | 39 | 2 | /s/ |
| 39 | 8 | /s/ | 39 | 6 | /r/ | 42 | 48 | /r/ |
| 42 | 46 | /s/ | 42 | 52 | /r/ | 48 | 138 | /r/ |
| 42 | 47 | /s/ | 42 | 53 | /r/ | | | |
| | | | 48 | 137 | /r/ | | | |
| | | | 48 | 142 | /s/ | | | |

TABLE 6.9. Distribution of clinicians and children by learning curve analyzed for therapy interactions on the Tone Keyboard.

ability and relevancy have played an important part in our thinking in recent years. This has forced us to seek more precise measures of accuracy of the target phoneme in conversation (see Chapter 7).

## Interaction Analysis of Therapy with Tone Keyboard (TKB)

As outlined in the Methodology chapter, we worked hard to obtain on-going information about the actual interaction between the clinician and child during therapy, but much of our efforts were futile. The TKB (Appendix C) was utilized and the clinicians sent weekly tapes to the project office to be decoded. Even though we believed that most of the bugs were worked out in our pilot Year 3, many—to our frustration—still remained. There were many human errors in providing accurate identification information in certain TKB entries. This resulted in misinformation when the tape was decoded and a large loss of valuable data. We also had calibration problems in converting the tones of computer tape for print-outs. Finally, available time and funds also constrained our analyses. Consequently, the data available to us via the TKB were greatly reduced.

After the KLMO curve types had been identified for the Year 4 children, we went back to the TKB data pool and located reliable tapes for 13 different children and three clinicians amounting to approximately 51 hours of therapy throughout the school year (Table 6.9). There were four "K" (2 /s/, 2 /r/), six "L" (1 /s/, 5 /r/), and three "M" (1 /s/, 2 /r/) curves represented.

## Total Antecedent, Child Response, and Subsequent Events

The events occurring during speech therapy can be defined in different ways (Diedrich, 1969; Johnson, 1969; Prescott, 1970; Boone and Prescott, 1971; Lingwall and Engmann, 1971; Schubert, 1974). See our description of the Tone Keyboard (TKB) in Appendix C. Table 6.10 summarizes all the clinician and child events by learning curve KLM and time period EU1-2 (first six weeks), EU2-3 (next six weeks) and EU3-4 (final 12 weeks) during the school year. Under Clinician Antecedent Event (AE) are listed two categories: talking (AG, F, V) and providing auditory models for the child to imitate. When the clinician said to the child, "Say the sound or word again" the Again (AG) key was pushed. Direction given to the child about movement or placement of his articulators was recorded as Feedback (F). All other talking by the clinician was indicated by the verbalization (V) key. Under auditory model was included Isolation, Syllable, Word, or Phrase/Sentence. No provision was made to describe visual stimuli on the Tone

| | Clinician AE | | Child Response | | Clinician SE | Total |
|---|---|---|---|---|---|---|
| | AG F V | Model | V DM Z | +/- | +/- | Events |
| **EU1-EU2** | | | | | | |
| K | 99 | 329 | 8 | 2017 | 440 | 2,893 |
| | 3 | 11 | 1 | 70 | 15 | |
| L | 243 | 817 | 39 | 1682 | 1082 | 3,863 |
| | 6 | 21 | 1 | 44 | 28 | |
| M | 129 | 212 | 36 | 464 | 304 | 1,145 |
| | 11 | 19 | 2 | 41 | 27 | |
| **EU2-EU3** | | | | | | |
| K | 35 | 25 | 3 | 1338 | 385 | 1,786 |
| | 2 | 1 | 0 | 75 | 22 | |
| L | 226 | 181 | 50 | 1780 | 631 | 2,868 |
| | 8 | 6 | 2 | 62 | 22 | |
| M | 143 | 48 | 68 | 666 | 297 | 1,222 |
| | 12 | 4 | 6 | 55 | 24 | |
| **EU3-EU4** | | | | | | |
| K | 40 | 3 | 3 | 1562 | 156 | 1,764 |
| | 2 | 0 | 0 | 89 | 9 | |
| L | 416 | 141 | 78 | 3171 | 598 | 4,404 |
| | 9 | 3 | 2 | 72 | 14 | |
| M | 175 | 55 | 3 | 1340 | 119 | 1,692 |
| | 10 | 3 | 0 | 80 | 7 | |
| **Total for The Year** | | | | | | |
| K | 174 | 357 | 14 | 4917 | 981 | 6,443 |
| | 3 | 6 | 0 | 76 | 15 | |
| L | 885 | 1139 | 167 | 6633 | 2311 | 11,135 |
| | 8 | 10 | 1 | 60 | 21 | |
| M | 447 | 315 | 107 | 2470 | 720 | 4,059 |
| | 11 | 8 | 2 | 61 | 18 | |
| **Grand Total** | | | | | | |
| | 1506 | 1811 | 289 | 14,019 | 4012 | 21,637 |
| | 7 | 8 | 1 | 65 | 19 | |

TABLE 6.10. Total number of clinician antecedent events (AE), child responses, and clinician subsequent events (SE), for four K, six L, and three M children reduced to the three time periods: EU 1-2 (first six weeks), EU 2-3 (next 12 weeks), and EU 3-4 (last 12 weeks) during the school year. The frequency of the event is above the line, percentage below the line, each row totals 100%.

Keyboard. Boone and Stech (1970) observed that 80-95% of the therapy process occurred at the verbal level; therefore, we believed that the auditory stimuli were the most important to describe. We have data on Picture and Graph stimuli reported earlier on the clinician's lesson plans.

Under Child Response two broad categories were summed. The first included any verbalization (V) by the child not specifically related to the clinician's stimuli, auditory discrimination (DM) responses, and when the child made a response which was recognized as an error and self-corrected (Z). The second category included all correct (+), approximations (/), and wrong (–) target phoneme responses.

Finally, under Clinician Subsequent Events (SE) consequations are included. For correct responses the clinician might have paid off in tokens, nonverbal responses (smiles, head nods, etc.), or verbal responses (good, okay, yes, correct). For approximations (/) the statements "that's better" or "it's closer" might have been used. Punishment (–) was usually verbal (that's wrong, no), but also included negative head nods, or token cost (removal of a chip, etc.).

The length of time for each event is not recorded, only when the event started. How can we determine an estimate of the amount of time spent under Clinician Antecedent Events, Child Response, and Clinician Consequation? Fortunately, Prescott (1970) asked that question and found a high relationship between the timed duration of events and the number of events described during speech therapy (r = .92). By summing the number of events for each category we can obtain an estimate of the amount of time spent for each group of learners.

The Lingwall and Engmann (1971) study evaluated 10,487 events (five clinicians and eight clients) from videotapes and found clinician antecedent events (visual and auditory) occurred 43% of the time, child response events 39%, and clinician subsequent events 18%. For 7,107 events (five clinicians and 36 clients) studied from audio tape, they found antecedent events (auditory alone) 42%, child response events 34%, and clinician subsequent events 24%.

In our study we obtained a grand total of 21,637 events from the Tone Keyboard and found the following interactions: antecedent events 15%, child response events 66%, and clinician subsequent events 19% (Table 6.10). These distributions of therapy effort were quite different from those reported by Lingwall and Engmann (1971), especially in the clinician antecedent and child response categories (Figure 6.2). These differences may be because in the TKB data no "O" curve or other types of inconsistent learning patterns were represented. The KLM children learned the target phoneme, which may account for the more frequent child responses reported on the TKB compared to the Lingwall and Engmann data. Other differences such as the length of each session studied, period of time in the year, etc., may also influence child output as well as antecedent events.

The data in Table 6.10 also provide a breakdown for our KLM learners and three time periods. The "K" group had the fewest AE's (14%) compared to the "L" (27%) and "M" (30%) for the first six weeks (EU1-2) of therapy. The "K's" also had far more child responses (71%) than the "L" (45%) and "M" (43%). Finally, clinician consequation (SE) was far fewer for "K" (15%) than "L" (28%) and "M" (27%).

During the next 12 weeks (EU2-3) the "K" group received very few auditory models (1%) while "L" had 6% and "M" 4%. The number of child responses have

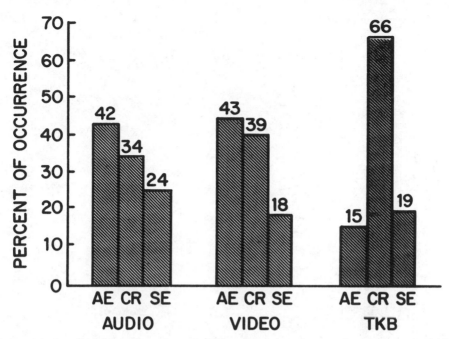

FIGURE 6.2. Bar diagram contrasts the percent frequency of occurrence of antecedent event (AE), child response (CR), and subsequent event (SE) described in the Lingwall-Engmann (1971) audio tape and video tape analysis compared with the Tone Keyboard (TKB) data collected in this study.

increased for "L" (62%) and "M" (55%). "M" also has increased discrimination (DM). "K's" increased in SE while L-M stayed about the same.

In the last 12 weeks of school (EU3-4) the KLM groups got little or no auditory stimulation and little change was noted in the Again, Feedback, and Verbalization category. All groups have increased child response: "K" is now at 89%, "L" at 72% and "M" at 80%. Frequency of clinician consequation diminished; in some cases less than half as often as in the previous time periods.

This analysis revealed that these clinicians spent most of their time presenting auditory models during the first six weeks of therapy and then very little after that. This supports the K-L lesson plan data reported in Tables E.35 and E.37, Appendix E which found high auditory model in the first six weeks and then large increases in picture and graphic (written) materials in the next 24 weeks. The other striking finding was the large amount of time consumed by child responses, especially for "K" in the first six weeks. "L" and "M" had far fewer. Since "M" had a 60% correct or better conversation level at baseline, it was surprising that these children were not responding at least as often as the "K" learners. The "M" group had many more clinician AE, too. The last major observation was that the "K" learners had little overt consequation especially in those first six weeks when they made their maximum gain. Additional comment will be made about this point in the next section when reinforcement ratios are discussed.

## Category Analysis of AE, CR, and SE

Table 6.11 has more reduction of the total events distribution. In this analysis each category AE or CR or SE represents 100% of the events. Our interest is in

| | Clinician AE | | | | | | | Child Response | | | | | | Clinician SE | | | Ratio | Ratio |
|---|---|---|---|---|---|---|---|---|---|---|---|---|---|---|---|---|---|---|
| | AG | F | V | I | S | W | Ph | V | DM | Z | + | / | - | + | / | - | C+/K+ | C-/K- |
| **EU1-EU2** | | | | | | | | | | | | | | | | | | |
| K | 37 | 20 | 43 | 1 | 7 | 85 | 7 | 0 | 0 | 0 | 92 | 1 | 7 | 83 | 5 | 12 | 20 | 38 |
| L | 35 | 24 | 41 | 17 | 32 | 43 | 8 | 1 | 1 | 0 | 80 | 5 | 13 | 78 | 7 | 15 | 62 | 69 |
| M | 43 | 14 | 43 | 6 | 72 | 22 | 0 | 2 | 0 | 5 | 55 | 9 | 29 | 62 | 14 | 24 | 69 | 50 |
| **EU2-EU3** | | | | | | | | | | | | | | | | | | |
| K | 15 | 31 | 54 | 0 | 0 | 100 | 0 | 0 | 0 | 0 | 92 | 2 | 6 | 82 | 4 | 14 | 26 | 67 |
| L | 6 | 18 | 51 | 4 | 30 | 66 | 0 | 1 | 1 | 0 | 88 | 2 | 8 | 82 | 7 | 11 | 32 | 50 |
| M | 34 | 8 | 58 | 0 | 4 | 90 | 6 | 4 | 0 | 0 | 83 | 1 | 6 | 84 | 6 | 10 | 41 | 69 |
| **EU3-EU4** | | | | | | | | | | | | | | | | | | |
| K | 38 | 20 | 42 | 0 | 0 | 100 | 0 | 0 | 0 | 0 | 98 | 0 | 2 | 95 | 0 | 5 | 10 | 21 |
| L | 28 | 21 | 51 | 3 | 1 | 91 | 5 | 1 | 1 | 0 | 90 | 1 | 7 | 79 | 6 | 15 | 16 | 37 |
| M | 22 | 10 | 68 | 0 | 2 | 64 | 34 | 0 | 0 | 0 | 89 | 2 | 9 | 50 | 13 | 37 | 5 | 37 |

AG = Again                I = Isolation          Ph = Phrase/Sentence      + = Correct        C+ = Clinician +

F = Feedback           S = Syllable          DM = Discrimination      / = Approximation     K+ = Child +

V = Verbalization     W = Word           Z = Self-correction

                                              - = Wrong

TABLE 6.11. The percent of clinician and child events for KLM learners. Each row represents 100% of the events for each category: Clinician AE, child response, and clinician SE. The reinforcement (C+/K+) and punishment (C-/K-) ratios also are indicated.

determining the percent occurrence of each variable under each category.

1. Clinician AE—AG, F, V. It can be observed that clinicians spend most of the auditory AE time talking (verbalization is about 40-50 percent); however, saying "again" contributed a large portion of the clinicians' AE repertoire, especially during the first six weeks (EU1-2).

2. Clinician AE—Auditory Models (I, S, W, Ph). The most obvious is the diminished use of isolation and syllable models during the first six weeks (EU1-2) which are replaced by word and phrase at EU2-3 and EU3-4 during the last 24 weeks. Of note here is that the "K" learners received 85% of their auditory models at the word level during the first six weeks of therapy.

3. Child Response—V, DM, Z. The percent occurrence of verbalization, discrimination, and self-correction is trivial in light of the high occurrence of target phoneme responses. These children spent very little time "just talking." These therapy samples appear very goal oriented.

4. Child Response—Correct (+), Approximation (/), and Wrong (-). Except for the "M" group during the first six weeks (EU1-2) which is at 55% correct, all the other percent correct tallies were at the 80-98% level. These clinicians perceived few approximation responses. We anticipated many more, especially during the early weeks of therapy. The "M" group had more than the K-L children. This was a reflection of one aspect of their problem, i.e., they still had trouble making on-target responses. They may also be inconsistent in their responses.

5. Clinician SE—Correct (+), Approximation (/), and Wrong (-). By far the greatest proportion of clinician consequation was for correct responses. Note that the "M" learners had the most punishment (-) events, 24% at EU1-2 and 37% at EU3-4.

6. Reinforcement and Punishment Ratios (C+/K+ and C-/K-). The clinicians for the "K" learners provided only a 20% positive reinforcement ratio during the first six weeks, while "L" and "M" had 62% and 69%. During EU2-3, the "K" group got increased positive reinforcement, but the "L" and "M" dropped almost in half. And for the 12 weeks, all groups greatly decreased their positive reinforcement ratio. The punishment ratio was quite different for the KLM groups, and across the three time periods. Except for "M" at EU1-2, all groups had a higher punishment ratio than a positive reinforcement ratio. The clinicians more often provided feedback when the child's target phoneme response was wrong.

## Discussion

An important observation is the clinician stimulus presentations. Here we note that clinicians of "K" learners provided fewer auditory stimuli than was given to the other two groups. "M" children had a few isolation drills, but lots of syllable drills, even more than the "L" children. Observe also that the "K" learners had more auditory stimuli presentations consisting of words and phrase/sentences. The "M" children (who have the target phonemes at 50% or better in conversation) were not getting much auditory stimulation at the word/phrase level. They may have received more visual (pictures, printed words, and sentences) stimuli than the other two groups.

We might infer that "K" learners needed less auditory stimuli because they could self-generate or initiate the target phoneme independent from clinician modeling. On the other hand the observation poses the interesting question: Were children who were given fewer auditory models helped to learn faster because they were forced early (or oftener) to self-generate their own production? It has been the first author's observation that beginning clinicians frequently provide too much auditory imitation behavior and do not give the child opportunities to produce the sound on his own initiative and effort. The above findings on "K" children coupled with the clinical supervisor's observation should be tested empirically.

The number of times that the clinician said "Again (Ag)" meaning "Say the sound or word again," was similar for all three groups. The number of times feedback (F) was provided to the child was also the same for all three learning groups. By feedback is meant that the clinician told the child something specific about his articulators, e.g., "Keep your tongue behind the teeth." We had originally thought that perhaps the good clinician was one who gave a lot of feedback to the child. Mowrer (1973) had made a similar observation. Since we do not have TKB data on high and low clinician performance this idea may still be true, but it did not differentiate the "K," "L," "M" groups.

Discrimination (DM) was not utilized often. For these "K" learners discrimination was not used and occurred infrequently for the "L" and most for "M." Discrimination was never entered on the daily lesson plans of these four "K" learners either. Our data analysis for the entire year indicated that discrimination activities made up only 2.8 percent of the daily lesson plan activity.

Ear training has a long history in the field (Van Riper, 1978) and automated auditory discrimination programs have been suggested by Holland and Matthews (1963). Garrett's (1973) data supported the notion that if a child were stimulable there was little reason to practice discrimination training. The clinicians in our study also thought there was little reason to practice discrimination.

Child self-correction (Z) occurred very infrequently for "K," "L," and "M" learners. We thought this behavior might be observed with higher frequency among the fast (K) learners. Not true. Reports in the literature (McReynolds, 1972; Gerber, 1973; and others) have also stressed the value of self monitoring and we believed that self-correction might be an index for that behavior. As you can see self-correction occurred only during the first six weeks of therapy for "M" children.

Productions of the target phoneme by the child which were not wrong or not correct and consequated by the clinician with "that's better" or "closer" were labeled approximations. Some persons (Winitz, 1975, p. 74) believe that the clinician should reinforce only correct responses. Reinforcement of partially correct responses may result in slowing down the acquisition of correct responses. Our data reported here would suggest that in the judgment of these clinicians, approximation responses either occurred very seldom in the output of the child or were considered wrong. It is interesting to note that the "M" children, those mastering the target phoneme at a slower acceleration than "K" or "L," also have the most approximation responses. But in none of the three groups do approximation responses surpass wrong responses. The clinician consequation for approximation occurred more often than the child production of approximation responses. Why? The clinician may have given some approximation consequation for correct responses. These tallies were not done on a point for point basis. It is difficult to say when or why this occurred. Sometimes the wrong key on the TKB was punched, the clinician meant to hit + and would hit − or the / key.

When all of the child's responses were counted, the correct one averaged 85% for all children. Maintaining a high level of correct response rate may be influenced by several factors:

a. The clinician cannot take failure, i.e., she likes to feel good.
b. The clinician believes that children cannot take failure.
c. The clinician programs well, i.e., a la Skinner errorless learning paradigm. It is unclear why the "M" children had only 55% correct in the first six weeks. They received lots of syllable drill and the target phonemes apparently were perceived as errors by the clinician. Perhaps the clinicians adapted to the production of the phoneme (five out of the six were /r/ children).

Stech (1969) reported correct response ratios in the 60-90% range. He pointed out that correct response ratios are a function of the client's problem. Severe stutterers or voice problems might result in almost 100% incorrect responses, but mild language or articulation disorders could result in almost 100% correct responses. Mowrer (1969) reported that an error rate greater than 25% was detrimental to acquisition of new articulation responses.

Boone (1970, p. 74-75) has stated "that the most effective speech therapy always starts where the client is and assures in every therapy session a high rate of correct response." K, L, M learners in our study were all successful and they all got stimuli which produced 80-89% correct responses. Unfortunately we do not have any "O" (poor learners) TKB data to compare and see if they had low percent correct response rates. Boone (p. 75) goes on to say: "It appears to me that the best therapy has 75-80% successful responses. If it's higher than that, then what we are doing is probably not difficult enough." We (WMD) intuitively agree with Boone, but the data (Table 6.11) suggest that "K" learners did very well with 92-98% total correct responses.

"K" children who learned faster were not given as much positive reinforcement (C+/K+) as the slower "L" and "M" articulation learners. One presumption is that fast learners know they are doing well and therefore the clinician intuitively provides less overt positive reinforcement. Or perhaps the clinician knows that an irregular reinforcement schedule is better now. However, when the fast learner (K curve) made an error, the clinician gave punishment much more often.

Stech (1969) reported positive reinforcement ratio values in the 60-95% range with a mean of 80% for most clinicians. He went on the say that "high rates of reinforcement were associated with outgoing and experienced clinicians." The values reported in our data are far below Stech's, but are more in line with those reported by Strong (1971) who analyzed three undergraduate senior clinicians each with 30 minutes of therapy with articulation clients. She found an average positive reinforcement of 45% (34%-53%) and incorrect responses corrected by the clinician 63% of the time (48% to 86%). This is in contrast to most of the Prescott (1970) data which indicated higher positive reinforcement than negative (punishment) reinforcement ratios for 10 out of 12 students studied.

In a more extensive study, Lingwall and Engmann (1971) evaluated 2,481 subsequent events with five clinicians and eight clients for 310 minutes of therapy from videotape. They found positive reinforcement occurred 43%, punishment 20%, no subsequent event 17%, and the remaining was other or irregular events. From 2,590 events audio tape recorded on five clinicians and 36 clients for 256 minutes, they found positive reinforcement 53%, punishment 7%, no subsequent event 32%, and the remaining other or irrelevant events. Our positive reinforcement rate was generally lower and our punishment ratio was much higher than

Lingwall and Engmann reported. The Tone Keyboard may have had the effect of alerting the clinician to indicate a punishment consequation.

Although our clinicians were instructed to punch the key which indicated positive reinforcement whenever they said "good," gave a token, provided an affirmative head nod or smiled, perhaps they failed to do so. Even if this did happen, it fails to account for the differential rate of positive consequation found in the KLM groups.

Ingmire and Schuckers (1975) reported on the category and frequency of verbal reinforcement utilized by clinicians in schools. They cited evidence from psychological literature that there are two types of verbal reinforcement—person oriented reinforcers (*good, fine, ok, great*) which connote praise or approval-disapproval, and performance reinforcers (*right, wrong, correct*) which relate to response accuracy. The authors stated that performance reinforcers demand a binary decision and person reinforcers operate on a subjective continuum of the clinician. We may go along with the two types of reinforcers, but disagree on the words chosen to be associated with both types. For example, *right* appears no less a person oriented word than a performance one. The reverse is true for the word *good*. It appears to us that the words themselves are not the critical issue, but the specific context in which the word is said and how the word is uttered is crucial. In evaluating the responses of 11 school clinicians, Ingmire and Schuckers found that 91% were in the person (approval-disapproval) category (80% consisted of *good, ok*, and *alright*). Only 9% of the total reinforcers were in the performance category (*right, yes, no*).

In a study of the effect of the verbal stimulus words *wrong, right*, and *tree* on dysfluency rates of stutterers and non-stutterers, Cooper, Cady, and Robbins (1970) found that the words significantly reduced dysfluencies in both groups. However, no differential effect was noted for any of the words. The authors concluded that 1) any verbal stimuli may act as a punisher in this situation and 2) a presumed affective content of contingent stimuli does not change dysfluency rates. The words *right* and *wrong* used by Cooper et al., would be classified by Ingmire and Schuckers as performance reinforcers and yet they did not have a differential effect. It seems we may not only presume affective content, but also semantic content and its effect on a response. As Cooper et al., have suggested, verbal stimuli in certain specified arrangements (i.e., speech therapy) may be interpreted quite differently by the listener.

Rosenhan and Greenwald (1965) cited by Ingmire and Schuckers believe that person reinforcers are more anxiety-reducing than performance reinforcers, i.e., they provide reassurance as compared to knowledge of results. Assuming this is true and assuming our clinicians also may have provided high person category reinforcement, then it is interesting to speculate that our clinicians somehow knew that fast learners (K) needed the least amount of reinforcement and "L" or "M" (the slow accelerators) needed the most.

Ingmire and Schuckers believe their data support the findings of Boone (1970) who reported that student clinicians were afraid to say *no* or to administer negative reinforcement. Data from Table 6.11 suggest a different interpretation. Clinicians provided stimuli for which children make a high percentage of correct responses which necessarily limits the number of wrong responses possible. Also, the clinicians more often gave punishment feedback then they did positive reinforcement. Apparently these clinicians were not afraid to say *no*. They also provided stimulus materials that encouraged a high level of correct responding on the part of the child. In addition, the clinician was sensitive to the child's overall speech level and capabilities as a learner in that situation. Clinicians who are more overtly supportive of the L-M learners find less "need" to give positive reinforcement to the fast learning "K" child. Another obvious hypothesis is that these clinicians were good programmers and knew that once the sound could be made, intermittent reinforcement was the best schedule.

## Total Therapy Time and Clinician-Child Response Time

Mowrer (1971) stressed that response accuracy and response frequency were two important factors for optimal learning in speech therapy. The total Tone Keyboard (TKB) time and clinician-child response times are listed in Table 6.12. The overall response frequency for all events that occurred in the therapy process was 7.0 per minute as recorded on the TKB during one school year. The antecedent events occurred at 1.1 per minute, child response rates at 4.6 per minute, and subsequent events at 1.3 per minute. Ingmire and Schuckers (1975) found frequency of verbal reinforcement varied from 1½ to 9 times per minute with an average rate for 11 clinicians of four per minute.

Of particular interest is that a differential response rate is evident across groups of learners and time during the year. During the first six weeks (EU1-2), there is no doubt that the "K" learners had fewer clinician AE's, more child responses, and fewer SE's than the LM groups. In the next 12 weeks the "K" learners had AE's that were still half of the LM, but child response rates and SE were about the same.

In the first two time blocks (EU1 and EU2 = 18 weeks), the LM groups have very similar response rates for AE, child response, and SE. During the last 12 weeks the "M" children had higher response rates (6.5) and fewer SE (0.6).

Mowrer (1969) cited Hurley (1969) who found a high of six responses to less than one per minute evoked by public school clinicians, with a mean of 2.79 for 10 therapy sessions studied. For three sessions on the S-Pack, Mowrer (1973) found over seven target /s/ responses per minute. He stated that initial response rates for isolation and words should be about 15-25 per minute down to 6-10 responses during connected speech. Lubbert et al. (1971) reported that when a child can make up to 20 responses per minute he was dismissed from therapy. Garrett (1974) said that up to 600 responses per session (20 per minute) are obtainable in articulation therapy. Our group therapy data was supportive of Hurley, but contained far fewer responses then the others have suggested for individual therapy articulation programs.

We read (Mowrer, 1969) that clinicians should increase the child's correct response rate. This presumably increases their rate of learning. The fact that children who learn faster can produce more responses per minute makes considerable clinical sense. When presented with a stimulus, fast learners usually make the response quickly and get ready for the next stimulus. The children who have trouble with imitation or self-production generally have a much slower response time to the stimulus. They work at it, often use subvocal rehearsal, and evidence start-stop response behavior, all of which increases the individual response time.

On the other hand, the findings of several workers have shown that increased response latency (between clinician stimulus and child response) may in fact improve acquisition. Locke (1971) cited the study by Romans and Milisen (1954)

| | Total Time | Total TKB Session | All Events Per Minute | AE Per Minute | Child Rsponse Per Minute | SE Per Minute |
|---|---|---|---|---|---|---|
| EU1–EU2 | | | | | | |
| K | 361 | 26 | 8.0 | 1.2 | 5.6 | 1.2 |
| L | 520 | 36 | 7.4 | 2.0 | 3.3 | 2.1 |
| M | 167 | 15 | 6.9 | 2.1 | 3.0 | 1.8 |
| EU2–EU3 | | | | | | |
| K | 304 | 23 | 5.9 | 0.2 | 4.4 | 1.3 |
| L | 405 | 27 | 7.1 | 1.0 | 4.5 | 1.6 |
| M | 210 | 19 | 5.8 | 0.9 | 3.5 | 1.4 |
| EU3–EU4 | | | | | | |
| K | 290 | 18 | 6.1 | 0.2 | 5.4 | 0.5 |
| L | 623 | 48 | 7.1 | 0.9 | 5.2 | 1.0 |
| M | 207 | 29 | 8.2 | 1.1 | 6.4 | 0.6 |
| Grand Mean | | | 7.0 | 1.1 | 4.6 | 1.3 |

TABLE 6.12. The total amount of time (minutes) recorded for each therapy session on the Tone Keyboard (TKB) for three learning groups KLM. Rates per minute have been computed for all events, antecedent events (AE), child response, and subsequent events (SE).

which found that adults' imitative articulatory responses improved in quality as stimulus-response latency was increased from zero to nine seconds. He also cited Hutchinson (1969) who observed better responses in misarticulating children at 12 seconds than at zero, four, or eight second intervals. Dick (1975) had children delay their responses 0.400, 3.0, and 10.0 seconds following stimulus presentation. She demonstrated better production of /r/ in the initial position at the syllable level with the 10-second delay. These children evidenced subvocal motor rehearsal during the preresponse interval, but the other children were not observed to be subvocalizing. Garrett (1973, p. 110) found 2.8 seconds an optimal time frame for presentation of nonsense syllables to elementary school children. It may be important to delay while the child is first learning to make the correct response. After he becomes proficient, speech drills which increase the rate of responding are important for some children (Bankson and Byrne, 1972).

One comment. If clinicians averaged one session per week for 20 weeks with "K" and up to 30 weeks for "L" and "M" groups the number of child responses for the year is approximately 1200 to 1800. For the rapid "K" learners, during the first six weeks, they made less than 500 responses. It seems extraordinary that a motor behavior such as speech, and more specifically a phoneme produced incorrectly, which may have had five years of practice for habituation (say age three to eight) and thousands of trials (8 /s/ per minute × 60 × 365 × 5 = 876,000) during the child's most formative years (cortically speaking), can be modified to a correct response in spontaneous speech in less than 500 trials, with some three hours of formal practice, over a period of six weeks. Only the 30 year, two-pack-a-day smoker who quits in one day comes to mind as one who can match or better this feat for adaptability of the organism.

As described in Chapter 2, Methodology, the events were punched on the TKB by the clinician and recorded on magnetic tape at a known speed. This permitted estimates for the number of times events occurred during the interaction

| Total Therapy Sessions | | Intervals Measured In Seconds | | | | | | | | | | | |
|---|---|---|---|---|---|---|---|---|---|---|---|---|---|
| | | 0 | 1 | 2 | 3 | 4 | 5 | 6 | 7 | 8 | 9 | 10 | 11+ |
| 75 sessions | Mean | 19 | 34 | 15 | 7 | 5 | 3 | 2 | 2 | 2 | 2 | 1 | 8 |
| Clinician A | ACC | 19 | 53 | 68 | 75 | 80 | 83 | 85 | 87 | 89 | 91 | 92 | 100 |
| 66 sessions | Mean | 7 | 28 | 19 | 10 | 6 | 4 | 4 | 3 | 3 | 3 | 1 | 12 |
| Clinician B | ACC | 7 | 35 | 54 | 64 | 70 | 74 | 78 | 81 | 84 | 87 | 88 | 100 |
| 16 sessions | Mean | 16 | 32 | 14 | 10 | 6 | 4 | 3 | 2 | 2 | 3 | 1 | 7 |
| Clinician C | ACC | 16 | 48 | 62 | 72 | 78 | 82 | 85 | 87 | 89 | 92 | 93 | 100 |
| 23 sessions | Mean | 13 | 36 | 18 | 8 | 6 | 3 | 2 | 2 | 2 | 2 | 1 | 7 |
| Clinician D | ACC | 13 | 49 | 67 | 75 | 81 | 84 | 86 | 88 | 90 | 92 | 93 | 100 |

TABLE 6.13. The time interval in seconds between two behavioral events punched on the Tone Keyboard. Data is summarized for mean percent and accumulated (ACC) percent of events that occurred between intervals up to 10 seconds for four clinicians. Anything greater than a 10 second interval was printed out as 11+.

between the clinician and the child. The computer printout summarized the percent of all the events for time periods from less than one second, for each second up to 10, and then anything above 10 seconds. Table 6.13 summarizes the mean and accumulated percent occurrence of events recorded by four clinicians. Clinician A was tallied with two "K" children, clinician B with two "L" and one "M," and clinicians C and D were with unspecified children. The measure is one of duration (in seconds) between the starting time of any two successive events and the frequency of those events. It is not a measure of event duration. About half of the events occurred in less than a two-second interval for three out of the four clinicians. From 70 to 81% of the events occurred in less than five seconds indicative of the swiftness of articulation therapy interaction. Less than 10% of the interactions had time intervals of more than 10 seconds between events. Jaffe and Feldstein (1970, p. 22) noted that the ". . . rhythmical unit in talking is a string of 2-10 words, averaging 5 . . ." with a mean duration of approximately 1.64 seconds in natural dialogue. Hesitation and juncture pauses ranged from .66 to .77 seconds. Combining the duration of talking with the pauses amounts to less than three seconds. Their figures provide some external validity for the duration of events collected on the TKB by our clinicians. It is interesting to observe that clinician A with "K" children had 53% of the events in less than two seconds while clinician B with "LM" children had only 35% in the same time period. Jaffe and Feldstein suggested (p. 117) that personality differences may determine the temporal bursts of speech and pauses used by different individuals. Was this the case here?

An indirect answer can be supplied by looking at the EOI (rapport) scores: Clinician A-123, B-108, C-123, and D-124. The mean EOI score for all clinicians was 117 (SD 7.2). All three clinicians with high EOI scores also had about 50% of their events in less than two seconds while clinician B had 35% in the same time period. However, when clinician performance level (CPL, Chapter 5) was evaluated, clinicians A, B, C, and D had average CPL scores of 25, 29, 26, and 34 respectively. These performance scores indicated that clinician D was better, yet her frequency of therapy event was very similar to clinicians A and C. Again, the analysis of one aspect of the therapy process (frequency of events) does not define the characteristics of a good clinician.

The complexity of the speech therapy task (discrimination, cognition, and motor production) is one thing, the speed at which we process this information is another. It is remarkable that any learning occurs on the part of the child under such circumstances. Similarly, in the training institution we expect the student clinician to master all the intricate and rapid moves of the speech therapy process. It is no surprise that clinical training takes time.

In summary, these data should be viewed with caution because of the few children and clinicians represented. However, the study does present one hypothesis: Within limits, the child appears to determine the response rate and not the clinician. The data presented indicated that there were considerable differences found on the KLM curves. Although there was great variation found among clinicians (Chapter 5), the differences found in the KLMO learning curves may be more child-bound, than clinician-bound.

# CHAPTER 7

# Conversation as a Measure of Articulation Learning[1]

The merits of conversation as a measure of articulation learning are examined in this chapter. Elementary school children with defective articulation were determined to have a significantly reduced word output compared to normal children. To our knowledge this is the first published report on a large number of cases suggesting this finding. Children with /r/ or /s/ errors did not use fewer /r/ or /s/ linguistic units because of these errors. Descriptive data about the frequency distribution of /r/ allophones and /s/ contexts from conversation are provided.

Clinicians have considerable concern about the generalization of their training to different speaking environments. The three-minute TALK task used in this study predicts target phoneme performance in the classroom and at home.

The last section explores the critical notion about termination criteria in articulation therapy. When should the clinician stop therapy? Cut-off measures based on samples of conversation are suggested.

For definitions of special terms and symbols used in this project refer to Appendix G in this book.

## Introduction

Although Travis (1931) noted that, in the evaluation of articulation disorders, a sample of conversation would be valuable, the classical articulation testing procedures have been the single word testing of the target phoneme in the initial, medial and final position. The type of error was usually noted as distortion, substitution, or omission. Single word testing has been the standard way of sampling articulation (Bryngelson and Glaspey, 1941; Templin and Darley, 1960). There also has been some effort to measure articulation intelligibility with a scaling technique from connected speech (Jordan, 1960) and more recently by spoken words (Mumm, 1974).

An historic shift in articulation measurement was proposed by McDonald (1964) wherein the phoneme was sampled more than three times (deep testing). The notion of coarticulation also was anticipated by using across-phoneme boundary speech samples, and speech was elicited in a spontaneous mode. This test was radically different from the classical initial, medial, and final articulation test samples.

A further shift in emphasis of articulation measurement was suggested by the Faircloths (1970a, 1970b) and by Dickerson (1971). They urged the evaluation of articulation from samples of conversation to obtain a more dynamic view of the child's phonological system. After finding significantly more articulation errors in spontaneous continuous speech compared to modeled continuous speech ("delayed imitation" used in the Goldman-Fristoe Articulation Test, 1969), DuBois and Bernthal (1976) concluded that "... spontaneous continuous speech

---

1. "Conversation as a measure of Articulation Learning" was contributed by W. Diedrich, J. Bangert, M. Denes, M. Elbert, and V. Wright.

sampling should be included in any evaluation of the articulation status of an individual."

We suggested a three-minute conversation sample for articulation impaired children (Diedrich, 1971b, 1972b, 1973b). A variety of programmed articulation learning packages have appeared in which probes of child-constructed stories (Mowrer, Baker, Schultz, 1968) or samples of conversation (Baker and Ryan, 1971; Lubbert et al., 1971; Irwin and Griffith, 1973) were being systematically used. Winitz (1975, p. 99) has developed principles for using conversation in drills and for transfer probes.

One other dimension of classical articulation testing is the notion of pre- and post-testing. Clinicians usually give a pre-test and sometimes they make a post-test. In this era of accountability there is an emphasis on continuous measurement of the process of learning. Aungst and McDonald (1973, p. 229) stated the need for more than just pre-post measures. They suggested that clinicians should have measures during therapy as well as for the evaluation of carryover effectiveness.

Audiologists struggled to standardize their audiometric procedures and results (Fowler, 1949), and once they did, the visual pattern of audiometric curves began to take on diagnostic significance. We had anticipated that once systematic SPT/TALK probes were accomplished over the school year, that learning curve patterns might be seen. Our isolation of the KLMO learning patterns substantiated our prediction (Chapter 3).

There are at least two questions regarding reliability of phoneme performance when judged by obtaining samples of conversation:
1. Can observers listen to conversation (live or from tape, without resorting to typescripts) and make reliable judgments of correct/wrong counts of the specified target phoneme?
2. Do field clinicians make reliable judgments of correct/wrong counts in the conversation of children they are treating?
These questions are evaluated in detail in Chapter 2.

The answer to the first question is yes. Our studies and those of Shelton et al. (1972) have given reliability coefficients or percent agreement scores in the 70-96 range.

For the second question, the answer is "it depends." Our data show that field clinicians make biased judgments (see details in Appendix D). Someone who works closely with the child will note subtle differences in production that are judged correct. An outside observer has not been in a position to perceive these changes and he judges the responses as wrong. The clinicians' judgments of percent correct in our studies ranged 10-20 percent higher than a neutral judge. We also found among large numbers of clinicians that some were better than others at judging correctness of the target phoneme. For some clinicians the agreement was good and for others it was poor. The phoneme in question also influences the perceptual judgment. Better agreement was obtained for /r/ than for /s/. Probes of conversation, independently judged (live or taped), would be necessary to demonstrate efficacy of some treatment variable.

The purpose of this section is fourfold:
1. To report a descriptive analysis of phoneme usage from samples of conversation for three groups of children, normal, defective /r/ and defective /s/.
2. To describe the generalization of a target phoneme from clinician-child conversation samples to other speaking environments.

3. To discuss prediction, sample size, and conversation probe measures in articulation learning.
4. To establish termination criteria from conversation for articulation learning.

## Descriptive Analysis of Three-Minute Conversation Samples

In a paper by Shriner, Holloway, and Daniloff (1969) it was suggested that someone ". . . might examine children's speech to see if they avoid attempting to produce those phonetic units which they misarticulate." Sommers (1969) also communicated the same possibility. Therefore, as a part of a larger study investigating articulation learning by children who misarticulate /r/ and /s/ phonemes, we attempted to answer the above question. In addition, we wished to examine more closely the several allophonic variations of /r/ in conversational speech in order to have better descriptive basis for clinical management decisions. The Curtis and Hardy (1959) study which described allophonic characteristics of /r/ generated interest among speech clinicians about the different types of /r/. More recent efforts in developing /r/ programs (Slipakoff, 1967; Butt and Peterson, 1971; and McDonald and McDonald, 1971; Jacobs and Sauer, 1972; Shriberg, 1975; Brown, 1975) would indicate a need for basic description of the frequency of occurrence for the /r/ allophones in children's speech on the premise that efforts should perhaps not be expended in training all the different allophones because some have low functional use in conversation. Elbert and McReynolds (1975) showed that most subjects increased the number of correct responses to items in several allophonic categories regardless of the specific allophone taught.

The purpose of this section is to examine whether children with articulatory errors on /r/ or /s/ use fewer words containing these phonemic elements when compared to normal children. A secondary objective is to describe the frequency of occurrence of three /r/ allophones (consonant, stressed, and unstressed) and position (I, M, F, Bl) of /s/ in children's conversational speech.

## Subjects

Children were chosen on the basis of a primary impairment of /r/ or /s/ determined by the McDonald Screening Deep Test of Articulation (see Chapter 8). They were without hearing loss, were not attending special education class, and did not exhibit obvious organic impairment of the speech mechanism. Most of the children were from predominantly white middle-class neighborhoods.

Children with defective /r/ and /s/ sounds who had a wide, representative range of baseline percent correct on TALK were chosen from a larger data base (Chapter 2). On the TALK task, the target phoneme is counted correct or wrong during three minutes of conversation between the clinician and child. The mean baseline scores for 63 /r/ children were 23% correct and for 75 /s/ children 16% correct, with a range of 0 to 77%. There was an approximately equal distribution of girls and boys in the first, second, third and fourth grades (35 boys and 29 girls for /r/ and 41 boys and 34 girls for /s/).

Thirty normal children were selected from a parochial school and 36 from a public school. The classroom teachers were asked to submit names of children who were average in school ability, free from known hearing losses, and without speech defects. Three boys and girls from grades 1, 2, 3, 4, and 5 were chosen in the parochial school. Six boys and six girls were chosen from grades 2, 3, and 4 in the

|  | /r/ words | | | /s/ words | | | Total words | | Average |
|---|---|---|---|---|---|---|---|---|---|
| Baseline | Mean | SD | % | Mean | SD | % | Mean | SD | WPM |
| /s/ children (N = 75) | 28.1 | 14.2 | 15.2 | 20.8 | 9.6 | 11.2 | 185.4 | 83.9 | 62 |
| /r/ children (N = 64) | 27.6 | 13.0 | 15.8 | 19.9 | 10.3 | 11.4 | 174.7 | 75.8 | 58 |
| Normal children (N = 65) | 41.6 | 13.0 | 15.5 | 30.3 | 9.6 | 11.3* | 268.9 | 75.2 | 90 |
| All males (N = 108) | 30.6 | 14.0 | | 21.5 | 9.9 | | 206.4 | 86.1 | 69 |
| All females (N = 96) | 34.2 | 15.3 | | 22.8 | 11.1 | | 211.2 | 91.8 | 70 |
| Midyear | | | | | | | | | |
| /s/ children (N = 75) | 33.5 | 15.5 | 16.0 | 23.5 | 9.8 | 11.2 | 209.9 | 81.3 | 70 |
| /r/ children (N = 64) | 28.3 | 11.8 | 15.0 | 21.9 | 9.3 | 11.3 | 187.2 | 78.2 | 62 |
| All males (N = 76) | 28.6 | 13.5 | | 22.1 | 10.2 | | 191.5 | 81.7 | 64 |
| All females (N = 63) | 34.1 | 14.3 | | 22.8 | 8.9 | | 209.0 | 78.4 | 70 |
| Children** | | | 13.0 | | | 8.0 | | | |
| Adults*** | | | 14.0 | | | 8.0 | | | |

*/s/ word counts were done on 29 normal children.

**90 children, thirty each at ages 5, 6, 7, adapted from Wepman and Haas (1969).

***500 adult telephone conversations, adapted from French, Carter, Koenig (1930).

TABLE 7.1. Means and standard deviations for /r/ words, /s/ words, and total words spoken in three minutes by different groups of children at baseline and midyear. Percent of /r/ and /s/ words compared to total words spoken and average words per minute also in indicated.

public school. This made a total of 32 boys (one was dropped) and 33 girls. Tape recordings revealed that these children were free from speech errors. The children lived in a middle-class predominantly white neighborhood.

We have checked to see whether sound interacts with demographic variables. Chi-square from a two-by-two table showed no significant difference in the distribution of the /r/ or /s/ sound by sex, nor of the articulation groups and normal group by sex. There was no difference in mean grade level of either /s/ or /r/ ($\overline{X}$ = 2.5 and 2.5 respectively), but the normals were slightly older ($\overline{X}$ grade = 3.0, F = 6.07, df2, 201, p < .01). No differences in age level (months) were found among the /s/, /r/, and normal groups (F = 1.4; $\overline{X}$ = 95.7, 96.3, 99.6 respectively).

## Procedures

All children were recorded in a quiet room in the school at 3¾ i.p.s. speed. The articulation impaired children were taped by the clinicians and the normal children by graduate students and one of the authors. Timed with stopwatches, three-minute conversation samples were obtained for the articulation impaired children in September and again in January (16-18 weeks apart). The normal children in public school were taped only in the fall and the parochial school children only in January. Topics of discussion included child's school activities, game play, TV programs, etc.

On the first listening the words-per-minute of child output were tallied with a hand counter. The three-minute time segment was also double checked for duration accuracy at this time. The definitions for counting words were taken from Johnson, Darley, and Spriesterbach (1963, p. 168). The tape was played a second time. For every word in which an /r/ or /s/ was heard, a written transcription was made. From this orthographic description the /r/ words were classified as consonant, unstressed vocalic, and stressed vocalic. Because of the controversy over classification of certain /r/ sounds, we established the following operational definition: consonant /r/ (rV, CrV, VrV); unstressed /ɚ/ (Vr—one syllable as in board, and CVr—second of two syllables—as in mother); stressed /ɝ/ (VrC as in girl). The /s/ words were classified according to position: initial, medial, final, and initial blends. Words in which the /s/ is pronounced as /z/ were not included, such as girls, was, etc.

## Reliability

Six graduate students listened to the normal children from the public schools and the percent agreement for spoken words-per-minute and total /r/ and /s/ words was in the nineties. Another judge heard the normals from parochial school and articulation impaired children. For this judge, 20 randomly chosen tape segments were analyzed by another judge. Intra and inter observer percent agreement was in the nineties for words per minute, and for /r/ and /s/ words with one exception—inter observer agreement for /s/ was 83%.

## Results

Table 7.1 contains data for all words, /r/ words, and /s/ words. Children with /r/ and /s/ errors at baseline (September) have a significantly lower output of /r/ words (F = 23.09; p < .001), /s/ words (F = 12.31; p < .001), and total words (F = 28.27; p < .001) than normal children. At midyear (January), after 16 weeks of therapy, the /s/ children compared with /r/ children had significantly more /r/

words (t = 2.21; .01 > p < .05), no difference in /s/ words (t = 1.45), and no difference in total words (t = 1.67) produced in three minutes of conversation. /r/ words occurred about 16% of the time and /s/ words about 11% of the time for all groups of children at both baseline (September) and midyear (January).

When all males were compared with all females no significant differences were found for total /r/ words, /s/ words, and total words spoken in three minutes at baseline. However, at midyear when only the /r/ and /s/ impaired children were compared, the females had significantly (t = 2.33; .01 < p < .05) higher /r/ word output than the males. No significant differences in /s/ word output was observed.

For comparison, the telephone conversation data collected by French, Carter, and Koenig (1930) on adults and children's descriptions of the TAT cards by Wepman and Hass (1969) are included. The proportion of /r/ and /s/ words in adult telephone conversations and child monologues is slightly less than the other three groups.

Table 7.2 illustrates the distribution of the three /r/ allophones and four /s/ positions comparing three groups of children at baseline (September). The normal children had a significantly higher output in all categories (except /s/ blends). This is simply a reflection of the greater number of words produced in three minutes by normals. At midyear (January), when the /s/ and /r/ children were compared, no differences were found across all categories except unstressed / ɚ /, where /s/ children spoke significantly more (t = 3.35; .01 < p < .001).

Raw data for /r/ allophones and /s/ positions at baseline and midyear were comparable and therefore combined in Table 7.2 with the percentage of the items also computed. The percents of occurrences of the three /r/ allophones and four /s/ positions are generally similar for all three groups of children. Of particular interest is the fact that the consonant /r/ and unstressed / ɚ / account for 90% of the /r/ words. Stressed / ɝ / makes up only 10% of the words. This has important implications for clinicians. If the consonant and unstressed / ɚ / were spoken correctly by the child, but the clinician was having difficulty teaching the stressed / ɝ /, therapy might be discontinued until later on the premise that the overall speech pattern would be quite intelligible (assuming no other errors).

The adult telephone conversations (French et al., 1930) and child monologues (Wepman and Hass, 1969) are included for comparison. The adult data indicate slight discrepancies—generally, higher unstressed / ɚ / and lower consonant /r/— while the children have higher stressed / ɝ / occurrences.

Inspection of the four /s/ positions, likewise illustrates a remarkable similarity among the three groups of children. Initial and final are the most frequent, followed by medial, and the least frequently occurring position were the initial blends. The adult data have a higher percentage for initial /s/ and fewer occurrences of the final and blend categories. The /s/ blends appear to increase at midyear for both /r/ and /s/ children and are higher than in normal children.

## Discussion

These data show that elementary school children with defective articulation have a significantly lower word output (60 wpm) compared with normals (90 wpm). Although normals averaged a half grade older, the ages were similar and it is doubtful that this discrepancy would account for the difference between the two groups. Lower word outputs in speech impaired children's conversation when

/r/ allophones     /s/ allophones

| | /r/ allophones | | | | | | | /s/ allophones | | | | | | | | |
|---|---|---|---|---|---|---|---|---|---|---|---|---|---|---|---|---|
| | Total | Conversation | Percentage | Unstressed | Percentage | Stressed | Percentage | Total | Initial | Percentage | Medial | Percentage | Final | Percentage | Blends | Percentage |
| /r/ children (N = 31) | 29.7 | 11.7 | 39 | 14.9 | 51 | 3.1 | 10 | 21.9 | 6.3 | 29 | 4.9 | 22 | 6.8 | 31 | 3.9 | 18 |
| /s/ children (N = 33) | 32.5 | 11.5 | 36 | 17.8 | 54 | 3.2 | 10 | 23.4 | 6.9 | 29 | 5.4 | 23 | 7.1 | 31 | 4.0 | 17 |
| Normal children | | | 36 | 23.6 | 54 | 4.5 | 10 | 32.4 | 9.9 | 30 | 7.7 | 24 | 10.3 | 32 | 4.5 | 14 |
| Normal children* | | | 27 | | 57 | | 16 | | | 39 | | 15 | | 30 | | 16 |
| Normal adults** | | | 31 | | 63 | | 6 | | | 40 | | 26 | | 25 | | 9 |

*Adapted from Wepman and Haas (1969).
**Adapted from French, Carter, and Koenig (1930).

TABLE 7.2. Percentage distribution of allophones of /r/ and positions of /s/ produced in three minutes of conversation (baseline and midyear averaged together).

compared to normals was also found by Dickerson (1971). In her study of ten articulation impaired children and ten normal children from ages 6-16 years, she found that children with articulation defects used 85 wpm and the normals spoke at 152 wpm. The differences between our study and hers may be due to age or manner in which the sample was elicited. In the Dickerson study the child was told he could earn money by talking for a minimum of two minutes. At the end of two minutes, five pennies were placed on the table and an additional penny was given for each minute of speech up to a maximum of five minutes. Previous studies have shown that systematic reinforcement markedly affects human behavior (Ferster and Perrott, 1968).

Children with articulation impairment display more than just sound errors. They also have a lower verbal output per unit of speaking time. This lends credence to suggestions that phonologic, morphemic, and syntactic development of the child must be considered as a complex developmental phonemenon. Further evaluation of verbal output appears warranted.

It is interesting to contrast these wpm rates of children with impaired articulation to other speaking interactions. Broen (1972) cites Maclay and Osgood (1967) as reporting adult speech rates from 122 to 181 wpm in relatively long utterances. In her work Broen found that 10 mothers averaged 69.2 wpm while talking with younger children (mean age 21 months) and 86.2 wpm while talking with older children (mean age 60 months) during free play. During story telling, rates were 115.1 wpm with the younger children and 127.5 wpm for the older children. Mean wpm for adult conversation was 132.4. Storytelling talking means the mother looked at pictures from a book and "told" a story from the pictures.

The percentage distribution of /r/ allophones or /s/ positions has about the same frequency as in normal children's speech. This answers the question posed by Shriner et al. (1969) as to whether children with a specified phonetic impairment, i.e., /r/ or /s/ errors, do not produce proportionately fewer total /r/ words or /s/ words than children with other articulation errors or children with normal speech. Dickerson also found a similar distribution of different phones (consonants, vowels, diphthongs) in the impaired articulation and normal groups. Her articulation group was longer on duration (took twice as long) and also had more pause-time as well as articulation-time than did the normal group.

The allophones of /r/ were studied in our second project year. We found that when 60 /r/ SPT items were sampled over a treatment period of one school year for approximately 300 /r/ children a definite rank order for allophones appeared (Wright and Diedrich, 1971). Mean scores of learned items were ranked, showing that the consonant /r/ items were most often produced correctly, followed by unstressed vocalic, and finally the stressed vocalic. These items were not taught or tested in this order. It is interesting to observe (Table 7.2) that 90% of the /r/ items were consonant and unstressed and 10% were stressed. If the stressed items are learned last, this may suggest some law of complexity and parsimony, i.e., more difficult motor units are used fewer times and are learned last. For example, consonant blends are usually mastered after other VC or CV combinations are acquired. Speech therapy did not change the order of these allophones over the school year. To our knowledge, this was the first long-term training study with a large population. This demonstrates that the allophonic differentiation is so powerful that it not only existed at the time of initial testing, but it was not greatly altered as the result of treatment. Although the number of correct responses increases substantially over time, the order of the items from those most often correct to those least often correct did not change markedly over time. This is true despite the fact that the design of the study permitted 20 clinicians to provide therapy of choice to the children they taught.

Some have questioned whether the three-minute samples in defective articulation children are large enough or representative enough of children's conversation. An average of 28 /r/ and 21 /s/ words are produced during a three-minute TALK sample for articulation impaired children. In addition, the distribution of the phoneme (CV, VC, VCV, etc.) is quite diversified. The percentage distribution of /r/ allophones and /s/ positions noted in the children's TAT descriptions adapted from Wepman and Hass (1969) and the adult telephone conversations by French et al. (1930) provides validity for the three-minute conversation samples between the clinician and child. For sounds that occur less frequently than /r/ and /s/, longer samples may be necessary.

Investigations of a given phonetic error in this study (/r/ or /s/) reveal that the frequency of use of that phoneme has a distribution similar to normal speakers. This indicates that the phonological model develops in a similar manner despite the articulation defect. Children with /r/ or /s/ errors did not use fewer /r/ or /s/ linguistic units because of these errors.

One might hypothesize (on an operant model of language learning) that a child who has a phonetic error, because of punishment for uttering these errors, would perhaps use fewer /r/ or /s/ sounds. The average age of our children was eight years. They had a minimum of three years beyond the time when general society (peers, teachers, parents) began to react to their speech if it was in error. Winitz (1969, pg. 76) states that children make all their sounds by three to four years of age. This means an eight-year-old has four to five years of mispractice on the phoneme. However, children in this study with /r/ or /s/ errors did not have a proportionately different frequency of erred words or allophones. This may support contentions that the deep structures are innate and one should thus not hypothesize that a difference in the use of phonemic structures would occur on the basis of surface phonetic errors.

There is further implication in using conversation for eliciting articulation responses. If children with articulation errors developed unique forms of language output (lacking in certain phonological characteristics) then samples of conversation used to determine the rate of progress in speech therapy could not be accurate without some adjustment because each child's output would be different. The results above would negate this concern.

## Generalization of the Target Phonemes in Different Speaking Environments

In evaluating how well articulation performance can be generalized to other speaking environments, Bankson and Byrne (1972) noted that speech performance measured on a final probe from a hidden tape recorder in a living room setting was comparable to speech performance that was tape recorded in the presence of the child (as in training) in that same living room. However, taped samples taken in the school and home had great variability (some had good agreement, others did not).

In order to determine if the three-minute conversations made each week by the field clinicians had any generalization outside the therapy setting, the following procedure was carried out by March 1 of our first project school year. Tape recordings were made of three-minute conversation samples from 37 children who were receiving therapy from three different female clinicians. Most of the recordings were obtained by an adult female, but some were by an adult male, both of whom were unknown to the children. The children were asked to describe various television programs they watched at home. About half the recordings were made in the speech clinicians' office, the remaining in other school rooms. The three field clinicians came to the project office about one month later and judged the same tapes. Reliability measures were obtained between the clinician's judgments done live during therapy compared to the clinician's counts from the tape recording made by another adult during that same week. Since we had earlier observed that there was a bias in the observations of clinicians vs. nonclinicians on the same children, this particular procedure would at least keep the bias in the same direction. We could determine whether or not there was generalization of the target phoneme to speaking arrangements other than speech between the child and the clinician. It was found that there were no significant differences in mean correct/wrong, total number of sounds and percentage correct (Table 7.3). Reliability was approximately .60 for total number of phonemes and number correct. The reason it was zero for number of wrong (and subsequently percent correct) is due to the few occurrences of wrong responses. Statistically, low variability results in low correlations.

Speech samples in three-minute TALKs during therapy by the clinician is representative of the child's speech when sampled outside therapy by another adult. The fact that a biased listener (the clinician) makes the judgments is irrelevant in this case. The question is, does the child use better, worse, or the same speech when talking with another person and when judged by the same perceptual criterion (the clinician)? Does the judge (in this case the clinician) perceive the child's speech in a similar manner in two different speaking environments? The clinicians heard the samples one month after they were taken. It is difficult to believe that they could remember the same number of correct or wrong responses the child used. We had established earlier that clinicians and different listeners did not perceive the same number of correct/wrong responses. These results indicated that the clinician did hear a similar number of correct/wrong phonemes spoken in two different situations.

|  | Live | | Tape | | | |
|---|---|---|---|---|---|---|
|  | Mean | SD | Mean | SD | t | r |
| Total Sounds (C+W) | 20.52 | 8.07 | 23.19 | 8.65 | 1.92 | .59** |
| Correct (C) | 19.94 | 8.01 | 21.29 | 8.73 | 0.92 | .57** |
| Wrong (W) | 0.58 | 1.31 | 1.65 | 3.86 | 1.41 | -.05 |
| C/C+W (%) | 90.0 | 20.0 | 94.0 | 19.0 | 1.38 | -.01 |

N = 31, df = 30, t.05 = 2.05*
N = 31, df = 29, r.05 = .335*; r.01 = .456**

TABLE 7.3. Three field clinicians' judgments on 32 children done live with the clinicians and from tapes made by another adult during the same week.

Another study during Year 2 (Denes and Diedrich, 1971) reported that tape recorded conversation samples made between a speech clinician and a child in a therapy room in the schools on 58 /r/ and /s/ children were judged not different from recorded samples between the teacher and the child in the classroom and between a parent and the child at home. Forty judges listened to 174 random tape segments and inter-judge agreement was .98. Mean percent correct scores in the three speaking environments were the same. There was no difference in children with high scores ($\overline{X}$ = 72% correct) or low scores ($\overline{X}$ = 49% correct) when compared across the three speaking conditions. Finally, correlations of percent correct across the three speaking conditions were in the nineties. In other words, correct/wrong target phoneme counts taken from the same child in three different speaking arrangements were judged to be similar. A criticism of this study is that the tape recorder might have been a discriminative stimulus for the child and, consequently, encouraged articulation responses that were similar in all three speaking situations. However, it is doubtful that a conditioned discriminative stimulus was formed. Few of the clinicians used the tape recorder in therapy. Also, the taped samples of conversation of speech sounded natural and did not appear to be exaggerated, forced or slowed.

Freilinger (1973) collected in the home (from a hidden recorder) taped samples of conversation made between child and an adult (ostensibly a baby-sitter). These were compared with tape recorded (visible to the children) conversations made by a speech clinician (this person was introduced to the child as a speech clinician interested in his improvement by the child's speech clinician) in the training environment. Comparison of correct production of the target phoneme (/r/ or /s/) made during conversation in the home and in the training environment were not significantly different between the children who received traditional therapy in the schools and the children who received paired stimuli therapy in a university clinic. However, when both therapy groups were combined, he did find that differences existed in correct/wrong counts between conversation samples made in therapy and those made at home. Therefore, caution should be used in predicting target phoneme performance outside therapy from samples made in therapy. As suggested in the section on Termination Criteria, the clinician should terminate therapy at 75% or better on two TALK tasks sampled one or two weeks apart, but continue to probe at four weeks and at eight weeks after termination to be sure the child is maintaining carryover.

Further support for the utility of the three-minute TALK task comes from a recent study by Longhurst and File (1977). They investigated Developmental Sentence Scores (DSS) in four different speaking conditions. An adult-child talking interaction with single object picture, toy, multiobject picture, and conversation. They found higher DSS scores in the adult-child conversation mode. Mastery of the phoneme is probably related to some hierarchy of speech performance, i.e., syllable, words, and conversation. With different conversations (describing action pictures, toys, and "talking") the Longhurst and File data demonstrate structural differences. The use of child-generated speech, which is necessary in a three-minute TALK task, is representative of the more complex forms of coarticulatory gestures. If a child evidences satisfactory performance on the target phoneme in this arrangement, the chances are very good that he or she will do so under other similar speaking conditions. Our data (noted above) which evaluated the adult-child speaking in the speech office, classroom, and home support this notion. All of this indicates that the conversation task is a very useful, and perhaps necessary tool for the clinician who wishes to demonstrate satisfactory performance of a child's newly acquired phoneme.

## Prediction, Sample Size, and Probe Measures

Pendergast, Dickey, and Soder (1969) followed children who had protrusional lisps for three years (beginning kindergarten to beginning third grade). They could predict 87% of the beginning third grade children who needed speech therapy on the basis of four items: 1) more misarticulations on the Photo Articulation Test, 2) substitutions on nine /s—z/ items, 3) open bite, and 4) articulation of /t-d-n-l/ with blade of the tongue.

McDonald and McDonald (1974) sampled on the Screening Deep Test of Articulation (SDTA) 521 children who received no speech therapy over a three-year period (beginning kindergarten to beginning third grade). Ten percent of the children had a problem (defined as less than three correct out of 10 items) on /s/ at the beginning of kindergarten. By the beginning of third grade only 6% of the same children were considered to have a problem. For /r/, 15% had a problem at the beginning of kindergarten, but by third grade only 6% still remained in the problem category. These results suggest that considerable change does result without therapy from age five to eight.

Barrett and Welsh (1975) did a study using the Predictive Screening Test of Articulation (PSTA) developed by Van Riper and Erickson (1973). Their findings indicate that some 90% of the first graders who scored above a cut-off score of 34 would have normal articulation by the third grade without therapy.

Predicting which children will be successful in therapy is another matter. In our project we used the McDonald Screening Deep Test of Articulation (1968) three times during the school year, September, January, and May. In addition, each child was probed with a Sound Production Task (SPT) which is an imitative sound, syllable, word, phrase test (Elbert, Shelton, Arndt, 1967; and Wright, Shelton, Arndt, 1969) and the three-minute conversation sample (TALK). The latter two probes were done once a week, twice a week, or once a month depending on whether the child was seen four times a week, twice a week, or once a week.

The pre-McDonald test had a good correlation with itself at midyear (.78) but had much smaller correlation with midyear TALK (–.26) tasks (Table 7.4). On the other hand the baseline SPT correlated .47 with midyear TALK and baseline TALK correlated .40 with midyear TALK (Table 7.5). The low correlation between the McDonald Test and TALK suggested that although the McDonald Test represents a sample of spontaneous speech performance of the child, speech obtained under the test conditions was not correlated highly with clinician-child spontaneous conversation. The baseline SPT and TALK correlations were higher than the McDonald Test, but even these would not be considered high. In other words, it is extremely difficult to predict at the beginning of the year how much a child will improve. In Freilinger's study (1973) the control children who had passed eight of ten items of the McDonald Test had a mean of 79% correct target phoneme counts from conversation at home. The experimental group, who also satisfied the same McDonald Test criterion, had mean scores of 57% correct during conversation at home. These findings support the notion that this articulation test is not a good predictor of future performance in conversation nor performance of conversation in another environment.

| | Pre-McD | Mid-McD | Post-McD | Pre-TALK | Mid-TALK | Post-TALK | Pre-Stim |
|---|---|---|---|---|---|---|---|
| Pre-McD | 100 | | | | | | |
| Mid-McD | 78 | 100 | | | | | |
| Post-McD | 67 | 86 | 100 | | | | |
| Pre-TALK | -26 | -28 | -23 | 100 | | | |
| Mid-TALK | -26 | -47 | -55 | 55 | 100 | | |
| Post-TALK | -19 | -42 | -58 | 21 | 86 | 100 | |
| Pre-Stim | -17 | -24 | -21 | 70 | 71 | 28 | 100 |

Partial Correlation – Pre-McD and Pre-TALK controlled

| | Mid-McD | Post-McD | Mid-TALK | Post-TALK | Pre-Stim |
|---|---|---|---|---|---|
| Mid-McD | 100 | | | | |
| Post-McD | 71 | 100 | | | |
| Mid-TALK | -43 | -56 | 100 | | |
| Post-TALK | -42 | -61 | 92 | 100 | |
| Pre-Stim | -14 | -11 | 22 | 20 | 100 |

TABLE 7.4. Correlations for 229 /r/ children for pretherapy stimulability scores for /r/ (number correct), total errors on the McDonald Test, and TALK percent correct scores for /r/ during the school year: pretherapy (September), midyear (January), and posttherapy (May).

|               | Base TALK | Base SPT | Base US | Mid TALK | Mid SPT | Mid US |
|---------------|-----------|----------|---------|----------|---------|--------|
| Baseline TALK | 100       |          |         |          |         |        |
| Baseline SPT  | 60        | 100      |         |          |         |        |
| Baseline US   | 77        | 94       | 100     |          |         |        |
| Midyear TALK  | 40        | 47       | 49      | 100      |         |        |
| Midyear SPT   | 28        | 46       | 45      | 79       | 100     |        |
| Midyear US    | 34        | 49       | 48      | 90       | 97      | 100    |

TABLE 7.5. Correlations for items correct on SPT and percent correct on TALK and Unified Scores (US) at baseline and midyear. Sample size varied for each cell from a minimum of 736 to a maximum of 900 children (/r/ and /s/ combined).

A Unified Score (Diedrich and Bangert, 1972) was developed wherein the total percent correct for both SPT and TALK were calculated to make a unified score for /r/ and a unified score for /s/ at different times during the school year (Table 7.6). Two things were clear from these results:
1. The /r/ children were always more stable than /s/ in predicting future performance. In other words, once the /r/ child got the new response in his repertoire he was more likely to maintain it than the /s/ child.
2. Systematic improvement in the prediction can be expected as the child continues in a therapy program (also see Chapter 3).

Shelton et al. (1967) had a similar finding, it took until the third lesson before a good prediction could be obtained on the child's final performance. It is obvious that speech clinicians have very little to go on at the beginning of the year from a diagnostic evaluation to predict how well any child will perform. However, after the child has been in treatment for awhile, the prediction of future performance is much better. This is suggestive of old fashioned diagnostic therapy discussed later.

|          | Base | 6 weeks | 18 weeks | 30 weeks |
|----------|------|---------|----------|----------|
| Baseline | 100  |         |          |          |
|          | 100  |         |          |          |
| 6 weeks  | 64   | 100     |          |          |
|          | 81   | 100     |          |          |
| 18 weeks | 37   | 62      | 100      |          |
|          | 62   | 79      | 100      |          |
| 30 weeks | 27   | 63      | 85       | 100      |
|          | 45   | 71      | 90       | 100      |

Note: With the effect of baseline scores eliminated, partial correlations resulted in similar predictions.

TABLE 7.6. Correlations of Unified Scores (SPT and TALK combined) over the school year for 488 /s/ and 508 /r/ children at baseline (September), six and 18 weeks after therapy began, and at 30 weeks, the end of therapy (May). Upper number is correlation for /s/ and lower number for /r/.

The last paragraph should be reminiscent of the stimulability concept of Carter and Buck (1958). Sommers et al. (1967) concluded that children with low stimulability scores showed more improvement with therapy than children with high stimulability scores. The Sound Production Task (SPT) contains items that are produced by the clinician and imitated by the child in isolation-syllables, words, and sentences, which in effect, makes the SPT a stimulability test. The correlations of SPT with TALK indicate that children's SPT scores were positively correlated with TALK scores at midyear (Table 7.5). Moore, Burke, and Adams (1976) have reported that stimulability was positively correlated with the correct number of /s/ productions for both clusters and words occurring with both high and low frequency. They also found that for imitation neither familiar or unfamiliar words, nor nonsense syllables, made any difference. These findings lend further support to the usefulness of the SPT as a probe tool.

To further test the notion of stimulability, the number produced correctly out of thirty nonsense syllable /r/ sounds among the sixty SPT /r/ items formed the basis for a stimulability score for 229 /r/ children. The distortion, substitution, and omission errors were counted to give a total error score for /r/ on the McDonald Test. Percent correct TALK scores for /r/ at baseline, midyear, and end of year were also included. Correlations and partial correlations for all three measures during the school year are shown in Table 7.4. As percent correct in TALK improved the McDonald Test error scores decreased (negative correlations). Also, children with more errors on the McDonald Test tended to have poorer stimulability scores (negative correlations). Again, as indicated earlier, pretherapy TALK scores are better correlated with mid-TALK scores than with post-TALK scores. Also, mid-TALK predicts better post-TALK than does pre-TALK. The partial correlations demonstrated a positive relationship of pretherapy stimulability scores with mid- and post-TALK scores (Table 7.4). Although low (.22 and .20) they were significant (p < .003). This indicated two things: 1) pretherapy evaluations of children using these measures separately (articulation test, talk, or stimulability scores) provide little predictive information about future progress in therapy, 2) children with higher stimulability scores who were placed in therapy tended to be associated with higher TALK scores after therapy.

Gerber (1977) noted that the packaged articulation programs currently available might be used to predict progress in therapy. Some programs improve a child's articulation pattern in a matter of hours. If the child does not move swiftly through a given program, with the help of a peer, aide, or the clinician, then obviously the clinician must provide the child with a more specific program to fit his needs. Both Garrett (1973) and Irwin (1974) commented that prediction from individual children was extremely difficult. Their highly systematic and structured programs provide big gains, for large numbers of children, in a very short time. However, it was difficult to determine at the beginning of the program which child would or would not succeed. Garrett (1973, p. 108) found that

> . . . the range of articulatory change of a target phoneme for stimulable children is for a mean of .25 on the properant in 179 minutes with the odds for such a change being 8 to 1, to a mean of .43 in 23 minutes with the odds being 3 to 1 for a change. When the child is not stimulable, data shows that program therapy can still be very efficient, but the clinician is not able to predict the time needed, the degree of change, nor the probability of that change occurring.

Another advantage in conversation samples is the use of a percent correct score for specific phonemes to compare performance across children and clinicians. The progress of specific children or groups of children can be described in objective terms. When one only uses the classification of distortion, substitution, or omission (DSO) to describe phoneme errors, it is extremely difficult to quantify the improvement and to discuss relative change. Elbert (1971) suggested that (for predicting the quantity and rate of articulation change) the error categories of substitution or distortion do not provide as much information as knowing whether the child makes correct or wrong responses (see Chapter 8). Jordan (1960) found that the number of defective sounds had the highest contribution to overall judged severity and that knowledge of DSO contributed minimally to the prediction. The complexity of the omission and substitution error interaction with phoneme type on listener judgments of intelligibility was demonstrated by Coston and Ainsworth (1972) which makes useless general statements like "omission errors should receive therapy first." Alcorn, Griffith, and Miner (1974) stressed that distinctive feature therapy should be considered in ranking severity of phoneme error production. Their work contradicted that of Milisen (1954) who concluded that severity occurred first by omissions, than substitutions, and lastly, distortions. Furthermore, when one looks in the literature (Van Riper, 1963) for evidence of how to use DSO information to determine therapy goals, it is found wanting. Turton (1973, p. 207) in discussing the analysis of DSO classification stated: "More importantly, we have not generated different therapy programs for each of these types of children." We submit that for children who have relatively few articulation errrors (as in /r/ or /s/) the DSO is not needed. However, children with multiple errors should have a distinctive feature analysis to assess their phonological system. The percent correct score can then be used to track improvement for a selected phoneme. See McReynolds and Engmann (1975) for a training manual on distinctive features and Costello (1975) and Costello and Onstine (1976) for a review of articulation instruction based on distinctive feature theory.

An obvious question concerning conversation is, "How much of a sample do you need?" Wright et al. (1969) used 30 occurrences of the phoneme in children's descriptions of pictures. Garrett (1973) proposed a minimum of 40 occurrences of the target phoneme and is using this as the criterion. Shelton, Johnson, and Arndt (1972) and Bankson and Byrne (1972) also used 40 items in conversation. In a number of the articulation learning programs conversation length of 5, 10, and 15 minutes has been suggested. Gray (1974) stated that the clinician must collect at least 10 target sounds while the student is talking in the classroom with the teacher and other students at an accuracy of 90%. From our data it was found that articulation impaired children in first through sixth grade averaged 22 /s/ and 30 /r/ words in three minutes of conversation. In this time one can obtain a good display of different /r/ allophones and /s/ positions as noted earlier (Table 7.2). In our opinion, a minimum of 10 but less than 20 seems reasonable to demonstrate target phoneme acquisition in conversation.

Another question is do you need both the SPT (an imitative probe) and TALK (a spontaneous speech sample) or could you use either one alone? We have described elsewhere our concept of a Unified Score (Diedrich and Bangert, 1972 and Chapter 3) which is the combined percent correct on SPT and TALK. There was a fairly high correlation of .79 between the SPT and TALK at midyear (Table 7.5). This would suggest that either one alone would be sufficient. However, there are advantages in using both to give the clinician different information. In systematically probing with the SPT items, the clinician can determine in what context the child is performing and thus guide therapy planning for the child (Wright et al., 1969). Turton (1973) has pointed out that imitative testing may reflect phonetic skills (the ability to produce the sound) and spontaneous speech may reflect phonemic skills (integration of the sound into a linguistic system). If the SPT is used alone, one may well have a child who is not generalizing, such as illustrated with child number 61 in Figure 7.1. The SPT and TALK tasks take about five minutes. That is no more time than clinicians generally expend in keeping daily log notes. If one were forced to choose only one task, then the three-minute TALK sample is probably better, since the goal of the clinician is to obtain correction for the child at the conversation level.

There is one other conspicuous finding about generalization when we visually compare the SPT and TALK learning curves over the school year. Forty children were pulled randomly from a pool of 1,108 children and their SPT/TALK learning curves were inspected. Six children were chosen for illustration (Figure 7.1). The most striking observation was that as the Sound Production Task improves, the TALK task follows right behind it as in /r/ child number 371 and /s/ child number 574. In children number 39 and number 72 there is practically a superimposed learning pattern with the peaks and valleys having astonishing similarity between the imitative SPT and conversation TALK. The exception to what we generally found was /r/ child number 61 whose SPT went to approximately 70% correct and the TALK task stayed at zero, demonstrating no generalization to conversation. However, this exception is the typical impression held by clinicians in speech pathology (including the first author until now). Somehow, we came to believe that until the child produces the response at an imitative level at some preestablished 100% criterion, he will not show much evidence of generalization to conversation. This view is contradicted by data presented here. In many cases, children show generalization to TALK long before they obtain 100% on the Sound Production Task (for more detail see Chapter 8).

The fact that the target phoneme may generalize relatively quickly in conversation should prompt clinicians to reevaluate their articulation programming procedures. Perhaps practice in sentences, reading, and conversations could be initiated much earlier and thereby achieve carryover sooner (see Chapter 6).

## Termination Criteria and Carryover in Articulation Learning

In speech pathology we have little empirical data to determine when someone should be dismissed from therapy. This is true for articulation, voice, dysfluency, or language. The clinician usually determines when to dismiss after listening to the client's speech and perhaps a report from parents, spouse, teachers, or the client himself about how well the client is doing outside the speech therapy office. A review of the literature revealed that little objective data are available to help the clinician determine when the child with an articulation problem should be terminated (Van Riper and Irwin, 1958; Chapman et al., 1961; Winitz, 1969; Van Hattum, 1969; Irwin, 1969; Black, 1970; Wolfe and Goulding, 1973; Sommers and Kane, 1974). Several articulation programs (Gerber, 1977) have specified the 90-100% level in conversational speech. The purpose of this section is to discuss

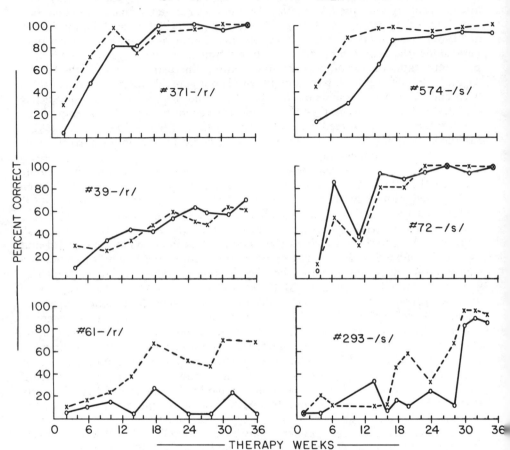

FIGURE 7.1. SPT/TALK generalization curves for selected children.

termination criteria and carryover in the case management of /r/ and /s/ impaired children by using systematic conversation probes.

## Procedures

A team of 20 speech clinicians from the greater Kansas City area representing a cross-section of different size school districts and socio-economic areas was selected to participate during project Year 2. The clinicians scheduled their cases in September and were asked to send to us a list of those children whose /r/ or /s/ errors represented the primary impairment as tested on the McDonald Articulation Screening Deep Test (1968). We randomly chose 15 /r/ and 15 /s/ children from each clinician. Children were in grades one through six, average grade level was 2.3. Group therapy size ranged from two to five children, average group size was 2.75. Several children were seen for individual therapy. Nine clinicians saw their children once a week. Eleven clinicians had therapy two times a week. Three clinicians were on the block system where they met four times a week for eight weeks of therapy, then eight weeks of no therapy, followed by eight more weeks of block therapy. Children were scheduled from 20 to 30 minutes of therapy time, most of them having 30 minute lessons. The children were not to have hearing losses, were not to be in special education classes, and were not to exhibit obvious impairment of the speech mechanism.

Articulation measures included the McDonald Articulation Test (1968) administered three times during the school year, baseline (September), midyear (January) and end of the year (May). The imitative Sound Production Tasks (SPT) modified by Elbert, Shelton, Arndt (1967) and Shelton, Elbert, Arndt (1967) for /r/ and /s/ and the three-minute TALK Task (Diedrich, 1971b) were systematically used as probes during the year. In the latter case the clinician engaged the child in conversation for three minutes and counts the target phoneme as correct or wrong. The SPT and TALK probes were given every week, two weeks, or each month depending on whether a child was scheduled four times a week, twice, or once a week, respectively, for therapy.

The children were enrolled in speech therapy and no specification of treatment procedures was given. The clinicians were told to dismiss the children from therapy whenever they believed a child was a "success."

No criteria were provided to determine when a child should be dismissed. The clinicians were asked to make SPT and TALK probes of the child's speech every four weeks after he was dropped from therapy. In the fall of the next year, another TALK probe of the child's speech was taken. These measures were obtained by the clinician in September before therapy was started for the year.

## Reliability

Sixteen of the 20 Year 2 clinicians had carryover data for us to analyze. Five graduate students in speech pathology checked seven of the 16 clinicians for reliability of correct and wrong counts. The students engaged the children in three-minute conversations during the same week the clinicians made their counts. We did not get counts from all of the clinicians because some had already been done when we were ready to do reliability. From two to seven children were sampled for each clinician (Table 7.7).

The correct/wrong counts show good agreement between the students and clinicians 4, 5, 6, 7. One child (number 5) for clinician three and two children (numbers 1 and 2) for clinician one had reversals in agreement, but agreed on all other children sampled. Clinician two and the graduate student disagreed on all six children.

When t-tests were run between the mean percent correct found by the clinicians and the students, the values were significantly different. The statistic fails to describe the basic trend of these data—when a conversation probe was made by two observers both agreed more often than not (30 out of 39 observations). The agreements were higher when you resolved some unique perceptual differences between clinician two and graduate student two. The judgment of whether the subsequent data are believable remains with the reader. Here, as with the reliability reported in Chapter 2, Methodology, one finds a range of agreement typical (in this project) for judgments of correct/wrong in conversation. Clearly, most of the time, most observers agree on most children.

**Clinician 1 / Student 1**

| | Clinician 1 C | Clinician 1 W | Student 1 C | Student 1 W |
|---|---|---|---|---|
| 1. | 26 | 0 | 14 | 21 |
| 2. | 20 | 1 | 4 | 20 |
| 3. | 21 | 0 | 15 | 7 |
| 4. | 49 | 0 | 16 | 3 |
| 5. | 36 | 0 | 25 | 1 |
| 6. | 16 | 0 | 16 | 9 |

**Clinician 2 / Student 2**

| | Clinician 2 C | Clinician 2 W | Student 2 C | Student 2 W |
|---|---|---|---|---|
| 1. | 29 | 0 | 14 | 17 |
| 2. | 12 | 0 | 11 | 25 |
| 3. | 14 | 0 | 8 | 35 |
| 4. | 19 | 3 | 14 | 39 |
| 5. | 12 | 5 | 11 | 29 |
| 6. | 7 | 1 | 14 | 28 |

**Clinician 3 / Student 3**

| | Clinician 3 C | Clinician 3 W | Student 3 C | Student 3 W |
|---|---|---|---|---|
| 1. | 22 | 8 | 43 | 10 |
| 2. | 16 | 1 | 33 | 10 |
| 3. | 16 | 1 | 14 | 5 |
| 4. | 18 | 1 | 26 | 0 |
| 5. | 13 | 2 | 8 | 28 |

**Clinician 4 / Student 4**

| | Clinician 4 C | Clinician 4 W | Student 4 C | Student 4 W |
|---|---|---|---|---|
| 1. | 13 | 0 | 9 | 3 |
| 2. | 27 | 1 | 21 | 3 |
| 3. | 28 | 2 | 32 | 2 |
| 4. | 30 | 0 | 14 | 4 |
| 5. | 37 | 1 | 12 | 4 |

**Clinician 5 / Student 5**

| | Clinician 5 C | Clinician 5 W | Student 5 C | Student 5 W |
|---|---|---|---|---|
| 1. | 27 | 0 | 39 | 0 |
| 2. | 29 | 2 | 10 | 4 |
| 3. | 35 | 0 | 54 | 1 |
| 4. | 26 | 1 | 37 | 0 |
| 5. | 22 | 0 | 33 | 1 |
| 6. | 20 | 5 | 17 | 8 |
| 7. | 35 | 2 | 53 | 0 |

**Clinician 6 / Student 5**

| | Clinician 6 C | Clinician 6 W | Student 5 C | Student 5 W |
|---|---|---|---|---|
| 1. | 22 | 0 | 20 | 0 |
| 2. | 14 | 0 | 32 | 0 |

**Clinician 7 / Student 5**

| | Clinician 7 C | Clinician 7 W | Student 5 C | Student 5 W |
|---|---|---|---|---|
| 1. | 24 | 0 | 28 | 0 |
| 2. | 22 | 0 | 25 | 0 |
| 3. | 16 | 0 | 24 | 0 |
| 4. | 12 | 0 | 13 | 4 |
| 5. | 13 | 0 | 16 | 0 |
| 6. | 28 | 0 | 26 | 0 |
| 7. | 20 | 0 | 29 | 0 |

TABLE 7.7. Target phoneme Correct (C) and Wrong (W) counts made from live three minute TALKs during the same week in September (carryover data) by the field clinician and a graduate student observer.

## Data Analyzed

We had available to us from our data the number of weeks a child had been in therapy, when the clinician decided the child was a success, and the follow-up probes conducted during the school year and the following fall. Out of the original 20 clinicians, seven did not designate any children as "success." The range in percent (defined as child dismissed from therapy with adequate speech) for 16 clinicians was 6% to 60% with an average for the group of 25%.

Since we had percent correct TALK scores on each child we could determine the level of percent correct set by the clinician for "success." In every case the clinician used the 100% correct level in conversation as their success criterion. By reviewing *post hoc* the probe data prior to the time each child was declared a "success" and dropped from therapy, it was determined for these 16 clinicians that the mean number of weeks of errorless (100%) conversation was six weeks (range 0-16 weeks) for /r/ and eight weeks (range 3-13 weeks) for /s/. In other words, after a child had reached 100% correct in conversation, these clinicians kept the child in therapy for an additional six to eight weeks of therapy.

For the purpose of choosing a possible termination criterion, an arbitrary cut-off point of 75% or better was selected. For several reasons not all children tested in May were probed again in September. The children could have moved, been sick, or the clinician had changed schools or resigned. In order to determine

|  |  | /r/ September | | |
|---|---|---|---|---|
|  |  | Present | Missing |  |
| May | above | 90 | 54 | 144 |
|  | below | 100 | 45 | <u>145</u> |
|  |  | 190 | 99 | 289 |

chi-square = 1.34

nonsignificant

|  |  | /s/ September | | |
|---|---|---|---|---|
|  |  | Present | Missing |  |
| May | above | 142 | 66 | 204 |
|  | below | 76 | 39 | <u>115</u> |
|  |  | 218 | 105 | 319 |

chi-square = 0.16

nonsignificant

TABLE 7.8. The number of /r/ and /s/ children who had scores above and below 75% correct during TALK in May. The number of children who were present or missing for carryover probes in September.

                          /r/ September
                    above              below

              above      75               18        93
        May
              below      11               86        97
                         86              104        190


                      chi-square = 92.05
                           p < .001


                          /s/ September
                    above              below

              above     116               27        143
        May
              below      10               65         75
                        126               92        218


                      chi-square = 92.68
                           p < .001

TABLE 7.9. The number of /r/ and /s/ children who had scores above and below 75% correct on TALK in May and for carryover in September.

if there was any systematic bias of children who were missing in September, a chi-square was computed for the number of children who were above and below 75% correct in May and present or missing in September (Table 7.8). No significant shifts were observed ($\chi^2$ = 1.34 for /r/ and .16 for /s/ children). We can conclude that the children who were available and probed (n = 190 /r/ and 218 /s/) were probably representative of the original sample.

It was observed that 81% of the 143 /s/ children who were equal to or above 75% in May remained there in September (Table 7.9). Eighty-one percent of the 93 /r/ children who were equal to or above 75% in May held that position in September. Two by two chi-square tests of these percentages are highly significant for /r/ ($\chi^2$ = 92.05; p < .001) and for /s/ ($\chi^2$ = 92.68; p < .001). In other words, one can predict that less than 19% of the children who have greater than 75% correct scores in conversation on the /r/ and /s/ phoneme in May will regress below that criterion in September.

We can also determine from Table 7.9 that 11% of the /r/ and 13% of the /s/ children who were below 75% in May, were above 75% in September. Thus, if approximately 19% of those children who were greater than 75% in May are below in September, about 12% of those who were below are now above 75% in September. That means a net loss of success of approximately 7% of the children who would need additional therapy in September based on this criterion score.

If a termination criterion of 75%, 85%, or 95% on Unified Scores were selected, then the numbers of children who would be dismissed from the "caseload" (57 clinicians with 996 children) could be estimated (Table 7.10).

For example, if one used 85% correct as the dismissal criterion, then about 5% of the children should not have been enrolled in therapy in September; 10% could have been dismissed after six weeks of therapy; 35% after eighteen weeks of therapy; and by the end of the school year (30 weeks), 53% or 561 children could have been dismissed.

## Discussion

The carryover data reported in the project Year 2 used only three-minute TALK scores. The Unified Scores (Table 7.10) were the total percent correct from both the SPT and the three-minute conversation measures (TALK). Correlations of the two scores at baseline (September) were .60 and at midyear (January) .79. By plotting separate curves for SPT and TALK percent correct, we have observed that the imitative SPT generally is better than spontaneous conversation, but that TALK is not far behind. Furthermore, sometimes the target phoneme does not generalize to TALK (see Chapter 8). Since our goal is adequate speech during conversation, we suggest that the criterion probe be determined by either SPT and TALK combined, or by TALK alone.

We think that the clinician could stop therapy when the percent correct in conversation is above 75% on two consecutive probes one to two weeks apart. But the conservative clinician may feel more comfortable by establishing the dismissal criterion at 85%. In his work with programmed articulation learning, Garrett (1973, p. 133) noted that little change occurred with additional therapy after the 70% level was achieved. We have made the same observation when children reach the 75-85% correct level in conversation. To obtain another 10-20% gain in the child's score which may take as much as 6-15 more therapy weeks is uneconomical (Table 7.11).

We selected the first 61 children (the N was arbitrary) in Year 2 who reached 75% correct or better on two successive probes during the school year. Clinicians in Year 2, who had no predetermined termination criterion, continued therapy another 14-15 weeks thereby increasing /r/ children from 87 to 91% correct and /s/ children showed no gain from 88 to 88% (Table 7.11).

Would children who were terminated from therapy at 75% correct during the school year continue to improve to 100% on their own? We attempted to answer this question in Year 3 by asking the clinicians to dismiss children from therapy who obtained 75% or better in two successive probes (one or two weeks apart). Unfortunately the clinicians would not cut the cord and follow through. By observing the clinician data cards in the project office, we could see that the clinicians were continuing to work with the child after 75% correct had been reached. When asked why they did not dismiss the child the clinicians would respond, ". . . I don't think the child is ready yet . . . let me work at it a little longer," etc. Consequently, the "weeks continued in therapy" column (Table 7.11) is not zero, but averages 3–5 weeks; substantially less than Year 2 and somewhat less than Year 4 clinicians who (like Year 2 clinicians) were not told when they should terminate therapy.

The *post hoc* data analysis presented in Table 7.11 for Years 2, 3, and 4 suggest:
1. Clinicians generally keep children in therapy until 90% or better is reached (Years 2 and 4).

Table 7.10. The number of children from a caseload of 996 (/r/ and /s/) who could be dismissed from speech therapy during the school year when a Unified Score (SPT + TALK) are specified.

| Dismissal Criteria | 75% Correct | | | 85% Correct | | | 95% Correct | | |
|---|---|---|---|---|---|---|---|---|---|
| | Percent | N | Total | Percent | N | Total | Percent | N | Total |
| Baseline | 9 | 105 | 105 | 5 | 65 | 65 | .5 | 1 | 12 |
| 6 weeks | 29 | 108 | 213 | 10 | 70 | 135 | 1 | 14 | 26 |
| 18 weeks | 46 | 270 | 483 | 35 | 248 | 383 | 8 | 150 | 176 |
| 30 weeks | 64 | 184 | 667 | 53 | 178 | 561 | 24 | 210 | 360 |

Table 7.11. Percent correct TALK scores at baseline and specified probe points in weeks during a school year for Project Years 2, 3, and 4.

| N | Sound | Baseline Percent Correct | Weeks to Criterion (75% Correct) | Average Percent Correct | Weeks Continued in Therapy | Average Percent Correct | Additional Weeks of No Therapy | Average Percent Correct |
|---|---|---|---|---|---|---|---|---|
| | | | | YEAR 2 | | | | |
| 61 | /r/ | 29 | 14 | 87 | 14 | 91 | 14 | 94 |
| 61 | /s/ | 8 | 13 | 88 | 15 | 88 | 15 | 88 |
| | | | | YEAR 3 | | | | |
| 24 | /r/ | 29 | 13 | 86 | 3 | - | 11 | 96 |
| 24 | /s/ | 23 | 9 | 81 | 5 | - | 11 | 86 |
| | | | | YEAR 4 | | | | |
| 39 | /r/ | 42 | 11 | 86 | 6 | 97 | 10 | 99 |
| 47 | /s/ | 29 | 9 | 87 | 6 | 96 | 11 | 98 |

2. The average amount of time spent in therapy after 75% was reached equaled the amount of time spent before 75% (Year 2) and was about 2/3 the time in Year 4. In other words, substantial therapy time is spent after 75% is reached.

The question remains is this additional therapy time warranted? Our suspicion is no (based on Year 3 results), but no definitive statement can be made on the basis of these data collection procedures. There are obviously wide individual differences in children which need to be taken into account when the decision is made to terminate therapy. For example, the turn-on-the-good-speech-for-clinician-child is one case. Here the child persists in using the error except when he walks in the speech therapy room where he easily obtains greater than 75% correct. This child should not be dismissed and will need a different approach to obtain target phoneme carryover into conversation.

Perhaps one reason clinicians do not drop children from therapy is administrative. If 12-15 weeks of therapy are needed for a child to reach 85% criterion, that means a calendar date between January 1 and February 1 of the school year (take out some weeks for testing in September, illnesses, and holidays). Since human effort is parsimonious and tends toward homeostasis, it is simpler to keep the children in therapy for the rest of the year (keep up average daily attendance) than to go through the hassle of scheduling additional children, working with the classroom teacher to get this done, and starting up a new therapy program.

Using a 75% correct criterion (Table 7.10) clinicians could dismiss 64% of the /r/ and /s/ children by the end of the school year compared to the yearly expected dismissal rate (30% average) reported by over 700 clinicians (Chapman et al., 1961). A management decision then would be to schedule children for about 15 weeks in the fall, drop all children who attain greater than 75% (or 85%) correct, and plan ahead to reschedule a new caseload for the spring. If this system were built into the clinical decision making of the speech clinician it might make the administrative rescheduling easier. Clinicians who operate on a six or eight week block system seem to have little difficulty changing schedules, once they educate the principal, teachers, and themselves to the format.

The September carryover data reported earlier noted that some 19% of the /r/ and /s/ children do regress below the 75% criterion level after an approximate four month lapse (16 weeks). This suggests that children should have periodic TALK followup probes to determine maintenance of carryover. Clinicians should probe the dismissed children in eight weeks to determine whether a child needs rescheduling for additional therapy during the last eight weeks of school. TALK probes should be made again in May (after 16 weeks) and only those children who are below 75-85% correct need to be checked again when they return to school in the fall.

This study was concerned with children who had a primary impairment of the /r/ or the /s/ sounds. It seems reasonable to believe, until otherwise demonstrated, that a TALK criterion score of 75% or better also would be justified in the termination from therapy of children with other phoneme errors as well.

## Summary

1. It is recommended that children with /r/ and /s/ errors be terminated from therapy when their TALK scores reach 75% or better on two successive probes.
2. Follow-up TALK probes should be carried out eight and 16 weeks after dismissal to ensure that carryover has been maintained.

3. Between May and September less than 19% of the sampled children regressed below 75% correct in conversation, but an additional 12% (who were below 75% in May) were better than 75% correct four months later (September).
4. There was an enormous inefficiency of clinician time by maintaining children in speech therapy long after maximal gains had been reached. From 53-64% of the /r/ and /s/ children could be dismissed each year if a 75-85% correct criterion score were used.

## Conclusions

This chapter has reviewed conversation as a measure for evaluating acquisition of the erred phoneme during therapy. The findings are summarized as follows:
1. Correct/wrong counts made by the child's clinician from three minute samples of conversation may be biased and not always reliable.
2. Systematic assessment of conversation to evaluate articulation learning seems to make a great deal of intuitive sense. If we want correction of speech in conversation then conversation probes should be our final criterion measure. Descriptive data of /r/ and /s/ from children's conversation were presented.
3. Clinician-child conversation samples collected in school may be representative of other adult-child speaking environments.
4. Phoneme generalization to conversation appears to occur in therapy earlier than we have generally believed. Sample size and repeated measures were discussed.
5. The concept of stimulability was discussed in terms of prediction of future performance in therapy and ultimate progress in achieving phoneme generalization in conversation.
6. Termination criteria from therapy based on samples of conversation were suggested.

CHAPTER 8

# Other Subanalyses of the Data

This chapter provides information about other phonological errors associated with primary /r/ or /s/ deficits. Is speed of learning of the target phoneme associated with other articulation errors? Also reviewed is our classic description of articulation errors as distortion, substitution, and omission.

The next section in the chapter deals with /s-z/ generalization. The evidence indicates that in most cases both /s/ and /z/ do not have to be treated. What notions about lateral and frontal /s/ learning or the effect of tongue thrust on /s/ learning does the reader have? Results from this study are described.

When generalization of the target phoneme from imitation to conversation is addressed, our findings have significant implications for clinical management. We learned that practice in contextual materials can be used earlier in therapy than is usually assumed.

The last series of studies evaluates different procedures for monitoring articulation learning, including the clinician, mother and child. Effects of child counting and charting their own progress is presented. The use of the Tone Keyboard to collect clinician-child interaction data did not appear to affect articulation learning.

For definitions of special terms and symbols used in this project refer to Appendix G in this book.

## McDonald Screening Deep Test of Articulation

### Project Year 2 Analysis of /s/ and /r/

To give the reader some idea of the severity of the /r/ and /s/ problems in children in this project, as well as the other errors most frequently associated with primary /r/ or /s/ deficits, an analysis of the McDonald Screening Deep Test of Articulation (1968) is included. These data come from Year 2 of our project. Year 2 had the largest sample of children for any project year. There were 307 /s/ and 277 /r/ and these children are representative of the majority of the children included in the project. Children were in grades one through six, average grade level was 2.3.

The 10 clinicians from Project Year 1 had 88% mean agreement in determining which sounds were in error and 76% mean agreement on type of error (distortion, substitution, and/or omission). Our 23 clinicians in Project Year 2 had a range of 73-77% agreement on type of error produced in listening to taped samples prior to beginning their baseline testing in the field. Their percent agreement scores on determining which sounds were defective were not available, but were assumed as good as demonstrated by the Year 1 clinicians (i.e., in the 80's).

With the McDonald, nine phonemes are sampled ten times, so the poorest score a child can receive is ten errors on any tested phoneme. At baseline the 277 /r/ child had a mean score of 7.79 /r/ errors (SD 2.16) and 307 /s/ children had a mean of 7.97 /s/ errors (SD 2.62).

A t-test for independent groups was nonsignificant which indicates that the two phonemes were similar in severity as measured by the McDonald Test. We had previously found (Chapter 3) no differences in baseline (EU1) scores for /r/ or /s/ when using the SPT/TALK as a probe measure. There were 71 (23%) out of

307 /s/ children who also had /r/ errors. The average /r/ error was 4.11 (SD 3.13) items wrong which was about half the number of errors of the children who had a primary /r/ problem. There were 84 (30%) out of 277 /r/ children who also had /s/ errors. The average /s/ error was 3.43 (SD 3.02) items wrong, which was also about half the number of errors of the children who had a primary /s/ disorder. In other words, the majority of primary /r/ and /s/ children did not have associated /r/ and /s/ defects. When such errors were present, the number of errors (severity) was much less. Another way of stating the infrequency of combined /s/ and /r/ errors is that only 11% of the 584 children had more than three errors on the /r/ and more than three errors on the /s/ (each sampled ten times) on the McDonald Test.

What about the other phonemes measured by the McDonald /l/, /θ/, /ʃ/, /tʃ/, /f/, /k/, /t/? Since very few of these /r/ and /s/ children had /f/, /k/, /t/ in error, these were disregarded. The remaining four phonemes were counted as defective if they had three or more of the ten items in error. Less than three errors were ignored and considered normal. This is a more stringent criterion than McDonald and McDonald (1974) who considered three errors within normal limits. Table 8.1 shows the distribution of /tʃ/ /θ/, /ʃ/,, and /l/ errors for the 307 /s/ and 277 /r/ children. Chi-square was used to test the association of errors with /s/ and /r/. The /tʃ/ and /ʃ/ errors occurred significantly more often in /s/ children, whereas /l/ occurred more often in the /r/ children. This finding was expected. The surprising observation was no difference in the proportion of /θ/ errors between the two groups. It was anticipated that the /s/ children would have significantly more.

From this analysis one gains some support for the notion of feature analysis. /s/ and /ʃ/ appear to have similar fricative features, whereas /θ/ also containing frication does not appear to be any more associated with /s/ than /r/. On the other hand the affricate /tʃ/ is more associated with /s/ errors. /r/ and /l/ are considered to be glides to or from certain vowel positions and /ɝ/ and /l/ (vowelized l) are considered vowel continuants (Kanter and West, 1941). The /r/ and /l/ are called semi-vowels by Fairbanks (1960). By whatever classification the /r/ and /l/ appear to be more related in errors than /s/ and /l/.

## Generalization of Training

Another question concerns how much generalization may occur with /r/ and /s/ training to the other phoneme errors, specifically the /tʃ/, /ʃ/, /θ/, and /l/. No strict control was maintained on the clinician as to whether they actually did

|  | /t ʃ/ | /θ/ | /ʃ/ | /l/ |
|---|---|---|---|---|
| /s/ | 123 | 130 | 136 | 54 |
| /r/ | 65 | 95 | 87 | 80 |
| $x^2$ | 9.89 | 1.94 | 4.89 | 6.29 |
| p | <.01 | NS | <.05 | <.02 |

Note: Any /s/ or /r/ child could have more than one phenome in error.

TABLE 8.1. The number of 307 /s/ and 277 /r/ children who had other errors on the McDonald Test. chi-square and p values are also reported.

work on these phonemes in addition to the primary /s/ or /r/ therapy. However, from our analysis of the data most clinicians worked only on /s/ and /r/ for that school year. Furthermore, we are assuming random therapy effort on these other erred phonemes for both /r/ and /s/ groups. Table 8.2 indicates the number of children who did or did not improve on a given phoneme over the school year (September-May). The criterion used was an improvement of one or more erred items out of ten on the McDonald Test (e.g., ten errors at baseline to nine at post therapy or five errors to three, etc.). Chi-square analysis for all four phonemes (/tʃ/, /θ/, /ʃ/, and /l/) was nonsignificant, indicating that neither the /s/ or the /r/ treated children had better generalization to these other phonemes. Both groups demonstrated an improvement for all phonemes but no differential improvement was noted. Because of distinctive feature notions, it had been anticipated that /s/ training would have a greater effect on the /tʃ/, /θ/, and /ʃ/ than /r/ training. But this did not occur. It might be hypothesized that the /ʃ/, /θ/, and /tʃ/ are complex sound units (typically occur later developmentally) and that the acquisition of /s/ and /r/ is a complex motor process, too. Sander (1972), after reviewing the developmental norms, had indicated that /s/ and /r/ take a long time to stabilize in the child's expressive repertoire (from 3 to 6 years of age for /s/ and 3 to 8 years of age for /r/). Therefore, generalization of /s/ and /r/ training to other phonemes might not only be considered along distinctive feature units, but along a motor complexity continuum as well (McReynolds, 1975).

Type of sound (/s/ or /r/) was not significantly different (Chapter 4) on baseline scores (EU1), previous therapy, grade, number in therapy group (NGP), and sessions per week; therefore, these variables would not influence any differences between /s/ and /r/ on the questions of generalization of learning to associated errors, i.e., /tʃ/, /θ/, /ʃ/, and /l/. This should strengthen the argument that training on one sound does have generalization to other errors. Training may not be sound specific, but may reflect a more general factor of learning better discrimination and/or how to use complex motor units. This conclusion must be considered tentative because of the lack of therapy control noted above. Also, no control group was observed to determine if the same degree of improvement would have been noted without therapy.

We did study a group of parochial school children (N = 47) with primary /r/ errors (mean grade 2.2, range 1-6 grade) who received no therapy. Their distribution on associated errors on the /tʃ/, /θ/, /ʃ/, and /l/ using chi-square analysis was similar to the children who received therapy (N = 27). Next we looked at the improvement of their scores on these error sounds (Table 8.3). There were no

| | /tʃ/ | | /θ/ | | /ʃ/ | | /l/ | |
|---|---|---|---|---|---|---|---|---|
| | Improve | No | Improve | No | Improve | No | Improve | No |
| /s/ | 94 | 29 | 90 | 40 | 105 | 31 | 39 | 15 |
| /r/ | 49 | 16 | 72 | 23 | 65 | 22 | 56 | .24 |
| χ² | 0.02* | | 1.17 | | 0.18 | | 0.08 | |

*All chi-squares were nonsignificant.

TABLE 8.2. The number of 307 /s/ and 277 /r/ children who had errors on other phonemes and those who improved after treatment during the school year on the post therapy McDonald Test.

|  | /t ʃ/ | | | /ʃ/ | | |
|---|---|---|---|---|---|---|
|  | Improved | No |  | Improved | No |  |
| Therapy /r/ | 49 | 16 | 65 | 65 | 22 | 87 |
| No Therapy /r/ | 3 | 3 | 6 | 7 | 2 | 9 |
|  | 52 | 19 | 71 | 72 | 24 | 96 |

$\chi^2 = 1.81$      $\chi^2 = 0.04$

Yates = 0.75      Yates = 0.04

|  | /θ/ | | | /l/ | | |
|---|---|---|---|---|---|---|
| Therapy /r/ | 72 | 23 | 95 | 56 | 24 | 80 |
| No Therapy /r/ | 8 | 3 | 11 | 5 | 2 | 7 |
|  | 80 | 26 | 106 | 61 | 26 | 87 |

$\chi^2 = 0.05$      $\chi^2 = 0.06$

Yates = 0.02      Yates = 0.12

TABLE 8.3. chi-square analyses compared on children who had treatment for /r/ and those who did not to determine improvement in several associated error categories.

significant differences between the two groups. One basic problem with these data is the small number of children in the no therapy group. However, if they can be supported with additional numbers then one would conclude that the no therapy /r/ group showed as much generalization for their associated errors as the treated group. This implies that both training and maturation (over a nine-month period) have an effect on the improvement of error sounds. What is surprising in all this is that the children who received therapy did not show greater improvement than the untreated group on their subset of errors. In contrast, we have shown that training on /s/ had marked generalization to /z/. The parochial school (untreated) children used for comparison also showed improvement on /z/, but not nearly to the extent of the treated group. One possible reason for not showing any differential improvement on the /tʃ/, /θ/, /ʃ/, and /l/) may be the grossness of the McDonald Test (albeit 10 items for each sound), contrasted to a 30 item SPT sample used for the /s-z/ study.

## Distortions, Substitutions, Omissions

It has been recommended in the literature that the classification of misarticulations as distortions, substitutions, or omissions is a more accurate way of describing articulation than the more simple assessment of correct or incorrect. The concept has been presented by Roe and Milisen (1942) that there is a developmental sequence from severe to mild articulations in which sounds are first omitted, then substituted, then distorted and finally correctly articulated. It has been suggested that identification by type of error is clinically important for diagnostic and treatment purposes (Van Riper, 1963, pages 221, 223).

Information concerning the change in the error categories of distortions, substitutions, and omissions over the school year from this project was presented earlier (Elbert, 1971). The definitions used to assign a misarticulation to an error category were as follows: Substitutions were errors that could be written in broad transcription as another phoneme by the clinician. An example of this would be the substitution of /w/ for /r/, or /θ/ for /s/. Omissions were those errors occurring any time there was a complete absence of a given sound within a word. A glottal stop was considered a substitution and not an omission because it can be transcripted phonetically. Distortions were errors in production that could not be transcribed as another phoneme, for example, the lateral lisp for /s/. Since less than 1% of the errors for these children were classified as omissions, this category was not included in this discussion. The clinicians achieved from 73 to 77% agreement on the type of error produced on audio tape samples heard at the beginning of the school year.

From the McDonald pretest in September, each child was designated as having either primarily substitution, omission, or distortion errors. All errors on the 10 items for /s/ or /r/ for each child were counted and when 75% or more of these errors were distortions, the child was designated as having primarily distortions. Substitutions were determined in the same way. There were no children classified as primarily omission errors so this category was not used. At midyear (January) and at the end of the school year (May), children were retested on the McDonald. If a child continued to make errors but they were less than 75% distortions or substitutions, he was then placed in the mixed category (Table 8.4).

|  | Pre | Mid | Post |
|---|---|---|---|
| **/s/ Substitutions** | | | |
| Substitution | 100% | 59% | 30% |
| Distortion |  | 7% | 5% |
| Mixed |  | 5% | 5% |
| No Errors |  | 29% | 60% |
| **/s/ Distortions** | | | |
| Distortion | 100% | 57% | 27% |
| Substitution |  | 7% | 9% |
| Mixed |  | 5% | 5% |
| No Errors |  | 31% | 59% |
| **/r/ Substitutions** | | | |
| Substitution | 100% | 76% | 55% |
| Distortion |  | 3% | 6% |
| Mixed |  | 8% | 4% |
| No Errors |  | 13% | 35% |

No children receiving therapy were considered /r/ distorters at pre-test.

TABLE 8.4. Change in type of error categories over time as measured by the McDonald Test.

For children with /s/ substitutions at the post test, 30% were still considered having primarily substitution errors while 5% were placed in a distortion category, 5% were in a mixed category, and 60% made no errors. The /s/ children were considered as having primarily distortion or substitution errors, however, for the /r/ sound no children were classified as having distortion errors. For the /s/ children who were classified as having distortion at the post-testing, only 27% were still considered to have distortions, 9% substitutions, 5% mixed, and 59% had no more errors. For the /r/ substitutions, 55% still had substitutions at the end of the school year, 6% had distortions, 4% were mixed, and 35% had no errors.

In summary, most of the misarticulations of the more than 500 children tested were typed as substitutions on the pretest and this classification did not change over time for these children. Instead of changing from one error category to another, most of the children tested either continued to make the same type of error, or corrected their misarticulations entirely. In a study of articulation learning (Elbert and McReynolds, 1978) using probes frequently during training, it was found that "omitters" went through a period when they marked the sound before they began to approximate the target sound. "Substituters" did not mark. Categorizing misarticulations as distortions, substitutions, or omissions, does not appear to be a functionally significant behavioral category for grade school children in our study. Furthermore, no known articulation training programs use these error categories as a basis for treatment and therefore appear to have little value to the clinician. Type of error category for children with multiple phoneme errors is important for distinctive feature analysis (McReynolds and Engmann, 1975) at least as far as the type of substitutions used is concerned. For children with only /s/ or /r/ errors, determining whether the sound is correct or wrong appears to be more important. Drash, Caldwell, and Leibowitz (1970) have made the point that

> . . . correct and incorrect response rates are sensitive, dependent variables against which the effects of independent variables such as stimulus complexity, schedules of reinforcement and E differences may be evaluated.

## KLMO Learning Curves and Articulation Errors

The next reasonable question about the errors reported on the McDonald Test concerns the KLMO learning groups. Do "K" children have fewer associated errors than the "O" children? Table 8.5 summarizes that the percent occurrence of other phoneme errors in addition to the primary /s/ or /r/ error as measured on the McDonald Screening Test.

*For the /s/ phoneme*
a. "L" learners had the most frontal /s/ errors.
b. "O" learners had the most lateral /s/ errors.[1]
c. KLMO and "Other" learners had similar frequency of associated errors for the /l/, /r/, /f/, /k/, /t/ phonemes.
d. "O" learners had half as many /θ/ and /t/ errors as other learners.

---

1. Although this would seem to indicate that lateral /s/ children are slower in learning, the reader is referred to the next section for a negation of this conclusion.

|  |  | /l/ | /r/ | /θ/ | /ʃ/ | /tʃ/ | /f/ | /k/ | /t/ | Frontal | Lateral | Other |
|---|---|---|---|---|---|---|---|---|---|---|---|---|
| /s/ | K (n = 70) | 6 | 13 | 30 | 43 | 30 | 1 | 0 | 0 | 74 | 8 | 17 |
|  | L (n = 60) | 7 | 12 | 37 | 27 | 22 | 5 | 3 | 5 | 83 | 5 | 12 |
|  | M (n = 51) | 6 | 14 | 31 | 27 | 23 | 2 | 2 | 2 | 69 | 12 | 20 |
|  | O (n = 41) | 5 | 17 | 15 | 24 | 12 | 2 | 2 | 0 | 54 | 34 | 12 |
|  | Other (n = 77) | 5 | 12 | 30 | 27 | 23 | 0 | 1 | 1 | 77 | 13 | 10 |

|  |  | /l/ | /s/ | /θ/ | /ʃ/ | /tʃ/ | /f/ | /k/ | /t/ |
|---|---|---|---|---|---|---|---|---|---|
| /r/ | K (n = 47) | 2 | 13 | 9 | 9 | 6 | 2 | 0 | 0 |
|  | L (n = 46) | 9 | 15 | 24 | 17 | 11 | 4 | 2 | 0 |
|  | M (n = 43) | 9 | 14 | 30 | 26 | 14 | 0 | 0 | 0 |
|  | O (n = 59) | 8 | 15 | 14 | 12 | 8 | 2 | 0 | 0 |
|  | Other (N = 87) | 10 | 14 | 28 | 16 | 13 | 0 | 1 | 2 |

TABLE 8.5. Percent of 282 /s/ and 299 /r/ children for different learning categories (KLMO and "Other") who had other phoneme errors on the McDonald Screening Test. The percent of frontal, lateral, and other error descriptions is indicated for each curve type for all /s/ children.

* Each phoneme was tested 10 times. If the child made less than three wrong on any given phoneme he was not included in the tally. Any given child might have had more than one phoneme in error.

e. "K" learners had almost one and a half times more /tʃ/ and /t/ errors as all "Other" learners; while "O" children had one and a half to three times fewer /tʃ/ errors.

*For the /r/ phoneme*

a. KLMO and "Other" learners had similar frequency distributions for /s/, /f/, /k/, and /t/.
b. "K" learners had fewer /l/, /θ/, /ʃ/, and /tʃ/ errors.
c. "O" learners had fewer /θ/, /ʃ/ and /tʃ/ errors than any group except "K."

## Conclusions

If one is looking for the reason why "O" learners demonstrate minimal gain over the school year, the explanation is not that they had more additional articulation errors than the other children—they did not. The easiest way to demonstrate that is to compare "O" learners with all "Other" learners and it becomes clear that the "O's" had similar or smaller error distributions. Speed of learning does not appear associated with other articulation errors, i.e., children who did acquire the /r/ or /s/ were as likely to have as many other defective phonemes as children who did not learn the /r/ or /s/.

## Generalization of /s-z/

Distinctive feature analysis has shed new light on the management of articulation problems (McReynolds and Huston, 1971; McReynolds and Engmann, 1975). Several studies have shown that training on one phoneme will have varying degrees of generalization to another untrained phoneme (Winitz and Bellerose, 1963; Park, 1968; McReynolds and Bennett, 1972). One aspect of this project was to study the generalization of /s/ training on /z/ errors in a public school clinical setting. Laboratory studies utilizing individual therapy had demonstrated such generalization (Elbert et al., 1967; Wright et al., 1969). Would the same effect be observed with larger numbers of children in group therapy in the schools? Furthermore, would children who had /s-z/ errors and who did not have /s/ therapy show any improvement on their /z/ scores?

## Methodology

As part of the larger study on articulation learning, 20 speech clinicians from the greater Kansas City area representing a cross-section of different size school districts and socio-economic areas participated. The clinicians scheduled their cases in September and submitted them to our project office. We randomly selected 30 children from their caseloads. Approximately half the children were working on the target phoneme /s/ and half on /r/. This made an original pool of 320 /s/ children and 280 /r/. Children with /s/ errors had an average of seven errors out of ten possible items on the McDonald Screening Deep Test of Articulation. The children were not to have hearing losses, not be in special education classes, nor exhibit obvious organic impairment of the speech mechanism. Children were in grades one through six, average grade level was 2.3. Group therapy size ranged from two to five children, average group size was 2.75. Nine clinicians saw the children once a week; eight clinicians had therapy two times a week; and three clinicians were on a block system. Children were scheduled from 20 to 30 minutes of therapy time each session.

|  | N | /s/ | | | | /z/ | | | |
|---|---|---|---|---|---|---|---|---|---|
|  |  | September | | May | | September | | May | |
|  |  | Mean | SD | Mean | SD | Mean | SD | Mean | SD |
| Untreated | 17 | 4.29 | 7.01 | 8.18 | 10.38 | 4.88 | 8.06 | 10.00 | 10.85 |
| Treated |  |  |  |  |  |  |  |  |  |
| Group I | 17 | 2.82 | 5.17 | 28.12 | 2.80 | 3.47 | 5.78 | 27.24 | 3.23 |
| Group II | 17 | 3.94 | 6.55 | 29.29 | 1.31 | 4.76 | 8.47 | 28.53 | 2.21 |

TABLE 8.6. Means and SD's for correct scores on the /s/ and /z/ Sound Production Tasks (SPT) for treated and untreated articulation groups at baseline (September) and end of year (May). There are 30 total items on each SPT list.

During the year, children who were trained on the /s/ target phoneme also were probed with the 30 items /s/ and /z/ Sound Production Tasks (SPT). Measures were taken at baseline and during the school year. Clinicians were asked to direct their therapy program to the training of the /s/ phoneme and ignore /z/.

A group of untreated parochial school children with /s/ errors was probed by three project staff clinicians during the school year. These children came from the same geographic location as the trained children in the project.

## Data Analysis

As it turned out, there were only 17 untreated /s/ children available with both baseline and end of year SPT /s/ and /z/ probes. From the original pool of 320 treated /s/ children, 17 (Treatment Group 1) were randomly chosen who matched the 17 untreated children on the basis of sound, grade, and baseline /s/ and /z/ SPT scores. Remember, in our data analyses reported earlier (Chapter 4), we found that the three most important independent variables to predict GAIN were sound, baseline score, and grade. Sex made no difference. If we control (match) for these then we come closer to making the children equivalent. For replication purposes, a second set of matched children was chosen randomly from the treated group (Treatment Group 2).

The 34 children in Treatment Groups 1 and 2 were taught by 16 different clinicians. Twenty children had therapy once/week, eight twice/week, and six were in block therapy. The mean age for the parochial school untreated children was 90.5 months (SD 17.3), 88.6 (SD 17.4) for Treatment 1, and 86.5 (SD 13.9) for Treatment 2. None of these are significantly different.

Treated Groups 1 and 2 are compared with the untreated group for September (baseline) and May (end of year) scores using the total number of correct out of a possible 30 items on the /s/ and /z/ SPT as the dependent variable.

## Results

Both the treated and untreated children started out (September) with similar mean baseline scores on the Sound Production Tasks (SPT) for /s/ and /z/ (Table 8.6). The mean and standard deviation for the end of year (May) SPT probes are also indicated. Figure 8.1 illustrates the distribution of children at the end of the year for the untreated children and their matched Treatment Groups 1 and 2 for /s/. The improvement in the treated groups is clear. Group 1 had 15 out of 17 children who achieved SPT scores in the 25-30 range (30 is maximum correct). All 17 of the Group 2 children achieved 25-30 SPT scores. In contrast, the untreated group had two children who had 25-30 correct.

The generalization to /z/ is just as apparent. For the treated groups all children had more than 20 items correct, most had better than 25 correct. The untreated children had a similar distribution of improvement to /z/ as they did on /s/ (Figure 8.2).

## Discussion

The answer to the original question would be that public school group therapy for /s/ does achieve generalization to the untreated phoneme /z/. Children who did not receive therapy demonstrated improvement on /s/ and /z/ after nine months maturation. This improvement clearly lags far behind that observed in the treated children.

One criticism of the study may be leveled at the bias of the judgments made on the observed speech changes. The clinicians made the judgments on the treated children and they have been shown to be biased toward more correct (Chapter 2, Reliability measures). Three project staff clinicians made judgments on the untreated parochial school children. It is possible that these judgments were also biased to counting more wrong. One alleviation of this criticism is that both randomly selected treated groups had practically the same amount of improvement (over 16 different clinicians). Furthermore, the clinicians did not know that any of their children would be selected for special comparison with other non-treated children.

These data suggest that /s/ training had an effect on /z/ learning. It is possible that training on other phonemes may also influence /z/ learning; however, Elbert et al. (1967) have demonstrated that /r/ training did not affect /z/ learning. The untreated children in parochial schools who were not given /s/ training also showed some /z/ improvement.

From previous data collected, we have established that for /r/ and /s/ there is a correlation of .79 between SPT percent correct scores and percent correct counts made in conversation at the middle of the school year. Therefore, it seems reasonable to assume that similar high correlations would exist between the /z/ SPT and /z/ counts made in conversation. Since as many as 15% of first grade children have /s/ errors and another 13% have /z/ errors (Pendergast et al., 1966) the implications of the above findings for case management would be that by treating /s/ alone, remediation of 28% of the articulation errors is potentially possible. In other words, the speech clinician can be parsimonious in clinical effort. In most cases both /s/ and /z/ do not have to be treated.

The finding that /z/ improves with /s/ training is perhaps "well known" to the experienced clinician, but it is reassuring to support our clinical hunches with some empirically derived data. Sometimes our insights and clinical "knowns" turn out to be clinical myths and should be abandoned (see the next section on lateral versus frontal /s/ learning).

Furthermore, these results were obtained in typical public school group therapy settings and they confirm the earlier cited laboratory reports with a limited number of cases in individual therapy. These clinical research data also support the distinctive feature model in articulation theory.


# Lateral and Frontal /s/ Learning

## Introduction

Many clinicians report that the lateral /s/ child is more difficult to manage and slower correction occurs than for the frontal /s/ condition (Van Riper, 1963, p. 220; Powers, 1971, p. 844). Some clinicians have noted less generalization to /z/ with correction of the lateral /s/ than to frontal /s/ children. From a theoretical point of view, as described in the section on /s/ to /z/ generalization, if one obtains good tongue placement for clear /s/ production, then generalization to /z/ should occur regardless of type of error.

The question is: "Are there differences between lateral and frontal /s/ children over the school year when compared on total percent GAIN, learning rates (GAMMA), and generalization to /z/?"

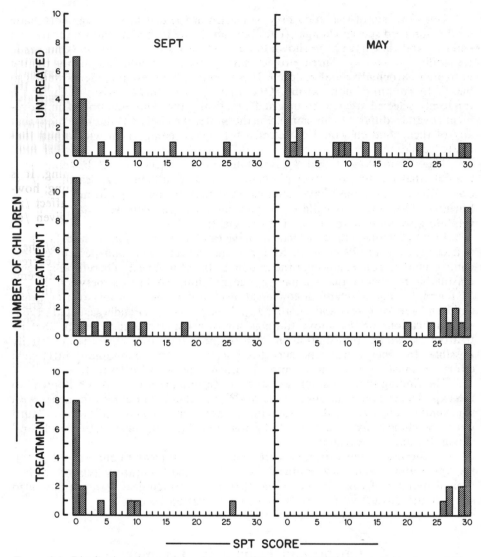

FIGURE 8.1. Distribution of untreated and treated children on /s/ SPT scores in September and May.

## Procedures

The clinicians classified the /s/ into three categories: frontal, lateral, other. For 386 /s/ children, 75% were frontal, 16% lateral, and 9% other. Each clinician used her own criteria for making these distinctions.

We had found that sound, grade, previous therapy, baseline scores, and number of therapy sessions per week had effects on our dependent variables: GAIN, GAMMA, and LEVEL (see Chapter 4). Thirty-two frontal and 32 lateral /s/ children in the data pool could be matched on the above criteria. Sex and the number of children in a therapy group had no effect on /s/ learning, so these

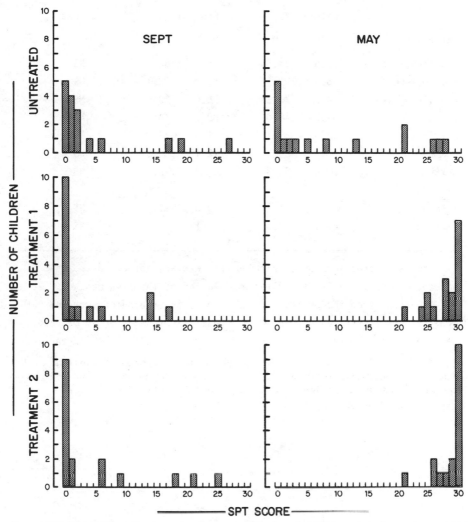

FIGURE 8.2. Distribution of untreated and treated children on /z/ SPT scores in September and May.

factors could be ignored in our matching. These 64 children had therapy with 35 different clinicians.

## Results

The two matched groups were compared by dependent t-tests and the results are shown in Table 8.7. There were no significant differences observed between lateral and frontal /s/ on EU1, 2, 3, 4, GAIN, GAMMA, LEVEL, pre- and post-/z/ scores. Both groups of children generalized their /s/ learning to the untrained /z/ phoneme. A frequency count of KLMO learners for the two groups displayed similar distributions (Table 8.8).

|                  | Lateral /s/ |      | Frontal /s/ |      | t-test |
|------------------|-------------|------|-------------|------|--------|
| Variables        | MEAN        | SD   | MEAN        | SD   |        |
| EU1 (Baseline)   | 30.8        | 31.8 | 28.1        | 32.0 | NS     |
| EU2 (6 weeks)    | 46.9        | 29.1 | 51.2        | 28.1 | NS     |
| EU3 (18 weeks)   | 74.3        | 23.5 | 78.0        | 20.5 | NS     |
| EU4 (30 weeks)   | 84.0        | 18.0 | 89.6        | 14.2 | NS     |
| GAIN             | 53.3        | 29.1 | 61.5        | 31.0 | NS     |
| GAMMA*           | 7.3         | 2.5  | 12.1        | 2.9  | NS     |
| LEVEL            | 60.0        | 22.3 | 62.4        | 19.0 | NS     |
| /s/ score**      |             |      |             |      |        |
| Pre              | 13.4        | 11.6 | 13.6        | 11.0 | NS     |
| Post             | 26.4        | 4.3  | 27.1        | 3.5  | NS     |

*GAMMA scores represent learning rate and are not expressed in percent correct; see Chapter 3 for explanation of these values.

**Derived from the 30 item /z/ SPT, means are the number correct out of 30 at baseline (pre) and end of a school year (post) for 16 matched children (total N=32); /z/ probes were not done on all /s/ children.

TABLE 8.7. Means and standard deviations on nine variables for 32 lateral and 32 frontal /s/ children matched on grade, previous therapy, EU1, and number of therapy sessions per week. Values represent percent correct on Unified Score except where indicated.

|       | Lateral /s/ | Frontal /s/ |
|-------|-------------|-------------|
| Type  | N           | N           |
| K     | 7           | 8           |
| L     | 7           | 10          |
| M     | 9           | 7           |
| 0     | 1           | 0           |
| Other | 7           | 5           |
| Total | 31          | 30*         |

*Two learning category types were missing.

TABLE 8.8. Frequency distribution for lateral and frontal /s/ by KLMO and "Other" learners.

# Discussion

Although the frontal /s/ had higher scores on all measures except baseline (Table 8.7), statistically these results tend to disprove the usual clinical impression that frontal /s/ cases make significantly more gain in shorter periods of time than lateral /s/. GAMMA was our indicator for rate of learning and it, too, did not differentiate the frontals and laterals.

Clinician effect may be interpreted in at least two ways. First, the biased belief that frontal /s/ is easier. This should have resulted in much better scores for the frontal /s/. In fact, although frontal scores were better than lateral, they were not statistically significant. Secondly, if some clinicians are better with frontals, and others with laterals, then having a large pool of clinicians (N = 35) should theoretically cancel out this particular clinician effect.

Another way of getting at clinician ability or quality is to compare the clinician performance levels (CPL, see Chapter 5) between the frontal and lateral groups. Mean CPL for the frontal /s/ and lateral /s/ children was not significant (t = 0.77). This provided further evidence that there were no clinician effects operating between the two groups of children.

What about the effects of tongue thrust in frontal /s/ learning? The frontal /s/ children had more evidence of tongue thrust ($p < .05$) than the lateral /s/ children. Some might say that since they were tongue thrusters this should slow their learning and perhaps account for the fact that they did not learn faster than the lateral /s/ children. The mean total tongue thrust scores (Appendix B) for 92 /s/ children in Year 4 was 4.2 (SD 2.1) compared to 4.8 (SD 1.7) for 16 of these frontal children for whom scores were available. It seems difficult to argue that these particular frontal /s/ children were much different from all others combined. In the next section on "Tongue Thrust" we have demonstrated no differences between GAIN scores for children who demonstrated tongue thrust and those who did not. Therefore, the tongue thrust argument does not appear to be a reasonable "cause" for the frontal /s/ children to do no better than the lateral /s/ children.

There were no differences in total dental scores or open bite for the two groups. Thus, another explanation for possible differences fails to materialize.

Since 75% of the /s/ children are classified as frontal and only 16% as lateral, there is little need to be concerned about laterals; they compose only a small portion of any given clinician's caseload. Neither frontal or lateral /s/ children should get prejudicial assignment in clinical management decision making. Some clinicians do better with certain cases and this may be the variable upon which to make a given decision rather than on inherent differences in the learning abilities of frontal or lateral /s/ children.

Finally, the equivalent /z/ generalization learning between frontal and lateral /s/ gives further credence to the notion that when /s/ is acquired in the response repertoire, no matter what the original error for /s/, the /z/ is acquired also. These clinical findings give further support to the distinctive feature theoretical base.

## Generalization of SPT/TALK

Thus far all of the data were analyzed by looking at combined SPT/TALK scores (our Unified Score) described in Chapters 2 and 3. We were curious to

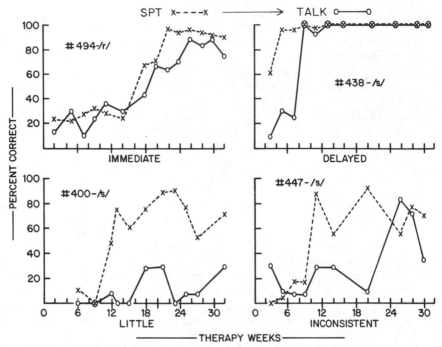

FIGURE 8.3. Four children from Year 4 who represented typical SPT/TALK generalization curves for the school year. For 85 children, 55% were Immediate, 31% Delayed, 7% Little, and 6% Inconsistent.

know what types of curve patterns might be discerned if the SPT and TALK probes were plotted separately. Early in the project we chose 40 children at random from the 1,108 children studied. The results of this first observation of both SPT and TALK curves were presented in Chapter 7. We were surprised to find that in many children the target phoneme generalized to conversation (TALK) as quickly as it was produced under an imitative condition (SPT).

When the high/low clinician performance level (CPL) lesson plan data were analyzed (Chapter 7) for 85 children, the SPT/TALK probes for these children in Year 4 were plotted. The resultant analyses disclosed that four basic SPT/TALK curves emerged over the school year. These curves were labeled Immediate, Delayed, Little, and Inconsistent generalization (Figure 8.3). These terms connote the rate or kind of generalization of the target phoneme on the conversation (TALK) probe as compared to phoneme acquisition on the imitative (SPT) probe. We defined immediate generalization as less than a 20% spread between SPT and TALK at baseline which was maintained throughout the year. Delayed generalization was defined as more than a 20% spread at baseline and less than 20% by the last two successive probes at the end of the year. Little generalization was defined as less than a 20% difference at baseline and greater than 30% spread on the last two probes. For inconsistent generalization, the curves may start together, or apart, and come together, or spread, during the year in no consistent fashion.

Over half (55%) of the children demonstrated immediate generalization, confirming the earlier findings noted above. Another 31% had delayed generalization and the remaining 13% demonstrated little or inconsistent generalization of the target phoneme to TALK (Table 8.9). Chi-square analysis of the immediate

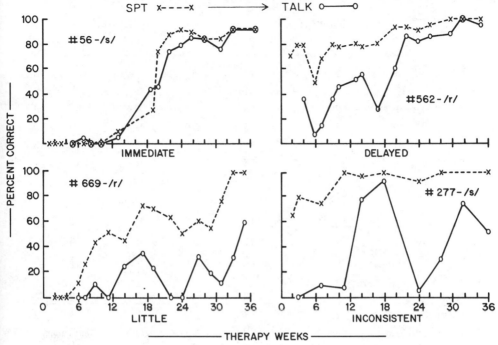

SPT x- - - -x ——————→ TALK o———o

FIGURE 8.4. Four children from Year 2 who represented typical SPT/TALK generalization curves for the school year. For 92 children, 51% were Immediate, 26% Delayed, 14% Little, and 9% Inconsistent.

and delayed curves by high and low clinician performance levels (CPL) was not revealing ($\chi^2$ = 2.86, df 1, $< .10 > .05$). In other words, the type of generalization curve was not associated with high or low CPL. We thought that high CPL might be associated with immediate generalization.

Selection of children from Year 4 was done by high/low performing clinicians and a bias in the types of curves is possible. It was decided to select /r/ and /s/ at random from our pool of 614 children in Year 2. These SPT/TALK scores were more readily available than the other years and 92 were plotted, (48 /s/ and 44 /r/). The same four basic generalization patterns noted above were observed (Figure 8.4). For these 92 children, 51% were immediate, 26% delayed, 14% little, and 9% had inconsistent generalization (Table 8.10). Over three-fourths were immediate and delayed and over half had immediate generalization—just as we found in the children of the high/low performance clinicians.

Additional findings were as follows:

1. /r/ and /s/ had similar distributions among the immediate and delayed curves. We anticipated that /r/ would be associated with immediate and /s/ with delayed because of their distributions in the high/low curves above.
2. The high/low clinician performance level (CPL) again was not associated ($\chi^2$ = 0.89, df 1, nonsignificant) with immediate or delayed generalization.
3. "K" curves (36%) were more often associated with immediate generalization than the other curves. "M" curves (58%) were more prevalent with delayed generalization than the other KLO curve patterns.

In summary, more than three-fourths of the children with /r/ and /s/ articulation disorders, when probed with the SPT and TALK tasks over a school year,

| | Immediate | | | | Delayed | | | |
|---|---|---|---|---|---|---|---|---|
| | /s/ | /r/ | N | % | /s/ | /r/ | N | % |
| K | 5 | 3 | 8 | 17 | 12 | 1 | 13 | 48 |
| L | 10 | 9 | 19 | 41 | 2 | 0 | 2 | 8 |
| M | 1 | 3 | 4 | 8 | 4 | 4 | 8 | 29 |
| 0 | 1 | 6 | 7 | 15 | 0 | 0 | 0 | 0 |
| Other | 0 | 9 | 9 | 19 | 0 | 4 | 4 | 15 |
| Total | 17 | 30 | 47 | 55 | 18 | 9 | 27 | 31 |

| | Little | | | | Inconsistent | | | |
|---|---|---|---|---|---|---|---|---|
| K | 1 | 0 | 1 | 17 | 2 | 0 | 2 | 40 |
| L | 0 | 1 | 1 | 17 | 0 | 0 | 0 | 0 |
| M | 0 | 0 | 0 | 0 | 0 | 1 | 1 | 20 |
| 0 | 1 | 1 | 2 | 33 | 0 | 0 | 0 | 0 |
| Other | 1 | 1 | 2 | 33 | 2 | 0 | 2 | 40 |
| Total | 3 | 3 | 6 | 7 | 4 | 1 | 5 | 6 |

TABLE 8.9. Distribution of 85 children from Year 4 by SPT/TALK generalization (Immediate, 55%; Delayed, 31%; Little, 7%; and Inconsistent, 6%), KLMO, and sound (42 /s/ and 43 /r/).

| | Immediate | | | | Delayed | | | |
|---|---|---|---|---|---|---|---|---|
| | /s/ | /r/ | N | % | /s/ | /r/ | N | % |
| K | 13 | 4 | 17 | 36 | 2 | 1 | 3 | 13 |
| L | 4 | 1 | 5 | 11 | 0 | 1 | 1 | 4 |
| M | 2 | 2 | 4 | 9 | 8 | 6 | 14 | 58 |
| 0 | 2 | 9 | 11 | 23 | 0 | 0 | 0 | 0 |
| Other | 1 | 9 | 10 | 21 | 2 | 4 | 6 | 25 |
| Total | 22 | 25 | 47 | 51 | 12 | 12 | 24 | 26 |

| | Little | | | | Inconsistent | | | |
|---|---|---|---|---|---|---|---|---|
| K | 2 | 1 | 3 | 23 | 0 | 0 | 0 | 0 |
| L | 1 | 2 | 3 | 23 | 0 | 0 | 0 | 0 |
| M | 0 | 0 | 0 | 0 | 2 | 1 | 3 | 38 |
| 0 | 3 | 0 | 3 | 23 | 1 | 2 | 2 | 38 |
| Other | 3 | 1 | 4 | 31 | 2 | 0 | 2 | 24 |
| Total | 9 | 4 | 13 | 14 | 5 | 3 | 8 | 9 |

TABLE 8.10. Distribution of 92 children from Year 2 by SPT/TALK generalization (Immediate, 51%; Delayed, 26%; Little, 14%; and Inconsistent, 9%), KLMO, and sound (48 /s/ and 44 /r/).

demonstrated two basic target phoneme generalization patterns, immediate and delayed. Fifty-one percent of the children acquired the target phoneme in conversation (TALK) as quickly as in the imitative (SPT) probe. Another 26% demonstrated an initial delay in target phoneme generalization conversation, but usually by midyear, percent correct in TALK catches up to the imitative task. These generalization patterns were found without regard to sound or clinician performance level. The remaining children (23%) demonstrated little or inconsistent generalization to TALK. Continued careful investigations are needed to determine the variables responsible for the generalization patterns described.

## Tongue Thrust

A heated controversy has ensued for many years over tongue thrust. Hanson (1967), Jann (1972), Fletcher (1974), and others believe that tongue thrusting should be managed through various forms of behavior control in elementary school-age children. Others take the view that remedial procedures for tongue thrusting should not be considered until puberty (Mason and Proffit, 1974). Our interest in this probelm is in the area of speech errors. A group of frontal /s/ tongue thrusters were matched with another group of frontal /s/ children who were not tongue thrusters. The question was: "Will speech therapy improve articulation errors without resorting to special myofunctional exercises?" The question does not include the issue of possible dental malformation.

## Procedures for Study I

Each clinician evaluated the children on indices of tongue thrust adapted from Larr (1962). The criterion for identification was five or more out of ten possible signs of tongue thrust (Appendix B). Twenty-three children were so identified from Project Year 4. We did not ask about tongue thrust in children from the other project years. Five of .the 23 tongue thrusters received varying amounts of tongue thrust therapy and were therefore removed from the group, leaving a final sample of 18 children. Another group of 18 who were not tongue thrusters were matched to grade, previous therapy and baseline score with the tongue thrusters. You will recall that these variables influenced our GAIN score reported in Chapter 4. A total of 18 different clinicians taught the 36 children, 12 with the tongue thrust group and 12 with the non-tongue thrust group (in other words, some clinicians had both kinds of children and some did not). All children in Project Year 4 had conventional speech therapy twice a week. Several children who were identified as tongue thrusters were labeled as lateral lispers and were not included in this group. All matched non-tongue thrust children also were frontal lispers. The mean grade for tongue thrusters was 2.2 (SD 1.0) and the mean grade for the non-tongue thrusters was 2.3 (SD 1.0). The difference was not significant.

*Results*: The mean and standard deviations on three variables are presented in Table 8.11. Both groups started at approximately 18% correct on their Unified Scores at baseline. GAIN between September and May and rate of learning (GAMMA) were not significantly different between the two groups.

*Discussion*: The basic question was whether frontal /s/ children who were identified as tongue thrusters, but who received no tongue thrust therapy, would respond to conventional speech therapy as well as children who were identified as having frontal /s/ impairment without tongue thrust. The answer is yes. There

| Variables | Tongue-Thrust | | Non-Tongue Thrust | | t-test |
|---|---|---|---|---|---|
| | Mean | SD | Mean | SD | P |
| EU1 (Baseline) | 17.9 | 22.8 | 17.9 | 27.9 | NS |
| GAIN | 71.7 | 23.9 | 76.8 | 28.1 | NS |
| GAMMA* | 26.6 | 28.7 | 23.2 | 42.3 | NS |
| Weeks dismissed | N = 8 | | N = 8 | | |
| from therapy | 9.6 | (3-19) | 8.4 | (2-16) | |

*GAMMA scores represent rate of learning and are not expressed in percent correct. See Chapter 3 for explanation. A higher score represents faster learning.

TABLE 8.11. Means and standard deviations on four variables for 18 tongue thrust and 18 non-tongue thrust frontal /s/ children matched on grade, previous therapy, baseline score, and number of sessions per week. Values represent percent correct on Unified Score (SPT/TALK). Also indicated is the mean number of weeks (range in parenthesis) a child had been dismissed from therapy before the end of a 30 week school year.

was no significant difference between the two groups on GAIN or rate of learning (GAMMA) over the school year.

## Procedures for Study II

Another way to define tongue thrust is to identify all the frontal /s/ children who had one or more tongue thrust lessons during the year. The assumption is that the clinician believed that thrust was present, and therefore provided therapy for it. Of the 19 children who conformed to this functional definition 14 had only one lesson (less than 12 minutes) and the remaining five had 27 to 219 minutes (Mean = 108) of tongue thrust therapy during the school year. (Four lateral /s/

| Variables | Tongue-Thrust | | Non-Tongue Thrust | | t-test |
|---|---|---|---|---|---|
| | Mean | SD | Mean | SD | P |
| EU1 (Baseline) | 8.1 | 11.2 | 7.8 | 15.0 | NS |
| GAIN | 79.7 | 18.1 | 82.0 | 18.0 | NS |
| GAMMA* | 13.6 | 30.7 | 31.9 | 35.3 | NS |
| Weeks dismissed | N = 9 | | N = 6 | | |
| from therapy | 9.7 | (2-17) | 11.8 | (4-23) | |

*GAMMA scores represent rate of learning and are not expressed in percent correct. See Chapter 3 for explanation. A higher score represents faster learning.

TABLE 8.12. Means and standard deviations for 19 tongue thrust children who had one or more lessons for tongue thrust matched with 19 non-tongue thrust frontal /s/ children on grade, previous therapy, baseline score, and number of sessions per week. Values represent percent correct on Unified Score (SPT/TALK). Also indicated is the mean number of weeks a child had been dismissed from therapy (range in parenthesis).

and 17 /r/ children also received tongue thrust therapy, but were excluded from this analysis.) Only three of the children who received tongue thrust therapy also were identified as having five or more tongue thrust behaviors on the Larr (1962) list. Nineteen non-tongue thrust frontal /s/ children were matched on grade, baseline score, previous therapy, and sessions per week. The mean grade for tongue thrusters was 2.4 (SD 0.9) and the mean grade for the non-tongue thrusters was 2.5 (SD 1.0). The difference was again not significant.

*Results*: The means and standard deviations on three variables are presented in Table 8.12. Both groups started at approximately 8% correct at baseline. Mean GAIN and mean rate of learning (GAMMA) were not significantly different between the two groups. This would indicate that the children who had tongue thrust and who received both myofunctional therapy and speech therapy made similar gains and in the same amount of time as those children who were without tongue thrust. Large standard deviations relative to the mean for GAMMA scores result partially from the fact that GAMMA can also be negative (five scores from minus five to minus 76 were observed).

*Discussion*: We did not take careful measures of changes in dentition, but Stansell (1970) did. She found a significant decrease in overjet in a group of 16 fourth to ninth grade children with tongue thrust and frontal /s/ errors who received only

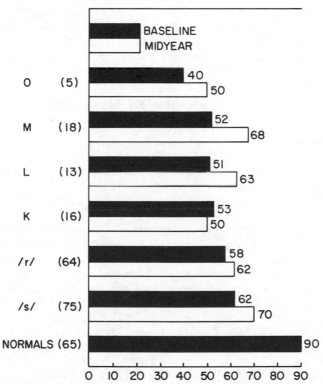

FIGURE 8.5. Median words-per-minute for normal, /s/, /r/, and KLMO children at baseline (September) and midyear (after 18 weeks of therapy). No data for normals at midyear. N for each group is in parenthesis.

speech training. Another matched group received only tongue thrust therapy and they too, had a significant decrease in overjet. There were no significant differences in amount of decrease between the two groups. Unfortunately no data were reported on the amount of speech improvement in both groups. The Stansell study is important because it provides evidence that dental alignment can be modified from articulation training alone.

What about the question of relapse of speech gains? From the clinician's reported data it was determined that eight of the 18 tongue thrusters and eight of the non-tongue thrusters had been dismissed from therapy before the end of the school year for periods of 2-19 weeks (Table 8.11) without any remission of their errors. The SPT/TALK probes done every two weeks showed no decrease in percent correct from the last measure taken when the child was dismissed from therapy. A similar finding appeared when the records of tongue thrusters who received myofunctional therapy were reviewed (Table 8.12). These partial data would suggest that once a tongue thrust child reached the clinician's dismissal criterion (greater than 90% correct) no regression in speech errors was noted with or without tongue thrust therapy.

Either way one defined presence of tongue thrust (operationally from a tongue thrust behavior checklist, or functionally from clinicians who performed tongue thrust therapy), the result is the same. Children with frontal /s/ impairment who have tongue thrust and receive speech therapy show no more (or less) mean percent GAIN when they receive or do not receive special tongue thrust exercises, compared to controls. The mean rate of learning (GAMMA) was also similar for the two groups. These results support the position (Mason and Proffit, 1974) that speech therapy for elementary school children without myofunctional therapy is justified in children who have evidence of tongue thrust and frontal /s/ errors.

## Speaking Rate and KLMO Curves

In Chapter 7 we discussed the word-per-minute (wpm) counts made by a group of normals (90 wpm) and defective /r/ and /s/ children (60 wpm) during three minute conversations. After deriving KLMO, we wondered what differences in speaking rate might be observed among children with different learning curves. KLMO curves were identified in 52 of the /r/ and /s/ children for whom word-per-minute data were available (see Chapter 7 for description of data collection procedures). These were "K" (13 /s/ + 3 /r/), "L" (6 /s/ + 7 /r/), "M" (14 /s/ + 4 /r/), and "O" (5 /r/). Table 8.13 contains the means, standard deviations, and medians for the KLMO groups. Data were collected in September (baseline) and January (midyear) of the school year. Figure 8.5 illustrates the pattern of word-per-minute rates for the different groups. In this figure the /r/ and /s/ have been combined for the KLMO curves. Because of the few cases, median scores were used to plot the diagrams. A trend of improvement is noted in median and mean scores from baseline to midyear except for the five /r/ children who had the "O" curve. The "K" curves show a slight decrease at midyear. We are at a loss to explain this, especially since "K" consisted mostly of /s/ children who generally improved at midyear.

Larger numbers would be necessary to derive any definite conclusions about word-per-minute rates and type of learning curves. The present data suggest that differences do exist. If the low word-per-minute rates evidenced by the "O" learners is real then it may provide additional evidence of poor linguistic skill.

Table 8.13. Means, standard deviations, and medians for word-per-minute (wpm) speaking rates at baseline and midyear and size of N for KLMO learning groups for /r/ and /s/.

| | | K | | L | | M | | O | |
|---|---|---|---|---|---|---|---|---|---|
| | | Baseline | Midyear | Baseline | Midyear | Baseline | Midyear | Baseline | Midyear |
| /r/ | Mean | 56* | 58 | 53 | 58 | 52 | 63 | 59 | 55 |
| | SD | 17 | 31 | 30 | 24 | 23 | 27 | 44 | 22 |
| | Median | 48 | 53 | 52 | 56 | 44 | 55 | 40 | 52 |
| | N | 3 | | 7 | | 4 | | 5 | |
| /s/ | Mean | 61 | 57 | 55 | 76 | 57 | 69 | | |
| | SD | 23 | 25 | 31 | 26 | 26 | 24 | | |
| | Median | 54 | 46 | 45 | 84 | 59 | 71 | | |
| | N | 13 | | 6 | | 14 | | | |
| Both | Mean | 60 | 57 | 54 | 66 | 56 | 67 | | |
| | SD | 22 | 25 | 29 | 25 | 25 | 24 | | |
| | Median | 53 | 50 | 51 | 63 | 52 | 68 | | |
| | N | 16 | | 13 | | 18 | | | |

*All numbers have been rounded to nearest whole number.

# Different Procedures for Monitoring Articulation Learning

## Clinician-Parent-Child Correct/Wrong (C/W) Counts

One of the early purposes of the project was to determine if children and parents could learn to count target phonemes in conversation. If parents could make reliable daily or weekly probes at home of their child's speech, then this information could help the clinician determine how well generalization occurred outside speech therapy. If the child developed self-monitoring skills (accurate C/W counts of his target phonemes during conversation), then this skill might also help phoneme acquisition and generalization.

In Project Year 1, clinicians taught parents to count the target phoneme in conversation with the child at home. Correct/Wrong (C/W) counts were made each day during a three-minute TALK. The child was also taught to make C/W counts of his/her live conversation with the clinician in school as well as with the parent at home. Home-school counts were within one week of each other.

Ten clinicians each had 10 children (100 total). Sufficient data to make early therapy (October) comparisons with mid-year (January) counts were obtained from 55 parents. The data were analyzed for 22 /r/ and 22 /s/ children (total of 44). The remaining eleven were discarded because they were children with other sound errors (ch, sh, th, etc.). From a sample of 100 children, slightly more than half (55%) of the parents participated for a meaningful length of time. Therefore, the data represent the abilities and biases of this particular group of parents who were willing to make C/W counts on their children and turn in the data to the speech clinician.

The design was a $2 \times 2 \times 2$ mixed ANOVA including judges (parent vs. clinician) and target phoneme (/r/ vs. /s/) as between-subjects variables, and two times (early vs. mid) as a repeated measure. Significant main effects were associated with time (early vs. midyear, Figure 8.6) ($F = 25.60$; df = 1,84; $p < .001$). Nonsignificant effects were found for parent vs. child counts ($F = 0.80$; df = 1,84; $p > .05$) and /r/ vs. /s/ ($F = 2.60$; df = 1,84; $> .05$). No significant interactions were observed.

The same design was used to compare clinician-child counts in school, sound and time. No significant interactions were observed. Significant main effects were

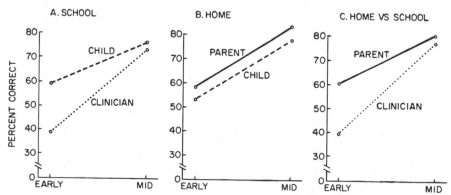

FIGURE 8.6. Data drawn represents 44 /r/ and /s/ children. ANOVA compared early-midyear percent correct counts for (A) clinician-child, (B) parent-child, and (C) parent-clinician.

found for clinician-child counts ($F = 6.10$; df = 1,84; $p < .05 > .01$). The clinician counts were lower (Figure 8.6). Again, midyear counts were significantly higher than early in treatment ($F = 49.47$; df = 1,84; $p < .001$).

The same ANOVA design was used to compare clinician-parent, sound, and time. One significant interaction was with time and subjects ($F = 5.86$; df = 1,84; $p < .05$). The gap between the clinician and parent was large early in the school year, but closed at midyear (Figure 8.6). The parent judged the child's speech significantly higher than the clinician ($F = 5.09$; df = 1.84; $p < .05$). There was no significant difference between /r/ and /s/ and midyear was significantly better than early ($F = 61.5$; df = 1,84; $p < .001$).

## General Conclusions

1. Parents and children counted significantly more correct phonemes during conversation than the clinician. However, this difference occurred early and not at midyear.
2. When counting together, the parent and child C/W counts were not significantly different. The counts may have been more overt at home, i.e., the child and parent knew when the other was tallying.
3. When the child talked with the clinician, the child counted significantly more correct target phonemes. This difference occurred early in therapy and not at midyear.
4. The parent, child and clinician all made significantly different counts across time, i.e., midyear (January) C/W counts were significantly higher than early (October) counts. Everyone agreed that the child was getting better.
5. Type of phoneme (/r/ and /s/) made no difference in parent-child-clinician counting. The /r/ appeared to be easier to count. This was reported by other listeners (Chapter 2, Reliability).

These data indicate that some (perhaps 50%) parents and children carried out C/W counts at home. They may not count accurately at the beginning of therapy, but by midyear their C/W counts were not unlike those of the clinician. This suggests that the clinician could get an idea of how well generalization has occurred in the home from some parents and children. Year 1 data were not analyzed according to KLMO (learning curves) and, therefore, the results do not indicate whether children who successfully perform C/W counts (self monitor) will learn faster or better than children who do not count.

## Effects of Staff Clinicians, Control Clinicians, and All Others

The purpose of this analysis was to determine if clinicians and their children who were not associated with the project made different progress than all other clinicians and children in the study.

An analysis was made of the dependent variables by three different groups of children: 1) children who received therapy from three project staff clinicians (group C), 2) children who were treated by the nine control clinicians (group D), and 3) all other clinicians (N = 49) and children in the project (groups ABEF). Group D (control children) was treated by clinicians who were not trained in the project procedures (SPT/TALK probes or charting). The probe data for group D was collected on a monthly basis by the staff clinicians (Table 8.14).

No significant differences were found at baseline (EU1) for the three groups of children. In other words, staff clinicians' correct/wrong counts were not dif-

| Year | Geography | Number of Clinicians And Children | | Group | SPT/Talk Probes Done By* | Conditions** |
|---|---|---|---|---|---|---|
| 1 | Kansas | 10, each with groups of 10 | 100 | 1 | clinician | a |
|  |  |  | 100 | 2 | clinician | b |
|  |  |  | 100 | 3 | clinician | c |
| 2 | Greater Kansas City | 20, each with 2 groups of 15 | 300 | A | clinician | a |
|  |  |  | 300 | B | clinician | d |
| 2 | Greater Kansas City | 3, approx. 20 each | 61 | C | staff | d |
| 2 | Greater Kansas City | No therapy | 61 | C | staff | e |
| 3 | Greater Kansas City | 9, approx. 20 each | 176 | D | staff | f |
| 3 | Greater Kansas City | 9, approx. 22 each | 207 | E | clinician | g |
| 4 | Jefferson County | 7, approx. 9 each | 65 | F | clinician | h |
| 4 | Minneapolis | 10, approx. 9 each | 93 | F | clinician | h |
| 4 | Wichita | 10, approx. 8 each | 84 | F | clinician | h |

a. No clinician or child charting.
b. Each week clinician and child counted simultaneously and each charted (graphed) and compared progress.
c. Weekly clinician and child counts and graphs; plus at home parent and child compare three minute counts five days a week.
d. Approximately every other week during child TALK, clinician and child simultaneously make correct/wrong counts of the target phoneme.
e. Parochial school children receive no therapy, staff make monthly probes.
f. Nine control clinicians provide therapy, staff make monthly SPT/TALK probes.
g. Seven clinicians from Year 2 and two clinicians from Year 1 use Tone Keyboard (TKB); charts of SPT/TALK progress shown to children approximately every other week.
h. Clinicians use Tone Keyboard but do not plot graphs of SPT/TALK.
* Probes were made by counting live child correct/wrong responses during SPT/TALK.
** Clinicians provided their own objectives, plans, and therapy procedures, none were superimposed by the project, except systematic SPT/TALK probes and conditions listed.

TABLE 8.14. Distribution of clinicians and children; persons doing probes; and various conditions of counting and charting target phoneme correct/wrong responses during four project years.

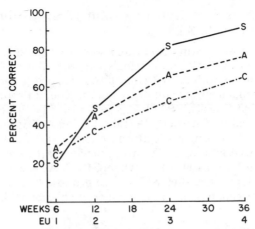

FIGURE 8.7. Learning curves for three groups of children: S—staff clinicians' (N = 61), C—control clinicians' (N = 176), and A—all others' (N = 871). Groups C and S were probed by staff clinicians.

ferent at baseline for their own children, the control children, or all others (Figure 8.7). Large differences ($< .001$) were found for all the other dependent variables (Table 8.15) in favor of the staff clinicians.

One interpretation is that the staff clinicians had a much better treatment program than the control and all other clinicians. A second reason might be that staff clinicians were biased and gave their children better scores than the rest of the clinicians. The fact that all children started at the same baseline level tends to negate this notion. A third possibility is neither of the above, but that systematic probes done by all clinicians except the controls sharpens the clinician's awareness about the child's learning and, consequently, they provide a "better" or more sensitive treatment program.

*Conclusion*: A better way to answer this question would have been for persons not associated with the project to make judgments of the progress accomplished by the three different groups of children.

| Groups | | EU1 | EU2 | EU3 | EU4 | GAIN | GAMMA |
|---|---|---|---|---|---|---|---|
| S | Mean* | 20 | 58 | 81 | 91 | 71 | 29 |
| | SD* | 25 | 29 | 22 | 16 | 26 | 35 |
| C | Mean | 25 | 37 | 52 | 65 | 40 | 0 |
| | SD | 27 | 31 | 30 | 27 | 20 | 14 |
| A | Mean | 27 | 45 | 66 | 77 | 50 | 0 |
| | SD | 29 | 29 | 30 | 26 | 31 | 28 |
| | p(F) | .098 | <.001 | <.001 | <.001 | <.001 | <.001 |

*Means and standard deviations have been rounded to the nearest whole number.

TABLE 8.15. Means and standard deviations for several dependent variables compared for three groups of children: S—Staff clinicians' children, C—Control clinicians' children, and A—All other children in the project.

## Effects of Teaching Children to Count (Self-Monitor) and Tone Keyboard (TKB)

Several different monitoring conditions were structured for the children and the clinicians. One of the early project goals was to establish systematic counting and charting procedures with school clinicians. The correct and wrong responses for a given target phoneme were counted from the Sound Production Task (SPT) and three-minute TALK tasks. SPT/TALK probes can be charted on graph paper and shown to the child (Diedrich, 1971ab; 1972ab; 1973ab). The question of whether counting and charting made any difference in articulation learning of the children was addressed in Year 2. Twenty clinicians participated in Year 2. Each had 30 children from their caseload for whom SPT/TALK data were collected for the project. The children were divided into two groups of 15 children. Each group (A and B) had approximately the same number of children with /r/ or /s/ sounds in error.

*Year 2, group A*: Clinicians took SPT/TALK probes approximately every two weeks but did not chart the child's progress.

*Year 2, group B*: Clinicians took SPT/TALK probes approximately every two weeks and the child was taught to count correct/wrong during (self-monitor) TALK with the clinician. The clinician made every effort to prevent cueing the child. The child was shown progress on both the SPT and TALK charts after each probe.

Clinicians for groups A and B were the same. There was at least one problem with the comparison. If the counting provided feedback to the clinician (group A) which resulted in treatment changes, this feedback could mask any effect that might be attributable to the counting and charting done by the child (group B). Thus the A-B comparison might not ferret that out.

Therefore in Year 3 nine clinicians were chosen who were not taught counting or charting procedures. These clinicians were selected in the same way that clinicians in Year 2 were chosen.

*Year 3, group D*: Nine clinicians each saw approximately 20 children. Once a month, three project staff clinicians went to the schools and made monthly SPT/TALK probes on these children throughout the school year. These children neither counted nor saw any progress charts. As indicated earlier, a possibility exists that the counting done with children in group D by the staff clinicians could be biased.

When the use of the Tone Keyboard was considered to collect therapy interaction data (see Chapter 2, Methodology and Appendix C), we were concerned that the instrument might interfere with the clinicians' usual therapy practices and make them less effective, or that the instrument would distract the children and therefore the children would show less articulation learning than might otherwise be expected. That problem needed to be resolved.

*Year 3, group E*: Nine clinicians who had participated in Year 1 or 2 volunteered to pilot the Tone Keyboard (TKB) for one school year. Each had approximately 20 children in their caseload for whom they collected data on the TKB. These clinicians collected SPT/TALK probes approximately every two weeks and charted their children's progress. The children were not taught to count, i.e., self-monitor during three-minute TALK.

Finally, in Year 4, group F contained 27 clinicians from three geographic

| SOUND | GRPS | N | | EU1 | EU2 | EU3 | EU4 | GAIN | GAMMA |
|---|---|---|---|---|---|---|---|---|---|
| | A | 151 | Mean | 28 | 53 | 74 | 85 | 57 | 13 |
| | | | SD | 31 | 29 | 27 | 19 | 31 | 33 |
| | B | 144 | Mean | 25 | 45 | 72 | 82 | 57 | 9 |
| | | | SD | 29 | 27 | 27 | 22 | 32 | 29 |
| /s/ | D | 50 | Mean | 27 | 45 | 66 | 76 | 48 | 8 |
| | | | SD | 27 | 27 | 27 | 26 | 27 | 23 |
| | E | 74 | Mean | 24 | 47 | 66 | 77 | 53 | 11 |
| | | | SD | 25 | 31 | 27 | 22 | 29 | 34 |
| | F | 93 | Mean | 28 | 55 | 81 | 90 | 62 | 18 |
| | | | SD | 33 | 27 | 21 | 16 | 33 | 30 |
| | | | p(F) | NS | <.05 | <.01 | <.001 | NS | NS |
| | A | 126 | Mean | 29 | 42 | 59 | 69 | 40 | 2 |
| | | | SD | 25 | 28 | 31 | 30 | 27 | 21 |
| | B | 137 | Mean | 28 | 40 | 56 | 69 | 41 | -1 |
| | | | SD | 28 | 29 | 30 | 29 | 30 | 23 |
| /r/ | D | 90 | Mean | 23 | 32 | 45 | 59 | 36 | -5 |
| | | | SD | 26 | 27 | 31 | 31 | 25 | 17 |
| | E | 86 | Mean | 21 | 31 | 46 | 61 | 41 | -6 |
| | | | SD | 25 | 29 | 34 | 34 | 30 | 24 |
| | F | 101 | Mean | 35 | 50 | 71 | 83 | 48 | 3 |
| | | | SD | 30 | 30 | 28 | 23 | 28 | 23 |
| | | | p(F) | <.01 | <.001 | <.001 | <.001 | NS | <.05 |

TABLE 8.16. ANOVA for five different groups of children compared on several dependent variables. Sound, number of children, mean, SD, and F probabilities are indicated.

locations (Kansas, Colorado, Minnesota), who used the Tone Keyboard. SPT/ TALK probes were collected every two weeks by the clinician, but the children were not taught to count and their progress was not charted (Table 8.14). No other therapy conditions were imposed on the clinicians. They could use whatever therapy procedures they chose.

Two big problems remain when comparisons of the groups are made. First, were the children who were assigned to all those groups of similar articulation ability? By comparing GAIN scores (which effectively eliminates any differences in baseline score) separately for /r/ and /s/, we could resolve the articulation ability issue, if not all other children's characteristics. As pointed out in the Results, Chapter 4, of the factors that affected a child's future articulation performance, sound and baseline score were the chief contributors.

Secondly, what effect would clinician ability have on the performance of children? We noted in Chapter 5 that there were enormous differences among clinicians. However, we have also demonstrated that these differences had little effect on overall GAIN scores by year. Therefore, the comparison of groups A, B, D, E, F still have validity.

*Results and Conclusions*: The ANOVA indicated in Table 8.16 demonstrated no difference in GAIN or GAMMA scores across all five groups for the /s/ sound. Also, no differences were found for GAIN on the /r/ sound, although GAMMA was just different at the .05 level. Although significant, the clinical difference in GAMMA was not large. Children (group B) who counted the target phoneme during conversation and who were supplied visual demonstration of their progress by charts did not make any more GAIN than children (group A) who did not have this experience. Groups A and B were taught by the same clinician, but significant differences were still not found when Group B was compared to children who were taught by clinicians who were not in the project and not taught to count or chart (group D). As a matter of fact, children who did have systematic probes but were not taught to count or chart in Year 4 (group F), also were not different from children in Year 2 (group B) who had both counting and charting. As a variable, then, counting by the child and charting of the target phoneme and showing it to the child (knowledge of results) did not appear to significantly affect children's GAIN scores in this project.

The question of whether the Tone Keyboard was an inhibitor of learning for the child and a possible distractor for the clinician was clearly resolved. Groups E and F had the TKB and they were not different from A, B, D. In fact, if anything, the children and clinicians exposed to the TKB in Year 4 (group F) had better overall GAIN and GAMMA scores than all other children. It appears that future investigations may use the TKB without concern that the instrument interferes with articulation learning as measured in this project.

# CHAPTER 9

# Final Summary

The major conclusions of this study are summarized, the dependent variables are reviewed and our explanation for generating four articulation learning curves is presented. The major independent variables, sound and baseline score (which accounted for half of the variance) are described. The importance of the clinician variable is again highlighted. Finally, lesson plans, therapy interactions, and generalization data are reviewed.

Eight decisions regarding clinical management which emerged from this project are presented. And, finally, areas for future studies are suggested.

For definitions of special terms and symbols used in this project refer to Appendix G in this book.

This has been a study with many subjects and many variables. We have presented some strong conclusions, and we have presented other conclusions that were not as strong or that were qualified for one reason or another.

We are not at this point able to say, "If you do such and such to these children, they will overcome articulation problems faster." We cannot boil all of the material down into a few short prescriptions for clinicians. We cannot really provide any prescriptions at all. We do not know what causes children to be fast learners or delayed learners.

This summary includes the highlights of this project. Chapters 1 and 2 contain details of the goals and procedures for the study and Chapters 3-8 contain the results. The global strategy was to identify effective teaching programs for children who achieve correct articulation performance in spontaneous speech. The clinician and child variables associated with the most effective learners were isolated.

The purpose of this section is to 1) summarize the major findings, 2) suggest some decisions regarding clinical management of /s/ and /r/, and 3) point some direction for future research.

In general terms this book has addressed the following:

1. Practical experience with various data collection procedures in the school clinical setting.
2. Evaluation of articulation learning.
3. Assessment of the differential effects of more than 40 variables on /r/ and /s/ learning.
4. Identification of four specific learning curve patterns that could be generalizable to other learning experiments.
5. Study of the specific differences between /r/ and /s/ articulation learning.
6. Generalization from imitation to spontaneous speech.
7. Evaluation of the effect of clinician characteristics, including age, experience, and rapport.
8. A method for the evaluation of clinician performance, i.e., identifying relatively successful and unsuccessful clinicians.
9. Data analysis on clinical issues such as lateral vs. frontal /s/ learning, tongue thrust, termination criteria, and /s/-/z/ generalization.
10. Analysis of lesson plans and therapy interactions between clinician and child.

# Major Conclusions

The data for analysis came from 61 clinicians and 1,108 children with /r/ or /s/ articulation errors. All of the statistical analysis of the primary results in Chapters 3-5 revolve around four items.

1. Dependent variables—EU2, GAIN, GAMMA,
2. KLMO as a measure of articulation learning pattern,
3. SNDEU1, the most important independent child-oriented variable, and
4. CPL, clinician performance level measures.

We started by wanting to measure articulation learning. In an experiment, or in clinical practice, how can one quantify the learning of the /s/ or /r/ phoneme? What we did was to establish measures of articulation, three-minute TALK and Sound Production Task (SPT), and then (by combining these) a Unified Score. This Unified Score tells us the level of a child's articulation at a particular time.

The problem in dealing with articulation learning is one of working with several articulation measurements taken over a period of time from the beginning to the end of the school year. We solve this by first estimating the values of four measurements, the EU numbers. These are averages of the Unified Scores, but the EU numbers (Equalized Unified score) can be considered as measured at fixed times in the therapy process: EU1 at the beginning, EU2 after six weeks of therapy, EU3 after 18 weeks, and EU4 at the end of the school year (30 weeks). Finally, these EU numbers are combined into three primary dependent variables: EU2; GAIN, which is the difference between EU4 and EU1; and GAMMA, which is a combination of all the EU numbers.

These three primary dependent variables cover the important aspects of learning. First, EU2 is a final score. If its value is high, then the child has quickly solved his articulation problem, whatever that problem might have been. By giving first place to EU2, we recognize that what we are interested in is solving these problems. Knowing the child's baseline score and adjusting for it is important in some learning studies, but in our case it is more important to focus on a final score, and on making that final score as high as possible.

The second of our primary dependent variables, GAIN, deals with the problem of baseline adjustments. Since it is the difference between the end of the year articulation, EU4, and the baseline score, EU1, it is sensitive to the child's change in articulation. Finally, we constructed a variable GAMMA, which measures the speed of learning. Children with high GAMMA start the year with low articulation and quickly solve their problems. Children with low GAMMA also start the year low, but it takes them longer to solve their problems.

These three variables can be useful in any learning study. They cover most of the conceptual ideas of learning, and they account for a large proportion of the raw variation.

However, they have the disadvantage of being obscure to the statistically unsophisticated reader. This is particularly true of GAMMA. Thus, we created a new variable, KLMO, to define groups of children by their learning curves. "K's" learn quickly; they are high GAMMA. "L's" learn, but slowly; they are low GAMMA. "M's" start the year with fairly good articulation; they make little progress and are thus high EU1, low GAIN. "O's" are the children whose articulation problem is not solved in one year. They are the low EU4's. The reader can react easily to the visual pattern of these four curves. Thus, KLMO is a dependent variable that can be used for the clarification of a learning study. It cannot be used as the primary dependent variable because it is not purely dependent. The definition of "K," for instance, depends on the baseline score, EU1. If this becomes a criterion in a study, then one would want to produce more "K's." But this implies both trying for high GAMMA, high EU2, and low EU1. The latter goal does not seem to be exactly what one wants in a learning experiment.

However, by using the graphic aspect of KLMO to explain what is going on in learning, and by using two-way tables instead of analyses of variance, clarity is brought to the analysis of learning. The concept of learning curve groups could be applied to many experiments.

After defining our dependent variables, the next step in our statistical analysis was to consider the independent variables. The important idea is that one particular variable, called SNDEU1, explains about half of the variation of the dependent variables, and that other variables are not very significant when adjusted for SNDEU1.

SNDEU1 divides the children into six groups, using the child's target phoneme (SND) and baseline score EU1. The first group is made up of children who had an /s/ problem and started therapy with a baseline score of six or less. These are the /s/ children who have a severe articulation problem. The next group is those /s/ children with baseline from seven to 33. The third group is /s/'s with baseline 34 to 100. We called these three /s/ low, /s/ medium, and /s/ high. There are three similar SNDEU1 groups for /r/ children. We discovered that the /r/ low children were special. They tend to learn much less and much slower than the /s/ lows. In most of our analyses, there was little difference between the /s/ highs and the /r/ highs. When we added other variables like the child's grade, or previous therapy status, we found that these might or might not be significant, depending on the dependent variable analyzed, but SNDEU1 was always significant and always explained the most variation of any independent variable. Thus, future articulation studies should use some simple baseline categories along with the target phoneme. It is of immediate interest to all of us to see if there are any child variables that contribute as strongly to explaining variation as does SNDEU1.

Finally, we know that there is one very important variable that our study was not set up to handle and that is the clinician herself. It is clear to us that clinician individual differences account for substantial proportions of variation explained in articulation learning. It appears that some clinicians do better than others in our study, but the reader must realize that, with suitable training, all clinicians might reach a high standard of performance. This is something we do not know.

Given the problems with our nonexperimental design, what we did show was a way that could be used with the next person experimenting in this area to establish levels of clinician performance. We created two variables, CPL2 and CPL4, which measure performance relative to the child's achievement after six weeks of therapy and at the end of the year. We have set up both formulas for calculating clinician performance level (CPL) and a general technique whereby performance measures might be calculated in other learning experiments. These procedures may also be used by the speech-language clinician to evaluate her performance.

A categorized form of CPL (QCPL) divides our clinicians into three groups. This was used to explore the statistical effect of the clinician, even though we do not consider this a strictly valid approach for our data. The result was that QCPL was always significant and always seemed to contribute to the variance explained. Moreover, QCPL seems to eliminate the effect of important clinical variables like number of sessions per week and number of children in the therapy group. Thus, we look for a future experiment in which clinicians are categorized at the outset by a performance measure, or else randomized, and children are divided into baseline and target phoneme groups in order to get a final assessment for these important clinical variables.

## Lesson Plans and Therapy Interactions

Our description of the therapy process had two components: clinician lesson plans and therapy interaction of clinician-child behaviors as recorded on the Tone Keyboard.

*Summary Statements Extracted from Lesson Plan Data Based on 27 Clinicians, 212 Children, and Over 19,000 Activities for the School Year:*
1. Standard drill (20%) was by far the most frequently used ACTIVITY in speech therapy followed by Free Conversation (13%). Discrimination and self-monitoring activities took up only 3% of the lesson plan activities for the school year.
2. The most frequent STIMULUS category was Child Generated (26%) (i.e., the child was expected to "make-up" words or sentences). Use of Pictures (24%), Graphic (21%), and Auditory Model (21%) came next.
3. CONTENT described the context of the target phoneme which included Isolation (5%), Syllable (6%), Words (33%), and Phrase/Sentences (54%).
4. Mixed POSITION of the target phoneme occurred 70% of the time (i.e., the target phoneme was used in the Initial, Medial, Final, or Blend Position). This was followed by Initial (18%), Final (7%), and Medial (3%).
5. The high occurrence of the mixed position and phrase/sentences (connected speech) suggest that these procedures were used to obtain carryover (generalization) of the target sounds into conversation.

*Summary Statements Extracted from Analysis of Lesson Plans Based on 17 Clinicians, 16 /s/ Children and 16 /r/ Children with KLO Learning Curves:*
1. These clinicians appeared to use similar teaching strategies for "K" and "L" learners. When the child was capable of one level of response the clinician moved to the next level in systematic fashion. There was a progressive use of Isolation, Syllable, Word, Phrase/Sentence and a predominant shift from the Initial to Mixed position with little use of the Medial or Final position as separate training categories.
2. "L" learners received more auditory stimuli than the "K" learners in the first six weeks of therapy. ˙
3. Different teaching strategies appeared to be used by the clinicians of "L" and "O" learners.
4. Considerable qualitative similarity was noted between /s/ and /r/ "L" curve learners. /s/ received more auditory stimulation and /r/ children had more word/phrase categories.
5. On a schedule of twice-a-week therapy for 20-30 minutes, the children were projected to receive (in a 30-week school year) 20-30 hours of therapy. The difference in real time spent in therapy reported by the clinicians was quite different from the expected time. Many children who were in therapy all year had 12 hours or less of actual therapy contact. Clinicians and administrators need to be aware of this when estimating "hours of therapy impact."
6. The average session was 17-18 minutes. A given activity lasted seven to eight minutes. These clinicians used two or three activities for each session.

# Summary Statements Extracted from the Tone Keyboard Data

(A total of 21,637 therapy events were recorded from three clinicians with 13 different children representing 51 hours of therapy over the school year.)

1. Antecedent events accounted for 15%, child response 66%, and clinician subsequent events 19%. These distributions are different from those reported in the literature.
2. The overall response frequency for all events was 7.0 per minute; antecedent event 1.1, child response 4.6, and subsequent events 1.3 per minute.
3. The fast learners were provided with fewer auditory stimuli than slow learners. Auditory discrimination activities were seldom used for fast or slow learners.
4. In the judgment of these clinicians, approximation responses (neither correct nor wrong) either occurred infrequently or were considered correct or wrong.
5. A high level of correct responding (average 85% for all 13 children) was maintained by these clinicians and is similar to that reported in the literature.
6. The positive reinforcement ratio used by these three clinicians was generally lower and the punishment ratio higher than previously reported.
7. From 70 to 81% of adjacent events (clinician-child or child-clinician) occurred in less than five seconds. About half of all the adjacent events were less than two seconds apart. That is indicative of the swiftness of articulation therapy interaction between clinician and child.

## Generalization

Four generalization curves (Immediate, Delayed, Inconsistent, and Little) were identified for acquisition of the target phoneme from imitation to conversation. Using the SPT and three-minute TALK as probes, 50% of the /s/ and /r/ children demonstrated a pattern of immediate generalization. This finding has important implications for speech training, i.e., clinicians may need to start programming for carryover early in therapy.

## Decisions Regarding Clinical Management

Since we cannot infer causes we cannot technically prescribe treatment. We cannot say what should be done on the basis of these results. The fact that our /s/ low children averaged 78% gain from the beginning to the end of the school year does not mean that concentrating on /s/ children will improve the overall gain. In order to be certain of the effect of such concentration, it is necessary to really run an experiment, and randomly assign children to a random sample of clinicians and then randomly assign these caseloads to the status of concentrated or not concentrated. This is the only way to know the effect of such a strategy.

Our data indicate what our children did, not what they would have done under other circumstances. What we are forced to do is return to the discussion at the beginning of the book (introductory statements regarding clinical experience). We will use our data and our experience to indicate what *may* work. These clinical decisions are derived not just from clinical experience, but also from our data base. Thus, we can proceed with some tentative clinicial management decisions.

Since we have so many independent variables, it may be comforting to know that the few (sound, group size, grade, and number of sessions per week), which do have some effect on the child's score, are variables that can be controlled by the clinician. Supervisors and administrators generally do not determine clinician rapport or years of experience. Likewise, clinicians cannot manipulate the child's baseline score, GFW, PPVTIQ, Token, Dental, and so on, but the *therapy arrangements* can be decided upon by the clinician.

## 1st Decision: Grade

Pendergast et al. (1969), McDonald and McDonald (1974), and Van Riper and Erickson (1973) cited by Barrett and Welsh (1975) have demonstrated prediction variables to determine whether kindergarten or first grade children with articulation errors should enter therapy immediately or wait until third grade. If these tests predict poor future articulation performance for /s/ and /r/ children, we may assume that they should be scheduled for therapy as soon as possible. However, if there are circumstances that defer therapy placement, our data indicate that, in general, children with /r/ or /s/ errors did better on GAIN and GAMMA in the older grades (3rd and 4th) than in the earlier grades (1st and 2nd). It does not appear that the older children did more poorly (which some previous workers have believed).

## 2nd Decision: Number of Sessions Per Week

GAMMA (speed of learning) and GAIN were not related to the number of sessions per week in therapy (once or twice) for /r/ and /s/, when the effect of the clinician performance level was removed. Unless otherwise demonstrable, once per week therapy would appear to be a more economical schedule.

## 3rd Decision: Number in Group

/s/ and /r/ showed no differences in GAIN or GAMMA when groups were composed of two, three, or four children. Therefore, maximizing group size should be more economical.

## 4th Decision: Previous Therapy

Children who have had previous therapy did not learn more or faster than those without previous therapy. In fact, by the end of the school year, children with previous therapy had no more GAIN than children who did not have a previous therapy experience. Therefore, in selecting children or groups, "previous therapy" can be ignored.

## 5th Decision: Multiple Sound Errors

Children who did acquire the /r/ or /s/ were as likely to have as many additional defective phonemes as children who did not learn the /r/ or /s/; therefore, using multiple additional errors for predicting success on /s/ or /r/ does not seem possible and could be disregarded in selecting children for therapy.

## 6th Decision: Other Factors

Children with lateral /s/ errors learn as well as those with frontal errors and children identified with tongue thrust learn as well with articulation training as non-tongue thrusters. Therefore, these factors can be ignored when choosing caseload.

## 7th Decision: Lesson Plans

Training the target sound in isolation, followed by the use of the target phoneme in the initial and then mixed position in words, phrases, and sentences was observed in the lesson plans of many of these clinicians. We know these procedures were used for many children who solved their problem and some who did not. We do not know if alternate procedures would obtain better or poorer results than those described here.

## 8th Decision: Termination Criteria

We believe that children who achieve 75% correct or better on the target phonemes /r/ or /s/ in conversation for two successive probes (one week apart) should be dismissed from therapy. A follow-up probe should be made at four weeks. If the child is still above 75%, but not at 95%, continue with eight-week interval probes. Stop follow-up probes when child is at 95% or better. Reinstate child in therapy if follow-up probes fall below 75% correct.

# Future Studies

We conclude by suggesting the need for future experimental studies on articulation learning. We have already alluded to a number of them in the body of the text. Several of the more obvious areas provoked by this study are as follows:
1. Better randomization of clinician selection.
2. Randomization of number of therapy sessions per week.
3. Selection of other personality variables in studying the clinician and child.
4. Investigation into different treatment approaches.
5. Continued work in describing and analyzing clinician-child interactions.
6. Reliability studies that contain independent observations of the speech changes measured in the children.
7. Continued studies of child performance level (KPL) and clinician performance level (CPL) measures to obtain comparable scores across children and clinicians.
8. Continued investigations of generalization of the target sound from imitation to conversation.

We hope this study spurs future investigators to examine other variables, use other measuring instruments, and develop different methodological strategies to discover more information about articulation learning.

Articulation disorders (as distinguished from disorders relating to language, voice, resonance, and prosody) comprise about two-thirds of all the problems that we treat in speech pathology. Most of these articulation disorders are found in children. Thus, we know what the major problem is and where it is to be found. It still remains for us to direct research toward helping children obtain better skills in articulation. Not only should more resources be directed toward overcoming articulation errors, there also should be concerted effort to prevent articulation disorders.

# Clinician Characteristics

## Educational Opinion Inventory (EOI)

The R Scale from the Educational Opinion Inventory (EOI) was administered to all of the participating clinicians in Years 2, 3, and 4 of the project. The scores obtained on the EOI was one of the clinician variables to be considered in the analysis of the results of the project.

The EOI is described by Richard Michael Krasno in *Teachers' Attitudes; Their Empirical Relationship to Rapport with Students and Survival in the Profession* (Technical Report No. 28), Stanford Center for Research and Development in Teaching, Stanford University, Stanford, California, June, 1972. The following was taken from the abstract of the report which describes the scale (p. *iii*):

> A sample of 30 male and 124 female prospective teachers were given a battery of inventories prior to teacher training. Included in this battery was a 300-item Educational Opinion Inventory (EOI). On the day immediately following the administration of each inventory, each subject taught a 40-minute lesson to 20 or 30 secondary school students. After the lessons, the students were asked to rate each subject on a 20-item Pupil Inventory that elicited responses from the students concerning the teacher-student rapport developed over the 40-minute lesson. From this rating each subject was assigned a rapport score based on the 11 items found through factor analysis to be highly loaded on the same factor, EOI responses of the highest and lowest 27% of the sample on teacher rapport scores were compared in order to find items that differentiated between the high- and low-rapport groups. A set of 62 items that differentiated the two groups on the basis of a chi-square test was designated as the R scale. Inspection of R Scale items indicated that high-rapport subjects differed from low-rapport subjects in their greater flexibility, higher sensitivity to needs of individual students, and generally more progressive educational philosophy.
>
> Discriminant analyses were performed using the predictor variables of (1) the California F-Scale, (2) the Kerlinger Scale of Educational Progressivism, (3) the Kerlinger Scale of Educational Traditionalism, (4) the Graduate Record Examination Verbal Test, (5) the Graduate Record Examination Quantitative Test. Results of the discriminant analyses indicated that these tests neither singly nor in combination could significantly or efficiently discriminate either high- from low-rapport students. . .

Comparison of R Scale Scores of High-Rapport and Low-Rapport Teachers

| Statistic | High Rapport | Low Rapport |
|---|---|---|
| N | 42 | 42 |
| Range | 146-83 (53) | 130-52 (78) |
| Mean | 128.95 | 100.20 |
| S.D. | 9.93 | 21.07 |
| S.E. | 1.61 | 3.33 |

*Table 12, p. 50 from Technical Report No. 28

There is some overlap between the two groups; but only one subject from the high-rapport group obtained an R Scale score below the mean of the low-rapport group, and only one subject from the low-rapport group received an R Scale score above the mean of the high-rapport group. The reliability of the R Scale was calculated to be .81 . . . (p. 49).

The Krasno report described the attitude patterns which differentiated high- and low-rapport subjects and the scoring procedures. It also lists the items related to the different categories which differentiated the high-rapport from the low-rapport subjects: goals of education, teacher beliefs, student characteristics, classroom techniques, and grading and evaluation.

# Child Characteristics

## Examination Procedures for Identification of Tongue Thrust and Dental Problems[1]

### Tongue Thrust Swallow Problems

| | Yes | No |
|---|---|---|
| 1. Does the tongue protrude when the child is saying words? | ___ | ___ |
| 2. Does the child have any distortion of the sibilant sounds?* | ___ | ___ |
| 3. In the rest position, does the tongue lie partly outside the dental arch?* | ___ | ___ |
| 4. Is it difficult for the child to bring the upper lip down to touch the lower? | ___ | ___ |
| 5. Does the child have an habitual grimace of tightness around the mouth? | ___ | ___ |
| 6. In your opinion is the child a mouth breather? | ___ | ___ |
| 7. Record the number of times the tongue-tip can touch the gum ridge. Ask the child to repeat 'da, da, da' and count the number of times during 15 seconds. | ___ | ___ |

### Observations of Swallow

| | Yes | No |
|---|---|---|
| 8. When you're holding the lower lip to break the seal, does the child retract the lip back as he attempts to swallow?* | ___ | ___ |
| 9. Is the child unable to swallow when the seal is broken?* | ___ | ___ |
| 10. Does the tongue protrude beyond the edges of any of the incisor teeth during swallow?* | ___ | ___ |
| 11. Can the child swallow easily without any of the behaviors noted in 8, 9, 10? | ___ | ___ |

## Discussion Sheet for Tongue Thrust Swallow Examination Procedures

The following suggestions and procedures refer to those items on the examination form which are marked with an asterisk.

A. In order to determine whether a child has any distortion of the sibilant sounds observe him during speech. Use short diagnostic speech test sentences or pictures to elicit a sample of sibilant sounds and note all sibilants that are even slightly distorted. (Question 2)

B. To determine whether a child's tongue lies partly outside the dental arch when the tongue is in the rest position, ask the child to drop his jaw open. If he protrudes his tongue deliberately (as he might if the doctor told him to open

[1]Modified after Larr, 1962; and Fletcher, Casteel and Bradley, 1961)

his mouth) tell him to close his mouth while you demonstrate what you wish him to do. Then tell him to drop his jaw again. (Question 3)

C. For observation of swallow, tell the child that you wish to "watch the way you swallow." Give the child a drink of water if he indicates his mouth is dry. To negate the seal used for swallow and to expose the tongue if it is thrust forward during swallow, depress the child's lower lip. Then make the observations for questions 8, 9, and 10.

## Dental Problems

Ask the child to "bite"; make sure the upper and lower molars are "fitting" properly. Check the appropriate blank.

|  | Yes | No |
|---|---|---|
| a. *Overjet*—Upper front teeth protrude beyond the lower teeth to a greater degree than normal. | ____ | ____ |
| b. *Undershot or underbite*—Lower jaw protrudes so that lower front teeth mask all or part of the upper front teeth. | ____ | ____ |
| c. *Open bite*—A space between the upper front and lower front teeth. | ____ | ____ |
| d. *Edentulous spaces*—Openings left by missing teeth. | ____ | ____ |
| e. *Interproximal spaces*—Openings between the teeth near the gums. | ____ | ____ |
| f. *Jumbling*—Irregularly placed or slanted teeth. | ____ | ____ |

## Language Battery

Several tests were included to provide an assessment of the language competency of the children in Year 4. Cynthia Shewan, Ph.D., provided the logic for this screening battery. Among the criteria for inclusion was the attempt to maximize information input and to minimize time output.

(a) Peabody Picture Vocabulary Test (Dunn, 1965)

(b) Token Test (Part V, modified after DeRenzi and Vignolo, 1962; and Noll, 1970)

(c) Detroit Test—Test 13, Auditory Attention Span for Related Syllables (Baker and Leland, 1959).

Two receptive tasks were selected to assess auditory comprehension. The Peabody Picture Vocabulary Test is a well-known test of single word vocabulary comprehension. Part V of the Token Test evaluates comprehension of certain grammatical concepts, specifically, spatial and temporal aspects, such as prepositions and constructs like "if-then." The two tests provide information about how the child understands both vocabulary and syntax.

The Detroit Test was used as an expressive language measure. While one may argue that imitative tasks are not necessarily representative measures of a child's typical linguistic performance, there is evidence that this method can be employed to assess grammatical competence (Fraser, Bellugi and Brown, 1963; Menyuk, 1963; Muma, 1971; and Berry-Luterman and Bar, 1971). Measures of performance, using analyses of language samples, require more time for evaluation and permit no control over the grammatical structures elicted.

# APPENDIX C

# Data Collection Methodologies

## Three-Minute TALK and Sound Production Task (SPT)

One of the basic concepts involved in this research project concerns the development of continuous measurement of articulation behavior changes. It is known that articulation testing on a pre- and post-basis over long periods of time (such as several months or an entire school year) does not describe the week-by-week changes in speech behavior that occurs with children. It is essential that we describe as accurately as possible the change in articulation as it occurs over time. For that reason a Three Minute TALK Task and a Sound Production Task is administered on a frequent basis throughout the year.

## Three-Minute TALK

Engage child in conversation for three minutes and during this time count the target phoneme Correct or Wrong. Tally your responses on a piece of paper or use counters. Use your stop watch to keep time. Clinician talking is limited to that amount necessary to keep the child talking and is included in the total three minutes. Use open-ended question, e.g., "What did you do at the fair?" not "Did you like the fair?".

## Sound Production Tasks

The Sound Production Tasks (SPT) are sounds, words, and phrases spoken by the clinician and imitated by the child. The procedures used at the University of Kansas (Elbert, Shelton, Arndt, 1967; Shelton, Elbert, Arndt, 1967; Wright, Shelton, Arndt, 1969) are a modification of the deep testing concept developed by McDonald (1964). There are 30 items for /s/ and 60 items for /r/. The items for /r/ have been systematically arranged to surround the /r/ with different vowels and consonant contexts, front-back vowels and consonants. Administration of the 30 items takes two and one-half minutes and the 60 items five minutes.

## Procedures

One three-minute TALK is administered during the baseline period (pre-therapy) and it is tape recorded. The Sound Production Task (SPT) is administered three times before therapy begins to get a baseline score. The last SPT can be given on the first day of therapy. Each item is marked either Correct or Wrong on the score sheet.

After therapy begins the three-minute TALK and SPT are given every two weeks throughout the course of therapy. When they are administered to the children *always* take the three-minute TALK first and then give the SPT. This procedure reduces the chance of cueing the child about the target phoneme in question. The three-minute TALK is tallied for Correct/Wrong productions of the target phoneme on a separate sheet of paper and transferred to the three-minute TALK and SPT score sheet.

When a child is put on CLINICAL REST, or is judged a SUCCESS, continue to probe his speech using the three-minute TALK and SPT every four weeks.

## Sound Production Task /s/

1. /us/
2. musty
3. /sae/
4. household
5. glasszoo
6. your side
7. placemat
8. missing
9. dog sits
10. houseknife

11. /s/
12. get some
13. Bob sent
14. /sa/
15. busboy
16. classday
17. breathe softly
18. clean suit
19. passthat
20. iceroom

21. home soon
22. husky
23. /is/
24. up Sunday
25. asleep
26. his seat
27. like soup
28. all silk
29. icewater
30. red socks

## Sound Production Task /r/

1. /ɝ/ (irk)
2. dear one
3. /kru/ (crew)
4. /ædɚ/ (adder)
5. girl
6. paper
7. rock
8. /kɝk/ (kirk)
9. /Iɚ/ (ear)
10. /ɝ/
11. /gru/ (grew)
12. beard
13. rabbit
14. bird
15. /agɚ/ (ahger)
16. /tɝt/ (tirt)
17. truck
18. hammer
19. /ræ/
20. turn

21. gargle
22. /tri/ (tree)
23. /itɚ/ (eater)
24. hurt
25. /oɚ/ (or)
26. /dræ/
27. board
28. fur
29. /ætɚ/ (atter)
30. grow
31. cooker
32. /gɝg/ (girg)
33. /ra/ (rah)
34. /ɛɚ/ (air)
35. wrong
36. mother
37. her
38. more things
39. /ri/ (ree)
40. /ugɚ/ (ooger)

41. read
42. /dɝd/ (dird)
43. /aɚ/ (are)
44. /kra/ (krah)
45. gurgle
46. brass
47. /dri/ (dree)
48. /akɚ/ (ahker)
49. crook
50. earn
51. /ru/ (rue)
52. /idɚ/ (eeder)
53. /gra/ (grah)
54. dirt
55. /træ/
56. door way
57. ran
58. /ukɚ/ (ooker)
59. grey
60. shirk

# Cognitive Lesson Plan

## Identification, Activity, and Feeling Sheet

| Clinician | # | Child Identification | | | |
|---|---|---|---|---|---|
| | | Seat | Pho | Name | Number |

Mo    Day    Year

Group Identity ⌊⌋

| ACTIVITY | | | THERAPY PLAN | | | | REINFORCEMENT | COST |
|---|---|---|---|---|---|---|---|---|
| # | Time Started | Seat | Pho. | Activity | Stim. | Cont. | Pos. | Token: Response | Token Response |

| How do you feel today about the following: | Before Therapy | | | | | | After Therapy | | | | | |
|---|---|---|---|---|---|---|---|---|---|---|---|---|
| | Clinician | | | Child | | | Clinician | | | Child | | |
| | Good | SoSo | Lousy | Good | SoSo | Lousy | Good | SoSo | Lousy | Good | SoSo | Lousy |
| Child #1 | | | | | | | | | | | | |
| Child #2 | | | | | | | | | | | | |
| Child #3 | | | | | | | | | | | | |
| Yourself | | | | | | | | | | | | |
| Therapy Conditions | | | | | | | | | | | | |
| Therapy Generally | | | | | | | | | | | | |

# Cognitive Lesson Plan

## Name of Activity

*Verbalization*
FC — Free Conversation
SS — Structured Speech
Rdg — Reading

*Other*
RA — Review Assignment
GA — Give Assignment
PP — Parent Participation
TP — Teacher Participation
PC — Parent Conference
TC — Teacher Conference
ChT — Chart Time
FT — Fun Time

*Drills*
SD — Standard Drill
GD — Game Drill
RD — Rate Drill
TD — Transfer Drill
TTh — Tongue Thrust Drill
Dis — Discrimination
SM — Self-Monitoring
NP — Negative Practice
Sh — Response Shaping
   ShD — Directions
   ShA — Auditory
   ShV — Visual
   ShK — Tactual (Kinesthetic)

*Stimulus*
M — Model (auditory)
P — Picture
MP — Model and Picture
T — Tape Recorder
E — Other Equipment
O — Object
G — Graphic
CG — Child Generated
SC — Sentence Completion
Ch — Chart

*Content*
I — Isolation
S — Syllable
W — Word
Ph — Phrase

*Position* (of target phoneme)
I — Initial position
M — Medial position
F — Final position
X — Mixed
Bl — Blends

## Description of Activities

## Verbalization

*FC — Free Conversation.* This refers to any spontaneous conversation activity (when the child is not on his guard). This type of activity is frequently utilized at the beginning of a therapy session. During this activity you may count each utterance of the child's target sound by indicating your judgment of the production (+, –, or /) on the Tone Keyboard or you may prefer to simply observe his use of the target phoneme without making judgments.

*SS — Structured Speech.* Any speech with a controlled format. This includes such things as (a) describing picture cards, (b) asking the child to tell a story, (c) speech where the child and/or clinician count Correct/Wrong productions of the target phoneme, (d) putting speech on loop tapes, Language Masters, etc. The child's target sound is judged (+, –, /) and recorded as such on the Tone Keyboard.

*Rdg — Reading.* Any reading that is used during the therapy session. Record each production of the target phoneme on the Tone Keyboard as (+, –, /).

# Other

*RA — Review Assignment.* Discussion with a child about work he was asked to do outside of the therapy room, for instance, checking his speech workbook.

*GA — Giving Assignment.* Discussion with the child about work you would want him to do outside of the therapy session.

*PP — Parent Participation.* Time during a therapy session when a parent is asked to either observe the session or to be trained to work at home with her child. The child is present during this time and the parent is participating in some way. Continue to use the Tone Keyboard but do not include any responses made by the parent.

*TP — Teacher Participation.* Time during a therapy session when a teacher is brought into the room to observe or receive training. The child is also present. Continue to use the Tone Keyboard but do not include teacher responses.

*PC — Parent Conference.* Time when a parent is seen without the child being present. This activity should be entered on the ID-ACTIVITY sheet but the Tone Keyboard is not used during the conference.

*TC — Teacher Conference.* Time when a teacher is seen without the child being present. Again, as with parent conference, this activity should be entered on the ID-ACTIVITY sheet, but the Tone Keyboard is not used during the conference.

*ChT — Chart Time.* This refers to time spent with a child working with charts. This can be time spent in explanation, discussion or actually plotting on charts or other visual aids.

*Ft — Fun Time.* Time spent in a therapy session that is unrelated to speech work. It should be noted on the ID-ACTIVITY sheet, but the Tone Keyboard is not used.

# Drill

We acknowledge the fact that this is a broad and varied activity category. The following divisions of this category are frequently used by clinicians.

*SD — Standard Drill.* This refers to the presentation of auditory, visual, or graphic stimuli to a child in order to prompt his verbal response to the material.

*GD — Game Drill.* Game drill is differentiated from SD on the assumption that in a game drill the child is not exclusively concerned with correct articulatory production of a sound in a word or phrase because of the other factors which may be present in a game situation. In addition to producing an articulatory response, the child may be attending to the rules of the game, and/or performance of other children who are competing. There may also be some stress involved in the situation. In some games, such as "Concentration," memory for card positions may be a competing factor.

*RD — Rate Drill.* Whenever stimulus material is presented to a child and his responses are evaluated in terms of correctness involving speed or ease of production, it is defined as a rate drill. An example might be the presentation of a list of 25 words containing a target sound. During the first reading the time would be noted and then on the second reading the child is asked to read the list more quickly with continued good articulation. He can either compete with himself on repeated reading or with other children on the basis of rate of correct articulations. Again, as with game drills, other competing factors are introduced which differentiate this category from the standard drill.

*TD — Transfer Drill.* When the child has learned to produce his target sound within a given context and this context is used to facilitate correct production within another context, this is considered a transfer drill.

*TTh — Tongue Thrust Swallow Drill.* This refers to time spent on drills and exercises designed to correct tongue thrust swallow. If you plan an entire period for non-verbal tongue thrust swallow therapy, do not use the Tone Keyboard.

*Dis — Discrimination Drill.* The child makes judgments of someone else's speech. For example, "Did you hear your sound in that word?" or "Was the sound at the beginning or end of the word?", etc.

*SM — Self-Monitoring.* The child makes discrimination judgments of his own productions; either from live speech or from taped speech.

*NP — Negative Practice.* The conditions for negative practice are described as whenever the clinician asks a child to contrast pairs of words (i.e. "Wabbit-Rabbit," "thoup-soup," etc.); or when specific requests are made for the child to produce his error sound intentionally.

*Sh — Response Shaping.* This category is utilized in a variety of situations. It may be selected as the major activity entry or it may be used intermittently during other activities as described on the Tone Keyboard.

*ShD — Directions.* All explanations to the child involving the sound being taught, as well as all motor directions which would assist the child in arranging his articulatory mechanism so as to facilitate correct productions of the desired response.

*ShA — Auditory.* The presentation of auditory models to the child for imitative responses. This category also includes information the clinician provides the child as to the correctness of the evoked response.

*ShV — Visual.* The shaping of responses by directing the child's observations of either his own articulatory responses in a mirror (mirror practice) or of the visual components of the clinician's articulation of the desired responses. For example, children with /s/ defects may sound almost correct and thus get little auditory feedback regarding the accuracy of their productions. They may need to focus their attention on the tongue protrusions by observing themselves in a mirror.

*ShK — Tactual.* Any touch cues provided by the clinician to assist in the evocation of a desired response. These cues may either be manual (i.e., touching the lower lip with a tongue depressor to indicate that the upper teeth should be placed there for the production of /f/ or /v/).

*Response Shaping* often embodies some, or all, of the above. If all of these categories are to be utilized during one activity period, then the entry placed in the brace would be ⌊s_ıh ı____⌋ only.

# Description of Stimulus, Content, and Position

## Stimulus

*M — Model.* An auditory model for the child to imitate (i.e. /s/ or "sur.")

*P — Picture.* Any picture used as a stimulus for the purpose of evoking a verbal response.

*MP — Model and Picture.* The use of an auditory stimulus coupled with a picture using this combination to evoke a response from the child.

*T — Tape Recorder.* When the tape recorder is used as a stimulus.

*E — Other Equipment.* This might include the Language Master.

*O — Object.* A real object or toy replica of the desired word.

*G — Graphic.* A written word, phrase, or sentence used as a stimulus.

*CG — Child Generated.* When the child himself is expected to "make up" the words or sentences without specific cues, such as picture cards.

*SC — Sentence Completion.* Whenever a word or phrase is evoked by preceding the response with a phrase, (i.e., "It shines during the day; it's called the _____.")

*Ch — Chart.* When a chart is used as a stimulus to evoke responses.

## Content

*I — Isolation*
*S — Syllable*
*W — Word*
*Ph — Phrase*
If necessary, two content categories may be used for one activity (i.e., I-S, or W-Ph).

## Position

Position of the target phoneme in a word.

*I — Initial Position*

*M — Medial Position*

*F — Final Position*

*X — Mixed Positions*

*Bl — Blends*

# Clinician-Child Therapy Interactions (Tone Keyboard)

The box with 16 keys is a Tone Keyboard used to record the clinician and child moment-to-moment interactions. Each key strikes a different tone which is recorded on tape at 1⅞ i.p.s. Later, the tape is played at 7½ i.p.s. through a decoder which puts the information onto computer tape.

On the Tone Keyboard, columns for Clinician, Model, Child Response, and Child Seat Number are spatially arranged.
1. Column 1 is the behavior of the Clinician (except Models).
2. Column 2 is for Models presented by the Clinician.
3. Column 3 is the response of the Child.
4. Column 4 identifies the child's Seat Number.

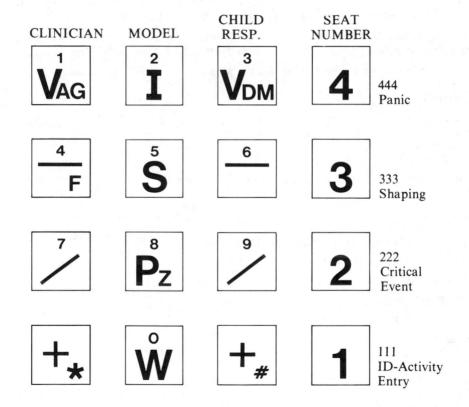

# Tone Keyboard Use

## Clinician Column

*V — Verbalization (Punch Key Once)*
Any verbalization of the clinician not covered by verbal consequation, feedback, or "again." Words used as fillers (ok, uhuh, etc.) need not be punched in.

*AG — Again (Punch Key Twice)*
The clinician wants the child to repeat what he has just said.

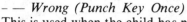

*- — Wrong (Punch Key Once)*
This is used when the child has produced a response and the clinician follows this response with a verbal "no," "that's wrong," a negative head nod, or token cost.

*F — Feedback (Punch Key Twice)*
Feedback statements made by the clinician immediately after a consequation (+, -, /) which tells the child something specific about his behavior, e.g., "that's good (+) you kept your tongue behind your teeth" (F), or "no, (-) you let your tongue come between your teeth" (F).

*/ — Approximation (Punch Key Once)*
Whenever the clinician follows the child's approximation response with the verbal "That's better," "That's closer," etc.

*+ — Correct (Punch Key Once)*
Whenever the clinician follows the child's correct response with a verbal statement such as, "good," a token, or an affirmative head nod.

*\* — Error Sign (Punch Key Three or More Times)*
The asterisk indicates that an error has been made in entering the ID-ACTIVITY information. Punch the asterisk key three or more times and re-enter all the correct ID-ACTIVITY information.

The error key should never be punched during therapy, i.e, while interaction is actually taking place. Errors made in punching during therapy are to be ignored.

*Note:* The small number at the top of a key is used when entering ID-ACTIVITY information.

# Model Column

### I — Isolation (Punch Key Once)

The sound in isolation is presented to the child as a model for him to imitate. (Note: If a clinician is developing the target phoneme by having the child say /i/-/r/ (ee-rr), the I key should be depressed only once for the /r/ sound. The child's production of /r/ is judged as (+, -, /); and entered under the Child Column).

### S — Syllable (Punch Key Once)

A syllable is presented to the child as a model for him to imitate.

### P — Phrase (Punch Key Once)

A phrase or sentence is presented to the child as a model for him to imitate.

### Z — Self-Correction (Punch Key Twice)

This is punched to indicate that a child has made a self-correction of his own production. This is the only key in this column to be depressed for anything except a clinician's verbal model.

### W — Word (Punch Key Once)

A word is presented to the child as a model for him to imitate.

When pairs of sounds, syllables, or words are used under Negative Practice (Rabbit-Wabbit), punch I, S, W, key twice in the Model Column and punch (+, -, /) twice in the Child Column.

*Note:* The small number at the top of a key is used when entering ID-ACTIVITY information.

## Child Response Column

*V — Verbalization (Punch Key Once)*
Statements or questions made by the child.

*DM — Discrimination (Punch Key Twice)*
The child is asked to monitor self, peer, clinician, or taped models of speech and make a judgment of correct or incorrect.

 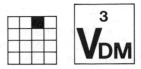

*- — Wrong (Punch Key Once)*
An incorrect articulation response, not judged as approximated.

*/ — Approximation (Punch Key Once)*
An articulation response which is partially, but not completely correct.

*+ — Correct (Punch Key Once)*
The response has been a correct response. For a child with a tongue protrusion on the /s/, the response must be visually as well as acoustically correct. A child whose response is exaggerated or prolonged would be counted as correct, if it is otherwise correctly produced.

*# — Space Bar (Punch Key Once)*
This symbol is used as a space bar function on a typewriter. It helps "space" the numbers for decoding purposes. It is used only in ID-ACTIVITY information entry. (Ex: 111 3 # 9 # 05 111)

*Note:* The small number at the top of a key is used when entering ID-ACTIVITY information.

## Seat Number Column

*4 — Seat number (Punch Key Once)*

*444 — Panic button (Punch key three or more times,)*
To be used whenever interruptions or systematic recording were not possible.

*3 — Seat number (Punch Key Once)*

*333 — Response Shaping (Punch key three or more times.)* If you have started on an ACTIVITY like Standard Drill and then decide to do some response shaping with one or more children, punch child's seat number, pause three seconds, and enter 333 to indicate "shaping" is being done. At the end of your shaping period, end with "333" and continue your Standard Drill.

(Example: Seat 3, (3 sec.), 333 ∿⟶ 333.)
                                  Time

*2 — Seat number (Punch Key Once)*

*222 — Critical Event (Punch key three or more times.)* Whenever you believe something "critical" occurred in the learning responses of the child punch this key. It is that point in time when you believe the child "has got it." You may feel that he has had several of these events during the course of learning the target phoneme. Punch child's seat number, pause three seconds, and enter 222.

(Example: 2, (3 sec.), 222)

*1 — Seat number (Punch Key Once)*

*111 — Activity Entry (Punch key three or more times.)* The "111" functions as a "Quote" symbol, before and after ID-ACTIVITY entries.

| ID Example: | 111 | 0 | # 25 | # 9 # 15 # 72 | # 3 | 111 |
|---|---|---|---|---|---|---|
| | | zero | Clin. no. | date | Grp. no. | |

| Activity Example: | 111 | 2 | # 10 # 07 | 111 |
|---|---|---|---|---|
| | | Activ. no. | Time | |

Figure C-1
Side View of Tone Keyboard

Figure C-2
Overhead View of Tone Keyboard

Figure C-3
Clinician using Tone Keyboard with child in therapy

APPENDIX D

# Reliability Measures of Conversation

Three different procedures were carried out during the project to establish the reliability of listener judgments in determining whether the target phoneme was correct or wrong during three minute conversations (TALK). The procedures involved 1) groups of listeners who heard talk samples from audio tape[1], 2) groups who heard from audio tape what the clinician heard live in the therapy session, and 3) listeners[2] who were with the clinician and child during the therapy. The reader will also note that different statistics and analyses were used with the different listening conditions: ANOVA and Pearson product moment correlations, means and standard deviations of correct/wrong count data.

## Group Listening

### Ten-Segment Tape

In the first year of the project, 10, tape recorded conversations were spliced together for judging. The conversations were selected from children in Year 1 of the project. The criteria for selection were target phoneme (a mix of /r/ and /s/ errors), range of severity, and fidelity of the tape. This tape sample was used to test the reliability of the clinicians in the first and second years of the project.

In the first experiment using the ten-tape criterion, ten field clinicians, three control clinicians and three staff clinicians were used, making a total of 16 listeners. The children in the ten taped conversations were unknown to these persons. Counts of correct or wrong were made by each listener of each conversation in each trial. The percent correct out of the total target phonemes heard was the raw data from which reliability calculations were made (Table D.1). The first two columns of this table are $r_{kk}$ estimates of the reliability of "K" listeners (Guilford, 1954, p. 395). The last column is the product-moment correlation of two trials. This estimates the reliability of tape listening across trials. All of these estimates of reliability were in the .90's for the group. The reliability for any one listener was .54. In the second project year, the same 10 samples were played to another 20 clinicians. The average $r_{kk}$ reliability for this group was .99.

### 22-Segment Tape

During our second project year we assembled another reliability tape. The tape contained 10 /r/ and 10 /s/ segments of three-minute conversations, one /r/ and one /s/ segment were repeated for internal reliability making a total of 22 tape segments spliced together randomly to make one tape. The segments were chosen

---

1. All taped material reported here was at 3 3/4 i.p.s. and obtained in the clinician's therapy room on a Realistic Model 505A tape recorder or Sony TC-104A. The tape listening was done either free field or with headphones and tapes played back on the Sony TC-104A.
2. Staff clinician(s) means person(s) with M.A. degrees in speech pathology whose average experience was seven years who were employed as project staff. The field and control clinicians had a B.A. or M.A. in speech pathology and were employed in the schools. The control clinicians were not provided with information about our project and were not taught to test (probe) or chart the child's progress.

| Clinicians | Number of raters = k | Reliability estimates for k raters | | Average correlation between trials |
|---|---|---|---|---|
| | | 1st trial | 2nd trial | |
| Field | 10 | .97 | .96 | .94 |
| Control | 3 | .93 | .97 | .95 |
| Staff | 3 | .98 | .96 | .96 |

TABLE D.1. Summary of reliability estimates for the ten-tape criterion sample and 16 raters.

from a pool of 174 for good tape fidelity and to represent a wide range of percent correct (from 1 to 100).

All listeners were given the same amount of preparatory training prior to the reliability tape presentation. This procedure consisted of listening to two, one-minute tape samples (one for /s/ and one for /r/) of children's conversation and making correct or wrong judgments of the specified target phoneme either /r/ or /s/. Three staff clinicians listened to the two, one-minute samples and obtained agreement on the total number of /s/ and /r/ words, and the correct/wrong counts for both phonemes. This became the standard for training all other listeners.

The listeners were shown lists of words containing samples of /r/ and /s/. Instructions covered the problem of two /r/'s in one word, e.g., *ruler* which was judged twice, *carrot*, judged once, etc. For /s/ they also were told not to judge /z/ as in *bees* but to count *piece*. For phrases such as *pass something*, the /s/ was judged once unless there was a pause between the words.

First, the listeners heard a one-minute sample of conversation and were asked to count the total number of /s/ sounds spoken by the child. After being told the standard count the tape was replayed and they counted total /s/ sounds again. Their counts were compared, a second time, with the standard and questions answered. Next, the listeners heard the same tape segment and counted the /s/ correct/wrong and that was compared to the standard. The tape was replayed one more time (the fourth time) and their correct/wrong counts again compared. The same procedure was followed for /r/ with another one-minute tape segment of conversation. The entire training procedure was accomplished in 20-30 minutes, whether it was speech clinicians or students.

The 22-segment tape was played to many different groups of listeners: a group of 40 nonspeech undergraduate and graduate students (J); six student nurses who heard the tape on two occasions ($N_1$, $N_2$); and the clinicians from three locales (11 from Minnesota; 12 from Kansas, 12 from Colorado); and another group of undergraduate students ($S_1$, $S_2$). (Table D.2).

One of the purposes of playing the 22-segment tape to a variety of listeners was to establish whether correct/wrong tallies were different. It was our intention to use these different groups to check the field clinicians' reliability. It will be noted from Table D.2 that some segments were judged differently by these groups, especially when individual clinicians were compared with the groups. However, there was more similarity of judgments than appears at first glance. The correlations in Tables D.3 and D.4 when broken out separately for /r/ and /s/ demonstrated moderate to high correlations for all group comparisons with /r/ more stable than /s/. The greatest difference in each table was in the individual clini-

| # | Sound | $N_1$ (N=6) % | $N_2$ (N=6) % | J (N=40) % | M (N=11) % | C (N=12) % | K (N=12) % | C (N=1) % | $S_1$ (N=6) % | $S_2$ (N=6) % |
|---|---|---|---|---|---|---|---|---|---|---|
| 1 | S | 45 | 32 | 95 | 53 | 62 | 47 | 94 | 43 | 36 |
| 2 | S | 53 | 46 | 66 | 73 | 79 | 60 | 23 | 45 | 38 |
| 3 | R | 28 | 21 | 44 | 17 | 48 | 19 | 7 | 10 | 12 |
| 4 | R | 57 | 83 | 70 | 83 | 76 | 69 | 84 | 65 | 53 |
| 5 | S | 49 | 50 | 62 | 69 | 71 | 60 | 0 | 33 | 38 |
| 6 | R | 24 | 24 | 22 | 37 | 32 | 29 | 17 | 15 | 17 |
| 7* | R reliability | | | 75 | 38 | 31 | 40 | | 19 | 17 |
| 8* | S reliability | | | 64 | 30 | 61 | 55 | | 33 | 30 |
| 9 | S | 42 | 71 | 83 | 60 | 72 | 68 | 100 | 44 | 31 |
| 10 | R | 24 | 29 | 85 | 30 | 33 | 24 | 94 | 13 | 17 |
| 11 | S | 23 | 11 | 24 | 03 | 17 | 02 | 88 | 06 | 10 |
| 12 | S | 34 | 54 | 75 | 66 | 85 | 66 | 0 | 30 | 32 |
| 13 | R | 71 | 98 | 99 | 99 | 97 | 95 | 100 | 80 | 20 |
| 14 | R | 33 | 24 | 42 | 42 | 49 | 36 | 26 | 26 | 22 |
| 15* | R reliability | | | 77 | 33 | 38 | 35 | | 13 | 28 |
| 16* | S reliability | | | 75 | 62 | 83 | 45 | | 41 | 32 |
| 17 | S | 36 | 33 | 68 | 61 | 56 | 44 | 60 | 60 | 28 |
| 18 | S | 47 | 72 | 62 | 68 | 88 | 66 | 0 | 63 | 51 |
| 19 | R | 76 | 90 | 93 | 88 | 90 | 86 | 76 | 70 | 67 |
| 20 | R | 45 | 52 | 61 | 47 | 43 | 24 | 68 | 49 | 44 |
| 21 | S | 42 | 68 | 72 | 83 | 82 | 64 | 81 | 56 | 21 |
| 22 | R | 30 | 28 | 44 | 34 | 40 | 25 | 59 | 20 | 26 |

*Tapes #7 and #15 and #8 and #16 were duplicates.

TABLE D.2. Mean percent correct on 22-tape segments for different groups of listeners.

cian's judgment of her child from the tape versus any composite judgment by a group.

The correlation for any individual listener with a group of listeners was always less than for the group. In our data the individual correlation was .54. That is the lower level of correlations found in Table D.3 for the /r/ sound. The /s/ phoneme was another matter. Much poorer (many negative) correlations were obtained between the individual and a group of listeners. With these data for /s/ one might question the clinician's skill, or else accept the data because we cannot get good agreement, at least from tape, for /s/. More will be said about /s/ judgments later on in this section.

A comparison of these different groups of listeners is presented in Table D.3 and D.4. The clinicians from each state correlated greater than .90 with one another for /r/ and /s/. The field clinicians from the three states had correlations with the 40 students in the 70's (for /s/ and /r/). Reliability of the six nurses and six students compared with the 40 students for /r/ was in the 70's, but for the /s/ tape segments these correlations are .49 to .60. The field clinician's taped observation of their child's correct/wrong response for one single child were compared to groups of judges. This resulted in reliabilities ranging from .51 to .87 for the /r/ and −.52 to +.42 for the /s/ sound.

The difficulty in judging /s/ as compared to /r/ is highlighted by an intra-reliability measure where one /s/ segment was repeated and one /r/ segment was repeated. Clinicians from the three states showed intra-reliability of .28 for the /s/ segment and .42 for the /r/ segment. The mean of the three means (one for each set of clinicians from the three states, Table D.2) for that /s/ segment was 49% correct (SD = 16) on the first listening and 63% correct on the second listening (SD = 19). The first time they heard the /r/ segment, there was a mean of 36% correct (SD = 5) and 35% correct on the second listening (SD = 3). It is clear that /s/ judged from these tapes was a much less reliable task.

Young (1969) had previously demonstrated that repeated exposure to many samples across sessions does not result in changes of the observer's ratings. We observed this phenomenon in the high correlations obtained for repeated judgments of the same tape after many hours of judging correct or wrong from samples of children's conversations. The nurses in our study listened to the 22-segment tape twice, 11 weeks apart. During the interim, they listened to tapes for about one and one-half hours, four times per week. The student nurses made 66 hours of correct/wrong judgments to samples of conversation on tape over an 11-week period ($N_1$ to $N_2$).

In another listening study, six undergraduate students heard the 22-segment tape twice, one week apart. During that week they listened daily to tapes, approximately two and one-half hours in the morning and two and one-half hours in the afternoon. Each undergraduate student heard 25 hours of tapes in one week ($S_1$ to $S_2$). Both groups had high correlations (upper nineties) with themselves for the nine /r/ segments, but lower correlations (.78 and .57) for the nine /s/ segments (Table D.3 and D.4). There was little practice effect or change in the listener's perceptual standard for /r/, but some on /s/.

Both student groups and the three groups of clinicians had inter-correlations in the 90's for the /r/ segments. However, the clinicians from the three states also had correlations with each other in the 90's for the /s/ segments. And finally, the clinicians from the three states had correlations with groups of non-clinicians for /r/ in the .70-.90 range and for /s/ in the .60-.80 range.

It would appear from these data that groups composed of six or more naive listeners provide sufficient reliability for taped judgments of correct/wrong /r/ or /s/ from conversation. Guilford (1954, p. 397) noted that "there is usually much (reliability) to be gained by adding the first two or three raters, but not much after reaching five."

## Clinician (Live) Versus Groups of Listeners (Tape)

### Year 2

In project Year 2 each clinician made a baseline (September) tape of three minutes of conversation with each child and again at midyear (January). Tapes were randomly selected from approximately 30 children for each clinician who

|  | $N_1$ | $N_2$ | 40 | MN | CO | KS | C* | $S_1$ | $S_2$ |
|---|---|---|---|---|---|---|---|---|---|
| Nurses$_1$ (6) | 100 | 97 | 75 | 95 | 95 | 93 | 60 | 97 | 98 |
| Nurses$_2$ (6) |  | 100 | 78 | 97 | 93 | 94 | 71 | 98 | 98 |
| Students (40) |  |  | 100 | 71 | 72 | 72 | 87 | 72 | 75 |
| Minnesota (11) |  |  |  | 100 | 92 | 97 | 66 | 97 | 96 |
| Colorado (12) |  |  |  |  | 100 | 96 | 51 | 91 | 90 |
| Kansas (12) |  |  |  |  |  | 100 | 58 | 91 | 91 |
| Clinician (1) |  |  |  |  |  |  | 100 | 66 | 69 |
| Students$_1$ (6) |  |  |  |  |  |  |  | 100 | 99 |
| Students$_2$ (6) |  |  |  |  |  |  |  |  | 100 |

TABLE D.3. Correlations among groups of listeners who made correct/wrong judgments from three-minute conversation on nine /r/ segments.

For nine observations, correlations must be .52 (5% level) and .69 (1% level). N listeners for each group are indicated in parenthesis.

*The clinician score represents her count made from that one child's tape segment (several different clinicians are represented on the nine segments).

| | N$_1$ | N$_2$ | 40 | MN | CO | KS | C* | S$_1$ | S$_2$ |
|---|---|---|---|---|---|---|---|---|---|
| Nurses$_1$ (6) | 100 | 54 | 56 | 75 | 71 | 71 | -36 | 59 | 78 |
| Nurses$_2$ (6) | | 100 | 57 | 77 | 86 | 89 | -28 | 61 | 54 |
| Students (40) | | | 100 | 73 | 71 | 79 | 04 | 60 | 49 |
| Minnesota (11) | | | | 100 | 97 | 92 | -41 | 76 | 59 |
| Colorado (12) | | | | | 100 | 97 | -52 | 66 | 72 |
| Kansas (12) | | | | | | 100 | 42 | 65 | 69 |
| Clinician (1) | | | | | | | 100 | -11 | -62 |
| Students$_1$ (6) | | | | | | | | 100 | 57 |
| Students$_2$ (6) | | | | | | | | | 100 |

For nine observations, correlations must be .52 (5% level) and .69 (1% level). N listeners for each group are indicated in parenthesis.

*The clinician score represents her count made from that child's tape segment (several different clinicians are represented on the nine segments).

TABLE D.4. Correlations among groups of listeners who made correct/wrong judgments from three-minute conversations on nine /s/ taped segments.

was participating in the project. A clinician's entire caseload would average about 80 children. For reasons of economy, between 16-20 children (average 17) were judged for each clinician. The taped three-minute TALK segments at baseline and midyear were randomized and judged by student nurses. Percent correct/wrong counts made by the clinician live in the school were averaged for all the children and compared to mean percent correct/wrong counts made from tape by the group of nurses. If the nurse judgments found a difference in the two scores (i.e., there was improvement in the mean gain for all the children judged on tape) and if the judgment was in agreement with the clinician's, then it was assumed that the clinician's correct/wrong counts were relatively reliable. The absolute amount of gain may not have been similar, but the trends for improvement were the same. All the clinician's believed that observable gains had occurred. Of the 20 clinicians, six were judged by the nurses to have no observable gains from baseline to midyear. In other words, the nurses agreed with 70% of the clinicians that improvement had been observed between baseline and midyear.

## Year 3

In Year 3, field clinicians obtained tape samples of the three-minute TALK recorded at baseline and again at midyear. These tapes were judged by six undergraduate students at a later time to obtain estimates of reliability on the field clinician's live judgments.

Mean correlations for the baseline and midyear tapes are summarized below for mean percent scores for the students compared to the clinician's counts done live.

|  | N | Base | Mid |
|---|---|---|---|
| Total (/r/ + /s/) | 464 | .30 | .60 |
| /r/ | 248 | .60 | .76 |
| /s/ | 216 | .30 | .49 |

N equals the number of tape samples judged by the student listeners.

It can be seen, again, that the /s/ is much more difficult to judge, especially during the baseline measure. We have observed that the clinicians have marked variability during the first three Sound Production Task measures taken during baseline. This indicates that they are not quite sure what their internal standard for that child will be. This is also noted for /r/ but the agreement is much better.

## Clinician Versus Individuals Within a Group

The problem of agreement for groups of listeners from tape compared to a given clinician's judgments in the field are exemplified in Table D.5. Here the clinician perceived little change in children 1, 2, and 3, but the listeners had wide differences. The clinician judged child 4 as getting worse, but only student 3 agreed with her. Children 5, 6, and 7 were judged by the clinician as getting better and the students had completely different judgments. All the students agreed that 7 had not improved. Disparities between live and tape judgments were demonstrated in the Stephens and Daniloff (1977) study.

Three more data sets are presented. High positive correlations are obtained in Table D.6 at baseline and midyear. Negative correlations at baseline and high positive correlations at midyear are presented in Table D.7. Finally, low negative

| Child Number | Phoneme | Clinician | | Five Student Listeners | | | | | | | | | |
|---|---|---|---|---|---|---|---|---|---|---|---|---|---|
| | | | | 1 | | 2 | | 3 | | 4 | | 5 | |
| | | Base | Mid | Base | Mid | Base | Mid | Base | Mid | Base | Mid | Base | Mid |
| 1 | /s/ | 0 | 0 | 22 | 0 | 0 | 0 | 22 | 95 | 33 | 0 | 67 | 54 |
| 2 | /r/ | 46 | 48 | 11 | 19 | 0 | 100 | 0 | 5 | 8 | 23 | 63 | 96 |
| 3 | /r/ | 0 | 4 | 20 | 0 | 33 | 0 | 0 | 19 | 0 | 0 | 0 | 47 |
| 4 | /r/ | 30 | 15 | 0 | 3 | 0 | 0 | 22 | 0 | 0 | 0 | 0 | 29 |
| 5 | /s/ | 59 | 89 | 70 | 37 | 100 | 100 | 31 | 100 | 74 | 36 | 96 | 100 |
| 6 | /s/ | 30 | 67 | 14 | 36 | 0 | 0 | 100 | 69 | 15 | 65 | 94 | 87 |
| 7 | /s/ | 0 | 82 | 0 | 0 | 0 | 0 | 7 | 0 | 0 | 0 | 0 | 0 |

TABLE D.5. Typical raw data for percent correct judgments done live by the clinician and from tape by student listeners at baseline and midyear.

| Child | Baseline Clinician | Baseline Listeners | Midyear Clinician | Midyear Listeners |
|---|---|---|---|---|
| 1 | 17% | 51% | 27% | 38% |
| 2 | 53 | 73 | 63 | 70 |
| 3 | 0 | 19 | 0 | 5 |
| 4 | 6 | 5 | 20 | 8 |
| 5 | 0 | 2 | 28 | 17 |
| 6 | 13 | 15 | 33 | 43 |
| 7 | 52 | 77 | 100 | 77 |
| 8 | 11 | 25 | 15 | 58 |
| 9 | 0 | 20 | 21 | 20 |
| 10 | 22 | 21 | 93 | 89 |
| Correlation | .90 | | .85 | |

TABLE D.6. Example of the correlations based on the percent correct raw data. This demonstrates good baseline and good midyear reliability for the same clinician.

correlations are noted at both baseline and midyear (Table D.8). The difficulty in obtaining good reliability between the clinician's live judgments and single listeners within a group from tape are obvious.

## Clinician (Live) Versus Other Listeners (Live)

In the first year, the reliability measures were made between 10 field clinicians and two staff clinicians. These were done live in the schools during the three-minute TALK task. In this analysis the staff clinicians' live observation of the field clinicians' children was from .69 to .83. When the raw data for total sounds, correct, wrong, and percent correct were analyzed, the staff clinicians counted a significantly different number of wrong responses when compared to the field cli-

| Child | Baseline Clinician | Baseline Listeners | Midyear Clinician | Midyear Listeners |
|---|---|---|---|---|
| 1 | 42% | 10% | 82% | 59% |
| 2 | 6 | 28 | 47 | 17 |
| 3 | 44 | 47 | 100 | 65 |
| 4 | 17 | 9 | 78 | 67 |
| 5 | 27 | 25 | 45 | 22 |
| 6 | 26 | 20 | 57 | 33 |
| 7 | 29 | 29 | 17 | 13 |
| 8 | 10 | 79 | 100 | 71 |
| 9 | 0 | 93 | 97 | 97 |
| 10 | 0 | 52 | 100 | 91 |
| Correlation | −.55 | | .92 | |

TABLE D.7. Example of the correlations based on the percent correct raw data. This demonstrates poor baseline and good midyear reliability for the same clinician.

| | Baseline | | Midyear | |
|---|---|---|---|---|
| Child | Clinician | Listeners | Clinician | Listeners |
| 1 | 19% | 24% | 43% | 25% |
| 2 | 46 | 46 | 44 | 48 |
| 3 | 18 | 17 | 48 | 30 |
| 4 | 0 | 53 | 0 | 59 |
| 5 | 0 | 82 | 6 | 61 |
| 6 | 75 | 54 | 91 | 57 |
| 7 | 19 | 24 | 43 | 25 |
| 8 | 46 | 46 | 44 | 48 |
| 9 | 18 | 17 | 48 | 30 |
| 10 | 0 | 53 | 0 | 59 |
| 11 | 0 | 82 | 6 | 61 |
| 12 | 75 | 54 | 91 | 57 |
| Correlation | -.10 | | -.26 | |

TABLE D.8. Example of the correlations based on the percent correct raw data. This demonstrates poor baseline and poor midyear reliability for the same clinician.

nician (Table D.9). In other words, the field clinicians made more estimates of correct responses than did the staff clinicians. In another analysis done in Year 1 between one staff clinician and three field clinicians made in the live situation with 91 children (mostly /r/ and /s/, but a few /l/, /sh/, /ch/, and /z/ errors), the reliability correlations were in the .80's and .90's. When one looked at the raw data for correct, wrong, and percent correct, significant differences were found between the staff and field clinicians. There was no significant difference between the total sounds heard in conversation by the staff clinician and the field clinicians (Table D.10). The clinician counted more correct and fewer wrong than the staff clinician.

Again, these two studies would support relatively good reliability (from .69 to .93), but significant differences are observed in the mean raw data counts of correct and wrong. The differences are generally in favor of the clinician. That is,

| | Field Clinicians | | Staff Clinician | | | |
|---|---|---|---|---|---|---|
| | Mean | SD | Mean | SD | t | r |
| Total Sounds (C + W) | 19.4 | 8.1 | 22.4 | 8.5 | 4.05*** | .83** |
| Correct (C) | 12.6 | 8.2 | 11.3 | 8.0 | 1.49 | .77** |
| Wrong (W) | 6.8 | 6.2 | 11.1 | 9.0 | 4.32*** | .69** |
| C/C + W (%) | 63.7 | 28.5 | 53.3 | 30.0 | 2.95** | .74** |

df = 42, t .05 = 2.02; t .01 = 2.70**; t .01 = 3.55***
df = 41, r .01 = .393**

TABLE D.9. Means, SD, t-tests, and correlations among ten field clinicians and two staff clinicians made during live three-minute TALK samples on 43 children.

|                      | Field Clinicians | | Staff Clinician | | | |
|----------------------|------|------|------|------|--------|--------|
|                      | Mean | SD   | Mean | SD   | t      | r      |
| Total Sounds (C + W) | 21.0 | 9.7  | 21.6 | 9.0  | 1.57   | .93**  |
| Correct (C)          | 15.2 | 10.2 | 13.8 | 9.9  | 2.813**| .90**  |
| Wrong (W)            | 5.9  | 7.6  | 7.9  | 7.8  | 4.20***| .84**  |
| C/C + W (%)          | 69.5 | 28.9 | 61.0 | 30.6 | 4.92***| .85**  |

t .05 = 1.99, r .05 = .205*; t .01 = 2.63**,
r .01 = .267**; t .001 = 3.42***

TABLE D.10. Means, SD, t-tests, and correlations between three field clinicians and a staff clinician on live C/W counts for 91 children combined for three different observations.

she is biased in counting more correct and the other observer counts more wrong. This may be because results reported in Tables D.9, D.10, D.11 and D.12 were done in the spring of the school year when the past year's progress is most apparent.

In Year 3, three staff clinicians listened live to the children of three field clinicians (total N = 9) at baseline and again at midyear. Each clinician had 20 children (total N = 180). Half the children were /s/ and half /r/. The range of correlations between staff clinicians and field clinicians for correct/wrong counts (converted to percent correct) was –.32 to .91 with a mean of .50 at baseline. For midyear the correlations ranged from a .46 to .93 with a mean of .75.

Fourteen senior undergraduate student speech clinicians testing a total of 111 children with 14 public school speech clinicians during the 1973 spring semester had good agreement in live listening of correct/wrong /r/ and /s/ phonemes in grade school children. The clinician and student made independent counts while the child was engaged in the three-minute TALK task. Tallies (hand movements) were screened from each other's view. When the mean percent correct scores were compared by t-tests, no significant differences were found between the students and the clinicians either at baseline or at the end of the semester. Pearson r's were .74 to .96 at baseline (January) and all were in the .90's at the end of therapy (May). The students observed the clinicians for about one week before the correct/wrong samples were taken; consequently, the students had an opportunity to learn the clinicians' standard for the sound. This may account for the fact that no differences were found between the students and the clinicians on correct/wrong counts. Of course the problem of bias still remains because the students were now doing the therapy for one semester.

In the first year of our project three field clinicians were checked for Sound Production Task (SPT) and TALK task reliability. Ten children from each of the three clinicians were checked for a total of 30 children. One staff clinician listened in the live situation with each of the three field clinicians. The children had mainly /s/ or /r/ problems. Correlations were run on percent correct between each of the clinicians and the staff observer. Each child had three measures (February, March, May). The reliability for SPT averaged over all three time periods between the observer and clinician one was .97, clinician two .97, and clinician three .97. The reliability for the same observer with these three field clinicians for correct/wrong

|  | Field Clinicians | | Staff Clinician | | | |
| --- | --- | --- | --- | --- | --- | --- |
|  | Mean | SD | Mean | SD | t | r |
| Total Sounds (C + W) | 24.4 | 12.4 | 28.6 | 15.3 | 4.01** | .84** |
| Correct (C) | 11.0 | 14.0 | 14.6 | 17.3 | 3.28** | .87** |
| Wrong (W) | 13.2 | 10.9 | 13.7 | 12.6 | 0.559 | .86** |
| C/C + W (%) | 43.8 | 34.2 | 48.7 | 33.8 | 1.67 | .79** |

df = 9, t .05 = 2.26*; t .01 = 3.25**
df = 8, r .05 = .602*; r .01 = .735**

TABLE D.11. Reliability of three field clinicians versus a staff clinician on ten taped judgments of C/W. Children have not had therapy with these clinicians.

counts (percent correct) during three minutes of conversation (TALK) was .97, .80 and .77 respectively. Our conclusion would be that (during live observation) reliability is better for SPT (imitation tasks) than for TALK (spontaneous speech). Another conclusion is that some observers have higher reliability with some clinicians than with others for TALK.

## Other Procedures

### Field Clinicians and Staff Clinician Listening to Two Different Tapes

The first tape contained samples of conversation on 10 children who were not in therapy with the three clinicians. A staff clinician and three field clinicians made correct/wrong judgments of these 10 samples (Table D.11). The reliability was .79 or better. These field clinicians counted fewer total sounds and fewer correct than the staff clinician. Remember, the judgments of the field clinicians were with children they did not know.

A second tape was played to the same three field clinicians and staff clinician. This tape had been made by another adult in the school with a sample of 37

|  | Field Clinicians | | Staff Clinician | | | |
| --- | --- | --- | --- | --- | --- | --- |
|  | Mean | SD | Mean | SD | t | r |
| Total Sounds (C + W) | 23.5 | 8.3 | 24.6 | 8.04 | 1.50 | .88** |
| Correct (C) | 22.2 | 8.0 | 17.2 | 8.62 | 3.74*** | .56** |
| Wrong (W) | 1.5 | 3.6 | 7.4 | 7.87 | 5.07*** | .49** |
| C/C + W (%) | 95.0 | 11.0 | 71.0 | 28.0 | 5.50*** | .39* |

N = 37, df = 35, t .05 = 2.03*; t .01 = 2.72**; t .001 = 3.60***
N = 37, df = 35, r .05 = .325*; r .01 = .418**

TABLE D.12. Three field clinicians from tape versus one staff clinician from tape counting target phoneme correct or wrong.

|  | N = 37 Treated | N = 10 Unknown | p |
|---|---|---|---|
| Total Sounds (C + W) | .88 | .84 | .69 |
| Correct (C) | .56 | .87 | .09 |
| Wrong (W) | .49 | .86 | .06 |
| C/C + W (%) | .39 | .79 | .11 |

Table D.13. Comparison of reliability measures on three field clinicians with a staff clinician judging two tapes of children. Tests of significance between the reliabilities are indicated.

children who were receiving therapy from these field clinicians. The clinicians were not present when the tape was being made. The clinicians knew they were hearing their own children, but did now know the names of children. Some clinicians could possibly identify children from their voices, but that is difficult.

Correlations between the clinician and the judgments of the staff clinician ranged from .39 to .88 for total sounds, correct, wrong, and percent correct (Table D.12). No significant differences were found for total target phonemes counted. Significant differences were found between the means of the correct, wrong, and percent correct.

The field clinicians were more reliable with the staff clinicians when listening to taped samples of children unknown to them. The field clinicians demonstrated bias when they were judging their own children, even when the tapes were made by another person. However, a test for the significance of the difference between these correlations did not reach the 5% level (Table D.13). In the reliability observations noted above, we generally found that after the clinician treats a child, she usually counts more corrects and fewer wrongs than the other observer.

## Clinician (Live) Versus Typescript

Another way of determining how reliable the clinician perceived the number of target phonemes in a child's verbal output is to compare the clinician's live

|  | Clinician Live | | Audio Typescript | | | | |
|---|---|---|---|---|---|---|---|
|  | Mean | SD | Mean | SD | t | p | r |
|  |  | /r/ phoneme | | | | | |
| Baseline (N = 31) | 26.6 | 12.4 | 32.9 | 16.3 | 2.64 | <.05 | .61 |
| Midyear (N = 28) | 29.9 | 12.2 | 31.0 | 13.0 | 0.73 | non | .80 |
|  |  | /s/ phoneme | | | | | |
| Baseline (N = 32) | 30.4 | 11.3 | 22.8 | 10.1 | 4.63 | <.01 | .62 |
| Midyear (N = 32) | 33.0 | 13.9 | 24.0 | 7.7 | 4.50 | <.01 | .59 |

Table D.14. Field clinicians live mean total correct/wrong tallies for a target phoneme compared to an audiotape typescript of the three-minute TALK task.

count with a taped transcript of the same conversation. In Year 4, samples of clinician-child three minute conversations were transcribed. The data presented in Table D.14 represented 21 different clinicians and 63 different children. The average percent correct determined by the clinicians for the /r/ was 32% correct at baseline and 80% correct at midyear.

These results indicated that the total correct/wrong counts tallied by the field clinicians during the three-minute TALK task at baseline were correlated .61 with the audio transcribed utterances. There was a significant difference in the means at less than the .05 level. The correlation improved to .80 at midyear, suggesting that the perception of the clinician became better with time and practice. There was no significant difference between means at midyear for /r/. The clinicians perceived fewer /r/ occurrences than actually were present at the beginning of the school year, but by midyear they seemed to perceive all of them. For /s/, the correlation at the baseline was .62 and the clinicians counted significantly (.01) more /s/ occurrences than was observed from the audio typescripts. At midyear the correlation was .59 and the same significant differences occurred between the means. Contrary to the perception of /r/, the clinicians did not improve by midyear in their discrimination of /s/ sounds. These data also were indicative of the high frequency of occurrence of the /r/ and /s/ sounds in the conversational speech of these children. The /r/ had a mean of about 11 per minute and the /s/ about eight per minute (see Chapter 7 for more detail about speaking rates and frequency distributions of /r/ and /s/).

## Tone Keyboard (TKB) Reliability

There were three reliability measures conducted on the TKB (I, II, and III) and are described in the text (page 22). The data are continued in Table D.15, page 266.

TABLE D.15 — Measures of Tone Keyboard Reliability I, II, and III

| | I Clinician Agreement | | Errors | | II Clinician Agreement | Present and Correct | Present Incorrect and Missing | | III Equipment Agreement | Audio Not Printed | |
|---|---|---|---|---|---|---|---|---|---|---|---|
| Clinician No. | % Agree | Agree | I | II | % Agree | | | % Agree | TKB Audio Tones | | % Agree |
| 39 | 71 | 188 | 52 | | 78 | 70 | 2 | 97 | 189 | 17 | 91 |
| 40 | 95 | 90 | 33 | | 73 | 51 | 1 | 98 | 360 | 21 | 94 |
| 41 | 78 | 131 | 30 | | 81 | 104 | 8 | 93 | 568 | 30 | 95 |
| 42 | 88 | 331 | 52 | | 86 | 26 | 24 | 52 | 177 | 7 | 96 |
| 43 | 83 | 269 | 75 | | 78 | 298 | 7 | 98 | 870 | 6 | 99 |
| 44 | 86 | 253 | 101 | 1 | 71 | 113 | 4 | 97 | 583 | 35 | 94 |
| 45 | 91 | 287 | 72 | 1 | 80 | 69 | 3 | 96 | 332 | 19 | 94 |
| 46 | 88 | 358 | 86 | 1 | 81 | 180 | 2 | 99 | 560 | 71 | 87 |
| 47 | 77 | 227 | 83 | 3 | 73 | 178 | 12 | 93 | 475 | 22 | 95 |
| 48 | 76 | 96 | 64 | | 60 | 96 | 22 | 81 | 291 | 18 | 94 |
| 49 | 76 | 137 | 65 | | 68 | 130 | 10 | 93 | 302 | 0 | 100 |
| 50 | 89 | | | | | 37 | 12 | 76 | 191 | 2 | 99 |
| 51 | 76 | | | | | 106 | 41 | 72 | 405 | 26 | 94 |
| 52 | 80 | 78 | 39 | | 67 | 171 | 25 | 87 | 569 | 40 | 93 |
| 54 | 99 | 188 | 92 | | 70 | 141 | 4 | 97 | 367 | 8 | 98 |
| 55 | 67 | | | | | 69 | 8 | 90 | 182 | 12 | 93 |
| 53 | 77 | 91 | 19 | | 83 | 108 | 30 | 78 | 484 | 52 | 89 |
| 56 | 82 | 108 | 70 | 1 | 60 | 111 | 11 | 91 | 387 | 25 | 94 |
| 57 | 69 | 340 | 160 | | 68 | 164 | 1 | 98 | 544 | 30 | 94 |
| 58 | 68 | 227 | 112 | 1 | 67 | 107 | 1 | 99 | 514 | 29 | 94 |
| 59 | 86 | 265 | 75 | | 78 | 111 | 6 | 95 | 538 | 42 | 91 |
| 60 | 84 | 212 | 88 | | 88 | 162 | 18 | 90 | 849 | 209 | 75 |
| 61 | 84 | | | | | 184 | 8 | 96 | 556 | 29 | 95 |
| 62 | 96 | 379 | 211 | 6 | 64 | 91 | 3 | 97 | 836 | 27 | 97 |
| 63 | 88 | 196 | 80 | | 71 | 118 | 2 | 98 | 663 | 92 | 86 |
| 64 | 88 | 157 | 88 | | 64 | 152 | 0 | 100 | 702 | 130 | 81 |
| 65 | 88 | 128 | 73 | | 64 | | | | | | |
| Total | | 4,736 | 1,820 | 14 | | 3,150* | 265 | | 12,494** | 999 | |
| Mean | 82 | 206 | 79 | .54 | 73 | 121 | 10 | 91 | 481 | 38 | 93 |
| SD | 9 | 92 | 41 | 1.6 | 8 | 57 | 10 | 11 | 202 | 45 | 6 |

*For middle one third of session
**For entire therapy session

TABLE D.15. Measures of Tone Keyboard Reliability I, II, and III for project Year 4 clinicians.

# APPENDIX E

# Tables Cited in Results (Chapters 3, 4, 5, and 6)

TABLE E.1. Number of children with a negative gain.

| Variable | Number of Children | Percent |
|----------|--------------------|---------|
| GAIN     | 34                 | 3.2     |
| GAIN12   | 131                | 11.8    |
| GAIN23   | 59                 | 5.3     |
| GAIN34   | 88                 | 10.0    |
| GAIN13   | 59                 | 5.3     |
| GAIN24   | 30                 | 3.5     |

FIGURES E.1a-d. Histograms and distributional statistics for EU numbers.

```
HISTOGRAM OF VARIABLE        EU1
                                SYMBOL  COUNT    MEAN       ST.DEV.
                                  X     1108     26.701     28.418
INTERVAL                                         FREQUENCY PERCENTAGE
NAME          50  100  150  200 250  300  350  400  INT. CUM.  INT.  CUM.
         +----+----+----+----+----+----+----+----+
  0.0000 +XXXXXXXXXXXXXXXXXX                          179  179   16.2  16.2
  5.0000 +XXXXXXXXXXXXXXXXXXX                         191  370   17.2  33.4
 10.000  +XXXXXXXXXXX                                 110  480    9.9  43.3
 15.000  +XXXXXXXX                                     75  555    6.8  50.1
 20.000  +XXXXX                                        54  609    4.9  55.0
 25.000  +XXXXX                                        53  662    4.8  59.7
 30.000  +XXXXX                                        54  716    4.9  64.6
 35.000  +XXXXX                                        54  770    4.9  69.5
 40.000  +XXXX                                         38  808    3.4  72.9
 45.000  +XXXX                                         36  844    3.2  76.2
 50.000  +XXX                                          26  870    2.3  78.5
 55.000  +XXX                                          33  903    3.0  81.5
 60.000  +XX                                           20  923    1.8  83.3
 65.000  +XXX                                          30  953    2.7  86.0
 70.000  +XXX                                          27  980    2.4  88.4
 75.000  +XX                                           20 1000    1.8  90.3
 80.000  +XXX                                          27 1027    2.4  92.7
 85.000  +XX                                           21 1048    1.9  94.6
 90.000  +XX                                           21 1069    1.9  96.5
 95.000  +XX                                           24 1093    2.2  98.6
100.00   +XX                                           15 1108    1.4 100.0
LAST     +                                              0 1108    0.  100.0
         +----+----+----+----+----+----+----+----+
```

FIGURE E.1a.

```
HISTOGRAM OF VARIABLE        EU2
                                  SYMBOL    COUNT       MEAN        ST.DEV.
                                     X       1108       44.899       29.314
INTERVAL                                                FREQUENCY  PERCENTAGE
NAME         50   100  150  200  250  300  350  400     INT. CUM.  INT.  CUM.
           +----+----+----+----+----+----+----+----+
 0.0000  +X                                              14    14   1.3    1.3
 5.0000  +XXXXXXXXX                                     103   117   9.3   10.6
10.000   +XXXXX                                          61   178   5.5   16.1
15.000   +XXXXX                                          60   238   5.4   21.5
20.000   +XXXXX                                          51   289   4.6   26.1
25.000   +XXXXX                                          61   350   5.5   31.6
30.000   +XXXXXXX                                        68   418   6.1   37.7
35.000   +XXXXXX                                         57   475   5.1   42.9
40.000   +XXXXX                                          51   526   4.6   47.5
45.000   +XXXXX                                          51   577   4.6   52.1
50.000   +XXXXX                                          50   627   4.5   56.6
55.000   +XXXXXX                                         56   683   5.1   61.6
60.000   +XXXXX                                          52   735   4.7   66.3
65.000   +XXXXX                                          51   786   4.6   70.9
70.000   +XXXXX                                          47   833   4.2   75.2
75.000   +XXXXXX                                         55   888   5.0   80.1
80.000   +XXXXX                                          45   933   4.1   84.2
85.000   +XXXXXX                                         56   989   5.1   89.3
90.000   +XXXXX                                          47  1036   4.2   93.5
95.000   +XXXX                                           42  1078   3.8   97.3
100.00   +XXX                                            30  1108   2.7  100.0
LAST     +                                                0  1108   0.   100.0
           +----+----+----+----+----+----+----+----+
```

FIGURE E.1b.

```
HISTOGRAM OF VARIABLE        EU3
                                  SYMBOL    COUNT       MEAN        ST.DEV.
                                     X       1108       64.910       30.207
INTERVAL                                                FREQUENCY  PERCENTAGE
NAME         50   100  150  200  250  300  350  400     INT. CUM.  INT.  CUM.
           +----+----+----+----+----+----+----+----+
 0.0000  +X                                               5     5   0.5    0.5
 5.0000  +XXX                                            29    34   2.6    3.1
10.000   +XXXX                                           41    75   3.7    6.8
15.000   +XXXX                                           37   112   3.3   10.1
20.000   +XX                                             24   136   2.2   12.3
25.000   +XXX                                            32   168   2.9   15.2
30.000   +XXX                                            31   199   2.8   18.0
35.000   +XXXX                                           41   240   3.7   21.7
40.000   +XXX                                            33   273   3.0   24.6
45.000   +XXXX                                           36   309   3.2   27.9
50.000   +XXX                                            32   341   2.9   30.8
55.000   +XXXXX                                          47   388   4.2   35.0
60.000   +XXXX                                           44   432   4.0   39.0
65.000   +XXXXXX                                         55   487   5.0   44.0
70.000   +XXXXX                                          48   535   4.3   48.3
75.000   +XXXXX                                          48   583   4.3   52.6
80.000   +XXXXXX                                         55   638   5.0   57.6
85.000   +XXXXXX                                         70   708   6.3   63.9
90.000   +XXXXXXXXX                                      87   795   7.9   71.8
95.000   +XXXXXXXXXXXX                                  116   911  10.5   82.2
100.00   +XXXXXXXXXXXXXXXXXXXX                          197  1108  17.8  100.0
LAST     +                                                0  1108   0.   100.0
           +----+----+----+----+----+----+----+----+
```

FIGURE E.1c.

```
HISTOGRAM OF VARIABLE      EU4
                             SYMBOL   COUNT      MEAN        ST.DEV.
                               X      1108       76.477      26.869
INTERVAL                                         FREQUENCY  PERCENTAGE
NAME          50  100  150  200  250  300  350  400  INT.  CUM.  INT.  CUM.
          +----+----+----+----+----+----+----+----+
  0.0000  +                                              3     3   0.3   0.3
  5.0000  +X                                            12    15   1.1   1.4
 10.000   +XX                                           16    31   1.4   2.8
 15.000   +XX                                           19    50   1.7   4.5
 20.000   +X                                            13    63   1.2   5.7
 25.000   +XXX                                          25    88   2.3   7.9
 30.000   +XXX                                          26   114   2.3  10.3
 35.000   +XX                                           15   129   1.4  11.6
 40.000   +XXX                                          26   155   2.3  14.0
 45.000   +XXX                                          25   180   2.3  16.2
 50.000   +XX                                           20   200   1.8  18.1
 55.000   +XXX                                          27   227   2.4  20.5
 60.000   +XXX                                          34   261   3.1  23.6
 65.000   +XXXX                                         35   296   3.2  26.7
 70.000   +XXXX                                         36   332   3.2  30.0
 75.000   +XXXXXX                                       57   389   5.1  35.1
 80.000   +XXXXXX                                       62   451   5.6  40.7
 85.000   +XXXXXXXX                                     75   526   6.8  47.5
 90.000   +XXXXXXXX                                     78   604   7.0  54.5
 95.000   +XXXXXXXXXXX                                 117   721  10.6  65.1
100.00    +XXXXXXXXXXXXXXXXXXXXXXXXXXXXXXXXXXXXXXXXX   387  1108  34.9 100.0
LAST      +                                              0  1108   0.  100.0
          +----+----+----+----+----+----+----+----+
           50  100  150  200  250  300  350  400
```

FIGURE E.1d.

TABLE E.2. Mean gain scores converted to common units of measurement.

| Variable | Time Interval Weeks | Raw Mean Gain | Average Gain for 10 Weeks |
|---|---|---|---|
| GAIN | 30 | 49.8 | 17 |
| GAIN12 | 6 | 18.3 | 31 |
| GAIN23 | 12 | 20.1 | 18 |
| GAIN34 | 12 | 11.6 | 10 |
| GAIN13 | 18 | 38.3 | 21 |
| GAIN24 | 24 | 31.6 | 13 |

FIGURES E.2a-f. Scattergrams showing the joint distribution between pairs of EU numbers.

```
           .+....+....+....+....+....+....+....+....X....+....+....+.
    105.0  +                                                        +
           .       1                                              2 1Y
           .    1            11  1           1       1      11   11 32 32.
           .11  1   1            1   1         1  1       1  1213 33142 12.
           .1    1                          11 2    1    1  11231 2332111.
    87.50  +2   1     1    11     11         1 121     212   4113111  121 +
           .21   1    1   2         1        2    1 21 311322 1 2212       .
           . 5111 1 11      112    11 1  1 1 12 121 212 32 1 121           .
           .11 11    1              11      1 11113 211 21    1  11         .
           .22 21    2    2 12 2 2213    3    3    21   1113                .
    70.00  +421 1     1    111 1 212 1 1222 2 311 2 1   1 1      1         +
  E        .521      1 1   112111 1 12   1 2112212 11                      .
  U        .3     111  2   112 12 11  1   1  11112          1        1     .
  2        .5212 3111121   12 221241122 1 1 1 11        1                  .
           .5 11 2 11    122 1 22 1 11111 2 1 1 11 1                       .
    52.50  +5222214132111 1211   2 21 2    1 1                            +
           .5121 13    21 3 12 32    1   1 2                              .
           .521 231   21231 11411 111        1                            .
           .62122 1131   3112 4  1    211                                 .
           .421222411 11 4313 4221   1  1                                 .
    35.00  +412213223 2 1  2113 11      1  1                              +
           .62 522311311 322   1    1 1                                   .
           .834413141223213131   1                                        .
           Y657242 3242 212 31    1      2                                 .
           .63232223132 3  2      111  1                                  .
    17.50  +742673122 1 2  1 1                                            +
           .8544331321 1                                                  .
           .CAA84213        1 1                                           .
           .7645611111           1                                        .
           X**913      1  1       1                                       .
    0.000  +*853                                                         +
           .+....+....+....+....+....+....+....+....+....+....+....+.
              10.     30.     50.     70.     90.
           0.0     20.     40.     60.     80.      100
  N= 1108
  COR= .716                        EU1

       MEAN    ST.DEV.    REGRESSION LINE     RES.MS.
  X    26.701   28.418   X= .69400*Y-4.4586    394.08
  Y    44.899   29.314   Y= .73845*X+ 25.181   419.31
```

FIGURE E.2a.

```
          .+....+....+....+....+....+..X.+....+....+....+....+....+.
    105.0 +                                                         +
          .52 131121      2 111 41   1 1221   1   3  11  112112222Y
          .*624312111 32111115 13  3 2131213 12 11625 12383221.
          .9341222 3411   3221 1 1 143212222325331332213321 123.
          .84132 1311 4 2213 1112       3    11121111      311131  .
    87.50 +A31413 321113113 2 111 1 1 131 211 112211   1          +
          .711 232 2  11 21   1      1    2   11      211 2       .
          .9237 12  1 1 1213 1314 11 1      1211   1 12    11 1   .
          .7 2  12     2 1111   4     1 1   11 1112    1 11       .
          .322711 3 2 11  1 32 112 12     11 1      1 1  1        .
    70.00 +4 1 1 32    1 11   1    1111 1   2       1             +
E         .3823212 2  12221 21 3221      12                       .
U         .44322 1   2 111 211 1 2 111     1 12    1              .
3         .2341 211 22 111 1321      11         1                 .
          .111 212 213   3112   1 12  1                        1  .
    52.50 +54245311 1 111   4 1    1    11          1            +
          Y2321 11 11     1 12  1  2 1         1                  .
          .51   21122121 1 11111    1                            .
          .141313 12    1   111 11                               .
          .43141 13 11 112      1       1 1                      .
    35.00 +54113211 21121 2     1       1                        +
          .62221112221 1  2111        1                          .
          .7113 1111     1          1                            .
          .243132 1212 2 2 1                                     .
          .52 11   11      1     1    1                          .
    17.50 +742 11 1    2       1                                 +
          .A34 21 1 11   1   11                                  .
          .84631111                                             .
          .794231                    1                          .
          .97412i   1                                           .
    0.000 X442                                                   +
          X+....+....+....+....+....+....+....+....+....+....+.
              10.      30.      50.      70.      90.
          0.0      20.      40.      60.      80.      100
N= 1108
COR= .473                          EU1

    MEAN     ST.DEV.    REGRESSION LINE       RES.MS.
X   26.701   28.418    X= .44487*Y-2.1753     627.58
Y   64.910   30.207    Y= .50263*X+ 51.489    709.06
```

Figure E.2b.

```
        .+....+....+....+....X....+....+....+....+....+....+.
 105.0 +                                                              +
       .*A59423422122231224122 1234231322154   2543134334245Y
       .HA4685533415314633462l 2332362156434322l 422217332 .
       .I449134221 1 3112141321 2  1111111112335   21222    .
       .A532214 21211 44 12   31 11 2    211  1 12   1 2 1   1.
 87.50 +3413432 23123412 22121 1 2112  1 11    2     1 1    +
       .3 14 1 3311112 211    21 1 11 1122 11     1    12    .
       .86626 4211221211      1  1 1   1           112 1     .
       .4624121 21  2211 23 1 11 11  1                       .
       .85212224 1    1 222 13331           1 2              .
 70.00 +231 41  2 1  1 1 3     1   1 2        1             +
   E   Y627311 111  11 11 2 1    11                          .
   U   .212114 21  1   11              11          1         .
   4   .311 1 111 1     13 11 1                              .
       .91 1  11 21   12211 1 1 11   1       1       1       .
 52.50 +2231 1 2211 11  1                                    +
       .21    2 1 111  1       1                             .
       .43 41 111  1 1      1        1         1             .
       .3211 1 1 1  2  1            1                        .
       .63 1121   11   1  11 1      1                        .
 35.00 +212 11   1  11     1                                +
       .33 1     2  1  2                                     .
       .214212 2    2 1          1    1                      .
       .85311      1                                         .
       .31211    11     1    1                               .
 17.50 +341 1  1   1                                        +
       .133111 1 1               1                           .
       .4511     1                                           .
       .322 2          1                                     .
       X53  2                                                .
 0.000 +311                                                 +
       X+....+....+....+....+....+....+....+....+....+....+.
          10.      30.      50.      70.      90.
        0.0     20.      40.      60.      80.      100
N= 1108
COR= .369                        EU1

    MEAN     ST.DEV.   REGRESSION LINE      RES.MS.
X   26.701   28.418   X= .39024*Y-3.1429    698.29
Y   76.477   26.869   Y= .34884*X+ 67.163   624.22
```

FIGURE E.2c.

```
         .+....+....+....+....+....+....+....+....+....X....+..Y.+.
 105.0 +                                                           +
       .                1   2 1   1   13 1   11 221   114111543168.
       .            1       1        111142223323 25326534844A5C853.
       .         1     1       1 111   231 15212586428C94666411   .
       .      1      1 1      114 142 21 42 51154423 333 12 1 .
 87.50 +      1 1     1 1 2   1  6232142512313273111123          +
       .      1 1 1 1    1  3  11111 215211 2   1 1 1111   1  .
       .    1 11 31     311111132221 332 34241 21112 11       .
       .         1       13211 2 134   31212113   1           .
       .       1   1 124332 321211  111231111 21              .
 70.00 +   1       1 2 11111 12     12212 11 1                +
   E   .        1221   2 2242313221 222 31211 1
   U   .    11 1 11132321  1 21212 21 111 1 1   1 1            .
   3   .    111 111123 12111 12311131                         .
       .     2 1   211121 2 2321 1 11     11   1              .
 52.50 + 21     21132144321113  2    11  1 1                  +
       .      11   12 31 1 1111 2   1  2 11                   .
       .   1111 121213 111211121                             .
       . 11      2 2 3 14 1132  1                             .
       . 2112112211 12 122 111        1                      .
 35.00 +   411 3 2 331333 2                                   +
       . 24   21111312321 1   1 111                          .
       .112   244    1   11    1                             .
       Y 2113512322121                                       .
       . 131211    12 1    1                                 .
 17.50 +122312 131 11      1                                 +
       . 3673321 1                                           .
       .334422411 1                                          .
       X26C 42       1                                       .
       .3E5 1  1                                             .
 0.000 +46                                                   +
         .+....+....+....+....+....+....+....+....+....+....+.
            10.       30.       50.       70.       90.
         0.0     20.       40.       60.       80.       100
 N= 1108
 COR= .831                        EU2

     MEAN     ST.DEV.    REGRESSION LINE      RES.MS.
 X   44.899   29.314   X= .80601*Y-7.4191     266.79
 Y   64.910   30.207   Y= .85584*X+ 26.483    283.28
```

FIGURE E.2d.

```
          .+....+....+....+....+....+....+....+...X+....+....+..Y.+.
  105.0 +                                                               +
       .              2  11    12  2221414322344243442376345497849 8D49A.
       .          2121332    13  11  1346253 22 45545476A88368838B66531.
       .      1   1311213  11216322131143  41214213453364721211       .
       .    1  11       2  22313212  113133513222224  1  11221  1  1    .
  87.50 +  21  11  2     11112212  1223  4513222  1223  1  11  1  1  1  1 +
       .    1  1   1      1122  12     11121314133  2   31111         1   .
       .  1121  21113132222  2261  31  143    1     11  1  11           .
       .  23111  1  2113113112113  1111  11  2  1      1                 .
       .  221  2  3   332222121  21211111121  21  1    1       1         .
  70.00 +    221112       11  221    1  1      22   11                   +
       .  22  1311111211  13  12    2   1  11  2         1               .
       .  1         21312221  1    1       1       11                    .
       .  111       22  1  1  13  2   2                                  .
       .  31      112  12  22322    3  2    1     1             1        .
  52.50 +   2   3131  1  1112      1  1                                  +
       .  1   1      1  2  23               1                           .
       Y2  212  2  21    1211  1      1          1                       .
       .2  1    1   1221111           1                                 .
       .  32   232   11     111111  1                                   .
  35.00 +  21  1  1  212               1                                +
       .  111  221    11  1   1                                         .
       .  413  2  13    11     11   1                                   .
       .  25613   1   1                                                 .
       .  13  51       1          1                                     .
  17.50 +  611  1   1   1                                               +
       X124  211     1  1                                               .
       .133  2  12                                                      .
       .114  21    1                                                    .
       .252    1                                                        .
  0.000 +32                                                             +
          .+....+....+....+....+....+....+....+....+....+....+....+.
            10.      30.      50.      70.      90.
          0.0     20.      40.      60.      80.      100
N= 1108
COR= .689                        EU2

        MEAN     ST.DEV.     REGRESSION LINE      RES.MS.
X      44.899   29.314   X= .75178*Y-12.595      451.72
Y      76.477   26.869   Y= .63158*X+ 48.120     379.50
```

FIGURE E.2e.

```
       .+....+....+....+....+....+....+....+....+....+....+..X.+.
 105.0 +                                                       Y
   .                                        1       122332476AH**.
   .                        1    1  1   11    1 2  1  12534388AH****F.
   .                        1  1        1    1271345342B234C89764.
   .                      2      111112222126341263615361 1.
  87.50 +        1 1          1       13 4 116362 245642 31 11 1+
   .                  1      11 2  3 3 3133 321 333212 11 .
   .            1  1      1 21 411 122 234344321123212      .
   .          1       1 11 2 21121 331 2 2331  1311 2 1     .
   .            1      11  11 122331512334141 21 111 1      .
  70.00 +       111    21    2  111    21212 11  1 11        +
 E .             2 222121    24 11 22312      1           1  .
 U .             1 21    121 11312 11   1   1             .
 4 .         1      1  1111112 131 11                     .
   .         11 1    131213 2 323 11  1      1 1 1         .
  52.50 +    1  1    1 231111 1   1 1  11      1            +
   . 1       1  21     12  1      2                        .
   .    1  1      2 1 113221111    2                       .
   .    11     2    1 322  11                              .
   .  1 11 1   1 23113113 1                                .
  35.00 + 1 1 1111  12  1  1                                +
   .             114   2 12   1                            .
   . 1213 1 2 2 3 2   11                                   .
 Y  1 3 14311131                                           .
   . 11 21 221                   1                 1       .
  17.50 + 112 22 1 1      1                                 +
   .1 13331                        1                       .
 X 114131 1                                                .
   . 131121 1                                              .
   .14112      1                                           .
  0.000 +32                                                 +
       .+....+....+....+....+....+....+....+....+....+....+.
          10.     30.     50.     70.     90.
        0.0     20.    40.    60.    80.    100

N= 1108
COR= .888                          EU3

      MEAN     ST.DEV.     REGRESSION LINE     RES.MS.
  X   64.910   30.207   X= .99837*Y-11.443     193.04
  Y   76.477   26.869   Y= .78991*X+ 25.204    152.73
```

FIGURE E.2f.

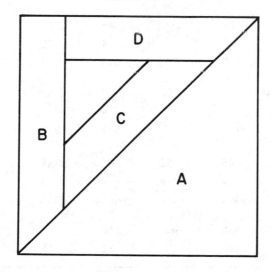

FIGURE E.3. Important areas in the EU scattergrams.

TABLE E.3. Joint distribution of GRADE and SNDEU1.

Independent Variable:  GRADE
Independent Variable:  SNDEU1
Cells are count over table percent over asd

| SOUND | CEU1 | GRADE | | | | |
| | | 1 | 2 | 3 | 4 | Total |
|---|---|---|---|---|---|---|
| /s/ | Low | 84 | 70 | 35 | 21 | 210 |
| | | 8 | 6 | 3 | 2 | 19 |
| | | 4.5 | 0.1 | -2.2 | 3.1 | |
| | Medium | 40 | 55 | 41 | 23 | 159 |
| | | 4 | 5 | 4 | 2 | 14 |
| | | -0.7 | 0.5 | 1.1 | -1.0 | |
| | High | 24 | 57 | 40 | 49 | 170 |
| | | 2 | 5 | 4 | 4 | 15 |
| | | -4.2 | 0.2 | 0.4 | 4.3 | |
| /r/ | Low | 65 | 66 | 45 | 12 | 188 |
| | | 6 | 6 | 4 | 1 | 17 |
| | | 2.4 | 0.7 | 0.6 | -4.3 | |
| | Medium | 46 | 55 | 47 | 42 | 190 |
| | | 4 | 5 | 4 | 4 | 17 |
| | | -1.1 | -1.3 | 0.9 | 2.0 | |
| | High | 45 | 62 | 40 | 44 | 191 |
| | | 4 | 6 | 4 | 4 | 17 |
| | | -1.3 | -0.2 | -0.5 | 2.3 | |
| | Total | 304 | 365 | 248 | 191 | 1108 |
| | | 27 | 33 | 22 | 17 | 100 |

chi-square = 74.3,  df = 15,  p <.001

TABLE E.4. Joint distribution of PREVT and SNDEU1.

Independent Variable:  PREVT
Independent Variable:  SNDEU1
Cells are count over row percent over asd

|        |        | PREVT |      |       |
|--------|--------|-------|------|-------|
| SNDEU1 |        | No    | Yes  | Total |
| /s/    | Low    | 156   | 54   | 210   |
|        |        | 74    | 26   | 100   |
|        |        | 5.0   | -5.0 |       |
|        | Medium | 98    | 61   | 159   |
|        |        | 62    | 38   | 100   |
|        |        | 0.8   | -0.8 |       |
|        | High   | 71    | 99   | 170   |
|        |        | 42    | 58   | 100   |
|        |        | -4.9  | 4.9  |       |
| /r/    | Low    | 134   | 54   | 188   |
|        |        | 71    | 29   | 100   |
|        |        | 3.8   | -3.8 |       |
|        | Medium | 105   | 85   | 190   |
|        |        | 55    | 45   | 100   |
|        |        | -1.1  | 1.1  |       |
|        | High   | 88    | 103  | 191   |
|        |        | 46    | 54   | 100   |
|        |        | -3.9  | 3.9  |       |
|        | Total  | 652   | 456  | 1108  |
|        |        | 59    | 41   | 100   |

chi-square = 67.5,   df = 5,   p < .001

```
HISTOGRAM OF VARIABLE        EU1T
                                 SYMBOL   COUNT      MEAN         ST.DEV.
                                   X      1108       26.116        29.594
INTERVAL                                             FREQUENCY  PERCENTAGE
NAME          50   100  150  200  250  300  350  400 INT.  CUM. INT.  CUM.
          +----+----+----+----+----+----+----+----+
 -40.000  +X                                           9     9   0.8   0.8
 -30.000  +XX                                         16    25   1.4   2.3
 -20.000  +XXXXX                                      45    70   4.1   6.3
 -10.000  +XXXXXXX                                    66   136   6.0  12.3
  0.0000  +XXXXXXXXX                                  86   222   7.8  20.0
 10.000   +XXXXXXXXXXX                               117   339  10.6  30.6
 20.000   +XXXXXXXXXXXXX                             141   480  12.7  43.3
 30.000   +XXXXXXXXXXXX                              129   609  11.6  55.0
 40.000   +XXXXXXXXXXXXXX                            148   757  13.4  68.3
 50.000   +XXXXXXXXXXXX                              116   873  10.5  78.8
 60.000   +XXXXXXXXX                                  92   965   8.3  87.1
 70.000   +XXXXXXX                                    66  1031   6.0  93.1
 80.000   +XXXX                                       38  1069   3.4  96.5
 90.000   +XX                                         24  1093   2.2  98.6
 100.00   +X                                           9  1102   0.8  99.5
 110.00   +X                                           6  1108   0.5 100.0
 120.00   +                                            0  1108   0.  100.0
 130.00   +                                            0  1108   0.  100.0
 140.00   +                                            0  1108   0.  100.0
 150.00   +                                            0  1108   0.  100.0
LAST      +                                            0  1108   0.  100.0
          +----+----+----+----+----+----+----+----+
           50   100  150  200  250  300  350  400
```

FIGURE E.4a.

```
HISTOGRAM OF VARIABLE        EU2T
                                 SYMBOL   COUNT      MEAN         ST.DEV.
                                   X      1108       45.289        23.722
INTERVAL                                             FREQUENCY  PERCENTAGE
NAME          50   100  150  200  250  300  350  400 INT.  CUM. INT.  CUM.
          +----+----+----+----+----+----+----+----+
 -40.000  +                                            0     0   0.    0.
 -30.000  +                                            0     0   0.    0.
 -20.000  +                                            0     0   0.    0.
 -10.000  +                                            0     0   0.    0.
  0.0000  +XXXX                                       41    41   3.7   3.7
 10.000   +XXXXXX                                     66   107   6.0   9.7
 20.000   +XXXXXX                                     71   178   6.4  16.1
 30.000   +XXXXXXXXX                                 111   289  10.0  26.1
 40.000   +XXXXXXXXXXXXXXXXX                         177   466  16.0  42.1
 50.000   +XXXXXXXXXXXXXXXX                          173   639  15.6  57.7
 60.000   +XXXXXXXXXXXXXXX                           162   801  14.6  72.3
 70.000   +XXXXXXXXXXXXX                             143   944  12.9  85.2
 80.000   +XXXXXXXX                                   92  1036   8.3  93.5
 90.000   +XXXX                                       42  1078   3.8  97.3
 100.00   +XX                                         19  1097   1.7  99.0
 110.00   +X                                          11  1108   1.0 100.0
 120.00   +                                            0  1108   0.  100.0
 130.00   +                                            0  1108   0.  100.0
 140.00   +                                            0  1108   0.  100.0
 150.00   +                                            0  1108   0.  100.0
LAST      +                                            0  1108   0.  100.0
          +----+----+----+----+----+----+----+----+
           50   100  150  200  250  300  350  400
```

FIGURE E.4b.

```
HISTOGRAM OF VARIABLE      EU3T
                          SYMBOL  COUNT     MEAN       ST.DEV.
                            X     1108      63.611      27.413
INTERVAL                                    FREQUENCY  PERCENTAGE
NAME        50  100  150  200  250  300  350  400   INT.  CUM.  INT.   CUM.
            +----+----+----+----+----+----+----+----+
 -40.000 +                                            0     0   0.     0.
 -30.000 +                                            0     0   0.     0.
 -20.000 +                                            0     0   0.     0.
 -10.000 +                                            0     0   0.     0.
  0.0000 +X                                          10    10   0.9    0.9
 10.000 +XX                                          19    29   1.7    2.6
 20.000 +XXXXX                                       46    75   4.2    6.8
 30.000 +XXXXXX                                      61   136   5.5   12.3
 40.000 +XXXXXXXXX                                   92   228   8.3   20.6
 50.000 +XXXXXXXXXXXX                               120   348  10.8   31.4
 60.000 +XXXXXXXXXXXXXXXX                           159   507  14.4   45.8
 70.000 +XXXXXXXXXXXXXXX                            148   655  13.4   59.1
 80.000 +XXXXXXXXXXXXXX                             140   795  12.6   71.8
 90.000 +XXXXXXXXXXXX                               116   911  10.5   82.2
100.00 +XXXXXXXXXX                                  103  1014   9.3   91.5
110.00 +XXXXX                                        51  1065   4.6   96.1
120.00 +XX                                           21  1086   1.9   98.0
130.00 +X                                            14  1100   1.3   99.3
140.00 +X                                             8  1108   0.7  100.0
150.00 +                                              0  1108   0.   100.0
LAST    +                                             0  1108   0.   100.0
        +----+----+----+----+----+----+----+----+
         50  100  150  200  250  300  350  400
```

FIGURE E.4c.

```
HISTOGRAM OF VARIABLE      EU4T
                          SYMBOL  COUNT     MEAN       ST.DEV.
                            X     1108      78.653      31.913
INTERVAL                                    FREQUENCY  PERCENTAGE
NAME        50  100  150  200  250  300  350  400   INT.  CUM.  INT.   CUM.
            +----+----+----+----+----+----+----+----+
 -40.000 +                                            0     0   0.     0.
 -30.000 +                                            0     0   0.     0.
 -20.000 +                                            0     0   0.     0.
 -10.000 +                                            0     0   0.     0.
  0.0000 +X                                            5     5   0.5    0.5
 10.000 +X                                             8    13   0.7    1.2
 20.000 +XX                                           18    31   1.6    2.8
 30.000 +XXX                                          32    63   2.9    5.7
 40.000 +XXXXXX                                       65   128   5.9   11.6
 50.000 +XXXXXXXX                                     77   205   6.9   18.5
 60.000 +XXXXXXXXXXX                                 105   310   9.5   28.0
 70.000 +XXXXXXXXXXXXXXXXX                           158   468  14.3   42.2
 80.000 +XXXXXXXXXXXXXX                              136   604  12.3   54.5
 90.000 +XXXXXXXXXXXX                               117   721  10.6   65.1
100.00 +XXXXXXXXXXXXX                               128   849  11.6   76.6
110.00 +XXXXXXXXX                                    86   935   7.8   84.4
120.00 +XXX                                          25   960   2.3   86.6
130.00 +XXXXXXXX                                     75  1035   6.8   93.4
140.00 +XXX                                          29  1064   2.6   96.0
150.00 +XXXX                                         44  1108   4.0  100.0
LAST    +                                             0  1108   0.   100.0
        +----+----+----+----+----+----+----+----+
         50  100  150  200  250  300  350  400
```

FIGURE E.4d.

```
HISTOGRAM OF VARIABLE       GAINT
                                    SYMBOL   COUNT      MEAN        ST.DEV.
                                       X     1108       52.774       34.270
INTERVAL                                                FREQUENCY PERCENTAGE
NAME          50   100  150  200  250  300  350  400    INT. CUM.  INT.  CUM.
           +----+----+----+----+----+----+----+----+
 -20.000   +                                              4     4   0.4   0.4
 -10.000   +X                                             7    11   0.6   1.0
   0.0000  +XXX                                          29    40   2.6   3.6
  10.000   +XXXXX                                        52    92   4.7   8.3
  20.000   +XXXXXXXXXX                                  109   201   9.8  18.1
  30.000   +XXXXXXXXXXX                                 122   323  11.0  29.2
  40.000   +XXXXXXXXXX                                  113   436  10.2  39.4
  50.000   +XXXXXXXXXXXXXX                              148   584  13.4  52.7
  60.000   +XXXXXXXXXX                                  108   692   9.7  62.5
  70.000   +XXXXXXXXXX                                  105   797   9.5  71.9
  80.000   +XXXXXXXX                                     82   879   7.4  79.3
  90.000   +XXXXXX                                       62   941   5.6  84.9
 100.00    +XXXXXX                                       62  1003   5.6  90.5
 110.00    +XXX                                          30  1033   2.7  93.2
 120.00    +XX                                           22  1055   2.0  95.2
 130.00    +XX                                           22  1077   2.0  97.2
 140.00    +XX                                           23  1100   2.1  99.3
 150.00    +X                                             5  1105   0.5  99.7
 160.00    +                                              2  1107   0.2  99.9
 170.00    +                                              1  1108   0.1 100.0
LAST       +                                              0  1108   0.  100.0
           +----+----+----+----+----+----+----+----+
            50   100  150  200  250  300  350  400
```

FIGURE E.4e.

```
HISTOGRAM OF VARIABLE       GAMMAT
                                    SYMBOL   COUNT      MEAN        ST.DEV.
                                       X     1108       -5.313       21.899
INTERVAL                                                FREQUENCY PERCENTAGE
NAME          50   100  150  200  250  300  350  400    INT. CUM.  INT.  CUM.
           +----+----+----+----+----+----+----+----+
 -60.000   +X                                            10    10   0.9   0.9
 -50.000   +XX                                           15    25   1.4   2.3
 -40.000   +XXXX                                         40    65   3.6   5.9
 -30.000   +XXXXXXXX                                     76   141   6.9  12.7
 -20.000   +XXXXXXXXXXXX                                121   262  10.9  23.6
 -10.000   +XXXXXXXXXXXXXXXXXXXX                        191   453  17.2  40.9
   0.0000  +XXXXXXXXXXXXXXXXXXXXXXXXXXX                 250   703  22.6  63.4
  10.000   +XXXXXXXXXXXXXXXXXXX                         187   890  16.9  80.3
  20.000   +XXXXXXXXXX                                   96   986   8.7  89.0
  30.000   +XXXXXX                                       59  1045   5.3  94.3
  40.000   +XXXX                                         37  1082   3.3  97.7
  50.000   +XX                                           18  1100   1.6  99.3
  60.000   +                                              4  1104   0.4  99.6
  70.000   +                                              1  1105   0.1  99.7
  80.000   +                                              1  1106   0.1  99.8
  90.000   +                                              2  1108   0.2 100.0
LAST       +                                              0  1108   0.  100.0
           +----+----+----+----+----+----+----+----+
            50   100  150  200  250  300  350  400
```

FIGURE E.4f.

TABLE E.5. Joint distribution of PREVT and GRADE.

Independent Variable: PREVT
Independent Variable: GRADE
Cells are count over row percent over asd

|  |  | PREVT |  |
| --- | --- | --- | --- |
| Grade | No | Yes | Total |
| 1 | 271 | 33 | 304 |
|  | 89 | 11 | 100 |
|  | 12.6 | -12.6 |  |
| 2 | 209 | 156 | 365 |
|  | 57 | 43 | 100 |
|  | -0.8 | 0.8 |  |
| 3 | 115 | 133 | 248 |
|  | 46 | 54 | 100 |
|  | -4.5 | 4.5 |  |
| 4+ | 57 | 134 | 191 |
|  | 30 | 70 | 100 |
|  | -9.0 | 9.0 |  |
| Total | 652 | 456 | 1108 |
|  | 59 | 41 | 100 |

chi-square = 197.9,  df = 3,  p <.001

```
HISTOGRAM OF VARIABLE        GAIN
                             SYMBOL   COUNT      MEAN        ST.DEV.
                               X      1108       49.776         31.082
INTERVAL                                         FREQUENCY  PERCENTAGE
NAME        50  100  150  200  250  300  350  400  INT. CUM.  INT.  CUM.
            +----+----+----+----+----+----+----+----+
 -40.000 +                                         0     0   0.     0.
 -35.000 +                                         1     1   0.1    0.1
 -30.000 +                                         2     3   0.2    0.3
 -25.000 +                                         2     5   0.2    0.5
 -20.000 +                                         2     7   0.2    0.6
 -15.000 +                                         3    10   0.3    0.9
 -10.000 +                                         1    11   0.1    1.0
 -5.0000 +X                                        11    22   1.0    2.0
  0.0000 +XX                                       22    44   2.0    4.0
  5.0000 +XXXXX                                    52    96   4.7    8.7
 10.000 +XXXX                                      44   140   4.0   12.6
 15.000 +XXXX                                      43   183   3.9   16.5
 20.000 +XXXXX                                     48   231   4.3   20.8
 25.000 +XXXXXX                                    57   288   5.1   26.0
 30.000 +XXXXX                                     61   349   5.5   31.5
 35.000 +XXXXXX                                    56   405   5.1   36.6
 40.000 +XXXXX                                     54   459   4.9   41.4
 45.000 +XXXXX                                     51   510   4.6   46.0
 50.000 +XXXX                                      44   554   4.0   50.0
 55.000 +XXXXX                                     45   599   4.1   54.1
 60.000 +XXXXX                                     50   649   4.5   58.6
 65.000 +XXXXXXX                                   68   717   6.1   64.7
 70.000 +XXXXXX                                    57   774   5.1   69.9
 75.000 +XXXXX                                     54   828   4.9   74.7
 80.000 +XXXXX                                     52   880   4.7   79.4
 85.000 +XXXXX                                     45   925   4.1   83.5
 90.000 +XXXXX                                     48   973   4.3   87.8
 95.000 +XXXXXX                                    59  1032   5.3   93.1
100.00 +XXXXXXXX                                   76  1108   6.9  100.0
LAST     +                                         0  1108   0.   100.0
            +----+----+----+----+----+----+----+----+
            50  100  150  200  250  300  350  400
```

FIGURE E.5a.

```
HISTOGRAM OF VARIABLE      GAMMA
                         SYMBOL   COUNT    MEAN       ST.DEV.
                           X      1108     6.630       28.356
INTERVAL                                  FREQUENCY  PERCENTAGE
NAME        50  100  150  200 250  300  350  400  INT. CUM.  INT.   CUM.
        +----+----+----+----+----+----+----+----+
 -80.000 +                                           0     0   0.    0.
 -75.000 +                                           1     1   0.1   0.1
 -70.000 +                                           1     2   0.1   0.2
 -65.000 +                                           2     4   0.2   0.4
 -60.000 +                                           2     6   0.2   0.5
 -55.000 +X                                          7    13   0.6   1.2
 -50.000 +X                                          5    18   0.5   1.6
 -45.000 +X                                         12    30   1.1   2.7
 -40.000 +X                                         10    40   0.9   3.6
 -35.000 +XX                                        17    57   1.5   5.1
 -30.000 +XXX                                       34    91   3.1   8.2
 -25.000 +XXXX                                      39   130   3.5  11.7
 -20.000 +XXXX                                      37   167   3.3  15.1
 -15.000 +XXXXX                                     54   221   4.9  19.9
 -10.000 +XXXXXXXX                                  79   300   7.1  27.1
 -5.0000 +XXXXXXXXXX                                99   399   8.9  36.0
  0.0000 +XXXXXXXXXXX                              108   507   9.7  45.8
  5.0000 +XXXXXXXXXXX                              108   615   9.7  55.5
 10.000 +XXXXXXXX                                   76   691   6.9  62.4
 15.000 +XXXXXXX                                    65   756   5.9  68.2
 20.000 +XXXXXX                                     59   815   5.3  73.6
 25.000 +XXXXX                                      47   862   4.2  77.8
 30.000 +XXX                                        33   895   3.0  80.8
 35.000 +XXXX                                       37   932   3.3  84.1
 40.000 +XXXX                                       39   971   3.5  87.6
 45.000 +XX                                         21   992   1.9  89.5
 50.000 +XXX                                        25  1017   2.3  91.8
 55.000 +XX                                         16  1033   1.4  93.2
 60.000 +XX                                         18  1051   1.6  94.9
 65.000 +X                                          14  1065   1.3  96.1
 70.000 +X                                          14  1079   1.3  97.4
 75.000 +X                                          10  1089   0.9  98.3
 80.000 +X                                           6  1095   0.5  98.8
 85.000 +X                                           5  1100   0.5  99.3
 90.000 +                                            3  1103   0.3  99.5
 95.000 +                                            4  1107   0.4  99.9
 100.00 +                                            0  1107   0.   99.9
LAST    +                                            1  1108   0.1 100.0
        +----+----+----+----+----+----+----+----+
         50  100  150  200 250  300  350  400
```

FIGURE E.5b.

```
HISTOGRAM OF VARIABLE        LEVEL
                                  SYMBOL   COUNT       MEAN        ST.DEV.
                                     X      1108       53.366       24.845
INTERVAL
NAME          50   100  150  200  250  300  350  400   FREQUENCY  PERCENTAGE
                                                       INT. CUM.  INT.  CUM.
              +----+----+----+----+----+----+----+----+
  0.0000  +                                              2     2   0.2   0.2
  5.0000  +XX                                           24    26   2.2   2.3
 10.000   +XXXX                                         41    67   3.7   6.0
 15.000   +XXXX                                         37   104   3.3   9.4
 20.000   +XXX                                          34   138   3.1  12.5
 25.000   +XXXX                                         38   176   3.4  15.9
 30.000   +XXXXXX                                       55   231   5.0  20.8
 35.000   +XXXXX                                        46   277   4.2  25.0
 40.000   +XXXXXX                                       64   341   5.8  30.8
 45.000   +XXXXXXX                                      69   410   6.2  37.0
 50.000   +XXXXXXX                                      72   482   6.5  43.5
 55.000   +XXXXXXX                                      72   554   6.5  50.0
 60.000   +XXXXXXXXX                                    85   639   7.7  57.7
 65.000   +XXXXXXXXX                                    91   730   8.2  65.9
 70.000   +XXXXXXXX                                     80   810   7.2  73.1
 75.000   +XXXXXXX                                      66   876   6.0  79.1
 80.000   +XXXXXX                                       55   931   5.0  84.0
 85.000   +XXXXXX                                       62   993   5.6  89.6
 90.000   +XXXX                                         43  1036   3.9  93.5
 95.000   +XXXXX                                        48  1084   4.3  97.8
100.00    +XX                                          24  1108   2.2 100.0
LAST      +                                             0  1108   0.  100.0
          +----+----+----+----+----+----+----+----+
              50   100  150  200  250  300  350  400
```

Figure E.5c.

TABLE E.6. Joint distribution of KSEX and SNDEU1.

Independent Variable:  KSEX
Independent Variable:  SNDEU1
Cells are count over row percent over asd

|        |        | KSEX | | |
|--------|--------|------|--------|-------|
| SNDEU1 |        | Male | Female | Total |
| /s/ | Low | 130 | 80 | 210 |
|     |     | 62 | 38 | 100 |
|     |     | 0.6 | -0.6 | |
| | Medium | 106 | 53 | 159 |
| |        | 67 | 33 | 100 |
| |        | 1.8 | -1.8 | |
| | High | 110 | 60 | 170 |
| |      | 65 | 35 | 100 |
| |      | 1.3 | -1.3 | |
| /r/ | Low | 99 | 89 | 188 |
|     |     | 53 | 47 | 100 |
|     |     | -2.3 | 2.3 | |
| | Medium | 97 | 93 | 190 |
| |        | 51 | 49 | 100 |
| |        | -2.8 | 2.8 | |
| | High | 125 | 66 | 191 |
| |      | 65 | 35 | 100 |
| |      | 1.6 | -1.6 | |
| | Total | 667 | 441 | 1108 |
| |       | 60 | 40 | 100 |

chi-square = 17.8,  df = 5,  p = .003

FIGURES E.6a-f. Scattergrams showing the joint distribution between pairs of EU2, GAIN, GAMMA, and LEVEL.

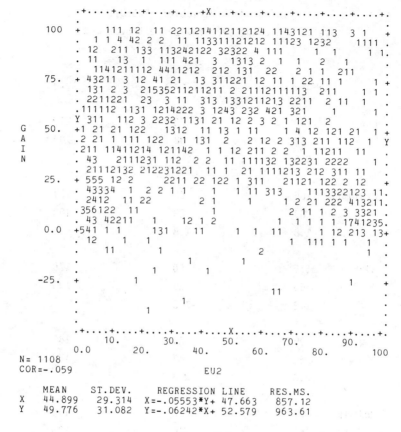

FIGURE E.6a.

```
        .+....+....+....+....+....+....+....+....+..*.+....+....+X
        .                                                      11 .
   90.  +                                               1  1  1+
        .                                             2  11111 .
        .                                          232 1        .
        .                                      2 2123   11   1 .
        .                                  21 3 31112  1 1 1 1 .
   60.  +    1           1                2  221211 1 12    1   +
        .                      1       1  1142141   12 1  1       .
        .                         1 2131241 31  1 11 23111     1 .
        .              1 1 1    1       1212 11212 1    1    31 1 .
  G     .            1   1 3343442122311 3311  1 1 2 1        Y
  A 30. +        11   21 1 121312331 1415 133 1 1121 1  1 +
  M     .      11    1 31 2 112123211 223131 121121121   11  1.
  M     .       1  1 1123113333321143121111211232 212414  2 1 .
  A     .   11121 2112134434223 2 121 2 21  13  1 12522136211.
        .122111314441312236 2 335   12 131 11233233 4122522424.
  0.0   +58A146124 14235535155 324 132 1223212221222 3252234+
        .14655253526544121 43 341141 221121 2 222 41311312   .
        .17611 473234216311  12 4 21116 211211212     12 311   .
        Y 3442322 42114112212 11 2 1 211 1    1 1 1         .
        .174 242321432121  11 1 1     1 11 1    1           .
  -30.  +243227 1123 3322 2 12            1  1             +
        .132 122     111  112  1   1  1   1               .
        .1421  22 1 1  1                                   .
        .12312                                             .
        .   111 1    1 1      1                           .
  -60.  +  221                                             +
        .  1    1                                          .
        .  1                                               .
        X 1                                                .
        .+....+....+....+....+....+....+....+....+....+....+.
          10.     30.     50.     70.     90.
        0.0    20.    40.    60.    80.    100
N= 1107
COR= .548                              EU2
```

| | MEAN | ST.DEV. | REGRESSION LINE | RES.MS. |
|---|---|---|---|---|
| X | 44.872 | 29.313 | X= .56947*Y+ 41.146 | 601.61 |
| Y | 6.5420 | 28.218 | Y= .52769*X-17.136 | 557.47 |

Figure E.6b.

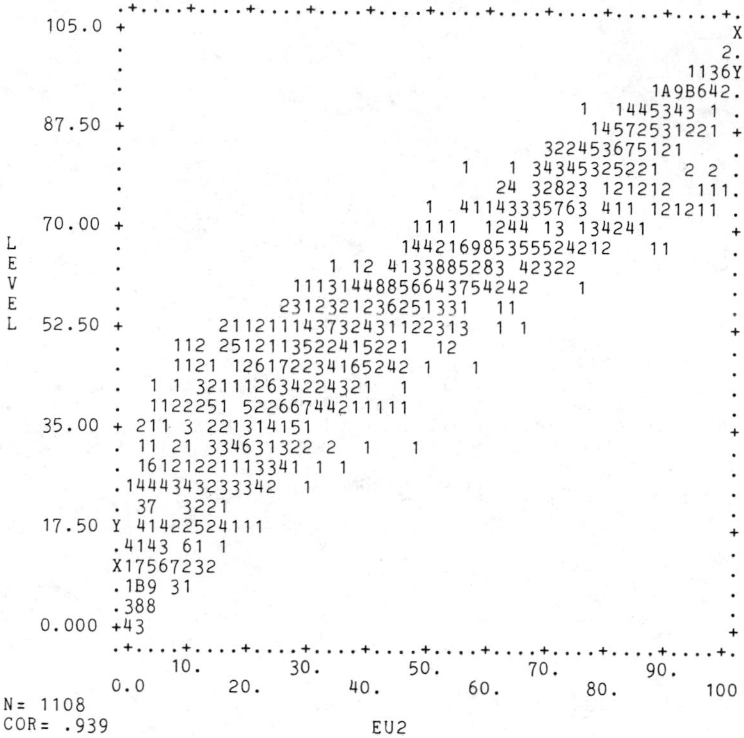

```
          .+....+....+....+....+....+....+....+....+....+....+.
  105.0 +                                                      X
       .                                                       2.
       .                                                    1136Y
       .                                                  1A9B642.
       .                                        1  1445343 1 .
  87.50 +                                         14572531221 +
       .                                       322453675121    .
       .                            1  1 34345325221   2 2 .
       .                             24 32823 121212  111.
       .                       1 41143335763 411 121211.
  70.00 +                    1111   1244 13 134241           +
L      .                 144216985355524212   11           .
E      .              1 12 4133885283 42322                .
V      .            11131448856643754242      1           .
E      .           2312321236251331  11                   .
L  52.50 +       211211143732431122313   1 1               +
       .     112 2512113522415221   12                    .
       .     1121 126172234165242 1   1                   .
       .   1 1 321112634224321   1                         .
       .   1122251 52266744211111                          .
  35.00 + 211 3 221314151                                  +
       . 11 21 334631322 2   1    1                        .
       . 16121221113341 1 1                                .
       .1444343233342  1                                   .
       . 37  3221                                          .
  17.50 Y 41422524111                                      +
       .4143 61 1                                          .
       X17567232                                           .
       .1B9 31                                             .
       .388                                                .
  0.000 +43                                                +
          .+....+....+....+....+....+....+....+....+....+....+.
          10.     30.     50.     70.     90.
       0.0     20.     40.     60.     80.     100
N = 1108
COR = .939                      EU2

      MEAN    ST.DEV.   REGRESSION LINE      RES.MS.
X    44.899   29.314   X= 1.1076*Y-14.208    102.22
Y    53.366   24.845   Y= .79557*X+ 17.646   73.428
```

FIGURE E.6c.

```
     .+....+....+....+....+....+....+....+....+.*..+....+X...+.
     .                                                    2   .
 90. +                                              1     2   +
     .                                        1        12  3  .
     .                                             1    1123  .
     .                                     111    2     44    .
     .                                   1 2  212      316    .
 60. +                       1           1  1  1221      225  +
     .                                   1      141111  335   .
     .                             1 1 312221 1 13625         .
     .         1          1 1           1114    4 2 11 1121   .
 G   .                              222 3151233 14253324      .
 A 30. +              1         21 51 232 135113322 2 3 6     Y
 M   .                     1   1  32  133222243224 23321 2    .
 M   .                  1      3222415425 2724 3225   23125   .
 A   .              11 323465345441223 2 41112131 33122       .
     .             11157443765421844 2 3245442121 332 4       .
 0.0 +        1    124BBBA534462634533113453223 1421 4311     +
     .          11 1  12297273B356A5214  221231243 521  13    .
     .          11  3313355636472362  45  12211341 112        .
     .      1       1  11113 132331122 431211 42 131  211     .
     .          1   111   3 532434311111121 2 12   21         .
-30. Y             2 1  12 1  1 21212222 34242312   1         +
     .    1  1    1        1     1212 1111 32  1  1  1         .
     .                1         1 1 1  2 32 1      21          .
     .            1               1   1 1121    1             .
     .           1           11            1   12             .
-60. +                                1     1 2   1           +
     .                                              11        .
     .                      1                     1           .
     .+....+....+....+..X.+....+....+....+....+....+....+....+.
     -45.      -15.       15.      45.       75.       105
         -30.       0.0       30.      60.       90.
 N= 1107
 COR= .394                        GAIN

     MEAN    ST.DEV.    REGRESSION LINE     RES.MS.
 X   49.762  31.093   X= .43434*Y+ 46.921   817.28
 Y   6.5420  28.218   Y= .35773*X-11.259    673.13
```

FIGURE E.6d.

```
          .+....+....+....+....+....+....+....+..X.+....+....+....+.
  105.0 +                                                              +
       .                          2
       .                        2531
       .                   1   26A842631
       .                      1 4 133254 2 1
   87.50 +                 111 1121341236 1221                         +
       .                   111   12 415132442513
       .                   12  1 1 1  2134223532   312 1
       .             1       1  1  11    131211 3  315 13 22    2     .
       .                  1  1       22 323211 2 12544144 11   233    .
   70.00 +        1             1   11   2 1 31121 241 1335            +
     L   .                    1     1211112 1 4111123623 21345124E    .
     E   .                    1 1          211 213 212322413122356B   .
     V   .        1       1           2 13 4211  34224223223246A3A    .
     E   .                        1   2 11 2 111252211   2421226     Y
     L  52.50 +               1        1 1121  41 2412 313144454       +
         Y             1        11    11 1 1131 2  12 34311 25154     .
       .                    21121311  1 1 232143356124221            .
       .                1 1         321 221  2321 4313 2 15           .
       .       1   1 1 1 1 11       41211 2112232342672121           .
   35.00 +                   1 4     12  3312 2132 1   1              +
       .                111 1 211111 3222213112 14 1                 .
       .              1 12 1   1   2 242 1 1  51112 11 1              .
       . 1         1      1 1 12 21 21322121 21 5212111 1            .
       .                1   1   1 222 1311  21                       .
   17.50 +         1      1    1  221 21522 1 2112                    +
       .                    11  22222211211                          .
       .              1  24 23 692 1111                              .
       .                 2122527211                                  .
       .               1114462                                       .
   0.000 +              151                                          +
          .+....+....+....+....+....+....+....X....+....+....+....+.
        -45.      -15.       15.       45.       75.        105
             -30.       0.0       30.       60.       90.
 N= 1108
 COR= .057                         GAIN

       MEAN     ST.DEV.    REGRESSION LINE      RES.MS.
  X   49.776    31.082   X= .07192*Y+ 45.938    963.76
  Y   53.366    24.845   Y= .04595*X+ 51.079    615.77
```

FIGURE E.6e.

```
        ...+....+....+....+....+....+..X.+....+....+....+....
 105.0 +                                                        +
   .                                2
   .                          1  523                            .
   .                          1155892741                        Y
   .                          13 415441 2 1                     .
  87.50 +                      11   1434661   1311              +
   .                    1  121343435532 121                     .
   .                    111 214214152313  3 11 2   1            .
   .                     1 124 14   141 3 31211111   2 1        .
   .                     2  33412 122163332122 12  2 1231       .
  70.00 +              1   1 2  22 1  51 11 111312341          +
L  .                   1 11 234212312332473121142942            .
E  .                    1  11125222245 3333756 211              .
V  .          1   11 11  43333 433451C75346 1                  *
E  .          1  1 1321343212522231 1 2                         .
L 52.50 +            311 1 26365484  211     1 1               +
   .           1   1123 236652314321                            .
   .            1   122455524A13322  11 1                       .
   .            1  31141224424 21131 1    2                     .
   .      1 112  1 2122 572693233 11 1 1                        .
  35.00 +       1 11323 1343112   1                            +
   .           1  33235431223 11  1 1                           .
   .        1 11   321143 2 1122 121  1  1                      .
   .     1 121111142234 252 3  4              1                 .
   .          1 2  111121 1421                                  .
  17.50 Y        2114 1233121312                               +
   .             2  2 3 1213222                                 .
   .            123 313763 21   1                               .
   .              21254451 1                                    .
   .               1 1764                                       .
  0.000 +              241                                     +
        ...+....+....+....X....+....+....+....+....+....+....
           -60.     -20.      20.       60.      100
       -80.     -40.      0.0      40.       80.
N= 1107
COR= .410                         GAMMA

   MEAN    ST.DEV.   REGRESSION LINE    RES.MS.
X  6.5420   28.218   X= .46510*Y-18.276   663.19
Y  53.361   24.855   Y= .36086*X+ 51.001   514.56
```

FIGURE E.6f.

TABLE E.7. Joint distribution of KSEX and GRADE.

Independent Variable:  KSEX
Independent Variable:  GRADE
Cells are count over row percent over asd

KSEX

| GRADE | Male | Female | Total |
|-------|------|--------|-------|
| 1 | 186 | 118 | 304 |
|   | 61 | 39 | 100 |
|   | 0.4 | -0.4 | |
| 2 | 213 | 152 | 365 |
|   | 58 | 42 | 100 |
|   | -0.9 | -0.9 | |
| 3 | 145 | 103 | 248 |
|   | 58 | 42 | 100 |
|   | -0.6 | 0.6 | |
| 4+ | 123 | 68 | 191 |
|   | 64 | 36 | 100 |
|   | 1.3 | -1.3 | |
| Total | 667 | 441 | 1108 |
|   | 60 | 40 | 100 |

chi-square = 2.4,  df = 3,  p = 0.502

FIGURE E.7. Mean transformed EU numbers for each SNDEU1 category.

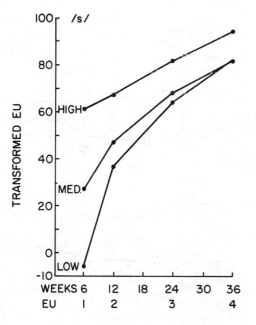
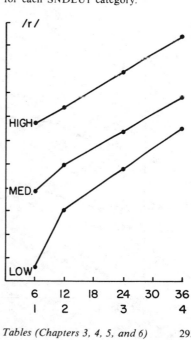

TABLE E.8. Joint distribution of KSEX and PREVT.

Independent Variable:  KSEX
Independent Variable:  PREVT
Cells are count over row percent over asd

|        |       | KSEX   |       |
|--------|-------|--------|-------|
| PREVT  | Male  | Female | Total |
| No     | 377   | 275    | 652   |
|        | 58    | 42     | 100   |
|        | -1.9  | 1.9    |       |
|        |       |        |       |
| Yes    | 290   | 166    | 456   |
|        | 64    | 36     | 100   |
|        | 1.9   | -1.9   |       |
|        |       |        |       |
| Total  | 667   | 441    | 1108  |
|        | 60    | 40     | 100   |

chi-square = 3.7,  df = 1,  p = 0.053

FIGURE E.8. Interaction plot.

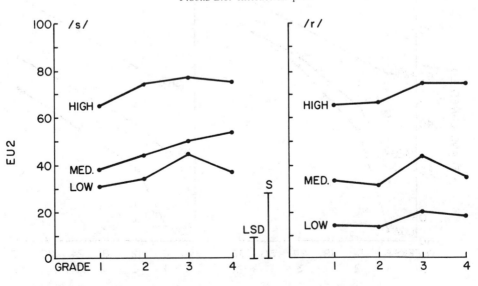

TABLE E.9. Summary of ANOVA. p(F) and $R^2$ for each primary dependent variable and each child prior independent variable in one-way ANOVA, N = 1108.

| Independent | EU2 | | GAIN | | GAMMA | |
|---|---|---|---|---|---|---|
| | p(F) | $R^2$ | p(F) | $R^2$ | p(F) | $R^2$ |
| SNDEU1 | <.001 | .48 | <.001 | .36 | <.001 | .09 |
| GRADE | <.001 | .06 | <.001 | .03 | .018 | .01 |
| PREVT | <.001 | .02 | <.001 | .04 | .104 | .00 |
| KSEX | .032 | .00 | .363 | .00 | .846 | .00 |

FIGURE E.9. Interaction plot.

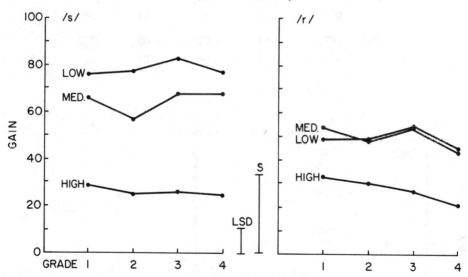

TABLE E.10. Summary of ANOVA, p(F) and $R^2$ for other dependent variables and each child prior independent variable in one-way ANOVA, N = 1108.

|  |  | Independent | | | |
| --- | --- | --- | --- | --- | --- |
| Dependent |  | SNDEU1 | GRADE | PREVT | KSEX |
| EU1 | p(F) | <.001 | <.001 | <.001 | .042 |
|  | $R^2$ | .82 | .06 | .06 | .00 |
| EU3 | p(F) | <.001 | <.001 | .028 | .317 |
|  | $R^2$ | .31 | .02 | .00 | .00 |
| EU4 | p(F) | <.001 | .014 | .343 | .271 |
|  | $R^2$ | .24 | .01 | .00 | .00 |
| GAIN12 | p(F) | <.001 | .004 | <.001 | .830 |
|  | $R^2$ | .19 | .01 | .01 | .00 |
| GAIN23 | p(F) | <.001 | <.001 | <.001 | .062 |
|  | $R^2$ | .16 | .02 | .02 | .00 |
| GAIN34 | p(F) | <.001 | <.001 | .003 | .962 |
|  | $R^2$ | .08 | .02 | .01 | .00 |
| GAIN13 | p(F) | <.001 | .003 | <.001 | .353 |
|  | $R^2$ | .30 | .01 | .02 | .00 |
| GAIN24 | p(F) | <.001 | <.001 | <.001 | .137 |
|  | $R^2$ | .20 | .04 | .02 | .00 |

FIGURE E.10. Interaction plot.

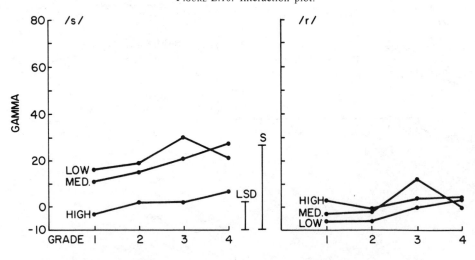

TABLE E.11. Mean transformed EU numbers for each SNDEU1 category.

| SNDEU1 | EU1T | EU2T | EU3T | EU4T |
|---|---|---|---|---|
| /s/ low | -6.0 | 36.6 | 63.9 | 81.8 |
| /s/ medium | 27.3 | 47.1 | 68.0 | 81.1 |
| /s/ high | 61.3 | 67.2 | 81.6 | 94.0 |
| /r/ low | -4.4 | 20.2 | 38.0 | 54.4 |
| /r/ medium | 28.2 | 39.8 | 54.0 | 68.0 |
| /r/ high | 57.2 | 64.0 | 78.4 | 93.9 |

FIGURE E.11. Interaction plot.

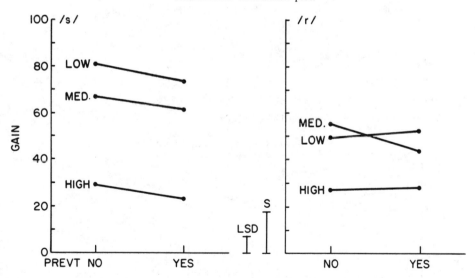

TABLE E.12. ANOVA tables.

Independent Variables:  SNDEU1, GRADE    N = 1108

Dependent Variable:  EU2, $R^2$ = .50

|  | SS | df | MS | F | p |
|---|---|---|---|---|---|
| SNDEU1 | 350090 | 5 | 70018 | 160.7 | <.001 |
| GRADE | 16364 | 3 | 5454 | 12.5 | <.001 |
| SNDEU1 X GRADE | 5530 | 15 | 369 | 0.8 | .626 |
| Error | 472179 | 1084 | 436 | | |
| Total | 951270 | 1107 | | | |

Dependent Variable:  GAIN, $R^2$ = .38

|  | SS | df | MS | F | p |
|---|---|---|---|---|---|
| SNDEU1 | 336798 | 5 | 67360 | 109.5 | <.001 |
| GRADE | 5171 | 3 | 1724 | 2.8 | .039 |
| SNDEU1 X GRADE | 8550 | 15 | 570 | 0.9 | .534 |
| Error | 666912 | 1084 | 615 | | |
| Total | 1069456 | 1107 | | | |

Dependent Variable:  GAMMA, $R^2$ = .12

|  | SS | df | MS | F | p |
|---|---|---|---|---|---|
| SNDEU1 | 73286 | 5 | 14657 | 20.2 | <.001 |
| GRADE | 12809 | 3 | 4270 | 5.9 | .001 |
| SNDEU1 X GRADE | 7504 | 15 | 500 | 0.7 | .796 |
| Error | 785366 | 1084 | 724 | | |
| Total | 890120 | 1107 | | | |

FIGURE E.12. Interaction plot.

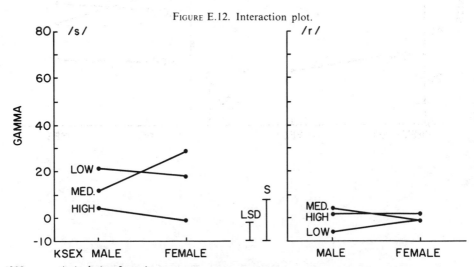

TABLE E.13. Means and standard deviations of primary dependent variables for each combination of SNDEU1 and GRADE.

| SNDEU1 | GRADE | EU2 Mean | EU2 SD | GAIN Mean | GAIN SD | GAMMA Mean | GAMMA SD | N |
|--------|-------|------|------|------|------|------|------|------|
| /s/ Low    | 1  | 30.5 | 24.7 | 76.1 | 25.5 | 15.8 | 36.1 | 84 |
|            | 2  | 33.5 | 25.2 | 78.0 | 24.7 | 18.6 | 36.4 | 70 |
|            | 3  | 45.4 | 27.6 | 83.4 | 24.0 | 30.1 | 36.7 | 35 |
|            | 4+ | 37.3 | 27.0 | 76.8 | 23.4 | 21.0 | 37.3 | 21 |
| /s/ Medium | 1  | 38.4 | 19.0 | 66.1 | 24.3 | 11.0 | 29.8 | 40 |
|            | 2  | 43.6 | 21.6 | 57.3 | 22.3 | 15.0 | 29.0 | 55 |
|            | 3  | 50.2 | 27.0 | 67.8 | 21.4 | 20.8 | 37.0 | 41 |
|            | 4+ | 54.4 | 23.3 | 67.7 | 14.8 | 26.7 | 33.1 | 23 |
| /s/ High   | 1  | 65.4 | 24.3 | 29.2 | 16.7 | -3.4 | 23.6 | 24 |
|            | 2  | 73.5 | 16.6 | 25.2 | 20.0 | 2.2 | 17.3 | 57 |
|            | 3  | 76.5 | 16.5 | 25.8 | 17.9 | 2.2 | 17.7 | 40 |
|            | 4+ | 75.1 | 18.5 | 24.8 | 20.7 | 6.7 | 20.1 | 49 |
| /r/ Low    | 1  | 14.2 | 18.9 | 49.4 | 34.1 | -5.7 | 27.4 | 65 |
|            | 2  | 13.0 | 15.5 | 48.7 | 32.4 | -6.1 | 21.3 | 66 |
|            | 3  | 18.6 | 21.5 | 54.3 | 31.3 | 0.4 | 30.3 | 45 |
|            | 4+ | 17.9 | 16.1 | 44.7 | 27.0 | 2.9 | 23.0 | 12 |
| /r/ Medium | 1  | 33.4 | 15.8 | 53.6 | 26.6 | -2.5 | 22.6 | 46 |
|            | 2  | 31.2 | 17.0 | 48.3 | 26.4 | -2.3 | 21.3 | 55 |
|            | 3  | 43.1 | 23.4 | 55.2 | 24.7 | 11.7 | 28.0 | 47 |
|            | 4+ | 33.5 | 10.5 | 43.1 | 26.8 | 0.3 | 23.0 | 42 |
| /r/ High   | 1  | 64.5 | 21.0 | 32.9 | 23.1 | 2.5 | 19.5 | 45 |
|            | 2  | 65.7 | 19.7 | 29.7 | 19.5 | 0.0 | 16.4 | 62 |
|            | 3  | 73.7 | 17.7 | 27.1 | 21.0 | 3.8 | 21.2 | 40 |
|            | 4+ | 74.3 | 20.4 | 20.7 | 21.8 | 3.6 | 17.0 | 44 |
| Total      |    | 44.9 | 29.3 | 49.8 | 31.1 | 6.6 | 28.4 | 1108 |

FIGURE E.13. Interaction plot.

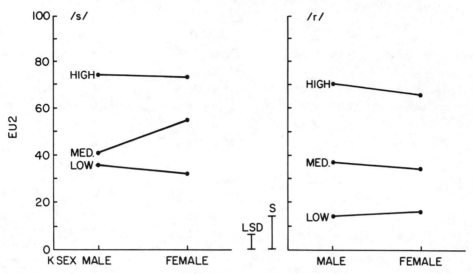

TABLE E.14. ANOVA tables.

Independent Variables:  SNDEU1, PREVT      N = 1108

Dependent Variable:  EU2, $R^2$ = .48

|              | SS      | df    | MS    | F     | p     |
|--------------|---------|-------|-------|-------|-------|
| SNDEU1       | 414569  | 5     | 82914 | 185.2 | <.001 |
| PREVT        | 147     | 1     | 147   | 0.3   | .566  |
| SNDEU1 X PREVT | 2992  | 5     | 598   | 1.3   | .246  |
| Error        | 490569  | 1096  | 448   |       |       |
| Total        | 951270  | 1107  |       |       |       |

Dependent Variable:  GAIN, $R^2$ = .37

|              | SS      | df    | MS    | F     | p     |
|--------------|---------|-------|-------|-------|-------|
| SNDEU1       | 321898  | 5     | 64380 | 105.0 | <.001 |
| PREVT        | 3971    | 1     | 3971  | 6.5   | .011  |
| SNDEU1 X PREVT | 5094  | 5     | 1019  | 1.7   | .141  |
| Error        | 671924  | 1096  | 613   |       |       |
| Total        | 1069456 | 1107  |       |       |       |

Dependent Variable:  GAMMA, $R^2$ = .10

|              | SS      | df    | MS    | F     | p     |
|--------------|---------|-------|-------|-------|-------|
| SNDEU1       | 60473   | 5     | 12095 | 16.6  | <.001 |
| PREVT        | 532     | 1     | 532   | 0.7   | .392  |
| SNDEU1 X PREVT | 8536  | 5     | 1707  | 2.3   | .039  |
| Error        | 796721  | 1096  | 727   |       |       |
| Total        | 890120  | 1107  |       |       |       |

FIGURE E.14. Interaction plot.

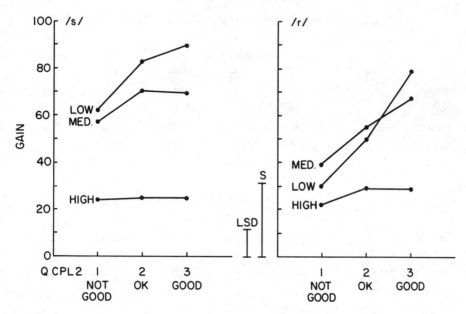

TABLE E.15. Means and standard deviations of primary dependent variables for each combination of SNDEU1 and PREVT.

| SNDEU1 | PREVT | EU2 Mean | EU2 SD | GAIN Mean | GAIN SD | GAMMA Mean | GAMMA SD | N |
|---|---|---|---|---|---|---|---|---|
| /s/ Low | No | 35.3 | 26.2 | 79.6 | 23.4 | 20.6 | 37.4 | 156 |
| | Yes | 32.9 | 25.4 | 73.4 | 28.1 | 16.6 | 33.8 | 54 |
| /s/ Medium | No | 48.3 | 22.8 | 65.6 | 21.4 | 22.4 | 30.8 | 98 |
| | Yes | 41.2 | 23.4 | 60.8 | 22.8 | 8.8 | 32.7 | 61 |
| /s/ High | No | 71.6 | 17.7 | 29.3 | 17.4 | 2.6 | 18.9 | 71 |
| | Yes | 74.9 | 19.1 | 23.3 | 20.1 | 2.8 | 19.7 | 99 |
| /r/ Low | No | 15.0 | 18.8 | 49.2 | 32.4 | -4.7 | 26.6 | 134 |
| | Yes | 15.2 | 17.0 | 52.0 | 32.2 | -1.7 | 24.4 | 54 |
| /r/ Medium | No | 35.9 | 18.2 | 54.8 | 24.4 | 0.8 | 25.7 | 105 |
| | Yes | 34.3 | 20.5 | 44.4 | 27.6 | 2.7 | 22.6 | 85 |
| /r/ High | No | 67.5 | 20.2 | 27.4 | 23.4 | 0.1 | 19.2 | 88 |
| | Yes | 70.4 | 20.0 | 28.2 | 19.9 | 4.0 | 17.4 | 103 |
| Total | | 44.9 | 29.3 | 49.8 | 31.1 | 6.6 | 28.4 | 1108 |

FIGURE E.15. Interaction plot.

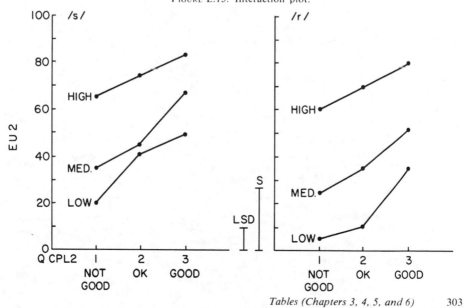

## Table E.16. ANOVA tables.

Independent Variables:  SNDEU1, KSEX      N = 1108

Dependent Variable:  EU2, $R^2$ = .49

|  | SS | df | MS | F | p |
|---|---|---|---|---|---|
| SNDEU1 | 426699 | 5 | 85340 | 192.9 | <.001 |
| KSEX | 62 | 1 | 62 | 0.1 | .708 |
| SNDEU1 X KSEX | 8855 | 5 | 1771 | 4.0 | .001 |
| Error | 484799 | 1096 | 442 |  |  |
| Total | 951270 | 1107 |  |  |  |

Dependent Variable:  GAIN, $R^2$ = .37

|  | SS | df | MS | F | p |
|---|---|---|---|---|---|
| SNDEU1 | 370422 | 5 | 74084 | 119.9 | <.001 |
| KSEX | 344 | 1 | 344 | 0.6 | .456 |
| SNDEU1 X KSEX | 3478 | 5 | 696 | 1.1 | .345 |
| Error | 677385 | 1096 | 618 |  |  |
| Total | 1069456 | 1107 |  |  |  |

Dependent Variable:  GAMMA, $R^2$ = .11

|  | SS | df | MS | F | p |
|---|---|---|---|---|---|
| SNDEU1 | 88477 | 5 | 17689 | 24.5 | <.001 |
| KSEX | 492 | 1 | 492 | 0.7 | .409 |
| SNDEU1 X KSEX | 13931 | 5 | 2786 | 3.8 | .002 |
| Error | 791443 | 1096 | 722 |  |  |
| Total | 890120 | 1107 |  |  |  |

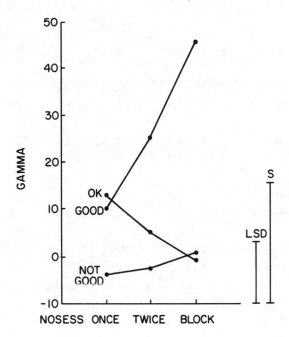

FIGURE E.16. Interaction plot.

TABLE E.17. Means and standard deviations of primary dependent variables for each combination of SNDEU1 and KSEX.

| SNDEU1 | KSEX | EU2 | | GAIN | | GAMMA | | N |
|---|---|---|---|---|---|---|---|---|
| | | Mean | SD | Mean | SD | Mean | SD | |
| /s/ Low | Male | 35.8 | 27.4 | 76.2 | 24.8 | 20.8 | 38.0 | 130 |
| | Female | 32.9 | 23.5 | 81.0 | 24.5 | 17.6 | 33.9 | 80 |
| /s/ Medium | Male | 41.0 | 21.3 | 61.7 | 22.8 | 11.5 | 29.4 | 106 |
| | Female | 54.8 | 24.4 | 67.8 | 20.1 | 28.6 | 34.6 | 53 |
| /s/ High | Male | 74.1 | 18.4 | 27.4 | 20.1 | 4.7 | 19.1 | 110 |
| | Female | 72.5 | 18.9 | 22.9 | 17.2 | -0.8 | 19.4 | 60 |
| /r/ Low | Male | 14.3 | 17.0 | 50.0 | 31.7 | -6.2 | 25.2 | 99 |
| | Female | 15.9 | 19.7 | 50.1 | 33.2 | -1.2 | 26.6 | 89 |
| /r/ Medium | Male | 36.7 | 19.1 | 51.2 | 25.9 | 3.9 | 25.0 | 97 |
| | Female | 33.6 | 19.3 | 49.0 | 26.8 | -0.6 | 23.5 | 93 |
| /r/ High | Male | 70.8 | 19.9 | 26.9 | 21.1 | 2.4 | 18.4 | 125 |
| | Female | 65.8 | 20.4 | 29.6 | 22.3 | 1.9 | 18.3 | 66 |
| Total | | 44.9 | 29.3 | 49.8 | 31.1 | 6.6 | 28.4 | 1108 |

F‌IGURE E.17. Interaction plot.

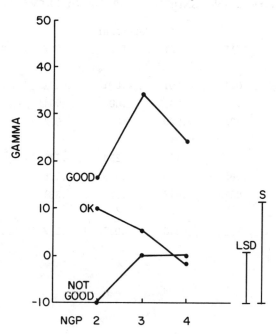

TABLE E.18. Summary of ANOVA, p(F) for *transformed* dependent variables in 3-way ANOVA, N = 1108. Independent Variables: SNDEU1 (S), GRADE (G), PREVT (P).

| | | | Dependent | | | |
|---|---|---|---|---|---|---|
| Independent | EU1T | EU2T | EU3T | EU4T | GAINT | GAMMAT |
| S | <.001 | <.001 | <.001 | <.001 | <.001 | <.001 |
| G | .014 | <.001 | .002 | .004 | .017 | .139 |
| P | .725 | .020 | .007 | .018 | .026 | .739 |
| SG | .162 | .179 | .238 | .179 | .197 | .699 |
| SP | .685 | .160 | .078 | .326 | .141 | .209 |
| GP | .061 | .647 | .536 | .389 | .172 | .384 |
| SGP | .161 | .006 | .017 | .027 | .101 | .667 |

TABLE E.19. Analysis of variance.

Dependent Variable: EU2

Independent Variables: SNDEU1 (S), GRADE (G), PREVT (P)

$R^2$ = .52   N = 1108

| | SS | df | MS | F | p |
|---|---|---|---|---|---|
| S | 245007 | 5 | 49001 | 114.4 | <.001 |
| G | 14716 | 3 | 4905 | 11.4 | <.001 |
| P | 3292 | 1 | 3292 | 7.7 | .006 |
| SG | 7909 | 15 | 527 | 1.2 | .241 |
| SP | 3338 | 5 | 668 | 1.6 | .169 |
| GP | 876 | 3 | 292 | 0.7 | .563 |
| SGP | 10543 | 15 | 703 | 1.6 | .057 |
| Error | 453924 | 1060 | 428 | | |
| Total | 951270 | 1107 | | | |

TABLE E.20. Means and standard deviations of EU2 for each combination of SNDEU1, GRADE, and PREVT.

| GRADE | PREVT | | /s/ Low | /s/ Medium | /s/ High | /r/ Low | /r/ Medium | /r/ High |
|-------|-------|------|------|--------|------|------|--------|------|
| 1 | No | Mean | 31.6 | 41.0 | 67.1 | 13.9 | 34.2 | 65.5 |
| | | SD | 24.9 | 18.9 | 22.4 | 19.1 | 16.1 | 20.1 |
| | | N | 77 | 34 | 21 | 61 | 42 | 36 |
| | Yes | Mean | 19.1 | 23.8 | 53.0 | 19.0 | 25.2 | 60.4 |
| | | SD | 21.2 | 12.2 | 39.0 | 17.2 | 10.4 | 25.1 |
| | | N | 7 | 6 | 3 | 4 | 4 | 9 |
| 2 | No | Mean | 33.3 | 46.1 | 73.8 | 14.7 | 35.0 | 62.8 |
| | | SD | 25.3 | 22.0 | 11.6 | 17.9 | 16.8 | 18.1 |
| | | N | 50 | 33 | 24 | 43 | 32 | 27 |
| | Yes | Mean | 34.2 | 39.9 | 73.3 | 10.0 | 25.9 | 67.9 |
| | | SD | 25.7 | 20.9 | 19.7 | 8.9 | 16.2 | 20.8 |
| | | N | 20 | 22 | 33 | 23 | 23 | 35 |
| 3 | No | Mean | 52.7 | 56.8 | 74.2 | 17.4 | 43.1 | 63.8 |
| | | SD | 26.6 | 24.2 | 18.5 | 20.6 | 23.4 | 20.0 |
| | | N | 23 | 23 | 14 | 23 | 19 | 13 |
| | Yes | Mean | 31.6 | 41.8 | 77.7 | 19.8 | 43.0 | 78.5 |
| | | SD | 24.8 | 28.7 | 15.5 | 22.8 | 23.8 | 14.6 |
| | | N | 12 | 18 | 26 | 22 | 28 | 27 |
| 4+ | No | Mean | 34.0 | 63.5 | 72.0 | 19.0 | 32.8 | 88.0 |
| | | SD | 29.1 | 26.2 | 18.4 | 19.8 | 19.5 | 13.7 |
| | | N | 6 | 8 | 12 | 7 | 12 | 12 |
| | Yes | Mean | 38.7 | 49.5 | 76.1 | 16.4 | 33.8 | 69.2 |
| | | SD | 27.0 | 20.9 | 18.6 | 10.8 | 18.4 | 20.2 |
| | | N | 15 | 15 | 37 | 5 | 30 | 32 |

TABLE E.21. Clinician data.

| CLIN | YEAR | DEGR | ASHA | AGE | CAGE | YRS EXP | SELF R | SELF S | EOI SUM | CEOI | NO SESS |
|---|---|---|---|---|---|---|---|---|---|---|---|
| 1 | 23 | 1 | 3 | 44 | 3 | 18 | 10 | 12 | 96 | 1 | 2.0 |
| 2 | 23 | 2 | 3 | 49 | 3 | 6 | 15 | 15 | 117 | 2 | 2.0 |
| 3 | 2 | 1 | 1 | 43 | 3 | 10 | 14 | 11 | 132 | 3 | 2.0 |
| 4 | 2 | 1 | 3 | 25 | 1 | 3 | 10 | 13 | 116 | 2 | 4.0 |
| 5 | 23 | 1 | 3 | 28 | 2 | 1 | | | | | 2.7 |
| 6 | 2 | 2 | 2 | 23 | 1 | 1 | 9 | 11 | 116 | 2 | 4.0 |
| 7 | 2 | 1 | 3 | 39 | 2 | 15 | 15 | 15 | 93 | 1 | 2.0 |
| 8 | 2 | 2 | 1 | 27 | 1 | 5 | 8 | 5 | 116 | 2 | 3.0 |
| 9 | 2 | 1 | 3 | 24 | 1 | 3 | 13 | 14 | 111 | 1 | 3.0 |
| 10 | 23 | 1 | 3 | 27 | 1 | 6 | 12 | 12 | 122 | 2 | 3.0 |
| 11 | 2 | 1 | 1 | 32 | 2 | 8 | 10 | 10 | 110 | 1 | 2.0 |
| 12 | 23 | 2 | 2 | 30 | 2 | 10 | 14 | 14 | 117 | 2 | 2.0 |
| 13 | 2 | 1 | 3 | 25 | 1 | 1 | 13 | 13 | 129 | 3 | 3.0 |
| 14 | 2 | 2 | 1 | 40 | 3 | 15 | 14 | 14 | 122 | 2 | 2.0 |
| 15 | 2 | 1 | 3 | 29 | 2 | 6 | 13 | 13 | 108 | 1 | 3.0 |
| 16 | 23 | 2 | 3 | 30 | 2 | 3 | 10 | 10 | 115 | 1 | 2.0 |
| 17 | 2 | 1 | 3 | 31 | 2 | 5 | 12 | 12 | | | 4.0 |
| 18 | 23 | 1 | 3 | 41 | 3 | 18 | 10 | 12 | 126 | 3 | 2.0 |
| 19 | 2 | 1 | 3 | 25 | 1 | 3 | 9 | 11 | 105 | 1 | 3.0 |
| 20 | 2 | 1 | 3 | 40 | 3 | 7 | 12 | 13 | 135 | 3 | 3.0 |
| 21 | 2 | 2 | 1 | 42 | 3 | 16 | 14 | 13 | 122 | 2 | 3.0 |
| 22 | 2 | 2 | 3 | 48 | 3 | 8 | 15 | 13 | 124 | 3 | 3.0 |
| 23 | 2 | 2 | 1 | 38 | 2 | 8 | 15 | 15 | 124 | 3 | 3.0 |
| 34 | 3 | 2 | 1 | 43 | 3 | 7 | 15 | 15 | 125 | 3 | 4.0 |
| 37 | 3 | 2 | 1 | 36 | 2 | 8 | 11 | 12 | 102 | 1 | 3.0 |
| 39 | 4 | 2 | 1 | 27 | 1 | 3 | 12 | 11 | 120 | 2 | 3.0 |
| 40 | 4 | 1 | 3 | 25 | 1 | 3 | 10 | 12 | 133 | 3 | 3.0 |
| 41 | 4 | 2 | 1 | 42 | 3 | 12 | 9 | 11 | 121 | 2 | 3.0 |
| 42 | 4 | 1 | 3 | 25 | 1 | 3 | 10 | 13 | 123 | 3 | 3.0 |
| 43 | 4 | 1 | 1 | 43 | 3 | 10 | 12 | 13 | 123 | 3 | 3.0 |
| 44 | 4 | 2 | 2 | 23 | 1 | 1 | 10 | 12 | 128 | 3 | 3.0 |
| 45 | 4 | 1 | 3 | 29 | 2 | 4 | 9 | 10 | 120 | 2 | 3.0 |
| 46 | 4 | 1 | 3 | 26 | 1 | 5 | 12 | 15 | 107 | 1 | 3.0 |
| 47 | 4 | 1 | 3 | 29 | 2 | 7 | 10 | 11 | 120 | 2 | 3.0 |
| 48 | 4 | 1 | 3 | 32 | 2 | 7 | 13 | 13 | 108 | 1 | 3.0 |
| 49 | 4 | 2 | 1 | 29 | 2 | 6 | 13 | 13 | 126 | 3 | 3.0 |
| 50 | 4 | 1 | 3 | 25 | 1 | 3 | 13 | 13 | 124 | 3 | 3.0 |
| 51 | 4 | 1 | 3 | 36 | 2 | 7 | 13 | 13 | 112 | 1 | 3.0 |
| 52 | 4 | 2 | 1 | 40 | 3 | 8 | 12 | 12 | 123 | 3 | 3.0 |
| 53 | 4 | 2 | 3 | 33 | 2 | 5 | 12 | 12 | 114 | 1 | 3.0 |

| CLIN | YEAR | DEGR | ASHA | AGE | CAGE | YRS EXP | SELF R | SELF S | EOI SUM | CEOI | NO SESS |
|------|------|------|------|-----|------|---------|--------|--------|---------|------|---------|
| 54 | 4 | 1 | 3 | 26 | 1 | 4 | 11 | 12 | 135 | 3 | 3.0 |
| 55 | 4 | 2 | 1 | 38 | 2 | 10 | 15 | 12 | 126 | 3 | 3.0 |
| 56 | 4 | 1 | 3 | 49 | 3 | 2 | 9 | 9 | 124 | 3 | 3.0 |
| 57 | 4 | 2 | 2 | 26 | 1 | 1 | 9 | 10 | 130 | 3 | 3.0 |
| 58 | 4 | 2 | 1 | 30 | 2 | 10 | 11 | 12 | 118 | 2 | 3.0 |
| 59 | 4 | 1 | 3 | 28 | 2 | 6 | 13 | 11 | 129 | 3 | 3.0 |
| 60 | 4 | 1 | 3 | 33 | 2 | 7 | 10 | 11 | 119 | 2 | 3.0 |
| 61 | 4 | 1 | 1 | 32 | 2 | 10 | 12 | 12 | 115 | 1 | 3.0 |
| 62 | 4 | 1 | 3 | 23 | 1 | 2 | 10 | 11 | 112 | 1 | 3.0 |
| 63 | 4 | 1 | 3 | 24 | 1 | 2 | 10 | 9 | 119 | 2 | 3.0 |
| 64 | 4 | 2 | 2 | 23 | 1 | 2 | 12 | 13 | 117 | 2 | 3.0 |
| 65 | 4 | 2 | 2 | 26 | 1 | 0 | 8 | 12 | 137 | 3 | 3.0 |
| 91 | 3 | | | | | | | | | | 2.0 |
| 92 | 3 | 1 | 3 | 24 | 1 | 2 | 9 | 11 | 127 | 3 | 2.0 |
| 93 | 3 | | | | | | | | | | 2.0 |
| 94 | 3 | 1 | 3 | 23 | 1 | 3 | 14 | 15 | 122 | 2 | 3.0 |
| 95 | 3 | 2 | 3 | 40 | 3 | 13 | 12 | 12 | 111 | 1 | 3.0 |
| 96 | 3 | 2 | 1 | 32 | 2 | 7 | 13 | 15 | 128 | 3 | 3.0 |
| 97 | 3 | | | | | | | | | | 2.0 |
| 98 | 3 | | | | | | | | | | 2.0 |
| 99 | 3 | 1 | 3 | 24 | 1 | 4 | 13 | 14 | 109 | 1 | 2.0 |

| CLIN | NO. KIDS | CASE LOAD | % S LOW | % S MED | % S HIGH | % R LOW | % R MED | % R HIGH | MEAN GRADE | % PREVT | % MALE |
|---|---|---|---|---|---|---|---|---|---|---|---|
| 1 | 43 | 87 | 14 | 21 | 14 | 19 | 14 | 19 | 2.3 | 9 | 63 |
| 2 | 49 | 125 | 20 | 20 | 8 | 18 | 27 | 6 | 2.6 | 39 | 57 |
| 3 | 28 | 75 | 18 | 29 | 14 | 7 | 7 | 25 | 2.5 | 57 | 68 |
| 4 | 26 | 75 | 27 | 4 | 12 | 19 | 19 | 19 | 2.0 | 42 | 46 |
| 5 | 44 | 120 | 16 | 23 | 5 | 39 | 11 | 7 | 1.6 | 30 | 61 |
| 6 | 29 | 40 | 7 | 21 | 21 | 7 | 34 | 10 | 2.8 | 38 | 55 |
| 7 | 28 | 125 | 39 | 7 | 25 | 14 | 11 | 4 | 1.8 | 0 | 71 |
| 8 | 28 | 85 | 11 | 18 | 11 | 14 | 43 | 4 | 2.1 | 39 | 57 |
| 9 | 30 | 81 | 23 | 3 | 13 | 0 | 13 | 47 | 2.1 | 30 | 50 |
| 10 | 46 | 90 | 37 | 15 | 11 | 13 | 11 | 13 | 2.8 | 41 | 57 |
| 11 | 29 | 115 | 3 | 21 | 31 | 0 | 14 | 31 | 1.8 | 90 | 72 |
| 12 | 51 | 108 | 22 | 6 | 18 | 31 | 12 | 12 | 2.0 | 65 | 61 |
| 13 | 26 | | 12 | 27 | 15 | 8 | 27 | 12 | 1.5 | 31 | 35 |
| 14 | 28 | 125 | 18 | 18 | 14 | 29 | 11 | 11 | 2.2 | 18 | 57 |
| 15 | 26 | 101 | 27 | 0 | 31 | 0 | 8 | 35 | 2.2 | 31 | 58 |
| 16 | 48 | 115 | 6 | 19 | 23 | 10 | 27 | 15 | 2.2 | 65 | 58 |
| 17 | 29 | 78 | 28 | 14 | 7 | 21 | 10 | 21 | 3.2 | 59 | 62 |
| 18 | 46 | 122 | 24 | 4 | 22 | 20 | 9 | 22 | 1.7 | 39 | 57 |
| 19 | 28 | 97 | 4 | 39 | 18 | 0 | 14 | 25 | 2.3 | 46 | 86 |
| 20 | 24 | 80 | 33 | 8 | 25 | 17 | 17 | 0 | 2.5 | 25 | 71 |
| 21 | 20 | 20 | 15 | 10 | 20 | 40 | 15 | 0 | 2.8 | 95 | 80 |
| 22 | 18 | 21 | 28 | 6 | 22 | 0 | 11 | 33 | 2.3 | 50 | 56 |
| 23 | 18 | 20 | 33 | 11 | 0 | 50 | 0 | 6 | 2.1 | 11 | 28 |
| 34 | 16 | 84 | 25 | 25 | 13 | 13 | 19 | 6 | 2.8 | 25 | 75 |
| 37 | 16 | 75 | 13 | 19 | 6 | 25 | 19 | 19 | 2.7 | 44 | 63 |
| 39 | 9 | 44 | 33 | 0 | 22 | 22 | 11 | 11 | 2.4 | 44 | 78 |
| 40 | 6 | 50 | 0 | 0 | 33 | 0 | 33 | 33 | 3.0 | 67 | 83 |
| 41 | 9 | 40 | 33 | 0 | 11 | 0 | 22 | 33 | 2.9 | 56 | 67 |
| 42 | 6 | 46 | 17 | 17 | 33 | 17 | 0 | 17 | 2.5 | 50 | 50 |
| 43 | 8 | 56 | 13 | 0 | 25 | 13 | 25 | 25 | 2.3 | 50 | 38 |
| 44 | 7 | 40 | 0 | 57 | 0 | 14 | 29 | 0 | 2.7 | 43 | 71 |
| 45 | 9 | 51 | 44 | 0 | 11 | 0 | 11 | 33 | 2.4 | 22 | 89 |
| 46 | 7 | 45 | 57 | 0 | 0 | 14 | 14 | 14 | 2.0 | 57 | 43 |
| 47 | 8 | 50 | 13 | 13 | 38 | 0 | 0 | 38 | 2.9 | 50 | 88 |
| 48 | 6 | 52 | 17 | 17 | 0 | 33 | 0 | 33 | 2.7 | 33 | 50 |
| 49 | 6 | 86 | 0 | 17 | 17 | 0 | 50 | 17 | 2.2 | 67 | 67 |
| 50 | 4 | 60 | 0 | 0 | 25 | 0 | 0 | 75 | 1.3 | 50 | 50 |
| 51 | 9 | 80 | 11 | 33 | 11 | 0 | 0 | 44 | 1.8 | 67 | 67 |
| 52 | 6 | 90 | 17 | 17 | 0 | 0 | 0 | 67 | 2.3 | 67 | 67 |
| 53 | 6 | 75 | 17 | 0 | 33 | 33 | 17 | 0 | 2.8 | 83 | 50 |

| CLIN | NO. KIDS | CASE LOAD | % S LOW | % S MED | % S HIGH | % R LOW | % R MED | % R HIGH | MEAN GRADE | % PREVT | % MALE |
|---|---|---|---|---|---|---|---|---|---|---|---|
| 54 | 6 | 70 | 0 | 0 | 33 | 0 | 33 | 33 | 2.0 | 17 | 17 |
| 55 | 6 | 90 | 33 | 0 | 0 | 50 | 17 | 0 | 2.2 | 67 | 33 |
| 56 | 9 | 73 | 11 | 22 | 11 | 11 | 22 | 22 | 3.4 | 67 | 44 |
| 57 | 7 | 80 | 14 | 43 | 0 | 0 | 29 | 14 | 2.0 | 57 | 57 |
| 58 | 6 | 60 | 17 | 33 | 17 | 0 | 33 | 0 | 2.5 | 50 | 83 |
| 59 | 8 | 51 | 25 | 0 | 25 | 25 | 13 | 13 | 2.6 | 50 | 38 |
| 60 | 7 | 85 | 0 | 29 | 14 | 0 | 29 | 29 | 2.0 | 43 | 43 |
| 61 | 7 | 47 | 57 | 14 | 0 | 14 | 0 | 14 | 2.6 | 43 | 14 |
| 62 | 8 | 115 | 25 | 0 | 25 | 13 | 13 | 25 | 1.9 | 50 | 38 |
| 63 | 7 | 52 | 0 | 29 | 14 | 43 | 0 | 14 | 2.9 | 43 | 71 |
| 64 | 8 | 85 | 38 | 0 | 13 | 25 | 25 | 0 | 2.5 | 63 | 75 |
| 65 | 9 | 95 | 33 | 0 | 0 | 0 | 44 | 22 | 2.1 | 56 | 67 |
| 91 | 15 | 25 | 20 | 27 | 20 | 20 | 13 | 0 | 2.7 | 73 | 73 |
| 92 | 9 | 100 | 0 | 22 | 11 | 22 | 33 | 11 | 2.1 | 44 | 44 |
| 93 | 7 |  | 0 | 14 | 14 | 0 | 43 | 29 | 2.9 | 43 | 86 |
| 94 | 17 | 70 | 0 | 12 | 29 | 12 | 6 | 41 | 2.9 | 0 | 94 |
| 95 | 17 | 48 | 12 | 12 | 24 | 29 | 12 | 12 | 2.4 | 0 | 59 |
| 96 | 19 | 80 | 5 | 0 | 0 | 58 | 26 | 11 | 1.9 | 0 | 68 |
| 97 | 17 |  | 29 | 0 | 12 | 29 | 29 | 0 | 2.9 | 12 | 41 |
| 98 | 20 |  | 5 | 10 | 10 | 10 | 25 | 40 | 2.3 | 35 | 70 |
| 99 | 19 | 147 | 26 | 11 | 0 | 26 | 21 | 16 | 1.9 | 47 | 53 |

| CLIN | MEAN EU1 | MEAN EU2 | MEAN EU3 | MEAN EU4 | MEAN GAIN | MEAN GAMMA | % K | % L | % M | % O | % OTHER |
|---|---|---|---|---|---|---|---|---|---|---|---|
| 1 | 25 | 43 | 63 | 70 | 45 | 11 | 23 | 12 | 12 | 19 | 35 |
| 2 | 18 | 29 | 49 | 75 | 57 | -15 | 10 | 33 | 10 | 14 | 33 |
| 3 | 28 | 54 | 85 | 93 | 65 | 18 | 32 | 18 | 21 | 4 | 25 |
| 4 | 24 | 46 | 67 | 84 | 60 | 5 | 27 | 15 | 15 | 15 | 27 |
| 5 | 13 | 31 | 58 | 67 | 54 | 9 | 20 | 30 | 7 | 32 | 11 |
| 6 | 31 | 43 | 56 | 67 | 35 | 0 | 10 | 17 | 21 | 31 | 21 |
| 7 | 19 | 47 | 78 | 92 | 73 | 13 | 32 | 25 | 18 | 0 | 25 |
| 8 | 22 | 49 | 78 | 87 | 65 | 18 | 43 | 25 | 11 | 0 | 21 |
| 9 | 44 | 54 | 68 | 77 | 33 | 2 | 10 | 13 | 23 | 17 | 37 |
| 10 | 20 | 26 | 48 | 63 | 43 | -8 | 15 | 13 | 9 | 33 | 30 |
| 11 | 35 | 45 | 67 | 74 | 38 | 3 | 3 | 17 | 10 | 7 | 62 |
| 12 | 22 | 27 | 34 | 47 | 25 | -7 | 4 | 10 | 14 | 49 | 24 |
| 13 | 29 | 45 | 64 | 76 | 48 | 4 | 19 | 27 | 12 | 15 | 27 |
| 14 | 24 | 37 | 61 | 74 | 50 | 0 | 11 | 29 | 21 | 21 | 18 |
| 15 | 47 | 65 | 77 | 84 | 37 | 11 | 12 | 15 | 42 | 4 | 27 |
| 16 | 33 | 40 | 54 | 69 | 36 | -6 | 6 | 10 | 21 | 25 | 38 |
| 17 | 22 | 61 | 78 | 83 | 61 | 34 | 34 | 10 | 17 | 14 | 24 |
| 18 | 34 | 50 | 76 | 88 | 54 | 5 | 9 | 37 | 37 | 4 | 13 |
| 19 | 34 | 35 | 44 | 60 | 26 | -14 | 0 | 11 | 18 | 36 | 36 |
| 20 | 20 | 63 | 89 | 92 | 71 | 41 | 67 | 0 | 17 | 0 | 17 |
| 21 | 16 | 42 | 79 | 88 | 72 | 16 | 15 | 40 | 10 | 15 | 20 |
| 22 | 35 | 59 | 78 | 90 | 55 | 12 | 22 | 11 | 28 | 0 | 39 |
| 23 | 9 | 75 | 88 | 95 | 86 | 59 | 83 | 6 | 6 | 6 | 0 |
| 34 | 22 | 78 | 85 | 92 | 70 | 49 | 69 | 6 | 19 | 0 | 6 |
| 37 | 21 | 50 | 74 | 86 | 65 | 17 | 25 | 38 | 6 | 6 | 25 |
| 39 | 31 | 60 | 87 | 97 | 66 | 19 | 44 | 22 | 33 | 0 | 0 |
| 40 | 57 | 72 | 79 | 93 | 36 | 1 | 17 | 17 | 67 | 0 | 0 |
| 41 | 31 | 38 | 61 | 81 | 50 | -13 | 0 | 33 | 33 | 11 | 22 |
| 42 | 46 | 69 | 83 | 92 | 46 | 13 | 33 | 0 | 50 | 0 | 17 |
| 43 | 36 | 53 | 79 | 90 | 54 | 6 | 13 | 25 | 38 | 13 | 13 |
| 44 | 21 | 60 | 87 | 97 | 75 | 29 | 86 | 14 | 0 | 0 | 0 |
| 45 | 29 | 39 | 71 | 87 | 58 | -4 | 11 | 33 | 33 | 11 | 11 |
| 46 | 14 | 39 | 63 | 76 | 62 | 12 | 29 | 14 | 14 | 14 | 29 |
| 47 | 48 | 76 | 91 | 94 | 46 | 25 | 25 | 0 | 50 | 0 | 25 |
| 48 | 31 | 39 | 58 | 79 | 48 | -13 | 0 | 33 | 33 | 17 | 17 |
| 49 | 32 | 51 | 67 | 79 | 47 | 7 | 17 | 0 | 33 | 17 | 33 |
| 50 | 78 | 85 | 94 | 96 | 18 | 6 | 0 | 0 | 100 | 0 | 0 |
| 51 | 44 | 62 | 87 | 88 | 44 | 17 | 33 | 0 | 44 | 0 | 22 |
| 52 | 37 | 29 | 52 | 75 | 38 | -30 | 0 | 33 | 0 | 0 | 67 |
| 53 | 30 | 46 | 70 | 81 | 51 | 6 | 0 | 33 | 33 | 17 | 17 |

| CLIN | MEAN EU1 | MEAN EU2 | MEAN EU3 | MEAN EU4 | MEAN GAIN | MEAN GAMMA | % K | % L | % M | % O | % OTHER |
|---|---|---|---|---|---|---|---|---|---|---|---|
| 54 | 47 | 56 | 69 | 77 | 29 | 1 | 0 | 0 | 50 | 33 | 17 |
| 55 | 6 | 31 | 86 | 93 | 87 | 19 | 0 | 83 | 0 | 0 | 17 |
| 56 | 27 | 66 | 89 | 91 | 64 | 38 | 44 | 0 | 0 | 0 | 56 |
| 57 | 22 | 35 | 61 | 69 | 46 | 5 | 14 | 29 | 14 | 43 | 0 |
| 58 | 24 | 42 | 68 | 76 | 53 | 10 | 33 | 17 | 17 | 17 | 17 |
| 59 | 27 | 37 | 61 | 71 | 44 | 0 | 0 | 25 | 25 | 25 | 25 |
| 60 | 43 | 59 | 74 | 86 | 43 | 4 | 14 | 29 | 43 | 0 | 14 |
| 61 | 14 | 54 | 81 | 92 | 78 | 29 | 43 | 43 | 14 | 0 | 0 |
| 62 | 44 | 63 | 90 | 98 | 55 | 11 | 25 | 25 | 50 | 0 | 0 |
| 63 | 28 | 62 | 79 | 87 | 59 | 27 | 29 | 29 | 29 | 14 | 0 |
| 64 | 16 | 42 | 66 | 82 | 66 | 10 | 25 | 13 | 13 | 13 | 38 |
| 65 | 18 | 56 | 88 | 97 | 79 | 29 | 33 | 44 | 0 | 0 | 22 |
| 91 | 19 | 24 | 38 | 46 | 27 | -2 | 7 | 13 | 7 | 53 | 20 |
| 92 | 23 | 41 | 59 | 68 | 45 | 8 | 33 | 11 | 0 | 33 | 22 |
| 93 | 36 | 50 | 57 | 62 | 27 | 9 | 0 | 0 | 14 | 29 | 57 |
| 94 | 52 | 64 | 77 | 88 | 36 | 1 | 6 | 18 | 47 | 6 | 24 |
| 95 | 32 | 48 | 58 | 75 | 43 | -1 | 18 | 12 | 35 | 29 | 6 |
| 96 | 12 | 22 | 41 | 62 | 50 | -9 | 5 | 26 | 5 | 42 | 21 |
| 97 | 13 | 23 | 43 | 51 | 38 | 2 | 0 | 24 | 6 | 59 | 12 |
| 98 | 31 | 41 | 56 | 70 | 39 | -3 | 0 | 15 | 15 | 25 | 45 |
| 99 | 11 | 26 | 49 | 58 | 46 | 6 | 5 | 16 | 5 | 37 | 37 |

| CL1N | MEAN NGP | GEOG | NEW CPL2 | CPL2 RANK | NEW QCPL2 | NEW CPL4 | RANK CPL4 | NEW QCPL4 | NO. B |
|---|---|---|---|---|---|---|---|---|---|
| 1 | 2.7 | 2 | 32 | 39 | 2 | 23 | 7 | 1 | 21 |
| 2 | 2.3 | 2 | 21 | 2 | 1 | 26 | 10 | 1 | 25 |
| 3 | 2.5 | 2 | 30 | 27 | 2 | 36 | 54 | 3 | 15 |
| 4 | 3.3 | 2 | 30 | 23 | 2 | 36 | 52 | 3 | 12 |
| 5 | 2.9 | 2 | 28 | 16 | 1 | 27 | 14 | 1 | 21 |
| 6 | 3.5 | 2 | 25 | 9 | 1 | 27 | 12 | 1 | 14 |
| 7 | 2.5 | 2 | 35 | 54 | 3 | 40 | 59 | 3 | 14 |
| 8 | 4.1 | 2 | 33 | 43 | 3 | 33 | 39 | 2 | 14 |
| 9 | 2.6 | 2 | 30 | 29 | 2 | 26 | 11 | 1 | 15 |
| 10 | 3.1 | 2 | 21 | 3 | 1 | 20 | 3 | 1 | 24 |
| 11 | 2.7 | 2 | 23 | 8 | 1 | 17 | 1 | 1 | 14 |
| 12 | 3.0 | 2 | 22 | 5 | 1 | 18 | 2 | 1 | 25 |
| 13 | 3.7 | 2 | 29 | 21 | 2 | 27 | 15 | 1 | 13 |
| 14 | 3.3 | 2 | 26 | 10 | 1 | 29 | 25 | 2 | 14 |
| 15 | 3.9 | 2 | 34 | 51 | 3 | 32 | 37 | 2 | 14 |
| 16 | 2.4 | 2 | 22 | 4 | 1 | 20 | 4 | 1 | 25 |
| 17 | 4.0 | 2 | 42 | 58 | 3 | 34 | 43 | 3 | 15 |
| 18 | 2.7 | 2 | 35 | 52 | 3 | 35 | 50 | 3 | 23 |
| 19 | 2.6 | 2 | 21 | 1 | 1 | 21 | 5 | 1 | 15 |
| 20 | 3.8 | 2 | 45 | 60 | 3 | 37 | 56 | 3 | 12 |
| 21 | 2.5 | 2 | 34 | 47 | 3 | 42 | 61 | 3 | 10 |
| 22 | 2.6 | 2 | 35 | 55 | 3 | 31 | 29 | 2 | 9 |
| 23 | 2.7 | 2 | 53 | 61 | 3 | 42 | 60 | 3 | 9 |
| 34 | 2.4 | 2 | 44 | 59 | 3 | 36 | 55 | 3 | 8 |
| 37 | 2.6 | 2 | 35 | 53 | 3 | 34 | 42 | 3 | 8 |
| 39 | 2.6 | 4 | 39 | 57 | 3 | 35 | 46 | 3 | 5 |
| 40 | 2.0 | 4 | 34 | 50 | 3 | 31 | 30 | 2 | 3 |
| 41 | 2.8 | 4 | 29 | 20 | 1 | 32 | 34 | 2 | 5 |
| 42 | 2.0 | 4 | 34 | 49 | 3 | 35 | 49 | 3 | 3 |
| 43 | 2.5 | 4 | 30 | 31 | 2 | 31 | 32 | 2 | 4 |
| 44 | 2.0 | 4 | 32 | 38 | 2 | 35 | 51 | 3 | 3 |
| 45 | 2.9 | 4 | 30 | 28 | 2 | 28 | 21 | 2 | 5 |
| 46 | 2.0 | 4 | 33 | 44 | 3 | 32 | 35 | 2 | 3 |
| 47 | 2.4 | 4 | 33 | 42 | 3 | 32 | 33 | 2 | 3 |
| 48 | 2.0 | 4 | 28 | 17 | 1 | 31 | 31 | 2 | 3 |
| 49 | 2.3 | 3 | 31 | 32 | 2 | 28 | 17 | 1 | 3 |
| 50 | 2.0 | 3 | 34 | 46 | 3 | 35 | 47 | 3 | 2 |
| 51 | 2.6 | 3 | 30 | 30 | 2 | 29 | 24 | 2 | 4 |
| 52 | 2.0 | 3 | 23 | 7 | 1 | 29 | 26 | 2 | 3 |
| 53 | 2.2 | 3 | 32 | 36 | 2 | 34 | 44 | 3 | 3 |

| CLIN | MEAN NGP | GEOG | NEW CPL2 | CPL2 RANK | NEW QCPL2 | NEW CPL4 | RANK CPL4 | NEW QCPL4 | NO. B |
|------|----------|------|----------|-----------|-----------|----------|-----------|-----------|-------|
| 54 | 2.0 | 3 | 31 | 35 | 2 | 30 | 28 | 2 | 3 |
| 55 | 2.0 | 3 | 33 | 40 | 2 | 36 | 53 | 3 | 3 |
| 56 | 2.3 | 1 | 34 | 48 | 3 | 34 | 45 | 3 | 5 |
| 57 | 2.3 | 1 | 26 | 14 | 1 | 24 | 9 | 1 | 3 |
| 58 | 2.0 | 1 | 26 | 12 | 1 | 28 | 20 | 1 | 3 |
| 59 | 2.0 | 1 | 29 | 22 | 2 | 29 | 22 | 2 | 4 |
| 60 | 2.0 | 1 | 30 | 25 | 2 | 27 | 13 | 1 | 4 |
| 61 | 2.4 | 1 | 31 | 33 | 2 | 32 | 36 | 2 | 4 |
| 62 | 2.0 | 1 | 34 | 45 | 3 | 35 | 48 | 3 | 4 |
| 63 | 2.0 | 1 | 36 | 56 | 3 | 38 | 58 | 3 | 3 |
| 64 | 2.0 | 1 | 33 | 41 | 2 | 33 | 41 | 2 | 4 |
| 65 | 2.7 | 1 | 32 | 37 | 2 | 38 | 57 | 3 | 4 |
| 91 | 2.9 | 2 | 22 | 6 | 1 | 23 | 8 | 1 | 8 |
| 92 | 3.0 | 2 | 29 | 19 | 1 | 28 | 18 | 1 | 4 |
| 93 | 4.1 | 2 | 30 | 24 | 2 | 28 | 19 | 1 | 3 |
| 94 | 2.3 | 2 | 31 | 34 | 2 | 33 | 40 | 2 | 8 |
| 95 | 2.1 | 2 | 26 | 11 | 1 | 29 | 23 | 2 | 8 |
| 96 | 2.7 | 2 | 30 | 26 | 2 | 33 | 38 | 2 | 10 |
| 97 | 4.2 | 2 | 27 | 15 | 1 | 27 | 16 | 1 | 9 |
| 98 | 3.1 | 2 | 26 | 13 | 1 | 23 | 6 | 1 | 10 |
| 99 | 2.7 | 2 | 28 | 18 | 1 | 29 | 27 | 2 | 10 |

TABLE E.22. Correlations between pairs of variables in the averages of child independent variables group. N = 57. Significance levels: .05, .269; .01, .349.

| | %S Low | %S Med | %S High | %R Low | %R Med | %R High | Mean GRADE | % PREVT | % Male |
|---|---|---|---|---|---|---|---|---|---|
| % S Low | 100 | | | | | | | | |
| % S Med | - 43 | 100 | | | | | | | |
| % S High | - 30 | - 27 | 100 | | | | | | |
| % R Low | 10 | - 17 | - 28 | 100 | | | | | |
| % R Medium | - 27 | 08 | - 10 | - 19 | 100 | | | | |
| % R High | - 23 | - 15 | 16 | - 55 | - 36 | 100 | | | |
| Mean GRADE | - 03 | 17 | 08 | 07 | 00 | - 23 | 100 | | |
| % PREVT | - 06 | 06 | 04 | - 17 | 13 | 04 | 10 | 100 | |
| % Male | - 19 | 22 | 19 | - 20 | 02 | 04 | 26 | 02 | 100 |

TABLE E.23. Correlations between clinician prior variables and child independent averages. N = 57. Significance levels: .05, .269; .01, .349.

| | %S Low | %S Med | %S High | %R Low | %R Med | %R High | Mean GRADE | % PREVT | % Male |
|---|---|---|---|---|---|---|---|---|---|
| DEGREE | 00 | 09 | - 29 | 26 | 38 | - 40 | 11 | 13 | 14 |
| ASHA | - 07 | - 09 | 33 | - 19 | - 19 | 23 | - 04 | - 18 | - 05 |
| AGE | 14 | 01 | - 08 | 13 | - 16 | - 07 | 17 | - 03 | - 05 |
| CAGE | 10 | - 01 | 02 | 10 | - 18 | - 03 | 18 | - 02 | 04 |
| YRSEXP | 19 | - 10 | 05 | 24 | - 27 | - 12 | - 10 | - 16 | 01 |
| SELFR | 24 | - 21 | - 04 | 36 | - 37 | - 06 | - 09 | - 17 | - 08 |
| SELFS | 25 | - 25 | - 08 | 23 | - 23 | 00 | - 16 | - 31 | - 02 |
| EOISUM | - 16 | - 06 | 00 | - 04 | 28 | 00 | 14 | 15 | - 05 |
| CEOI | - 18 | - 01 | - 05 | 02 | 25 | 00 | 07 | 04 | - 06 |

TABLE E.24. Correlations between clinician dependent variables. N = 57. Significance levels: .05, .269; .01, .349.

| | | MEAN | | | | | | % | | | | |
|---|---|---|---|---|---|---|---|---|---|---|---|---|
| | | EU1 | EU2 | EU3 | EU4 | GAIN | GAMMA | K | L | M | O | Other |
| Mean | EU1 | 100 | | | | | | | | | | |
| | EU2 | 55 | 100 | | | | | | | | | |
| | EU3 | 26 | 83 | 100 | | | | | | | | |
| | EU4 | 23 | 75 | 94 | 100 | | | | | | | |
| | GAIN | - 68 | 09 | 48 | 56 | 100 | | | | | | |
| | GAMMA | - 25 | 64 | 74 | 61 | 67 | 100 | | | | | |
| % | K | - 31 | 50 | 55 | 51 | 65 | 83 | 100 | | | | |
| | L | - 39 | - 42 | - 02 | 11 | 42 | - 15 | - 28 | 100 | | | |
| | M | 87 | 57 | 33 | 32 | - 50 | - 14 | - 27 | - 30 | 100 | | |
| | O | - 25 | - 66 | - 83 | - 89 | - 46 | - 48 | - 43 | - 11 | - 24 | 100 | |
| | Other | - 07 | - 39 | - 39 | - 40 | - 24 | - 35 | - 33 | - 14 | - 39 | 09 | 100 |

TABLE E.25. Factor loadings for clinician dependent variables.

| | | Factor | | |
|---|---|---|---|---|
| Variable | I | II | III | IV |
| % O | -.93 | -.22 | -.12 | -.12 |
| MEAN EU4 | .91 | .32 | .14 | -.16 |
| MEAN EU3 | .86 | .41 | -.02 | -.18 |
| MEAN EU2 | .77 | .30 | -.46 | -.24 |
| CPL4 | .57 | .52 | .26 | -.29 |
| % M | .56 | -.47 | -.42 | -.52 |
| CPL2 | .50 | .69 | -.09 | -.26 |
| % K | .23 | .89 | -.13 | -.07 |
| MEAN GAMMA | .34 | .87 | -.12 | -.12 |
| MEAN GAIN | .29 | .74 | .57 | .00 |
| % L | .04 | -.13 | .96 | -.11 |
| % Other | -.09 | -.24 | -.12 | .94 |
| Variance Explained | 4.18 | 3.55 | 1.79 | 1.47 |

N = 61, Total percent variance explained = 92

TABLE E.26. Summary of ANOVA. p(F) and R² for dependent variables versus QCPL2 and QCPL4 in one-way ANOVA, N = 555 (B sample).

|  |  | Independent | | |
|---|---|---|---|---|
| Dependent |  | QCPL2 | QCPL4 | CLINO |
| EU1 | P(F) | .268 | .410 | .003 |
|  | $R^2$ | .00 | .00 | .16 |
| EU2 | p(F) | < .001 | < .001 | < .001 |
|  | $R^2$ | .14 | .08 | .30 |
| EU3 | p(F) | < .001 | < .001 | < .001 |
|  | $R^2$ | .20 | .16 | .27 |
| EU4 | p(F) | < .001 | < .001 | < .001 |
|  | $R^2$ | .17 | .16 | .26 |
| GAIN | p(F) | < .001 | < .001 | < .001 |
|  | $R^2$ | .09 | .13 | .25 |
| GAMMA | p(F) | < .001 | < .001 | < .001 |
|  | $R^2$ | .16 | .13 | .35 |

TABLE E.27. Summary of analysis of variance. p(F) and R² for CPL2 and CPL4 with SNDEU1 for the primary dependent variables, N = 555 (B sample).

|  |  | Dependent | | | | |
|---|---|---|---|---|---|---|
|  | EU2 | | GAIN | | GAMMA | |
| Independent | p(F) | $R^2$ | p(F) | $R^2$ | p(F) | $R^2$ |
| SNDUE1 | <.001 | | <.001 | | <.001 | |
| QCPL2 | <.001 | | <.001 | | <.001 | |
| S X Q | .107 | | <.001 | | <.001 | |
| All Factors | | .60 | | .50 | | .30 |
| SNDEU1 | <.001 | | <.001 | | <.001 | |
| QCPL4 | <.001 | | <.001 | | <.001 | |
| S X Q | .102 | | <.001 | | .039 | |
| All Factors | | .57 | | .51 | | .25 |

TABLE E.28. Means and standard deviations of primary dependent variable for each combination of SNDEU1 and QCPL2.

| SNDEU1 | QCPL2 | EU2 Mean | EU2 SD | GAIN Mean | GAIN SD | GAMMA Mean | GAMMA SD | N |
|---|---|---|---|---|---|---|---|---|
| /s/ low | Not good | 21.1 | 23.3 | 62.4 | 29.4 | 4.2 | 31.9 | 40 |
| | OK | 40.7 | 21.7 | 84.7 | 19.6 | 28.0 | 32.8 | 25 |
| | Good | 49.3 | 26.1 | 89.9 | 11.8 | 37.8 | 36.8 | 43 |
| /s/ medium | Not good | 34.5 | 18.2 | 57.3 | 24.3 | 1.3 | 28.0 | 44 |
| | OK | 45.8 | 15.8 | 70.1 | 14.1 | 20.5 | 23.5 | 21 |
| | Good | 67.7 | 25.1 | 69.0 | 16.8 | 48.8 | 27.4 | 15 |
| /s/ high | Not good | 67.4 | 21.3 | 25.0 | 17.0 | -0.6 | 17.0 | 34 |
| | OK | 73.3 | 17.7 | 25.9 | 22.4 | 5.0 | 19.6 | 19 |
| | Good | 82.2 | 11.6 | 27.0 | 20.5 | 10.0 | 18.6 | 28 |
| /r/ low | Not good | 6.3 | 6.4 | 30.4 | 27.9 | -8.7 | 17.5 | 44 |
| | OK | 10.6 | 10.8 | 52.1 | 33.2 | -14.0 | 19.7 | 21 |
| | Good | 35.6 | 26.6 | 78.3 | 21.8 | 19.6 | 32.1 | 29 |
| /r/ medium | Not good | 26.5 | 14.0 | 38.5 | 29.7 | -7.4 | 17.4 | 47 |
| | OK | 36.0 | 14.0 | 54.7 | 20.7 | 2.6 | 16.7 | 28 |
| | Good | 55.2 | 18.6 | 68.0 | 13.8 | 24.5 | 25.0 | 26 |
| /r/ high | Not good | 61.3 | 21.5 | 21.8 | 19.3 | -5.0 | 16.8 | 34 |
| | OK | 70.4 | 18.9 | 29.4 | 22.9 | 2.6 | 19.0 | 31 |
| | Good | 81.1 | 16.2 | 28.8 | 17.0 | 9.1 | 13.3 | 26 |
| Total | | 45.1 | 29.4 | 50.1 | 31.1 | 7.7 | 28.8 | 555 |

TABLE E.29. Summary of ANOVA. p(F) and R² for NOSESS with QCPL2 in two-way ANOVA. N = 555 (B sample).

| | Dependent | | | | | |
|---|---|---|---|---|---|---|
| | EU2 | | GAIN | | GAMMA | |
| Independent | p(F) | $R^2$ | p(F) | $R^2$ | p(F) | $R^2$ |
| QCPL2 | < .001 | | < .001 | | < .001 | |
| NOSESS | .087 | | .497 | | .189 | |
| N X Q | .106 | | .204 | | .001 | |
| All Factors | | .16 | | .11 | | .20 |

TABLE E.30. Summary of ANOVA. p(F) and R² for NGP with QCPL2 in two-way ANOVA. N = 555 (B Sample).

| | Dependent | | | | | |
|---|---|---|---|---|---|---|
| | EU2 | | GAIN | | GAMMA | |
| Independent | p(F) | $R^2$ | p(F) | $R^2$ | p(F) | $R^2$ |
| QCPL2 | < .001 | | < .001 | | < .001 | |
| NGP | .629 | | .172 | | .014 | |
| N X Q | .496 | | .238 | | .026 | |
| All Factors | | .17 | | .12 | | .21 |

TABLE E.31. Means and standard deviations of primary dependent variables for each combination of QCPL2 and NGP. N = 555 (B Sample).

| | | EU2 | | GAIN | | GAMMA | | |
|---|---|---|---|---|---|---|---|---|
| QCPL2 | NGP | Mean | SD | Mean | SD | Mean | SD | N |
| Not good | Two | 33.8 | 26.6 | 41.8 | 28.7 | -10.3 | 23.2 | 82 |
| | Three | 36.4 | 29.0 | 38.6 | 28.8 | 0.2 | 23.0 | 123 |
| | Four | 26.4 | 24.3 | 39.4 | 34.3 | -0.4 | 21.4 | 34 |
| OK | Two | 47.8 | 29.4 | 51.0 | 29.3 | 9.7 | 24.3 | 68 |
| | Three | 46.4 | 23.1 | 55.1 | 31.1 | 6.4 | 26.8 | 60 |
| | Four | 44.1 | 28.3 | 49.2 | 35.2 | -0.8 | 30.0 | 17 |
| Good | Two | 60.8 | 29.6 | 59.5 | 32.0 | 17.9 | 31.8 | 59 |
| | Three | 58.1 | 27.8 | 71.6 | 28.3 | 33.1 | 31.9 | 51 |
| | Four | 61.7 | 24.4 | 57.4 | 29.8 | 24.8 | 27.2 | 49 |
| Total | | 45.1 | | 49.9 | | 7.6 | | 555 |

TABLE E.32. Joint distribution of QCPL2 and YEAR.

Independent Variables: YEAR, QCPL2
Cells are count over row percent over asd
N = 555 (B Sample)

|  |  | Year |  |  |
| QCPL2 | Two | Three | Four | Total |
|---|---|---|---|---|
| Not good | 129 | 97 | 17 | 243 |
|  | 53 | 40 | 7 | 100 |
|  | -1.1 | 6.0 | -5.7 |  |
| OK | 70 | 27 | 48 | 145 |
|  | 48 | 19 | 33 | 100 |
|  | -2.1 | -2.6 | 5.8 |  |
| Good | 110 | 26 | 31 | 167 |
|  | 66 | 16 | 18 | 100 |
|  | 3.2 | -4.0 | 0.5 |  |
| Total | 309 | 150 | 96 | 555 |
|  | 56 | 27 | 17 | 100 |

chi-square = 67.7,     df = 4,     $p < .001$

TABLE E.33. Clinician and child number for selected K and L /s/ and L and O /r/ learning curves.

| /s/ |  |  |  | /r/ |  |  |  |
|---|---|---|---|---|---|---|---|
| K |  | L |  | L |  | O |  |
| Clin. | Child | Clin. | Child | Clin. | Child | Clin. | Child |
| 39 | 8 | 41 | 36 | 39 | 1 | 46 | 113 |
| 39 | 10 | 45 | 92 | 39 | 6 | 48 | 139 |
| 42 | 46 | 46 | 106 | 40 | 20 | 57 | 406 |
| 42 | 47 | 46 | 109 | 41 | 40 | 57 | 407 |
| 44 | 80 | 48 | 142 | 42 | 53 | 59 | 448 |
| 55 | 217 | 52 | 293 | 48 | 137 | 59 | 449 |
| 62 | 419 | 52 | 294 | 62 | 417 | 58 | 491 |
| 56 | 438 | 64 | 507 | 53 | 453 |  |  |
|  |  |  |  | 64 | 509 |  |  |

TABLE E.34. Characteristics for eight K /s/ and eight L /s/ children, including average percent GAIN for each group at three time periods, clinician, child, EU1 (baseline percent correct), Peabody IQ, reading percentile, total raw score on the Token Test (Subtest IV), Detroit (memory for syllables), geography, grade, number in therapy group (NGP), and previous therapy. All children had therapy twice a week.

| Group | Clinician No. | Child No. | EU1 | IQ | Reading | Token | Detroit | Geography | Grade | NGP | Previous Therapy |
|---|---|---|---|---|---|---|---|---|---|---|---|
| K /s/ | 39 | 8 | 0 | 116 | 34 | 15 | 49 | 4 | 3 | 3 | No |
| (n = 8) | 39 | 10 | 0 | 95 | 58 | 14 | 46 | 4 | 3 | 3 | No |
| Average GAIN | 42 | 46 | 32 | 90 | 64 | 18 | 79 | 4 | 3 | 2 | No |
| EU1-EU2 56% | 42 | 47 | 0 | 114 | 37 | 18 | 37 | 4 | 3 | 2 | No |
| EU2-EU3 32% | 44 | 80 | 17 | 111 | 60 | 19 | 78 | 4 | 4 | 2 | Yes |
| EU3-EU4 1% | 55 | 217 | 0 | 110 | 22 | 20 | 46 | 3 | 2 | 2 | No |
| | 56 | 438 | 1 | 98 | 89 | 19 | 64 | 1 | 4 | 2 | No |
| | 62 | 419 | 0 | 127 | NA | 18 | 65 | 1 | 1 | 2 | No |
| Mean | | | 6.3 | 108 | 52 | 18 | 58 | 3.4 | 2.9 | 2.3 | |
| SD | | | 12.0 | 12.3 | 22.6 | 2.1 | 15.7 | 1.1 | 1.0 | 0.5 | |
| | | | | | | | | | | | |
| L /s/ | 41 | 36 | 1 | 91 | 15 | 13 | 43 | 4 | 2 | 3 | No |
| (n = 8) | 45 | 92 | 3 | 98 | 75 | 12 | 45 | 4 | 1 | 3 | No |
| Average GAIN | 46 | 106 | 0 | 105 | 30 | 16 | 43 | 4 | 1 | 2 | No |
| EU1-EU2 2% | 46 | 109 | 4 | 91 | 41 | 13 | 37 | 4 | 1 | 2 | Yes |
| EU2-EU3 31% | 48 | 142 | 3 | 111 | 72 | 16 | 26 | 4 | 2 | 2 | No |
| EU3-EU4 34% | 52 | 293 | 11 | 116 | 89 | 17 | 57 | 3 | 3 | 2 | Yes |
| | 52 | 294 | 6 | 116 | 93 | 16 | 65 | 3 | 2 | 2 | Yes |
| | 64 | 507 | 1 | 101 | N/A | 9 | 22 | 1 | 1 | 2 | Yes |
| Mean | | | 3.5 | 104 | 59 | 14 | 42 | 3.1 | 1.6 | 2.3 | |
| SD | | | 3.6 | 10.1 | 30.5 | 2.7 | 14.4 | 1.4 | 0.7 | 0.5 | |
| t | | | 0.54 | 0.62 | 0.60 | 4.30 | 1.86 | 1.0 | 3.03 | 0 | |
| p | | | NS | NS | NS | <.01 | NS | NS | <.05 | NS | |

time periods: EU1-2, EU2-3, and EU3-4.

## L /s/ N=8

### ACTIVITY NAME

| TIME | FC | SS | Rdg | Cht | SD | GD | DM | SH | Asn | Oth |
|---|---|---|---|---|---|---|---|---|---|---|
| EU1–EU2 6 wks. | 10 | 1 | 0 | 12 | 42 | 3 | 4 | 7 | 8 | 11 |
| EU2–EU3 12 wks. | 16 | 2 | 1 | 14 | 32 | 12 | 1 | 1 | 12 | 9 |
| EU3–EU4 12 wks. | 13 | 11 | 8 | 13 | 25 | 10 | 0 | 0 | 11 | 9 |

### STIMULUS / CONSEQUATION REIN COST

| TIME | M | P | MP | G | CG | Oth | REIN | COST |
|---|---|---|---|---|---|---|---|---|
| EU1–EU2 6 wks. | 63 | 6 | 4 | 2 | 17 | 8 | 37 | 1 |
| EU2–EU3 12 wks. | 34 | 25 | 10 | 3 | 16 | 12 | 16 | 2 |
| EU3–EU4 12 wks. | 6 | 31 | 6 | 20 | 32 | 5 | 21 | 10 |

### CONTENT / POSITION

| TIME | I | S | W | PH | I | M | F | X | Bl |
|---|---|---|---|---|---|---|---|---|---|
| EU1–EU2 6 wks. | 60 | 12 | 24 | 4 | 69 | 0 | 9 | 22 | 0 |
| EU2–EU3 12 wks. | 10 | 26 | 33 | 31 | 47 | 2 | 7 | 41 | 3 |
| EU3–EU4 12 wks. | 1 | 0 | 45 | 54 | 6 | 2 | 1 | 84 | 7 |

## K /s/ N=8

### ACTIVITY NAME

| TIME | FC | SS | Rdg | Cht | SD | GD | DM | SH | Asn | Oth |
|---|---|---|---|---|---|---|---|---|---|---|
| EU1–EU2 6 wks. | 19 | 3 | 6 | 0 | 41 | 8 | 6 | 2 | 11 | 4 |
| EU2–EU3 12 wks. | 23 | 15 | 11 | 0 | 23 | 13 | 3 | 0 | 5 | 7 |
| EU3–EU4 12 wks. | 34 | 6 | 9 | 13 | 14 | 17 | 0 | 0 | 0 | 5 |

### STIMULUS / CONSEQUATION REIN COST

| TIME | M | P | MP | G | CG | Oth | REIN | COST |
|---|---|---|---|---|---|---|---|---|
| EU1–EU2 6 wks. | 30 | 10 | 2 | 28 | 27 | 3 | 29 | 12 |
| EU2–EU3 12 wks. | 6 | 31 | 1 | 26 | 35 | 1 | 4 | 5 |
| EU3–EU4 12 wks. | 4 | 20 | 0 | 20 | 34 | 22 | 22 | 42 |

### CONTENT / POSITION

| TIME | I | S | W | PH | I | M | F | X | Bl |
|---|---|---|---|---|---|---|---|---|---|
| EU1–EU2 6 wks. | 6 | 15 | 41 | 38 | 31 | 6 | 6 | 57 | 0 |
| EU2–EU3 12 wks. | 0 | 0 | 18 | 82 | 2 | 3 | 1 | 94 | 0 |
| EU3–EU4 12 wks. | 0 | 0 | 0 | 100 | 0 | 0 | 0 | 100 | 0 |

FC – Free Conversation
SS – Structured Speech
Rdg – Reading
Cht – Charting
SD – Standard Drill

GD – Game Drill
SH – Shaping
Asn – Assignment
Oth – Other Activities
DM – Discrimination

M – Auditory Model
P – Picture
MP – Model & Picture
G – Graphic
CG – Child Generated

I – Isolation
S – Syllable
W – Word
PH – Phrase/Sent.

I – Initial
M – Medial
F – Final
X – Mixed
Bl – Blend

TABLE E.36. Characteristics for seven O /r/ and nine L /r/ children include average percent GAIN for each group at these three time periods, clinician, child EU1 (baseline percent correct), Peabody IQ, reading percentile, total raw score on the Token Test (Subtest IV), Detroit (memory for syllables), geography, grade, number in therapy group (NGP), and previous therapy. All children had therapy twice a week.

| Group | Clinician No. | Child No. | EU1 | IQ | Reading | Token | Detroit | Geography | Grade | NGP | Previous Therapy |
|---|---|---|---|---|---|---|---|---|---|---|---|
| O /r/ | 46 | 113 | 1 | 90 | 35 | 17 | 34 | 4 | 3 | 2 | Yes |
| (n = 7) | 48 | 139 | 0 | 97 | N/A | 14 | 12 | 4 | 2 | 2 | No |
| Average GAIN | 57 | 406 | 13 | 82 | N/A | 15 | 45 | 1 | 3 | 2 | Yes |
| EU1-EU2    1% | 57 | 407 | 18 | 100 | N/A | 17 | 39 | 1 | 1 | 2 | No |
| EU2-EU3   10% | 58 | 491 | 20 | 116 | 82 | 17 | 75 | 1 | 3 | 2 | Yes |
| EU3-EU4    9% | 59 | 448 | 3 | 102 | 35 | 14 | 70 | 1 | 2 | 2 | No |
|  | 59 | 449 | 0 | 97 | 11 | 14 | 56 | 1 | 3 | 2 | No |
| Mean |  |  | 7.9 | 98 | 41 | 15 | 47 | 1.9 | 2.4 | 2 |  |
| SD |  |  | 8.2 | 9.7 | 25.8 | 1.4 | 20.2 | 1.4 | 0.9 | 0 |  |
|  |  |  |  |  |  |  |  |  |  |  |  |
| L /r/ | 39 | 3 | 5 | 104 | 50 | 19 | 44 | 4 | 2 | 3 | No |
| (n = 9) | 39 | 6 | 27 | 90 | N/A | 16 | 58 | 4 | 2 | 2 | Yes |
| Av. GAIN | 40 | 20 | 25 | 108 | 77 | 17 | 54 | 4 | 1 | 2 | Yes |
| EU1-EU2    3% | 41 | 40 | 10 | 90 | N/A | 10 | 33 | 4 | 3 | 2 | Yes |
| EU2-EU3   36% | 42 | 53 | 0 | 111 | 11 | 11 | 53 | 4 | 2 | 2 | No |
| EU3-EU4   34% | 48 | 137 | 0 | 108 | 30 | 17 | 69 | 4 | 3 | 2 | Yes |
|  | 62 | 417 | 13 | 121 | N/A | 13 | 42 | 1 | 1 | 2 | No |
|  | 59 | 453 | 9 | 112 | 8 | 19 | 61 | 1 | 4 | 2 | Yes |
|  | 64 | 509 | 1 | 102 | 86 | 8 | 39 | 1 | 2 | 2 | Yes |
| Mean |  |  | 10.0 | 105 | 44 | 14 | 50 | 3.0 | 2.2 | 2 |  |
| SD |  |  | 9.6 | 9.5 | 30.2 | 3.8 | 11.0 | 1.4 | 0.9 | 0 |  |
| t |  |  | 0.04 | 0.05 | 0.01 | 0.05 | 0.02 | 1.53 | 0.46 | 0 |  |
| p |  |  | NS | NS | NS | NS | NS | NS | NS | NS |  |

TABLE E.3/. Percent of activities for L and O learning curves for 16 /r/ children summarized for three time periods: EU1-2, EU2-3, EU3-4.

## L /r/ N=9

### ACTIVITY NAME

| TIME | FC | SS | Rdg | Cht | SD | GD | DM | SH | Asn | Oth |
|---|---|---|---|---|---|---|---|---|---|---|
| EU1-EU2 6 wks. | 13 | 3 | 0 | 3 | 53 | 1 | 7 | 8 | 8 | 4 |
| EU2-EU3 12 wks. | 17 | 3 | 2 | 6 | 39 | 15 | 0 | 0 | 12 | 6 |
| EU3-EU4 12 wks. | 23 | 7 | 11 | 12 | 21 | 11 | 0 | 0 | 10 | 5 |

| TIME | STIMULUS | | | | | | CONSEQUATION | |
|---|---|---|---|---|---|---|---|---|
| | M | P | MP | G | CG | Oth | REIN | COST |
| EU1-EU2 6 wks. | 41 | 8 | 15 | 12 | 19 | 5 | 21 | 5 |
| EU2-EU3 12 wks. | 10 | 41 | 5 | 11 | 25 | 8 | 26 | 13 |
| EU3-EU4 12 wks. | 3 | 35 | 0 | 24 | 31 | 7 | 16 | 7 |

| TIME | CONTENT | | | | POSITION | | | | |
|---|---|---|---|---|---|---|---|---|---|
| | I | S | W | PH | I | M | F | X | Bl |
| EU1-EU2 6 wks. | 27 | 30 | 34 | 9 | 64 | 2 | 11 | 22 | 1 |
| EU2-EU3 12 wks. | 1 | 7 | 58 | 34 | 27 | 7 | 16 | 50 | 0 |
| EU3-EU4 12 wks. | 0 | 0 | 25 | 75 | 4 | 4 | 1 | 78 | 13 |

## O /r/ N=7

### ACTIVITY NAME

| TIME | FC | SS | Rdg | Cht | SD | GD | DM | SH | Asn | Oth |
|---|---|---|---|---|---|---|---|---|---|---|
| EU1-EU2 6 wks. | 19 | 2 | 1 | 8 | 29 | 10 | 8 | 6 | 17 | 0 |
| EU2-EU3 12 wks. | 21 | 1 | 0 | 9 | 27 | 21 | 2 | 1 | 13 | 5 |
| EU3-EU4 12 wks. | 24 | 3 | 0 | 6 | 27 | 17 | 1 | 1 | 17 | 4 |

| TIME | STIMULUS | | | | | | CONSEQUATION | |
|---|---|---|---|---|---|---|---|---|---|
| | M | P | MP | G | CG | Oth | REIN | COST |
| EU1-EU2 6 wks. | 45 | 10 | 3 | 18 | 23 | 1 | 19 | 6 |
| EU2-EU3 12 wks. | 30 | 14 | 4 | 14 | 32 | 6 | 18 | 4 |
| EU3-EU4 12 wks. | 30 | 13 | 2 | 21 | 27 | 7 | 25 | 13 |

| TIME | CONTENT | | | | POSITION | | | | |
|---|---|---|---|---|---|---|---|---|---|
| | I | S | W | PH | I | M | F | X | Bl |
| EU1-EU2 6 wks. | 14 | 12 | 47 | 27 | 47 | 5 | 0 | 47 | 1 |
| EU2-EU3 12 wks. | 6 | 13 | 40 | 41 | 49 | 4 | 6 | 41 | 0 |
| EU3-EU4 12 wks. | 3 | 9 | 42 | 46 | 31 | 8 | 13 | 44 | 5 |

FC  - Free Conversation
SS  - Structured Speech
Rdg - Reading
Cht - Charting
SD  - Standard Drill

GD  - Game Drill
DM  - Discrimination
SH  - Shaping
Asn - Assignment
Oth - Other Activities

M  - Auditory Model
P  - Picture
MP - Model & Picture
G  - Graphic
CG - Child Generated

I  - Isolation
S  - Syllable
W  - Word
PH - Phrase/Sent.

I  - Initial
M  - Medial
F  - Final
X  - Mixed
Bl - Blend

Table E.38. Summary means for the amount of time (in minutes), number of therapy sessions, and number of different therapy activities, spent by each learning curve group for the three blocks of time EU1-2, 2-3, and 3-4 during the school year.

| | K /s/ N = 8 | | | L /s/ N = 8 | | | L /r/ N = 9 | | | O /r/ N = 7 | | |
|---|---|---|---|---|---|---|---|---|---|---|---|---|
| | Time (Min.) | No. Sess | No. Act | Time (Min.) | No. Sess | No. Act | Time (Min.) | No. Sess | No. Act | Time (Min.) | No. Sess | No. Act |
| EU1–EU2 6 wks. | 113 | 8 | 17 | 127 | 8 | 17 | 122 | 8 | 22 | 232 | 12 | 30 |
| EU2–EU3 12 wks. | 173 | 10 | 21 | 200 | 11 | 26 | 183 | 11 | 25 | 203 | 12 | 26 |
| EU3–EU4 12 wks. | 118 | 8 | 17 | 222 | 14 | 30 | 269 | 13 | 35 | 288 | 16 | 41 |
| Total | 404 | 26 | 55 | 549 | 33 | 73 | 574 | 32 | 82 | 723 | 40 | 97 |
| X̄ Time | | 17 | 7 | | 17 | 8 | | 18 | 7 | | 18 | 7 |
| X̄ Act/Sess | | | 2.3 | | | 2.2 | | | 2.6 | | | 2.4 |

TABLE E.39. Comparison of children between high and low Clinician Performance Level. CPL2 (at 6 weeks) and CPL4 (at 30 weeks) on several categories (sound, EU1, EU2, GAIN, and GAMMA).

| | CLINO | CPL2 | CPL4 | Number of Children | /s/ Low <7 | /s/ Medium 7-33 | /s/ High >33 | /r/ Low <7 | /r/ Medium 7-33 | /r/ High >33 | EU1 | EU2 | GAIN | GAMMA |
|---|---|---|---|---|---|---|---|---|---|---|---|---|---|---|
| High | 63 | 36 | 38 | 7 | 0 | 2 | 1 | 3 | 0 | 1 | 28 | 62 | 59 | 27 |
| | 56 | 34 | 34 | 9 | 1 | 2 | 1 | 1 | 2 | 2 | 27 | 66 | 64 | 38 |
| | 44 | 32 | 35 | 7 | 0 | 4 | 0 | 1 | 2 | 0 | 21 | 60 | 75 | 29 |
| | 65 | 32 | 38 | 9 | 3 | 0 | 0 | 0 | 4 | 2 | 18 | 56 | 79 | 29 |
| | 39 | 39 | 35 | 9 | 3 | 0 | 2 | 2 | 1 | 1 | 31 | 60 | 66 | 19 |
| | 42 | 34 | 35 | 6 | 1 | 1 | 2 | 1 | 0 | 1 | 46 | 69 | 46 | 13 |
| | 61 | 31 | 32 | 7 | 4 | 1 | 0 | 1 | 0 | 1 | 14 | 54 | 78 | 29 |
| MEAN | | 34.0 | 35.3 | | | | | | | | 26.4 | 61.0 | 66.7 | 26.3 |
| SD | | 2.6 | 2.0 | | | | | | | | 9.7 | 4.9 | 11.0 | 7.5 |
| Low | 52 | 23 | 29 | 6 | 1 | 1 | 0 | 0 | 0 | 4 | 37 | 29 | 38 | -30 |
| | 45 | 30 | 28 | 9 | 4 | 0 | 1 | 0 | 1 | 3 | 29 | 39 | 58 | -4 |
| | 41 | 29 | 32 | 9 | 3 | 0 | 1 | 0 | 2 | 3 | 31 | 38 | 50 | -13 |
| | 57 | 26 | 24 | 7 | 1 | 3 | 0 | 0 | 2 | 1 | 22 | 35 | 46 | 5 |
| | 59 | 29 | 29 | 8 | 2 | 0 | 2 | 2 | 0 | 1 | 27 | 37 | 44 | 0 |
| | 58 | 26 | 28 | 6 | 1 | 2 | 1 | 0 | 2 | 0 | 24 | 42 | 53 | 10 |
| | 48 | 28 | 31 | 6 | 1 | 1 | 0 | 2 | 0 | 2 | 31 | 39 | 48 | -13 |
| MEAN | | 27.3 | 28.7 | | | | | | | | 28.7 | 37.0 | 48.1 | -7.6 |
| SD | | 2.2 | 2.4 | | | | | | | | 4.6 | 3.8 | 6.0 | 12.5 |
| t | | 4.82 | 5.21 | | | | | | | | -0.52 | 9.50 | 3.64 | 11.34 |
| p | | <.001 | <.001 | | | | | | | | N | <.001 | <.01 | <.001 |

Tables E.40-E.50. All lesson plan data was tallied for each child. The total number of events for all children in high or low CPL were tabulated. Each cell represents the proportion for each event under each category. Each row represents 100% of all the events listed for each category: ACTIVITY NAME, STIMULUS, CONTENT, and POSITION for each of three time periods, first six weeks of therapy, the next 12 weeks, and the final 12 weeks. Consequation represents the number of times (in percent) the clinician planned to use reinforcement or cost for all the activities performed within that time period.

TABLE E.40. Percent of activities summarized for three time periods (EU1-EU2, EU2-EU3, EU3-EU4) for high and low CPL and for low baseline /r/ children.

**HIGH CPL for /r/ LOW (0-6%), N=10**

ACTIVITY NAME

| TIME | FC | SS | Rdg | Cht | SD | GD | DM | SH | Asn | Oth |
|---|---|---|---|---|---|---|---|---|---|---|
| EU1-EU2 6 wks. | 9 | 3 | 1 | 10 | 36 | 5 | 8 | 7 | 12 | 10 |
| EU2-EU3 12 wks. | 17 | 3 | 6 | 3 | 29 | 10 | 3 | 4 | 21 | 5 |
| EU3-EU4 12 wks. | 21 | 15 | 8 | 9 | 22 | 9 | 1 | 1 | 7 | 7 |

| | STIMULUS | | | | | | CONSEQUATION | |
|---|---|---|---|---|---|---|---|---|
| TIME | M | P | MP | G | CG | Oth | REIN | COST |
| EU1-EU2 6 wks. | 39 | 22 | 15 | 10 | 14 | - | 30 | 100 |
| EU2-EU3 12 wks. | 14 | 28 | 5 | 32 | 21 | - | 43 | - |
| EU3-EU4 12 wks. | 9 | 37 | 2 | 20 | 33 | - | 26 | - |

| | CONTENT | | | POSITION | | | | |
|---|---|---|---|---|---|---|---|---|
| TIME | S | W | PH | I | M | F | X | Bl |
| EU1-EU2 6 wks. | 16 | 50 | 23 | 38 | 8 | 19 | 30 | 5 |
| EU2-EU3 12 wks. | 8 | 38 | 53 | 18 | 7 | 8 | 60 | 7 |
| EU3-EU4 12 wks. | 3 | 26 | 71 | 6 | 5 | 5 | 84 | - |

Note: HIGH CONTENT/POSITION leading column (I): 11, 1, - for the three time periods.

**LOW CPL for /r/ LOW (0-6%), N=4**

ACTIVITY NAME

| TIME | FC | SS | Rdg | Cht | SD | GD | DM | SH | Asn | Oth |
|---|---|---|---|---|---|---|---|---|---|---|
| EU1-EU2 6 wks. | 27 | 1 | - | 4 | 35 | 13 | 2 | 3 | 13 | 1 |
| EU2-EU3 12 wks. | 30 | - | - | - | 32 | 24 | 1 | - | 8 | 5 |
| EU3-EU4 12 wks. | 36 | 2 | 5 | 1 | 31 | 16 | - | - | 5 | 4 |

| | STIMULUS | | | | | | CONSEQUATION | |
|---|---|---|---|---|---|---|---|---|
| TIME | M | P | MP | G | CG | Oth | REIN | COST |
| EU1-EU2 6 wks. | 37 | 13 | 6 | 9 | 34 | - | 41 | 44 |
| EU2-EU3 12 wks. | 31 | 21 | 3 | 7 | 38 | - | 30 | 0 |
| EU3-EU4 12 wks. | 35 | 23 | - | 9 | 33 | - | 30 | 56 |

| | CONTENT | | | | POSITION | | | | |
|---|---|---|---|---|---|---|---|---|---|
| TIME | I | S | W | PH | I | M | F | X | B1 |
| EU1-EU2 6 wks. | 33 | 18 | 27 | 22 | 59 | - | 5 | 36 | - |
| EU2-EU3 12 wks. | 12 | 30 | 23 | 36 | 73 | 6 | 3 | 18 | - |
| EU3-EU4 12 wks. | 1 | 13 | 37 | 49 | 21 | 20 | 10 | 50 | - |

TABLE E.41. Percent of activities summarized for three time periods (EU1-EU2, EU2-EU3, EU3-EU4) for high and low CPL and medium baseline /r/ children.

**HIGH CPL for /r/ MEDIUM (7-33%), N=8 — ACTIVITY NAME**

| TIME | FC | SS | Rdg | Cht | SD | GD | DM | SH | Asn | Oth |
|---|---|---|---|---|---|---|---|---|---|---|
| EU1-EU2 6 wks. | 16 | 7 | 2 | - | 44 | 2 | 10 | 3 | 5 | 10 |
| EU2-EU3 12 wks. | 15 | 9 | 9 | - | 33 | 6 | 11 | - | 9 | 7 |
| EU3-EU4 12 wks. | 21 | 17 | 10 | 4 | 19 | 12 | 3 | - | 7 | 7 |

**LOW CPL for /r/ MEDIUM (7-33%), N=8 — ACTIVITY NAME**

| TIME | FC | SS | Rdg | Cht | SD | GD | DM | SH | Asn | Oth |
|---|---|---|---|---|---|---|---|---|---|---|
| EU1-EU2 6 wks. | 19 | 2 | 2 | 1 | 28 | 8 | 12 | 7 | 17 | 4 |
| EU2-EU3 12 wks. | 16 | 2 | - | 4 | 25 | 22 | 4 | 1 | 22 | 6 |
| EU3-EU4 12 wks. | 19 | 4 | 1 | 3 | 28 | 16 | 1 | 1 | 21 | 6 |

**HIGH CPL — STIMULUS / CONSEQUATION**

| TIME | STIMULUS | | | | | | CONSEQUATION | |
|---|---|---|---|---|---|---|---|---|
| | M | P | MP | G | CG | Oth | REIN | COST |
| EU1-EU2 6 wks. | 50 | 17 | - | 10 | 23 | - | 50 | - |
| EU2-EU3 12 wks. | 34 | 16 | 1 | 21 | 27 | - | 17 | - |
| EU3-EU4 12 wks. | 15 | 27 | 1 | 22 | 36 | - | 33 | - |

**LOW CPL — STIMULUS / CONSEQUATION**

| TIME | STIMULUS | | | | | | CONSEQUATION | |
|---|---|---|---|---|---|---|---|---|
| | M | P | MP | G | CG | Oth | REIN | COST |
| EU1-EU2 6 wks. | 37 | 10 | 4 | 24 | 25 | - | 33 | 30 |
| EU2-EU3 12 wks. | 23 | 20 | 5 | 20 | 32 | - | 33 | 20 |
| EU3-EU4 12 wks. | 20 | 25 | 1 | 30 | 23 | - | 33 | 50 |

**HIGH CPL — CONTENT / POSITION**

| TIME | CONTENT | | | | POSITION | | | | |
|---|---|---|---|---|---|---|---|---|---|
| | I | S | W | PH | I | M | F | X | Bl |
| EU1-EU2 6 wks. | 6 | 12 | 51 | 31 | 26 | 5 | 15 | 53 | 2 |
| EU2-EU3 12 wks. | 4 | 5 | 46 | 46 | 14 | 4 | 8 | 65 | 8 |
| EU3-EU4 12 wks. | - | - | 23 | 77 | - | 3 | 9 | 83 | 5 |

**LOW CPL — CONTENT / POSITION**

| TIME | CONTENT | | | | POSITION | | | | |
|---|---|---|---|---|---|---|---|---|---|
| | I | S | W | PH | I | M | F | X | Bl |
| EU1-EU2 6 wks. | 11 | 7 | 52 | 30 | 41 | 1 | 4 | 54 | 1 |
| EU2-EU3 12 wks. | 2 | 9 | 51 | 38 | 32 | 4 | 7 | 57 | - |
| EU3-EU4 12 wks. | 2 | 3 | 49 | 46 | 19 | 5 | 7 | 65 | 5 |

TABLE E.42. Percent of activities summarized for three time periods (EU1-EU2, EU2-EU3, EU3-EU4) for high and low CPL and for high baseline /r/ children.

## HIGH CPL for /r/ HIGH (34-100%), N=2

### ACTIVITY NAME

| TIME | FC | SS | Rdg | Cht | SD | GD | DM | SH | Asn | Oth |
|---|---|---|---|---|---|---|---|---|---|---|
| EU1-EU2 6 wks. | 7 | 7 | 11 | 30 | 7 | - | 15 | - | 4 | 19 |
| EU2-EU3 12 wks. | 13 | 6 | 15 | 4 | 23 | 4 | - | 4 | 23 | 8 |
| EU3-EU4 12 wks. | - | - | - | - | - | - | - | - | - | - |

### STIMULUS / CONSEQUATION

| TIME | M | P | MP | G | CG | Oth | REIN | COST |
|---|---|---|---|---|---|---|---|---|
| EU1-EU2 6 wks. | 18 | 24 | 18 | 18 | 24 | - | 100 | - |
| EU2-EU3 12 wks. | 14 | 11 | - | 47 | 28 | - | - | - |
| EU3-EU4 12 wks. | - | - | - | - | - | - | - | - |

### CONTENT / POSITION

| TIME | I | S | W | PH | I | M | F | X | BI |
|---|---|---|---|---|---|---|---|---|---|
| EU1-EU2 6 wks. | 6 | - | 41 | 53 | 13 | 6 | - | 69 | 13 |
| EU2-EU3 12 wks. | - | 3 | 25 | 72 | 6 | 6 | - | 89 | - |
| EU3-EU4 12 wks. | - | - | - | - | - | - | - | - | - |

## LOW CPL for /r/ HIGH (34-100%), N=6

### ACTIVITY NAME

| TIME | FC | SS | Rdg | Cht | SD | GD | DM | SH | Asn | Oth |
|---|---|---|---|---|---|---|---|---|---|---|
| EU1-EU2 6 wks. | 18 | 2 | - | 4 | 36 | 8 | 10 | 2 | 13 | 7 |
| EU2-EU3 12 wks. | 13 | - | 7 | 5 | 21 | 19 | 1 | - | 20 | 14 |
| EU3-EU4 12 wks. | 44 | 22 | 22 | - | 11 | - | - | - | - | - |

### STIMULUS / CONSEQUATION

| TIME | M | P | MP | G | CG | Oth | REIN | COST |
|---|---|---|---|---|---|---|---|---|
| EU1-EU2 6 wks. | 41 | 11 | 6 | 13 | 29 | - | 100 | 100 |
| EU2-EU3 12 wks. | 11 | 38 | 5 | 26 | 21 | - | - | - |
| EU3-EU4 12 wks. | 29 | 29 | - | 29 | 14 | - | - | - |

### CONTENT / POSITION

| TIME | I | S | W | PH | I | M | F | X | BI |
|---|---|---|---|---|---|---|---|---|---|
| EU1-EU2 6 wks. | 13 | 19 | 50 | 19 | 40 | 3 | 6 | 51 | - |
| EU2-EU3 12 wks. | 2 | 11 | 50 | 28 | 48 | 2 | 3 | 47 | - |
| EU3-EU4 12 wks. | - | - | 20 | 80 | 20 | - | - | 80 | - |

TABLE E.43. Percent of activities summarized for the entire year for high and low CPL and for low and medium baseline /r/ children combined.

**HIGH CPL for /r/ LOW & MEDIUM, N=18**

TIME: 30 wks.

| ACTIVITY NAME | | | | | | | | | |
|---|---|---|---|---|---|---|---|---|---|
| FC | SS | Rdg | Cht | SD | GD | DM | SH | Asn | Oth |
| 17 | 9 | 6 | 5 | 29 | 8 | 5 | 2 | 11 | 8 |

| STIMULUS | | | | | | CONSEQUATION | |
|---|---|---|---|---|---|---|---|
| M | P | MP | G | CG | Oth | REIN | COST |
| 24 | 26 | 4 | 20 | 26 | - | | |

| CONTENT | | | | POSITION | | | | |
|---|---|---|---|---|---|---|---|---|
| I | S | W | PH | I | M | F | X | Bl |
| 3 | 7 | 38 | 52 | 16 | 5 | 10 | 64 | 5 |

**LOW CPL for /r/ LOW & MEDIUM, N=12**

TIME: 30 wks.

| ACTIVITY NAME | | | | | | | | | |
|---|---|---|---|---|---|---|---|---|---|
| FC | SS | Rdg | Cht | SD | GD | DM | SH | Asn | Oth |
| 23 | 2 | 2 | 2 | 29 | 16 | 3 | 2 | 16 | 5 |

| STIMULUS | | | | | | CONSEQUATION | |
|---|---|---|---|---|---|---|---|
| M | P | MP | G | CG | Oth | REIN | COST |
| 28 | 20 | 3 | 20 | 29 | - | | |

| CONTENT | | | | POSITION | | | | |
|---|---|---|---|---|---|---|---|---|
| I | S | W | PH | I | M | F | X | Bl |
| 7 | 10 | 44 | 39 | 32 | 6 | 6 | 54 | 2 |

TABLE E.44. Percent of activities summarized for the entire year for high and low CPL and for low, medium, and high baseline /r/ children combined.

**HIGH CPL for /r/ LOW, MEDIUM, & HIGH, N=20**

TIME: 30 wks.

| ACTIVITY NAME | | | | | | | | | |
|---|---|---|---|---|---|---|---|---|---|
| FC | SS | Rdg | Cht | SD | GD | DM | SH | Asn | Oth |
| 16 | 9 | 7 | 5 | 29 | 8 | 5 | 2 | 11 | 8 |

| STIMULUS | | | | | | CONSEQUATION | |
|---|---|---|---|---|---|---|---|
| M | P | MP | G | CG | Oth | REIN | COST |
| 24 | 25 | 4 | 21 | 26 | - | | |

| CONTENT | | | | POSITION | | | | |
|---|---|---|---|---|---|---|---|---|
| I | S | W | PH | I | M | F | X | Bl |
| 3 | 7 | 37 | 53 | 15 | 5 | 10 | 65 | 5 |

**LOW CPL for /r/ LOW, MEDIUM, HIGH, N=18**

TIME: 30 wks.

| ACTIVITY NAME | | | | | | | | | |
|---|---|---|---|---|---|---|---|---|---|
| FC | SS | Rdg | Cht | SD | GD | DM | SH | Asn | Oth |
| 23 | 2 | 2 | 3 | 29 | 16 | 4 | 2 | 16 | 6 |

| STIMULUS | | | | | | CONSEQUATION | |
|---|---|---|---|---|---|---|---|
| M | P | MP | G | CG | Oth | REIN | COST |
| 28 | 20 | 3 | 20 | 28 | - | | |

| CONTENT | | | | POSITION | | | | |
|---|---|---|---|---|---|---|---|---|
| I | S | W | PH | I | M | F | X | Bl |
| 7 | 11 | 45 | 37 | 34 | 5 | 6 | 53 | 1 |

TABLE E.45. Percent of activities summarized for three time periods (EU1-EU2, EU2-EU3, EU3-EU4) for high and low CPL and for low baseline /s/ children.

## HIGH CPL for /s/ LOW (0-6%), N=12

### ACTIVITY NAME

| TIME | FC | SS | Rdg | Cht | SD | GD | DM | SH | Asn | Oth |
|---|---|---|---|---|---|---|---|---|---|---|
| EU1-EU2 6 wks. | 10 | 1 | 3 | 4 | 32 | 8 | 15 | 6 | 14 | 8 |
| EU2-EU3 12 wks. | 19 | 9 | 9 | 2 | 27 | 20 | 2 | - | 6 | 7 |
| EU3-EU4 12 wks. | 29 | 13 | 12 | 7 | 12 | 21 | - | - | 2 | 3 |

### STIMULUS / CONSEQUATION

| TIME | M | P | MP | G | CG | Oth | REIN | COST |
|---|---|---|---|---|---|---|---|---|
| EU1-EU2 6 wks. | 49 | 17 | 2 | 20 | 12 | - | None reported | |
| EU2-EU3 12 wks. | 17 | 33 | 6 | 22 | 22 | - | None reported | |
| EU3-EU4 12 wks. | 6 | 38 | - | 21 | 35 | - | None reported | |

### CONTENT / POSITION

| TIME | I | S | W | PH | I | M | F | X | Bl |
|---|---|---|---|---|---|---|---|---|---|
| EU1-EU2 6 wks. | 12 | 14 | 37 | 37 | 45 | 1 | 3 | 51 | - |
| EU2-EU3 12 wks. | - | 1 | 39 | 60 | 12 | 3 | 5 | 80 | - |
| EU3-EU4 12 wks. | - | - | 17 | 83 | 3 | 1 | 1 | 95 | - |

## LOW CPL for /s/ (0-6%), N=13

### ACTIVITY NAME

| TIME | FC | SS | Rdg | Cht | SD | GD | DM | SH | Asn | Oth |
|---|---|---|---|---|---|---|---|---|---|---|
| EU1-EU2 6 wks. | 17 | 2 | - | - | 39 | 6 | 7 | 5 | 11 | 12 |
| EU2-EU3 12 wks. | 17 | 5 | 4 | 3 | 28 | 17 | 1 | 1 | 18 | 6 |
| EU3-EU4 12 wks. | 21 | 8 | 5 | 6 | 25 | 11 | 1 | - | 13 | 11 |

### STIMULUS / CONSEQUATION

| TIME | M | P | MP | G | CG | Oth | REIN | COST |
|---|---|---|---|---|---|---|---|---|
| EU1-EU2 6 wks. | 48 | 10 | 4 | 14 | 24 | - | 29 | 60 |
| EU2-EU3 12 wks. | 26 | 30 | 3 | 20 | 22 | - | 36 | 20 |
| EU3-EU4 12 wks. | 34 | 41 | 2 | 9 | 14 | - | 36 | 20 |

### CONTENT / POSITION

| TIME | I | S | W | PH | I | M | F | X | Bl |
|---|---|---|---|---|---|---|---|---|---|
| EU1-EU2 6 wks. | 25 | 10 | 33 | 31 | 52 | - | 3 | 44 | 1 |
| EU2-EU3 12 wks. | 4 | 9 | 42 | 45 | 35 | - | 5 | 59 | 2 |
| EU3-EU4 12 wks. | 1 | 1 | 30 | 68 | 15 | 4 | 5 | 77 | - |

TABLE E.46. Percent of activities summarized for three time periods (EU1-EU2, EU2-EU3, EU3-EU4) for high and low CPL and for medium baseline /s/ children.

## HIGH CPL for /s/ MEDIUM (7-33%), N=10

### ACTIVITY NAME

| TIME | FC | SS | Rdg | Cht | SD | GD | DM | SH | Asn | 0th |
|---|---|---|---|---|---|---|---|---|---|---|
| EU1-EU2 6 wks. | 19 | 2 | 4 | 10 | 26 | 4 | 9 | 5 | 14 | 8 |
| EU2-EU3 12 wks. | 20 | 15 | 12 | 5 | 23 | 7 | 4 | - | 8 | 6 |
| EU3-EU4 12 wks. | 11 | 16 | 12 | 1 | 12 | 11 | 1 | 1 | 15 | 12 |

### STIMULUS / CONSEQUATION

| TIME | M | P | MP | G | CG | 0th | REIN | COST |
|---|---|---|---|---|---|---|---|---|
| EU1-EU2 6 wks. | 35 | 15 | 6 | 25 | 16 | - | 67 | 67 |
| EU2-EU3 12 wks. | 18 | 18 | 2 | 25 | 37 | - | 0 | 0 |
| EU3-EU4 12 wks. | 10 | 16 | 1 | 35 | 38 | - | 33 | 33 |

### CONTENT / POSITION

| TIME | I | S | W | PH | I | M | F | X | Bl |
|---|---|---|---|---|---|---|---|---|---|
| EU1-EU2 6 wks. | 13 | 15 | 29 | 43 | 24 | - | 7 | 69 | - |
| EU2-EU3 12 wks. | - | 2 | 30 | 68 | 6 | 1 | 4 | 89 | - |
| EU3-EU4 12 wks. | - | 1 | 12 | 87 | 4 | - | 1 | 94 | 2 |

## LOW CPL for /s/ MEDIUM (7-33%), N=7

### ACTIVITY NAME

| TIME | FC | SS | Rdg | Cht | SD | GD | DM | SH | Asn | 0th |
|---|---|---|---|---|---|---|---|---|---|---|
| EU1-EU2 6 wks. | 15 | - | - | 2 | 26 | 2 | 19 | 6 | 15 | 15 |
| EU2-EU3 12 wks. | 17 | 4 | 3 | 6 | 23 | 17 | 3 | - | 16 | 12 |
| EU3-EU4 12 wks. | 16 | 7 | 9 | 11 | 10 | 16 | 1 | - | 17 | 13 |

### STIMULUS / CONSEQUATION

| TIME | M | P | MP | G | CG | 0th | REIN | COST |
|---|---|---|---|---|---|---|---|---|
| EU1-EU2 6 wks. | 46 | 8 | 2 | 24 | 20 | - | 35 | - |
| EU2-EU3 12 wks. | 22 | 17 | 2 | 40 | 20 | - | 65 | - |
| EU3-EU4 12 wks. | 14 | 21 | - | 44 | 21 | - | 0 | - |

### CONTENT / POSITION

| TIME | I | S | W | PH | I | M | F | X | Bl |
|---|---|---|---|---|---|---|---|---|---|
| EU1-EU2 6 wks. | 9 | 8 | 40 | 44 | 35 | 3 | 1 | 60 | 1 |
| EU2-EU3 12 wks. | 3 | 7 | 21 | 69 | 14 | 1 | 3 | 82 | 2 |
| EU3-EU4 12 wks. | 1 | - | 22 | 78 | 17 | 11 | 11 | 61 | - |

TABLE E.47. Percent of activities summarized for three time periods (EU1-EU2, EU2-EU3, EU3-EU4) for high and low CPL and for high baseline /s/ children.

## HIGH CPL for /s/ HIGH (34-100%), N=3

### ACTIVITY NAME

| TIME | FC | SS | Rdg | Cht | SD | GD | DM | SH | Asn | Oth |
|---|---|---|---|---|---|---|---|---|---|---|
| EU1-EU2 6 wks. | 18 | - | - | 3 | 38 | 10 | - | - | - | 31 |
| EU2-EU3 12 wks. | 25 | 15 | 6 | 2 | 11 | - | - | - | 8 | 34 |
| EU3-EU4 12 wks. | - | - | - | - | - | - | - | - | - | 100 |

### STIMULUS / CONSEQUENCE

| TIME | M | P | MP | G | CG | Oth | REIN | COST |
|---|---|---|---|---|---|---|---|---|
| EU1-EU2 6 wks. | 25 | 13 | - | 21 | 42 | - | 100 | - |
| EU2-EU3 12 wks. | 8 | 5 | - | 53 | 35 | - | 0 | - |
| EU3-EU4 12 wks. | - | - | - | - | - | - | 0 | - |

### CONTENT / POSITION

| TIME | I | S | W | PH | I | M | F | X | Bl |
|---|---|---|---|---|---|---|---|---|---|
| EU1-EU2 6 wks. | - | - | 33 | 66 | - | - | 4 | 96 | - |
| EU2-EU3 12 wks. | - | 8 | 8 | 85 | - | - | - | 100 | - |
| EU3-EU4 12 wks. | - | - | - | - | - | - | - | - | - |

## LOW CPL for /s/ HIGH (34-100%), N=3

### ACTIVITY NAME

| TIME | FC | SS | Rdg | Cht | SD | GD | DM | SH | Asn | Oth |
|---|---|---|---|---|---|---|---|---|---|---|
| EU1-EU2 6 wks. | 3 | - | 2 | - | 21 | 17 | 3 | - | 19 | 7 |
| EU2-EU3 12 wks. | 35 | - | - | - | 10 | 25 | - | - | 23 | 7 |
| EU3-EU4 12 wks. | 47 | 5 | 5 | - | 8 | 18 | - | - | 8 | 8 |

### STIMULUS / CONSEQUENCE

| TIME | M | P | MP | G | CG | Oth | REIN | COST |
|---|---|---|---|---|---|---|---|---|
| EU1-EU2 6 wks. | 30 | 11 | - | 11 | 49 | - | 33 | 100 |
| EU2-EU3 12 wks. | 13 | 18 | - | 7 | 56 | - | 66 | - |
| EU3-EU4 12 wks. | 5 | 13 | - | 13 | 69 | - | 0 | - |

### CONTENT / POSITION

| TIME | I | S | W | PH | I | M | F | X | Bl |
|---|---|---|---|---|---|---|---|---|---|
| EU1-EU2 6 wks. | - | 2 | 19 | 79 | - | - | - | 100 | - |
| EU2-EU3 12 wks. | 2 | 5 | 2 | 91 | 2 | - | - | 98 | - |
| EU3-EU4 12 wks. | - | - | 3 | 97 | - | - | - | 100 | - |

**HIGH CPL for /s/ LOW & MEDIUM, N=22** — EU1–EU2 6 wks.

ACTIVITY NAME

| FC | SS | Rdg | Cht | SD | GD | DM | SH | Asn | Oth |
|----|----|-----|-----|----|----|----|----|-----|-----|
| 15 | 1 | 3 | 7 | 29 | 6 | 12 | 5 | 14 | 8 |

STIMULUS / CONSEQUATION

| M | P | MP | G | CG | Oth | REIN | COST |
|---|---|----|---|----|-----|------|------|
| 43 | 16 | 4 | 23 | 14 | - | | |

CONTENT / POSITION

| I | S | W | PH | I | M | F | X | Bl |
|---|---|---|----|---|---|---|---|----|
| 12 | 15 | 33 | 40 | 35 | - | 5 | 60 | - |

**LOW CPL for /s/ LOW & MEDIUM, N=20** — EU1–EU2 6 wks.

ACTIVITY NAME

| FC | SS | Rdg | Cht | SD | GD | DM | SH | Asn | Oth |
|----|----|-----|-----|----|----|----|----|-----|-----|
| 16 | 1 | - | 1 | 33 | 4 | 13 | 5 | 13 | 14 |

STIMULUS / CONSEQUATION

| M | P | MP | G | CG | Oth | REIN | COST |
|---|---|----|---|----|-----|------|------|
| 47 | 9 | 3 | 19 | 22 | - | | |

CONTENT / POSITION

| I | S | W | PH | I | M | F | X | Bl |
|---|---|---|----|---|---|---|---|----|
| 17 | 9 | 37 | 37 | 43 | 2 | 2 | 52 | 1 |

**HIGH CPL for /s/ LOW & MEDIUM, N=22** — 30 wks.

ACTIVITY NAME

| FC | SS | Rdg | Cht | SD | GD | DM | SH | Asn | Oth |
|----|----|-----|-----|----|----|----|----|-----|-----|
| 18 | 10 | 9 | 5 | 24 | 12 | 5 | 2 | 9 | 7 |

STIMULUS / CONSEQUATION

| M | P | MP | G | CG | Oth | REIN | COST |
|---|---|----|---|----|-----|------|------|
| 22 | 23 | 3 | 24 | 27 | - | | |

CONTENT / POSITION

| I | S | W | PH | I | M | F | X | Bl |
|---|---|---|----|---|---|---|---|----|
| 4 | 5 | 29 | 63 | 14 | - | 4 | 81 | 1 |

**HIGH CPL for /s/ LOW & MEDIUM, N=20** — 30 wks.

ACTIVITY NAME

| FC | SS | Rdg | Cht | SD | GD | DM | SH | Asn | Oth |
|----|----|-----|-----|----|----|----|----|-----|-----|
| 17 | 5 | 3 | 5 | 26 | 12 | 4 | 2 | 15 | - |

STIMULUS / CONSEQUATION

| M | P | MP | G | CG | Oth | REIN | COST |
|---|---|----|---|----|-----|------|------|
| 30 | 21 | 2 | 26 | 21 | - | | |

CONTENT / POSITION

| I | S | W | PH | I | M | F | X | Bl |
|---|---|---|----|---|---|---|---|----|
| 7 | 6 | 32 | 55 | 27 | 2 | 5 | 65 | 1 |

TABLE E.50. Percent of activities summarized for the entire year for high and low CPL and for low, medium, and high baseline /s/ children combined.

## HIGH CPL for /s/ LOW, MEDIUM, HIGH, N=25

| TIME | ACTIVITY NAME | | | | | | | | | |
|---|---|---|---|---|---|---|---|---|---|---|
| | FC | SS | Rdg | Cht | SD | GD | DM | SH | Asn | Oth |
| 30 wks. | 19 | 10 | 9 | 5 | 23 | 11 | 4 | 2 | 9 | 9 |

| TIME | STIMULUS | | | | | | CONSEQUATION REIN COST |
|---|---|---|---|---|---|---|---|
| | M | P | MP | G | CG | Oth | |
| 30 wks. | 22 | 23 | 3 | 25 | 8 | - | |

| TIME | CONTENT | | | | POSITION | | | | |
|---|---|---|---|---|---|---|---|---|---|
| | I | S | W | PH | I | M | F | X | Bl |
| 30 wks. | 3 | 5 | 28 | 64 | 14 | 1 | 3 | 81 | 1 |

## HIGH CPL for /s/ LOW, MEDIUM, HIGH, N=23

| ACTIVITY NAME | | | | | | | | | |
|---|---|---|---|---|---|---|---|---|---|
| FC | SS | Rdg | Cht | SD | GD | DM | SH | Asn | Oth |
| 20 | 4 | 3 | 4 | 24 | 13 | 4 | 2 | 16 | 10 |

| STIMULUS | | | | | | CONSEQUATION REIN COST |
|---|---|---|---|---|---|---|
| M | P | MP | G | CG | Oth | |
| 29 | 20 | 2 | 24 | 25 | - | |

| CONTENT | | | | POSITION | | | | |
|---|---|---|---|---|---|---|---|---|
| I | S | W | PH | I | M | F | X | Bl |
| 5 | 6 | 29 | 59 | 24 | 2 | 4 | 68 | 1 |

# APPENDIX F

# Computer Programs Used in the Statistical Analysis

This book would have been impossible without the use of a computer and canned statistical programs. The volume and complexity of data would take years to analyze by hand. Besides specific analyses reported here, there are many large piles of computer output which were used to explore different variables and hypotheses.

All of the analyses reported in the text were run on programs from the BMDP series (Dixon and Brown, 1977). In particular, what was used were the versions of BMDP converted for Honeywell computers by the Academic Computer Center of the University of Kansas.

The following lists the major programs used with their revision date:

BMDP2D—February 7, 1975, KU Version 2.OA 3/18/76—means, standard deviations and other univariate summary statistics.

BMDP5D—February 7, 1975—histogram plots.

BMDP6D—February 7, 1975—scattergrams.

BMDP1F—July 7, 1975, KU Version 2.OA 7/26/76—two-way tables and chi-square.

BMDP3F—August, 1976, KU Version 3.OA 6/10/77—multi-way tables and log-linear models.

BMDP2V—February 7, 1975, KU Version 2.OA 2/13/76—analysis of variance.

BMDP4M—October 7, 1974—factor analysis.

BMDP6R—February 7, 1975, KU Version 2.OA 3/10/76—multiple regression.

The BMDP programs were developed at the Health Sciences Computing Facility, UCLA, sponsored by NIH Special Research Resources Grant RR-3.

# Glossary of Frequently Used Symbols

AU Number—A measure of a child's articulation ability. The AU number is an average of Unified Scores.

CPL—A clinician variable. CPL (Clinician Performance Level) measures the performance of a clinician in correcting /r/ and /s/ articulation problems. It is calculated relative to the sample of children in this project. There were two CPL variables: CPL2 for performance after six weeks of therapy, and CPL4 for performance at the end of the year (thirty weeks of therapy).

Child prior variable—A child variable which measures a property which the child had prior to the beginning of therapy. SOUND, the child's target phoneme, is a child prior variable. EU2, the child's articulation level after six weeks of therapy, is not a child prior variable.

Child Variable—A variable like baseline score or target phoneme which is a property of the child. This is contrasted with a clinician variable.

Clinician Variable—A variable like last degree granted or years of clinical experience which is a property of the clinician. This is contrasted with a child variable.

EU Number—A measure of the child's articulation ability computed from SPT and TALK. The EU number has a value between 0 and 100. It estimates articulation at a particular time. The set of EU numbers form the basis for the primary dependent variables in our project.

EU1—Baseline EU number.

EU2—Estimate of the child's articulation six weeks after the beginning of therapy.

EU3—Estimate of the child's articulation eighteen weeks after the beginning of therapy.

EU4—Estimate of the child's articulation thirty weeks after the beginning of therapy.

GAIN—A measure of the child's articulation improvement from the beginning to the end of the year. GAIN is the difference between EU4 and EU1. It is one of the primary dependent variables.

GAMMA—A measure of the curvature or speed of the child's learning curve. GAMMA is derived from the EU numbers. It is one of the primary dependent variables.

K—One of the KLMO categories. The K child starts with low articulation and rises quickly to a high level.

KLMO—A categorical variable which divides children into five groups based on the shape of their learning curve. It is used as a criterion or dependent variable.

KPL—A child variable, KPL (Kid Performance Level) measures the performance of a child relative to the sample of children in this project. Its primary use is to calculate the clinician performance level CPL. There are two KPL variables: KPL2 for performance after six weeks of therapy and KPL4 for performance at the end of the year (thirty weeks of therapy).

L—One of the KLMO categories. The L child starts low and ends the year with a high level of ability, but does not rise as quickly as K.

Learning Curve—A sequence of articulation measures on one child and one variable. The idea that a sequence of measures is called a "learning curve" is primarily a matter of visualization.

M—One of the KLMO categories. The M child starts the year with a high score and ends the year with a higher score.

NGP—A child independent variable. NGP indicates the number of children in this child's therapy group.

NOSESS—A child independent variable. NOSESS indicates the number of therapy sessions per week which the child had.

O—One of the KLMO categories. The O child starts the year with a very low ability and makes little improvement.

PREVT—A child independent variable. PREVT (Previous Therapy) indicates whether the child has had articulation therapy prior to the beginning of the project year.

SNDEU1—A child independent variable. SNDEU1 divides children into six groups based on target phoneme and baseline scores.

SOUND—A child independent variable. SOUND indicates the child's target phoneme, $/r/$ or $/s/$.

SPT—Sound Production Task, a measure of imitative speech ability.

TALK—A measure of spontaneous conversation between clinician and child; time interval was three minutes.

Unified Score—A single measure of a child's articulation ability which is a combination of TALK and SPT.

# References

Alcorn, S., Griffith, J., & Miner, L. E. Comparison of articulation severity ratings of /s/ and /r/ by lower-, middle-, and upper socio-economic groups. *J. Commun. Dis.*. 1974, 7, 79-87.

Arlt, P. B., & Goodban, M. T. A comparative study of articulation acquisition as based on a study of 240 normals, aged three to six. *Language, Speech and Hearing Services in Schools*, 1976, 7, 173-180.

Aronin, M. *An experimental study of position generalization in articulation training*. Unpublished masters thesis, University of Kansas, 1971.

Aungst, L. F., & McDonald, E. T. Evaluating articulation therapy. In W. D. Wolfe and D. J. Goulding (Eds.), *Articulation and learning*, Springfield, IL: Charles C. Thomas, 1973.

Baker, H. J., & Leland, B. *Detroit tests of learning aptitude*. Indianapolis, IN: Bobbs-Merrill Co., 1959.

Baker, R. D., & Ryan, B. P. *Programmed Conditioning for Articulation*. Monterey, CA: Monterey Learning Systems, 1971.

Bankson, N. W. *The effect of word drill with a contingency for rate and accuracy of production on automatization of articulatory responses*. Unpublished doctoral dissertation, University of Kansas, 1970.

Bankson, N. W., Byrne, M. C. The effect of a timed correct sound production task on carryover. *J. Speech Hearing Res.*, 1972, 15, 160-168.

Barker, R. G., & Wright, H. F. *Midwest and its children: The psychological ecology of an American town*. New York: Harper and Row, 1955.

Barrett, M. D., & Welsh, J. W. Predictive articulation screening. *Language, Speech. Hearing Services in Schools*, 1975, 6, 91-95.

Bellack, A. A., Kliebard, H. M., Hyman, R. T., & Smith, F. L., Jr. *The Language of the Classroom*. Columbia University, NY: Teachers College Press. 1966.

Berry-Luterman, L., & Bar, A. The diagnostic significance of sentence repetition for language impaired children. *J. Speech and Hearing Dis.*. 1971, 36, 29-39.

Bingham, D., Van Hattum, R., Faulk, M., & Taussig, E. Program organization and management. In F. Darley (Ed.), Public School Speech and Hearing Services. *J. Speech Hearing Dis., Monograph Supplement #8*, 1961, 33-49.

Bishop, Y. M. M., Feinberg, S. E., & Holland, P. W. *Discrete multivariate analysis: Theory and practice*. Cambridge, MA: MIT Press, 1975.

Black, M. E. School speech therapy. Pittsburgh, PA: Stanwix House. 1970.

Boone, D. R. A close look at the clinical process. In J. L. Anderson (Ed.), *A conference on supervision of speech and hearing programs in the schools*. Bloomington, IN: Speech and Hearing Center, Indiana Univ., 1970.

Boone, D. R., & Prescott, T. E. *Speech and hearing therapy scoring manual*. Bureau for Education of the Handicapped, Office of Education, Grant No. OEG-0-70-4758-607, University of Denver, 1971.

Boone, D. R., & Stech, E. L. *The development of clinical skills in speech pathology by audiotape and videotape self-confrontation*. Final Report, Project No. 1381, Div. of Research, Bureau of Education for the Handicapped, U.S. Dept. Health, Education, and Welfare, Washington, DC, 1970.

Broen, P. A. The verbal environment of the language-learning child. *American Speech and Hearing Association, Monograph No. 17*. Washington, DC, 1972.

Brown, J. C. Techniques for correcting /r/ misarticulations. *Language, Speech and Hearing Services in Schools*, 1975, 6, 86-91.

Bryngelson, B., & Glaspey, E. *Speech in the classroom*. Chicago, IL: Scott, Foresman Co., 1941.

Butt, D., & Peterson, D. *R-Kit for articulation therapy (Research Edition)*. Albuquerque, NM: Speech Systems, 1971.

Carter, E. T., & Buck, M. Prognostic testing for functional articulation disorders among children in the first grade. *J. Speech Hearing Dis.*. 1958, 16, 124-133.

Chapman, M. E., Herbert, E. L., Avery, C. B., & Selmar, J. W. *VI. Clinical practice: Remedial procedures*. In F. Darley (Ed.), Public School Speech and Hearing Services. *J. Speech Hearing Dis. Monograph Supplement #8*, 1961, 48-77.

Cooper, E. B., Cady, B. B., & Robbins, C. J. The effect of the verbal stimulus words WRONG, RIGHT, and TREE on the disfluency rates of stutterers and nonstutterers. *J. Speech Hear. Res.*, 1970, *13*, 239-244.

Costello, J. M. Articulation instruction based on distinctive features theory. *Language, Speech and Hearing Services in Schools*, 1975, *6*, 61-71.

Costello, J. M. Programmed instruction. *J. Speech Hear. Dis.*, 1977, *42*, 3-28.

Costello, J. M. & Onstine, J. M. The modification of multiple articulation errors based on distinctive feature therapy. *Journal of Speech and Hearing Disorders*, 1976, *41*, 199-215.

Costley, M. S., & Broen, P. A. *The nature of listener disagreement in judging misarticulated speech*. Unpublished ASHA Convention paper, Houston, TX, 1976.

Coston, G. N., & Ainsworth, S. H. The effects of omissions and substitutions of selected consonants on intelligibility. *Brit. J. Disord. Communication*, 1972, *7*, 184-188.

Cronbach, L. J., Gleser, G. C., Nanda, H., & Rajaratnam, N. *The dependability of behavioral measurements*. New York: John Wiley and Sons, 1972.

Curlee, R. F. Manpower resources and needs in speech pathology/audiology. *American Speech and Hearing Association*, 1975, *17*, 265-273.

Curtis, J. F., & Hardy, J. C. A phonetic study of misarticulation of /r/. *J. Speech Hearing Res.*, 1959, *2*, 244-257.

Datamyte. Electro/General Corporation, Minnetonka, MN, 1969.

Denes, M., & Diedrich, W. M. Phoneme generalization in different speaking conditions. *American Speech and Hearing Association*, 1971, *13*, 549.

DeRenzi, E., & Vignolo, L. A. The Token Test: A sensitive test to detect receptive disturbances in aphasics. *Brain*, 1962, *83*, 665-678.

Dick, L. The effects of imposed preresponse time delay on the production of /r/ in the initial position at the syllable level. *J. Kans. Speech Hear. Assoc.*, 1975, *15*, 56-65.

Dickerson, M. V. *An investigation of a method of sampling spontaneous connected speech for the evaluation of articulatory behavior*. Unpublished doctoral dissertation, Florida State University, 1971.

Diedrich, W. M. Analysis of the clinical process. *J. Kansas Speech Hear. Assoc.*, 1969, *10*, 1-8

Diedrich, W. M. *Training speech clinicians in the recording and analysis of articulatory behavior*. OEG-0-71-1689 (603). U.S. Office of Education, Dept. HEW, Washington, DC, 1971a, 1972a, 1973a.

Diedrich, W. M. Procedures for counting and charting a target phoneme. *Language, Speech and Hearing Services in Schools. ASHA 5th booklet*, 1971b, 18-32.

Diedrich, W. M. *Counting and charting target phonemes in conversation*. Film Services, University of Kansas, Lawrence, KS., 1972b. (16mm color sound film)

Diedrich, W. M. *Charting speech behavior*. Lawrence, KS: Extramural Independent Study Center, University of Kansas, Lawrence, KS, 1973b.

Diedrich, W. M., & Bangert, J. A unified score for imitation and spontaneous speech. *American Speech Hearing Association*, 1972, *14*, 481.

Dixon, W. J., & Brown, M. B. *BMDP-77, Biomedical Computer Programs, P-Series*, Berkeley, CA: University of California Press, 1977.

Drash, P. W., Caldwell, L. R., & Leibowitz, J. M. Correct and incorrect response rates as basic dependent variables in the operant conditioning of speech in non-verbal subjects. *Psychol. Aspects of Disability*, 1970, *17*, 16-23.

DuBois, E. M., & Bernthal, J. E. The effects of three speech sampling methods on articulatory responses of children. *ASHA Convention Papers*, Houston, TX, 1976.

Dublinske, S., & Bruntzel, M. *Determining perceived and real program activity time in the public schools*. Unpublished ASHA Convention Paper, 1974.

Duguay, M. J. *The comparative effectiveness of an auditory discrimination program focusing on the error rather than the correct phoneme*. Unpublished doctoral dissertation, University of New York at Buffalo, 1971.

Dunn, L. M. *Peabody Picture Vocabulary Test*. Circle Pines, MN: American Guidance Service, 1965.

Elbert, M. The effects of therapy on distortion, substitution, and omission errors. *American Speech and Hearing Association*, 1971, *13*, 550.

Elbert, M., Shelton, R. L., & Arndt, W. B. A task for evaluation of articulation change: I. Development of methodology. *J. Speech Hearing Res.*, 1967, *10*, 281-289.

Elbert, M., & McReynolds, L. V. Transfer of /r/ across contexts. *Journal Speech and Hear. Dis.*, 1975, *40*, 380-387.

Elbert, M., & McReynolds, L. V. An experimental analysis of misarticulating children's generalization. *J. Speech Hear. Res.*, 1978, *21*, 136-150.

Fairbanks, G. *Voice and Articulation Drillbook*. (2nd ed.) New York: Harper and Bros., 1960.

Faircloth, M. *An analysis of the articulatory behavior of a selected group of speech defective children in spontaneous connected speech and in isolated word responses.* Unpublished doctoral dissertation, Florida State University, 1970.

Faircloth, M., & Faircloth, S. An analysis of the articulatory behavior of a speech defective child in connected speech and in isolated word responses. *J. Speech Hearing Dis.*, 1970, *35*, 51-61.

Ferster, C. G., & Perrott, M. C. *Behavior Principles*. New York: Appleton-Century-Crofts, 1968.

Flanders, N. A. Teacher influence, pupil attitudes, and achievement. OE-25040. *Cooperative Research Monograph No. 12*, U.S. Government Printing Office, Washington, DC, 1965.

Fletcher, S. G., Casteel, R. L., & Bradley, D. P. Tongue-thrust swallow, speech articulation, and age. *J. Speech Hearing Dis.*, 1961, *26*, 201-208.

Fletcher, S. G. Tongue thrust in swallowing and speaking. *Learning Concepts*. Austin, TX, 1974.

Fowler, E. P., Jr. Standard audiogram recording. *Acta Otolaryngologica Supplement*, 1949, *78*, 173-182.

Fraser, C., Bellugi, U., & Brown, R. Control of grammar in imitation, comprehension, and production. *J. of Verbal Learning and Verbal Behavior*, 1963, *2*, 121-135.

Freilinger, J. J. *Generalization of newly acquired phonemic responses in the home environment*. Unpublished doctoral dissertation, University of Kansas, 1973.

French, N. R., Carter, C. W., Jr., & Koenig, W., Jr. The words and sounds of telephone conversations. *Bell System Tech. J.*, 1930, *9*, 290-324.

Garrett, E. R. Programmed articulation learning. In W. D. Wolfe, and D. J. Goulding (Eds.), *Articulation and Learning*. Springfield, IL: Charles C. Thomas, 1973.

Garrett, E. Personal communication, 1974.

Gerber, A. *Goal: Carryover*. Philadelphia, PA: Temple University Press, 1973.

Gerber, A. Programming for articulation modification. *J. Speech Hear. Dis.*, 1977, *42*, 29-43.

Goldman, R., & Fristoe, M. *Test of Articulation*. Circle Pines, MN: American Guidance Service, Inc., 1969.

Goldman, R., Fristoe, M., & Woodcock, R. W. *Test of auditory discrimination*. Circle Pines, MN: American Guidance Service, 1970.

Gray, B. B. A field study on programmed articulation therapy. *Language, Speech, Hearing Services in Schools*, 1974, *5*, 119-131.

Griffiths, H., & Craighead, W. E. Generalization in operant speech therapy for misarticulation. *J. Speech Hear. Dis.* 1972, *35*, 485-494.

Guilford, J. P. *Psychometric Methods*. (2nd ed.) New York: McGraw-Hill, 1954.

Haberman, S. J. The analysis of residuals in cross-classified tables. *Biometrics*, 1973, *29*, 205-220.

Hanson, M. L. Some suggestions for more effective therapy for tongue thrust. *J. Speech Hear. Dis.*, 1967, *32*, 75-79.

Herbert, J. *A system for analyzing lessons*. New York: Columbia University, Teachers College Press, 1967.

Holland, A. L., & Matthews, J. Application of teaching machine concepts to speech pathology and audiology. *American Speech and Hearing Association*, 1963, *5*, 474-482.

Hurley, M. *An analysis of children's verbal responses during speech therapy sessions*. Unpublished masters thesis, Arizona State University, 1969.

Hutchinson, B. O. A pilot study: The effect of selected latency intervals upon articulation therapy. *Illinois Speech Hear. J.*, 1969, *2*, 6-10.

Ingmire, S. M., & Schuckers, G. *The category and frequency of verbal reinforcement utilized by clinicians in schools*. Unpublished paper, University of Indiana, 1975.

Irwin, R. B. *Speech and Hearing Therapy*. Pittsburgh, PA: Stanwix House, 1969.

Irwin, J. V. Personal communication, 1974.

Irwin, J. V., & Griffith, F. A. A theoretical and operational analysis of the paired stimuli technique. In W. D. Wolfe, and D. J. Goulding (Eds.), *Articulation and Learning*. Springfield, IL: Charles C. Thomas, 1973.

Jacobs, K. E., & Sauer, J. K. *The /r/ Program*. St. Paul, MN, 1972.

Jaffe, J., & Feldstein, S. *Rhythms of Dialogue*. New York: Academic Press, 1970.

Jann, G. R. *Lisping and tongue thrusting*. Unpublished paper, Dept. of Speech, State University College, Brockport, NY, 1972.

Johnson, T. S. *The development of a multidimensional scoring system for observing the clinical process in speech pathology*. Unpublished doctoral dissertation, University of Kansas, 1969.

Johnson, W., Darley, F. L., & Spriesterbach, D. C. *Diagnostic Methods in Speech Pathology*. New York: Harper and Row, 1963.

Jordan, E. P. Articulation test measures and listener ratings of articulation defectiveness. *J. Speech Hearing Res.*, 1960, *3*, 303-319.

Kanter, C. E., & West, R. *Phonetics*. New York: Harper and Bros., 1941.

Kenney, D. A. A quasi-experimental approach to assessing treatment effects in the non-equivalent control group design. *Psych. Bulletin.*, 1975, *82*, 345-362.

Kent, R. N., O'Leary, K. D., Diament, C., & Dietz, A. Expectation biases in observational evaluation of therapeutic change. *J. Consult. Clinical Psychol.*, 1974, *42*, 774-780.

Krasno, R. M. *Teachers' attitudes: Their empirical relationship to rapport with students and survival in the profession*. (Technical Report No. 28). Stanford, CA: Stanford Center for Research and Development in Teaching, Stanford University, 1972.

Larr, A. *Tongue thrust and speech correction*. Belmont, CA: Fearon Publications, 1962.

Lingwall, J., & Engmann, D. E. Event model of the clinical process. *ASHA Convention Paper*, 1971.

Locke, J. The child's acquisition of phonetic behavior. *Acta Symbol.*, 1971, *2*, 28-32.

Longhurst, T. M., & File, J. J. A comparison of developmental sentence scores from head-start children collected in four conditions. *Language, Speech and Hearing Services in Schools*, 1977, *8*(1), 54-64.

Lord, F. M. Statistical adjustments when comparing pre-existing groups. *Psychological Bulletin*, 1969, *72*, 336-337.

Lubbert, L., Johnson, K., Brenner, C., & Aldersen, A. *Behavior modification program for speech aides*. Tempe, AZ: Ideas, 1971.

Maclay, H., & Osgood, C. E. Hestitation phonemes in spontaneous speech. In L. A. Jakobovits & M. S. Milton (Eds.), *Readings in the psychology of language*. Englewood Cliffs, NJ: Prentice-Hall, 1967.

McDonald, E. *Articulation testing and treatment: A sensory-motor approach*. Pittsburgh, PA: Stanwix House, 1964.

McDonald, E. *A screening deep test of articulation*. Pittsburgh, PA: Stanwix House, 1968.

McDonald, E. Personal communication, 1974.

McDonald, E. T., & McDonald, J. M. *Norms for the Screening Deep Test of Articulation: Based on a longitudinal study of articulation development from beginning kindergarten to beginning third grade*. Project #73024. Department of Special Education, Penn. State Univ., State College, PA, 1974.

McDonald, G., & McDonald, J. *The teaching of "R" by a programmed method*. Hollidaysburgh, PA: Blair County Public Schools, 1971.

McLean, J. E. Extending stimulus control of phoneme articulation by operant techniques. In F. L. Girardeau & J. E. Spradlin (Eds.), *A functional approach to speech and language*. Washington, DC: American Speech and Hearing Association, ASHA Monographs Number 14, 1970, pp. 24-47.

McLean, J. & Raymore, S. *Programmatic research on a systematic articulation therapy program*. Carry-over of phoneme responses to untrained situations for normal-learning public school children. Report No. 6, Parsons, KS: Parsons Research Center Reports, 1972.

McNeil, D. R. *Interactive data analysis*. New York: John Wiley and Co., 1977.

McReynolds, L. V. Personal communication, 1975.

McReynolds, L. V. Articulation generalization during articulation training. *Language and Speech*, 1972, *15*, 149-155.

McReynolds, L. V., & Bennett, S. Distinctive feature generalization in articulation training. *J. Speech Hear. Dis.*, 1972, *37*, 462-470.

McReynolds, L. V., & Engmann, D. L. *Distinctive feature analysis of misarticulations*. Baltimore: University Park Press, 1975.

McReynolds, L. V., & Huston, K. A distinctive feature analysis of children's misarticulations. *J. Speech Hear. Dis.*, 1971, *76*, 155-166.

Mason, R. M., & Proffit, W. R. The tongue thrust controversy: Background and recommendation. *J. Speech Hear. Dis.*, 1974, *39*, 115-132.

Menyuk, P. A preliminary evaluation of grammatical capacity in children. *Journal of Verbal Learning and Verbal Behavior*, 1963, *2*, 429-439.

Milisen, R. The disorders of articulation: A systematic clinical and experimental approach. *J. Speech Hear. Dis., Monograph Supplement 4*, 1954.

Moore, W. H., Jr., Burke, J., & Adams, C. The effect of stimulability on the articulation of /s/ relative to cluster and word frequency of occurrence. *J. Speech Hearing Res.*, 1976, *19*, 458-466.

Mosteller, F., & Tukey, J. W. *Data analysis and regression.* Reading, MA: Addison-Wesley, 1977.

Mowrer, D. E. Evaluating speech therapy through precision recording. *J. Speech Hear. Dis.*, 1969, *34*, 239-244.

Mowrer, D. E. Transfer of training in articulation therapy. *J. Speech Hear. Dis.*, 1971, *36*, 427-446.

Mowrer, D. E. Accountability and speech therapy in the public schools. *American Speech and Hearing Association*, 1972, *14*, 111-115.

Mowrer, D. E. A behavioristic approach to modification of articulation. In W. D. Wolfe & D. J. Goulding (Eds.), *Articulation and learning.* Springfield, IL: Charles C. Thomas, 1973.

Mowrer, D. E., Baker, R. L., & Schultz, R. E. *Modification of the frontal lisp programmed articulation control kit.* Tempe, AZ: Education Psychological Research Assoc., 1968.

Muma, J. R. Language intervention: *A psycholinguistic approach.* Short course presented at the 47th Annual American Speech and Hearing Assoc. Convention, Chicago, IL, November, 1971.

Mumm, M. N. A comparison of the results of "behavior modification" versus "traditional" approaches in the treatment of misarticulations in a public school setting. *American Speech and Hearing Association*, 1974, *16*, 562.

Noll, J. D. *The use of the token test with children.* Presented to the 46th Annual American Speech and Hearing Association Convention, New York, 1970.

Ott, L. *An introduction to statistical methods and data analysis.* North Scituate, MA: Duxbury Press, 1977.

Park, K. *The effects of speech therapy upon the articulation profiles of kindergarten children.* Unpublished masters thesis, University of Kansas, 1968.

Pendergast, K., Dickey, S. E., & Soder, A. L. *A study of protrusional lisps to identify children requiring speech therapy.* Final report. Project No. 5-0319. Contract No. OE-5-10-180. Office of Education, U.S. Dept. HEW. (Seattle Public School, 815-4th Ave. North, Seattle, Washington 98109), 1969.

Pendergast, K., Soder, A., Barker, J., Dickey, S., Gow, J., & Selmar, J. An articulation study of 15,255 Seattle first grade children with and without kindergarten. *Execptional Chlidren*, 1966, *32*, 541-547.

Plutchik, R. *Foundations of experimental research.* New York: Harper and Row, 1968.

Poole, I. Genetic development of articulation of consonant sounds in speech. *Elem. Eng. Rev.*, 1934, *2*, 159-161.

Powell, J., & McReynolds, L. V. A procedure for testing position generalization from articulation training. *J. Speech Hear. Res.*, 1969, *12*, 629-645.

Powers, M. H. Functional disorders of articulation—Symptomatology and etiology. In L. E. Travis (Ed.), *Handbook of Speech Pathology.* New York: Appleton-Century-Crofts, 1971.

Prather, E., Hedrick, D. E., & Kern, C. A. Articulation development in children aged two to four years. *J. Speech Hearing Dis.*, 1974, *60*, 179-191.

Prescott, T. E. *The development of a methodology for describing speech therapy.* Unpublished doctoral dissertation, University of Denver, 1970.

Raymore, D., & McLean, J. E. A clinical program of carry-over of articulation therapy with retarded children. In J. E. McLean, D. E. Yoder, & R. L. Schiefelbusch (Eds.), *Language intervention with the retarded.* Baltimore: University Park Press, 1972.

Roe, V., & Milisen, R. The effect of maturation upon defective articulation in elementary grades. *J. Speech Hear. Dis.*, 1942, *1*, 37-45.

Romans, E. F., & Milisen, R. Effects of latency between stimulation and response on reproduction of sounds. *J. Speech Hear. Dis., Monograph Supplement No. 4*, 1954, pp. 71-78.

Rosenhan, D., & Greenwald, J. The effects of age, sex, and socio-economic class on responsiveness of two classes of verbal reinforcement. *J. Personality*, 1965, *33*, 108-121.

Ruscello, D. M. The importance of word position in articulation therapy. *Language, Speech and Hearing Services Schools*, 1975, *6*(4), 190-196.

Sander, E. When are speech sounds learned? *J. Speech Hear. Dis.*, 1972, *37*, 55-63.

Schubert, G. W. *The analysis of behavior of clinicians (ABC) system*. Grand Forks: University of North Dakota, 1974.

Sharf, D. J. Distinctiveness of "defective" fricative sounds. *Lang. Speech*, 1968, *2*, 38-45.

Shelton, R. L., Elbert, M., & Arndt, W. B. A task for evaluation of articulation change: II. Comparison of task scores during baseline and lesson series testing. *J. Speech Hear. Res.*, 1967, *10*, 578-586.

Shelton, R. L., Johnson, A. F., & Arndt, W. B. Monitoring and reinforcement by parents as a means of automating articulatory responses. *Perceptual Motor Skills*, 1972, *35*, 759-767.

Shelton, R. L., Johnson, A., & Arndt, W. B. Variability in judgment of articulation when observer listens repeatedly to the same phone. *Perceptual Motor Skills*, 1974, *39*, 327-332.

Shriberg, L. D. A response evocation program for /r/. *J. Speech Hear. Dis.*, 1975, *40*, 92-105.

Shriner, T. H., Holloway, M. S., & Daniloff, R. G. The relationship between articulatory deficits and syntax in speech defective children. *J. Speech Hear. Res.*, 1969, *12*, 319-325.

Slipakoff, E. L. An approach to the correction of the defective /r/. *J. Speech Hear. Dis.*, 1967, *32*, 71-74.

Smith, B. D., & Meux, M. O. in collaboration with J. Coombs, D. Eierdem, & R. Szoke. *A study of the logic of teaching*. Urbana: University of Illinois Press, 1970.

Sommers, R. Personal communication, 1969.

Sommers, R. K., Leiss, R. H., Delp, M. A., Gerber, A. J., Fundrella, D., Smith, R. M., II, Revucky, M. V., Ellis, D., & Haley, V. A. Factors related to effectiveness of articulation therapy for kindergarten, first, and second grade children. *J. Speech Hear. Res.*, 1967, *10*, 428-437.

Sommers, R. K., & Kane, A. R. Nature and remediation of functional articulation disorders. In S. Dickson (Ed.), *Communication disorders: Remedial principals and practices*. Glenview: Scott, Foresman, and Co., 1974.

Stansell, B. J. Effects of deglutition and speech training on dental overjet. *J. South. Calif. Dent. Assn.*, 1970, *38*, 423-437.

Stech, E. L. Quick analysis methods for continuous interaction scoring in speech therapy. Appendix A reprinted in D. R. Boon and E. L. Stech. 1970. The development of clinical skills in speech pathology by audiotape and videotape self-confrontation. Final report. Project No. 1381, Div. of Research, Bureau of Education for the Handicapped, U.S. Dept. HEW. Washington, D.C., 1969.

Stephens, M. I., & Daniloff, R. A methodological study of factors affecting the judgment of misarticulated /s/. *J. Communications Dis.*, 1977, *10*, 207-220.

Strong, C. Analysis of verbal behavior in articulation therapy. In T. S. Johnson (Ed.), *Clinical interaction and its measurement*. Dept. of Communicative Disorders, Utah State University, 1971.

Tekieli, M. E., & Lass, N. J. The verbal transformation effect: Consistency of subjects' reported verbal transformations. *J. of General Psychology*, 1972, *86*, 231-245.

Templin, M. C., & Darley, F. L. *The Templin-Darley Tests of Articulation*. Iowa City: Bureau of Educational Research and Service, State University of Iowa, 1960.

Travis, L. E. *Speech Pathology*. New York: D. Appleton, 1931.

Tukey, J. W. *Exploratory Data Analysis*. Reading, MA: Addison-Wesley, 1977.

Turton, L. J. Diagnostic implications of articulation testing. In W. D. Wolfe and D. J. Goulding (Eds.), *Articulation and learning*. Springfield, IL: Charles C. Thomas, 1973.

Van Hattum, R. J. *Clinical Speech in the Schools*. Springfield, IL: Charles C. Thomas, 1969.

Van Riper, C. *Speech Correction: Principles and methods*. (1st ed.). New York: Prentice-Hall, 1939.

Van Riper, C. *Speech Correction: Principles and methods*. (4th ed.) Englewood Cliffs, NJ: Prentice-Hall, 1963.

Van Riper, C. *Speech Correction: Principles and methods*. (5th ed.) Englewood Cliffs, NJ: Prentice-Hall, 1972.

Van Riper, C. *Speech Correction: Principles and methods.* (6th ed.) Englewood Cliffs, NJ: Prentice-Hall, 1978.

Van Riper, C., & Erickson, R. *Predictive screening test of articulation* (manual, 3rd ed.). Kalamazoo, MI: Continuing Education Office, Western Michigan, Univ., 1973.

Van Riper, C., & Irwin, J. V. *Voice and articulation.* Englewood Cliffs, NJ: Prentice-Hall, 1958.

Warren, R. M. Illusory changes of distinct speech upon repetition—the verbal transformation effect. *Brit. J. Psychol.*, 1961, *52*, 249-258.

Wepman, J. & Hass, W. *Spoken word counts.* Chicago, IL: Language Research Assoc., 1969.

Winer, B. J. *Statistical principals in experimental design.* (2nd ed.) New York: McGraw-Hill, 1971.

Winitz, H. *Articulatory acquisition and behavior.* New York: Appleton-Century-Crofts, 1969.

Winitz, H. *From syllable to conversation.* Baltimore: University Park Press, 1975.

Winitz, H., & Bellerose, B. Phoneme-sound generalization as a function of phoneme similarity and verbal unit of test and training stimuli. *J. Speech Hear. Res.*, 1963, *4*, 379-391.

Wolfe, W. D., & Goulding, D. J. *Articulation and learning.* Springfield, IL: Charles C. Thomas, 1973.

Wright, V., & Diedrich, W. M. Context analysis of /r/ and /s/. *American Speech and Hearing Association*, 1971, *13*, 549.

Wright, V., Shelton, R. L., & Arndt, W. B. A task for evaluation of articulation change: III. Imitative task scores compared with scores for more spontaneous tasks. *J. Speech Hear. Res.*, 1969, *12*, 875-884.

Young, M. A. Observer agreement: Cummulative effects of rating many samples. *J. Speech Hear. Res.*, 1969, *12*, 135-143.

# Index

# Author Index

Leland, B., *238*
Lingwall, J., *23, 158, 160, 165*
Locke, J., *167*
Longhurst, T.M., *181*
Lord, F.M., *62*
Lubbert, L., *167, 172*

Maclay, H., *178*
Mason, R.M., *215*
Matthews, J., *164*
McDonald, E., *7, 171, 173, 218*
McDonald, E.T., *172, 198, 232*
McDonald, G., *191*
McDonald, J.M., *173, 198, 232*
McLean, J., *155, 156*
McReynolds, L.V., *154-156, 164, 173, 186, 199, 202*
Menyuk, P.A., *238*
Meux, M.O., *1*
Milisen, R., *167, 186, 200*
Miner, I.E., *186*
Moore, W.H., Jr., *185*
Mosteller, F., *120*
Mowrer, D.E., *164, 165, 167, 172*
Muma, J.R., *238*
Mumm, M.N., *171*

Nanda, H., *19*
Noll, J.D., *238*

O'Leary, K.D., *20*

Osgood, C.E., *178*
Ott, L., *72-73*

Park, K., *204*
Pendergast, K., *182, 207, 232*
Perrott, M.C., *178*
Peterson, D., *173*
Plutchik, R., *xiv, 58*
Poole, I., *17*
Powell, J., *155*
Powers, M.H., *207*
Prather, E., *17*
Prescott, T.E., *158, 160*
Proffit, W.R., *215*

Rajaratnam, N., *19*
Raymore, D., *155*
Robbins, C.J., *166*
Roe, V., *200*
Romans, E.F., *167*
Rosenhan, D., *166*
Ruscello, D.M., *155*
Ryan, B.P., *172*

Sander, E., *17, 199*
Sauer, J.K., *173*
Schubert, G.W., *158*
Schuckers, G., *166*
Schultz, R.E., *172*
Selmar, J.W., *187, 195, 207, 232*
Sharf, D.J., *21*
Shelton, R.L., *6, 19, 21, 156, 172, 182, 184, 186, 189, 239*
Shriberg, I.D., *173*

Shriner, T.H., *173*
Slipakoff, E.L., *173*
Smith, B.D., *1*
Soder, A., *182*
Sommers, R., *173*
Sommers, R.K., *ix, 157, 173*
Spriesterbach, D.C., *175*
Stansell, B.J., *217*
Stech, E.I., *160, 165*
Stephens, M.I., *20, 258*
Strong, C., *165*

Taussig, E., *18*
Tekieli, M.F., *21*
Templin, M.C., *17, 171*
Travis, I.E., *171*
Tukey, J.W., *120*
Turton, I.J., *186*

Van Hattum, R.J., *18, 187*
VanRiper, C., *143, 164, 182, 186, 200, 207, 232*
Vignolo, L.A., *238*

Warren, R.M., *21*
Welsh, J.W., *182, 232*
Wepman, J., *176, 179*
West, R., *198*
Winer, B.J., *62, 63*
Winitz, H., *156, 164, 172, 179*
Wolfe, W.D., *187*
Woodcock, R.W., *9*
Wright, V., *1, 156, 178, 182, 186, 204, 239*

Young, M.A., *255*

# Date Due

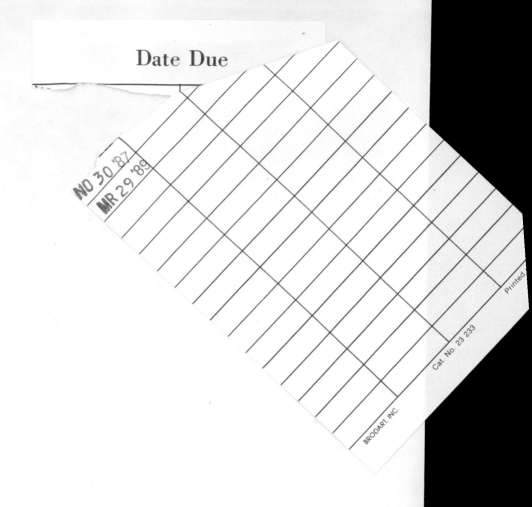